HANDBOOK OF FORMATIVE ASSESSMENT IN THE DISCIPLINES

The *Handbook of Formative Assessment in the Disciplines* meaningfully addresses current developments in the field, offering a unique and timely focus on domain dependency. Building from an updated definition of formative assessment, the book covers the integration of measurement principles into practice; the operationalization of formative assessment within specific domains, beyond generic strategies; evolving research directions including student involvement and self-regulation; and new approaches to the challenges of incorporating formative assessment training into pre-service and in-service educator training.

As supporters of large-scale testing programs increasingly consider the potential of formative assessments to improve teaching and learning, this handbook advances the subject through novel frameworks, intersections of theory, research, and practice, and attention to discernible disciplines. Written for instructors, graduate students, researchers, and policymakers, each chapter provides expert perspectives on the procedures and evaluations that enable teachers to adapt teaching and learning in-process toward student achievement.

Heidi L. Andrade is Professor of Educational Psychology and Methodology in the School of Education at the University at Albany, State University of New York, USA.

Randy E. Bennett is Norman O. Frederiksen Chair in Assessment Innovation in the Research and Development Division at Educational Testing Service, USA.

Gregory J. Cizek is Guy B. Phillips Distinguished Professor of Educational Measurement and Evaluation at the University of North Carolina at Chapel Hill, USA.

HANDBOOK OF FORMATIVE ASSESSMENT IN THE DISCIPLINES

Edited by

Heidi L. Andrade, Randy E. Bennett, and Gregory J. Cizek

NEW YORK AND LONDON

First published 2019
by Routledge
52 Vanderbilt Avenue, New York, NY 10017

and by Routledge
2 Park Square, Milton Park, Abingdon, Oxon, OX14 4RN

Routledge is an imprint of the Taylor & Francis Group, an informa business

© 2019 Taylor & Francis

The right of Heidi L. Andrade, Randy E. Bennett, and Gregory J. Cizek to be identified as the authors of the editorial material, and of the authors for their individual chapters, has been asserted in accordance with sections 77 and 78 of the Copyright, Designs and Patents Act 1988.

All rights reserved. No part of this book may be reprinted or reproduced or utilised in any form or by any electronic, mechanical, or other means, now known or hereafter invented, including photocopying and recording, or in any information storage or retrieval system, without permission in writing from the publishers.

Trademark notice: Product or corporate names may be trademarks or registered trademarks, and are used only for identification and explanation without intent to infringe.

Library of Congress Cataloging-in-Publication Data
Names: Andrade, Heidi L., editor. | Bennett, Randy Elliot, 1952-
 editor. | Cizek, Gregory J., editor.
Title: Handbook of formative assessment in the disciplines / edited
 by Heidi L. Andrade, Randy E. Bennett, and Gregory J. Cizek.
Description: New York, NY : Routledge, 2019. | Includes
 bibliographical references and index.
Identifiers: LCCN 2018061176 (print) | LCCN 2019008362
 (ebook) | ISBN 9781315166933 (eBook) | ISBN
 9781138054349 (hardback) | ISBN 9781138054363 (pbk.)
Subjects: LCSH: Educational evaluation. | Education, Higher—
 Evaluation. | Universities and colleges—Curricula—
 Evaluation. | Educational tests and measurements. | Academic
 achievement—Testing.
Classification: LCC LB2822.75 (ebook) | LCC LB2822.75 .H356
 2019 (print) | DDC 378—dc23
LC record available at https://lccn.loc.gov/2018061176

ISBN: 978-1-138-05434-9 (hbk)
ISBN: 978-1-138-05436-3 (pbk)
ISBN: 978-1-315-16693-3 (ebk)

Typeset in Bembo
by Swales & Willis Ltd, Exeter, Devon, UK

CONTENTS

List of Figures		*vii*
Preface		*ix*

PART I
Theoretical Advances   **1**

1   Formative Assessment: History, Definition, and Progress   3
    Gregory J. Cizek, Heidi L. Andrade, and Randy E. Bennett

2   Integrating Measurement Principles into Formative Assessment   20
    Randy E. Bennett

PART II
Intersections of Theory, Research, and Best Practices in Formative
Assessment in the Disciplines   **33**

3   Formative Assessment in Mathematics   35
    Hugh Burkhardt and Alan Schoenfeld

4   Scenario-Based Formative Assessment of Key Practices
    in the English Language Arts   68
    Paul Deane and Jesse R. Sparks

5   Formative Assessment in Science Education:
    Mapping a Shifting Terrain   97
    Erin Marie Furtak, Sara C. Heredia, and Deb Morrison

Contents

6 Formative Assessment in the Arts   126
Heidi L. Andrade, Joanna Hefferen, and Maria E. Palma

7 Formative Assessment in Higher Education:
An Example from Astronomy   146
Anders Jönsson and Urban Eriksson

PART III
Professional Preparation in Formative Assessment   171

8 Creating Formative Assessment Systems in the Teaching
of Writing, and Harnessing Them as Professional Development   173
Lucy Calkins, Mary Ehrenworth, and Diana Akhmedjanova

9 Teacher Preparation in Mathematics   207
Margaret Heritage and Caroline Wylie

10 Conclusion: Why Formative Assessment is Always Both
Domain-General and Domain-Specific and What Matters is the
Balance Between the Two   243
Dylan Wiliam

List of Contributors   *265*
Index   *271*

FIGURES

2.1	Guidelines for what constitutes a quality argument essay.	24
3.1	The key roles of formative assessment in powerful mathematics classrooms.	43
3.2	Mean scores on pre, post and delayed post-tests (Birks, 1987).	46
3.3	Tasks designed to promote the surfacing and subsequent resolution of misconceptions.	48
3.4	Two genres of learning activity.	49
3.5	Pre-assessment for percent changes.	52
3.6	Common Issues table for percent changes.	53
3.7	Up and down percentage.	54
3.8	The poster with multiply-by-decimals and multiply-by-fractions arrow cards.	55
3.9	The task from the boomerangs lesson.	57
3.10	The first part of the Common Issues table for boomerangs.	57
3.11	Sample student work by Alex (a), Danny (b) and Jeremiah (c).	58
3.12	The ITMA microworld, Eureka.	61
4.1	Introductory scenario for *A Meal in Ancient Rome*.	79
4.2	Introduction to three phases of research and virtual avatars from *A Meal in Ancient Rome*.	80
4.3	Opening screen from the task, "Evaluating Sources about Clouds."	86
4.4	Informational screen from the task, "Evaluating Sources about Clouds."	86
4.5	Relevance item screen from the task, "Evaluating Sources about Clouds."	88
4.6	Informational screen from the task, "Evaluating Sources about Clouds."	89
4.7	Credibility item screen from the task, "Evaluating Sources about Clouds."	89
4.8	Bias item screen from the task, "Evaluating Sources about Clouds."	90
4.9	Expertise item screen from the task, "Evaluating Sources about Clouds."	91
4.10	Screen showing final classification of relevant sources from the task, "Evaluating Sources about Clouds."	91
5.1	Example formative assessment tool: The red fox task.	100
5.2	Formative Assessment Design Cycle.	105
6.1	Typical theory of action for formative assessment.	129

Figures

6.2	Theory of action with no explicit reference to standards or criteria.	129
6.3	*Keeping Learning on Track® Program* Theory of Action for Formative Assessment.	130
6.4	Theory of Action for Formative Assessment in Arts Education.	131
6.5	Visual gradation rubric.	133
6.6	The Ladder of Feedback.	137
6.7	Peer feedback template.	138
6.8	Peer feedback about a self-portrait.	139
6.9	Result of revision after peer feedback.	139
6.10	Peer feedback scaffolding used by Angela Fremont, elementary visual arts.	140
7.1	Astronomers have found that there is a relationship between the period and luminosity of variable stars that can be used for distance determinations.	151
7.2	The scientific explanation for a solar eclipse visualized by blocking the light from a flashlight (representing the Sun) with a ball (representing the Moon).	153
7.3	Diagram explaining the apparent retrograde motion of an outer planet as seen from Earth (gray circles), in this case Mars (black circles).	155
7.4	A hot source emits electromagnetic radiation, such as visible light.	162
7.5	Simplified version of the Toulmin model.	163
8.1	Excerpt from third-grade checklist for narrative writing.	181
8.2	Teachers and students learn to annotate exemplars as tools to raise the level of writing.	186
9.1	A framework for cultivating teachers' formative assessment expertise.	208
9.2	Contrasting examples of learning goals and success criteria.	209
9.3	A misconception item targeting understanding of a diagonal.	231
9.4	An item targeting understanding of fractions.	231
9.5	Proportional reasoning problem and three student responses.	232

PREFACE

Heidi L. Andrade, Gregory J. Cizek, and Randy E. Bennett

As a field, formative assessment has rapidly matured. Its general principles are by now fairly well established: The fundamental purpose of formative assessment is to provide feedback that is used to adjust teaching and learning with the goal of improving students' achievement of intended instructional outcomes (American Educational Research Association, American Psychological Association, National Council on Measurement in Education [AERA, APA, NCME], 2014). The broad features of formative assessment are also clear: A comprehensive approach includes information about learning goals (Where are we going?), current states (How are we doing?), and methods for closing any gaps between the two (What next?) (Hattie & Timperley, 2007). Although there is still work to be done on the implementation of generic formative assessment processes (e.g., setting learning goals, asking questions), the popularity of some types of formative assessment is an indication that students and teachers are more systematically collecting data, interpreting it, and using it to give and act upon feedback about student learning.

This is a heartening development, even more so where formative assessment is closely linked to curriculum and embedded in instruction (Penuel & Shepard, 2016). Here we make a distinction between formative assessment practices that are genuinely useful to and used by teachers and students, and commercial products that are labeled "formative" but are in fact mini-summative assessments. Although not all of the assessment tools introduced in the chapters in this book are developed by teachers, they differ fundamentally from interim or benchmark assessments designed to predict how well students will do on state accountability tests.

So what is next for the field of formative assessment? Our answer is *discipline specificity*. We knew from theory, research, and experience that formative assessment practices differed by discipline (Bennett, 2011). For example, in the writing of persuasive essays, our questioning behavior with students might productively be focused on the claims-reasons-evidence structure of that form, whereas in the solving of word problems in mathematics it might more sensibly be directed to the processes of translating language to symbolic representation, understanding the representation, planning a solution, and executing the plan. Differences like these reflect the nature of the intellectual work being done in each subject area. As clearly revealed by work on learning progressions (Heritage, 2009), attention to the epistemology of a subject can productively guide the design of curriculum, instruction, and assessment: Formative assessment needs to follow suit. This *Handbook* is an exploration of how the nature of the disciplines shapes the goals that are set, the questions that are asked, the types of behaviors that constitute evidence, the interpretations given to that evidence, and the actions taken.

Preface

The organization of the *Handbook* flows from a reconceptualization of formative assessment described in detail in Chapter 1. The *Handbook* comprises three parts. The first part, Theoretical Advances, contains our opening chapter that provides context on the history of formative assessment, and presents a suggested reconceptualization and next-generation definition. Part I also includes a chapter on the integration of measurement principles in formative assessment by Randy Bennett, who brings disciplinary ideas directly into play.

The second part, Intersections of Theory, Research, and Best Practices in Formative Assessment in the Disciplines, includes chapters that begin to illustrate what formative assessment looks like when it is conceptualized from a disciplinary perspective. The first four chapters in Part II are focused on K-12 contexts: there are chapters by Hugh Burkhardt and Alan Schoenfeld on mathematics, Paul Deane and Jesse Sparks on English language arts, Erin Furtak, Sara Heredia, and Deb Morrison on science, and Heidi Andrade, Joanna Hefferen, and Maria Palma on the arts. The final chapter in the part, by Anders Jonsson and Urban Eriksson, is about science in higher education.

The third part of this *Handbook*, Professional Preparation in Formative Assessment, extends consideration of formative assessment to post-secondary teacher education and professional development. Part III has a chapter by Lucy Calkins, Mary Ehrenworth, and Diana Akhmedjanova on professional development for English language arts teachers, and by Margaret Heritage and Caroline Wylie on teacher preparation in mathematics. The book closes with a synthesis, critique and discussion of future directions for formative assessment research and practice by Dylan Wiliam.

Although the second and third parts of this book include disciplinary chapters related to the English language arts, mathematics, science, and the arts, there are no chapters at the elementary or secondary level about social studies, or at the university level for the humanities, social sciences, or applied sciences, among other areas. This absence was not intentional but rather reflects the lack of formative assessment research and theory development within these specific disciplines. We hope this book will pave the way for new scholarship in these areas.

This *Handbook* is likely to be of interest to individuals working in the field of assessment, or whose work is affected by it. These individuals include researchers, teacher educators, assessment developers, federal and state policy makers, and school district staff members, especially teachers and school leaders—in short, all those whose work is centered on improving student achievement. Finally, this *Handbook of Formative Assessment in the Disciplines* is intended to provide information about cutting edge research and applications for graduate students wrestling with current challenges in curriculum, assessment, educational psychology, and education policy. Of course, ultimately, we hope that this work serves students.

This book would not have been possible with the contributions of many people. First, we acknowledge the generous contributions of our chapter authors, whom we regard as the most qualified authorities in the field. Each chapter author has tackled the challenging task of describing a key aspect of disciplinary formative assessment in a rigorous, contemporary, and practical fashion. Their collective willingness to disseminate knowledge, extend research, and promote improved formative assessment practice is a considerable service to the field. We are indebted to them.

We are also indebted to the reviewers of the prospectus for this book, who provided support and sound advice. Individually, the editors of this book would like to acknowledge many others. I (HLA) am grateful for this opportunity to continue the work that Greg Cizek and I started with the publication of the *Handbook of Formative Assessment* (2010), and for his suggestion that we invite Randy Bennett to join us. Randy's perspective informed the topic of this book and sharpened its focus. Collaborating with both Greg and Randy has been an honor and a treat. I am also appreciative of Taja Young's help with the preparation of the book manuscript, and Mark Schmidt's work on many of the images. For me (REB), working with Heidi, Greg, and the chapter authors has been an incredibly valuable learning experience, extending my knowledge of and perspective on formative assessment. Finally, I (GJC) echo those sentiments about the great learning opportunity it

Preface

has been for me to work with such thoughtful colleagues. In addition, I gratefully acknowledge the love, support, and patience extended to me in the enduring challenge of keeping (too many) balls in the air by, most notably, my wife, Julie Cizek. Collectively we share the optimism that the work represented in this volume has its desired effect of improving the learning and lives of the students, educators, and parents who are ultimately most affected by thoughtful research and policy making on formative assessment.

References

American Educational Research Association, American Psychological Association, National Council on Measurement in Education [AERA, APA, NCME]. (2014). *Standards for educational and psychological testing.* Washington, DC: American Psychological Association.

Andrade, H. & Cizek, G. (Eds.) (2010). *Handbook of formative assessment.* New York, NY: Routledge.

Bennett, R. E. (2011). Formative assessment: A critical review. *Assessment in Education: Principles, Policy and Practice, 18*(1), 5–25. DOI: 10.1080/0969594X.2010.513678.

Hattie, J. & Timperley, H. (2007). The power of feedback. *Review of Educational Research, 77*, 81–112.

Heritage, M. (2009). *The case for learning progressions.* San Francisco, CA: Stupski Foundation.

Penuel, W. R. & Shepard, L. A. (2016). Assessment and teaching. In D. H. Gitomer & C. A. Bell (Eds.), *Handbook of research on teaching* (5th ed.) (pp. 787–850). Washington, DC: American Educational Research Association.

PART I

Theoretical Advances

1
FORMATIVE ASSESSMENT
History, Definition, and Progress

Gregory J. Cizek, Heidi L. Andrade, and Randy E. Bennett

If you ask five teachers what formative assessment is, you're likely to get five different answers.

The above observation about formative assessment was the opening sentence of a recent examination of the topic published in *Education Week* (Gewertz, 2015, p. S2). Indeed, as we will see later in this chapter, although the term *formative assessment* has experienced a long history and increasing contemporary interest, it is used in diverse ways—including ways that overlap other usages of the term and ways that are synonymous with other assessment concepts.

Despite the diversity of usage, the concept of formative assessment has attracted the attention of researchers, educators, and policy makers as a promising mechanism for increasing student learning. As one of us has written, policy initiatives that rely on mandated large-scale summative assessments have likely reached a point of diminishing returns as a mechanism for spurring increased achievement. Thus, formative assessment may represent "the next best hope for promoting greater achievement gains for students" (Cizek, 2010, p. 15).

In general, large-scale summative testing, such as the assessments mandated by the *No Child Left Behind Act* (2001) and the *Every Student Succeeds Act* (2015), remains a cornerstone of state and federal educational policy and enjoys fairly broad public support. For example, one recent national survey found that 63% of adults support or strongly support the federal requirement that all students be tested in mathematics and reading each year in grades 3–8 and once in high school (West et al., 2018). Another poll revealed that 67% of respondents indicated that "using tests to measure what students have learned" was rated as either important or very important for improving the quality of public schools (Kernan-Schloss & Starr, 2015, p. K12).

At the same time, there are hints of an increasing lack of faith that summative assessment will continue to be an effective policy lever for improving American education, and some level of disillusionment is evident. The reliance on summative assessments for boosting achievement may have run its course. For example, it is clear that an increasingly large constituency of parents is not content with the status quo, either believing that the amount of testing time should be reduced or supporting "opting out" of state-wide summative tests altogether (Bennett, 2016; Kernan-Schloss & Starr, 2015). Perhaps one way to reconcile the somewhat contradictory findings about mandated summative assessment is to observe that although parents still approve of mandated summative testing for *monitoring* achievement and supporting policy actions, they do not view that form of assessment as highly valuable for *increasing* achievement.

Educators, too, have become less enthusiastic about large-scale summative assessments. Perhaps mostly because these measures have increasingly been appropriated for use in personnel and organizational evaluation and accountability systems, large-scale mandated summative testing is not seen as a valuable tool for directing attention to teaching and learning of the type that would generate classroom learning gains (see Kernan-Schloss & Starr, 2015; Wang, Beckett, & Brown, 2006).

Some Beginning Definitions

Before further examining the characteristics and potential of formative assessment as a complement to summative testing, it seems appropriate to define some key terms somewhat more formally. We have already used the term *summative assessment* in this chapter. To be clear, we are using this term to mean a form of information gathering about students that is conducted primarily for the purposes of making judgments about the status of individual learners or determinations about the effectiveness of educational programs or systems. For the most part, those judgments or determinations occur at single time points and are evaluative; that is, they represent primarily conclusions about what has occurred, either in terms of student accomplishment or attainment of institutional goals. For example, at the student level, summative assessment would be exemplified by the use of test performance to assign grades; at the system level, an example of summative assessment would be the use of aggregated test performance to create accountability indicators such as *adequate yearly progress* or *value added* indices for teachers, schools, or state education systems.

A succinct definition of summative assessment is provided in the *Standards for Educational and Psychological Testing*: "The assessment of a test taker's knowledge and skills typically carried out at the completion of a program of learning, such as the end of an instructional unit" (American Educational Research Association, American Psychological Association, and National Council on Measurement in Education [AERA, APA, & NCME], 2014, p. 224; hereafter, *Standards*). Foreshadowing what we will see in definitions of formative assessment, this definition highlights the characteristic of summative assessment as being "at the completion" of an educational experience. This characteristic, for example, would apply to student grades on report cards, end-of-course or end-of-grade examinations, and to monitoring mechanisms such as yearly school report cards or other such annual accountability reporting systems.

As has been pointed out previously, the information yielded by any type of assessment and the use of that information are separate, but related, measurement issues (see Cizek, 2016). Accordingly, a summative assessment may have one of many targets (e.g., the measurement of ability, achievement, interest, college readiness, vocational aptitude), and may be of any format (e.g., oral questioning, portfolio, multiple-choice test items, performance tasks). It is not necessarily the target or format of an assessment that determines what kind of an assessment it is; rather, it is *how the assessment information is used* that is the primary driver in its classification. Put another way, one might not be able to tell simply by looking that an assessment was summative; one would need to know what use was being made of the assessment results in order to ascertain what type of an assessment had occurred.

That said, there is also another consideration in assigning the label *formative* to an assessment: the intended use of an assessment should be a central focus in its design. Whereas an assessment that was explicitly designed as a summative assessment *could* be used in a formative manner (and vice versa), that would clearly not be an optimal situation. Rather, a characteristic of any sound assessment is that it is used in the way it was designed. It follows that the optimal instantiation of a formative assessment is one that is both *designed* and actually *used* that way. To build a useful assessment, one needs to begin with a clear sense of its purpose; the actual use of an assessment can define its function, but that intended function should also be focused and improved by design.

Although it is sometimes portrayed as an alternative to summative assessment, we view formative assessment as a complementary activity designed to address very different aims. The *Standards* define formative assessment as "an assessment process used by teachers and students during instruction that provides feedback to adjust ongoing teaching and learning with the goal of improving students' achievement of intended instructional outcomes" (AERA, APA, & NCME, 2014, p. 219). As an aside, we note that, other than a definition of formative assessment in a glossary, there is no other explicit attention to formative assessment in the *Standards*—no best practices, no guidelines for construction or use, and no individual standards for formative assessment. Nonetheless, at least three aspects of the definition of formative assessment found in the *Standards* are noteworthy and stand in contrast to the characteristics of summative assessment.

First, assessment typically involves two parties: educators and students. In summative assessment contexts, educators help design, write, score, and use results, whereas students provide the responses—a comparatively passive form of involvement. Those responses on summative assessments are then used by educators to serve the purposes of grading, monitoring, accountability, and so on. On the other hand, formative assessment typically engages both parties to a greater degree. The preceding definition highlights the distinction that, in contrast to summative assessments, formative assessment is a more collaborative endeavor that involves both educators *and* students in more elaborated and differentiated roles. For example, in a formative assessment context, educators play a role in designing and leading instructional events, but students can also play a role in setting learning goals. Formative assessment provides information that teachers can use to focus or redirect instruction; it also provides information that students can use to assess their own and each other's learning. In short, formative assessment calls for more of an interaction between educators and students than does summative assessment.

Second, whereas summative assessments occur at the end of an instructional program, the above definition characterizes formative assessment as occurring alongside, or even within instruction. In this regard, the labeling of an assessment can—though not always does—provide a clue as to the type of assessment. For example, the term *end-of-course testing* frequently implies a summative assessment, whereas some versions of formative assessment have been described as *embedded assessments*.

Third, whereas summative assessments are *primarily* conducted for the purposes of making evaluative decisions about individuals or programs, with allowances for formative uses of summative data, the focus of formative assessment is squarely on providing feedback and information for adjusting ongoing teaching and learning. Numerous writers have characterized the difference in these primary summative and formative goals as "assessment of learning" versus "assessment for learning" (see, for example, Assessment Reform Group, 1999; Stiggins, 2005). A widely-cited metaphor by the prolific contributor to the field of program evaluation, Robert Stake, captured the distinction between summative and formative assessment in this way: "When the cook tastes the soup, that's formative; when the guests taste the soup, that's summative" (Miller et al., 2016, p. 288).

Although that dichotomous way of categorizing assessments is somewhat useful, we think a more nuanced approach is warranted. Recalling Stake's analogy, it is certainly possible for the guests to both taste the soup and judge it overall, but also to offer suggestions for improving it. Assuming some soup remained in the pot or the chef planned to prepare the recipe again, the guests' suggestions would represent a formative use of summative information. In a testing context, this means that summative tests can yield formatively useful information.

The same does not hold as neatly for formative assessment. Although it is not uncommon for teachers to use impressions gained from a series of formative assessments to inform their judgments in assigning grades or otherwise documenting achievement, such uses can too easily corrupt the formative assessment process and so, we assert, summative uses of formative assessment should be discouraged. Thus, an important distinction between summative and formative assessment lies in their potential uses: Summative assessment data can be used formatively, but formative assessment information should, in general, be used only formatively.

Although the distinctions between summative and formative assessment just presented may be clear in concept, there is at present a serious—and, we believe, consequential—lack of clarity about the definition of formative assessment. In subsequent portions of this chapter, we will describe the variety of definitions and instantiations of what is called formative assessment, and we will identify the deficiencies in those conceptualizations. Then, we will suggest a next-generation definition that we believe best captures the characteristics of formative assessment that are associated with improvements to teaching and learning. For now, however, we turn to a brief historical tracing of the concept.

Evolving Notions of Formative Assessment: An Historical Review

Nearly all attempts to identify the origins of the concept of formative assessment trace beginning usages of *formative* to Michael Scriven, who coined the term *formative evaluation*. Scriven invoked the term in the course of responding to a 1963 article by Lee Cronbach regarding the evaluation of educational programs in which Cronbach asserted that "evaluation, used to improve the course while it is still fluid, contributes more to improvement of education than evaluation used to appraise a product already placed on the market" (p. 236). In a research monograph published later that year, Scriven countered that prioritizing one evaluation focus over another was needless: "Fortunately we do not have to make this choice [between summative and formative evaluation]. Educational projects, particularly curricular ones, clearly must attempt to make best use of evaluation in both these roles" (1963, p. 6). Scriven went on to provide a rudimentary definition of formative evaluation: "This kind of research can be called process research, but it is of course simply outcome evaluation at an intermediate stage. . ." (p. 16).

The distinction between summative and formative aims in evaluation was quickly popularized through the work of Benjamin Bloom and his associates via the *Handbook of Formative and Summative Evaluation of Student Learning* (Bloom, Hastings, & Madaus, 1971). Although that volume is widely known for its elaboration of taxonomies of educational objectives, the authors considered the distinction between formative and summative evaluation to be foundational and they provided the most formal definitions of the terms at that time. In describing summative evaluation, they noted:

> We have chosen the term *summative evaluation* to indicate the type of evaluation used at the end of a term, course, or program for purposes of grading, certification, evaluation of progress, or research on the effectiveness of a curriculum, course of study, or educational plan . . . Perhaps the essential characteristic of summative evaluation is that a judgment is made about the student, teacher, or curriculum with regard to the effectiveness of learning or instruction after the learning or instruction has taken place.
>
> *(p. 117)*

Bloom, Hastings, and Madaus then contrasted summative evaluations with evaluations that served the different purposes prioritized by Cronbach—that is, those that were "used to improve the course while it is still fluid" (1963, p. 236). According to Bloom, Hastings, and Madaus (1971), formative evaluation:

> is for us the use of systematic evaluation in the process of curriculum construction, teaching and learning for the purpose of improving any of these three processes. . . . This means that in formative evaluation one must strive to develop the kinds of evidence that will be most useful in the process, seek the most useful method of reporting the evidence, and search for ways of reducing the negative effect associated with evaluation, perhaps by reducing the judgmental aspects of evaluation or, at least, by having the users of the formative evaluation (teachers, students, curriculum makers) make the judgments.
>
> *(p. 118)*

Formative Assessment

Table 1.1 Formative Assessment Definitions

Formative assessment is . . .	*Citation*
. . . concerned with how judgments about the quality of student responses (performances, pieces, or works) can be used to shape and improve the student's competence by short-circuiting the randomness and inefficiency of trial-and-error learning.	Sadler, 1989, p. 120
. . . assessment carried out during the instructional process for the purpose of improving teaching and learning.	Shepard, 2006, p. 627
. . . a planned process in which assessment-elicited evidence of students' status is used by teachers to adjust their ongoing instructional procedures or by students to adjust their current learning tactics.	Popham, 2008, p. 6
. . . [classroom practice in which] evidence about student achievement is elicited, interpreted, and used by teachers, learners, or their peers, to make decisions about the next steps in instruction that are likely to be better, or better founded, than the decisions they would have taken in the absence of the evidence that was elicited.	Black & Wiliam, 2009, p. 9
. . . the formal and informal processes teachers and students use to gather evidence for the purpose of improving learning. It is the use of the information gathered, by whatever means, to adjust teaching learning that merits the formative label.	Chappius, 2009, p. 12
. . . an active and intentional learning process that partners teachers and students to continuously and systematically gather evidence of learning with the express goal of improving student achievement.	Moss & Brookhart, 2009, p. 6
. . . [the use of] information from a particular assessment to track learning, give students feedback, and adjust instructional strategies in a way intended to further progress toward learning goals.	Greenstein, 2010, p. 21
. . . a process that occurs during teaching and learning and involves both teachers and students gathering information so they can take steps to keep learning moving forward to meet the learning goals.	Heritage, 2010, p. 8
. . . a process tied to learning goals that is used while instruction is occurring.	Marzano, 2010, p. 8
. . . the collaborative processes engaged in by educators and students for the purpose of understanding students' learning and conceptual organization, identification of strengths, diagnosis of weaknesses, areas for improvement, and as a source of information that teachers can use in instructional planning and students can use in deepening their understandings and improving their achievement.	Cizek, 2010, p. 6
. . . a planned process by which teachers or students use assessment-elicited evidence to improve what they're doing.	Popham, 2011, p. 2

Adapted from "Definitions that Explain the Essence of Formative Assessment."

Retrieved from https://cesp.rutgers.edu/sites/default/files/eight-definitions-of-formative-assessments.pdf.

At least one thing is clear regarding the evolution of the term *formative*: In their definitions of formative and summative evaluation, Bloom, Hastings, and Madaus (1971) extended those terms beyond the narrow focus on program and product evaluations that were central to Scriven's (1963) notions. In their more formal definitions, Bloom and his colleagues expanded the notion of formative and summative evaluations to the assessment of learning for individual students, and the modifiers "formative" and "summative" were quickly associated with the core concept of assessment. Although the study of formative and summative assessment became more closely associated with educational

Table 1.2 Ten Characteristics of Formative Assessment

1	Focuses on goals that represent valuable educational outcomes with applicability beyond the learning context
2	Communicates clear, specific learning goals
3	Provides examples of learning goals including, when relevant, the specific grading criteria or rubrics that will be used to evaluate the student's work
4	Identifies student's current knowledge/skills and necessary prerequisites for the desired goals.
5	Requires development of plans for attaining the desired goals
6	Includes frequent assessment, including student self-assessment, peer assessment, and assessment embedded within learning activities
7	Includes feedback that is non-evaluative, specific, timely, related to the learning goals, and provides recommendations for how to improve
8	Encourages students to self-monitor progress toward the learning goals
9	Promotes metacognition and reflection by students on their work
10	Encourages students to take responsibility for their own learning

Adapted from Cizek (2010).

measurement, those concepts shared the aim introduced in the context of educational program evaluation; namely, improving teaching and learning.

Since the 1960s, there has been relative consensus regarding summative assessment as a type of measurement activity conducted primarily for the purposes of documenting learning, achievement, or some other educational outcome. Regrettably, definitional clarity regarding formative assessment has not advanced as far; by some accounts, it may even have degraded. In their 2009 review of the research literature on formative assessment, Dunn and Mulvenon concluded that "there is no agreed upon lexicon with regard to formative assessment" (p. 1). Similarly, Bennett (2011, p. 19) concluded that the term *formative assessment* "does not yet represent a well-defined set of artifacts or practices."

When specialists in formative assessment use the term, some commonalities are apparent, however. For example, Table 1.1 shows several definitions of formative assessment attributed to scholars working in the field of classroom assessment or educational measurement more broadly. Several common elements can be discerned in these definitions. Cizek (2010) provided a list that attempted to capture the relevant characteristics of formative assessment; that list is provided in Table 1.2. As can be seen from Tables 1.1 and 1.2, early work on formative assessment began along a potentially fruitful path and at least some commonality of high-level characteristics can be distilled from the simple, conceptual definitions of formative assessment suggested in the 1980s and 1990s. However, definitional commonality and clarity diminished around the turn of the century as the term *formative assessment* was invoked, applied, and (mis)appropriated in ways that were often antithetical to the core characteristics that are linked to its presumed efficacy. In a chapter titled "Formative Assessment: Caveat Emptor," Shepard (2005) described the co-opting of formative assessment that transpired:

> Potentially powerful classroom-based learning and teaching innovation [of formative assessment] was overshadowed almost immediately by the No Child Left Behind Act (January 2002) with its intense pressure to raise scores on external accountability tests. The title of my chapter is prompted by the recent burgeoning of so-called "formative assessments" offered by commercial test publishers to help raise test scores for NCLB. "Everyone knows that formative

Table 1.3 Types of Assessments: A Head-to-Head Comparison

Formative Learning Assessment	Formative Diagnostic Assessment	Benchmark/Interim Assessment	Summative Assessment
What is it?			
Formative learning is the process of teaching students how to set goals for their learning, to identify their growth toward those goals, to evaluate the quality of their work, and to identify strategies to improve.	Formative diagnostic assessment is a process of questioning, testing, or demonstration used to identify how a student is learning, where his strengths and weaknesses lie, and potential strategies to improve that learning. It focuses on individual growth.	Benchmark or interim assessment is a comparison of student understanding or performance against a set of uniform standards within the same school year. It may contain hybrid elements of formative and summative assessments, or a summative test of a smaller section of content, like a unit or semester.	Summative assessment is a comparison of the performance of a student or group of students against a set of uniform standards.
Who is being measured?			
Individual students are measuring themselves against their learning goals, prior work, other students' work, and/or an objective standard or rubric.	Individual students. The way they answer gives insight into their learning process and how to support it.	Individual students or classes.	The educational environment: Teachers, curricula, education systems, programs, etc.
How often?			
Ongoing: It may be used to manage a particular long-term project, or be included in everyday lessons. Feedback is immediate or very rapid.	Ongoing: Often as part of a cycle of instruction and feedback over time. Results are immediate or very rapid.	Intermittent: Often at the end of a quarter or semester, or a midpoint of a curricular unit. Results are generally received in enough time to affect instruction in the same school year.	Point in time: Often at the end of a curricular unit or course, or annually at the same time each school year.

(continued)

Table 1.3 (continued)

Formative Learning Assessment	Formative Diagnostic Assessment	Benchmark/Interim Assessment	Summative Assessment
For what purpose?			
To help students identify and internalize their learning goals, reflect on their own understanding and evaluate the quality of their work in relation to their own or objective goals, and identify strategies to improve their work and understanding.	To diagnose problems in students' understanding or gaps in skills, and to help teachers decide next steps in instruction.	To help educators or administrators track students' academic trajectory toward long-term goals. Depending on the timing of assessment feedback, this may be used more to inform instruction or to evaluate the quality of the learning environment.	To give an overall description of students' status and evaluate the effectiveness of the educational environment. Large-scale summative assessment is designed to be brief and uniform, so there is often limited information to diagnose specific problems for students.
Self-evaluation and metacognition, analyzing work of varying qualities, developing one's own rubric or learning progressions, writing laboratory or other reflective journals, peer review, etc.	Rubrics and written or oral test questions, and observation protocols designed to identify specific problem areas or misconceptions in learning the concept or performing the skill.	Often a condensed form of an annual summative assessment, e.g. a shorter term paper or test. It may be developed by the teacher or school, bought commercially, or be part of a larger state assessment system.	Summative assessments are standardized to make comparisons among students, classes, or schools. This could a single pool of test questions or a common rubric for judging a project.

Adapted from Sparks (2015).

Formative Assessment

assessment improves learning," said one anonymous test maker, hence the rush to provide and advertise "formative assessment" products. But are these claims genuine?. . . Commercial item banks may come closer to meeting the timing requirements for effective formative assessment, but they typically lack sufficient ties to curriculum and instruction to make it possible to provide feedback that leads to improvement.

(p. 2)

This turn of events resulted in the application of the label *formative assessment* to a diverse menu of educational programs and practices, many of which share little in common with the aspects of formative assessment listed in Table 1.2. For example, the term *formative assessment* has often been used interchangeably—as if synonymous—with the terms *benchmark assessment, interim assessment, progress assessment*, and others. Further, formative assessment has often been dissected along lines demarcating the primary consumer of the information yielded, as in formative *for the student* and formative *for the teacher*. The recent coverage of formative assessment by *Education Week* attempted to distinguish formative and summative assessment while also further subdividing types of formative assessment based on answers to questions such as Who is being measured? How often? For what purpose? and What strategies are used? (see Table 1.3).

Overall, and despite some attempts at definitional clarity, a wide variety of formative assessment conceptualizations persists, including in terms of materials and practices such as:

* brief, teacher-made quizzes used for grading purposes only;
* commercially-marketed or locally-produced "benchmark" or "interim" assessments that may be nothing more than miniature summative assessments;
* item pools that educators can use to create customized assessments for in-depth measurement to ascertain student mastery of specific knowledge or skills;
* "exit questioning" that teachers use to gauge student understandings/misunderstandings and that occur as informal exchanges at the end of a class period;
* rich, longer-term performance tasks designed to serve as instructional activities as well as assessment events; and
* student-developed rubrics for evaluating work in a specific subject area or for use in conducting peer assessments of work products.

Whereas each of these versions is called formative assessment, they do not individually or collectively comprise a coherent and comprehensive description of formative assessment for teaching and learning. Ultimately, although each of these tools or practices may be somewhat helpful for promoting student learning, we assert this minimal good is overshadowed by the untoward consequences of the absence of a clear, specific, consensus definition of formative assessment. The lack of definition that drives the principled design and implementation of formative assessment: 1) results in instructional products and practices that can be widely variable in their form and efficacy; 2) enables inconsistent classroom implementation; 3) presents barriers to scaling up formative assessment; and 4) impedes the ability to conduct high-quality research on and evaluation of formative assessment. One of the main goals of this volume is to address these threats by advancing a clearer, more theoretically-sound and more practically-relevant definition.

Some Observations on the Research Literature on Formative Assessment

The research on formative assessment can be conceptualized as falling into two broad categories: research on individual elements of commonly cited components of formative assessment, and research on combinations of elements that interact to yield more comprehensive and potentially more effective treatments. The following paragraphs provide an introduction and commentary on these two research streams.

The first category is research on the individual elements most often mentioned as key components of formative assessment. Clearly, if formative assessment is to be effective, it must be implemented in ways that maintain fidelity with the core features presumed to account for its efficacy—what have been referred to in the literature on fidelity of implementation as "critical components" (Century, Rudnick, & Freeman, 2010, p. 201). Among others, the elements most often cited as comprising formative assessment include making learning goals explicit, questioning, providing feedback, engaging in peer assessment, and fostering students' ownership of their learning. The seminal literature review by Black and Wiliam (1998a) covered some of these topics as well as others tied to formative assessment. Those authors concluded in a related publication (Black & Wiliam, 1998b) that effect sizes between 0.40 and 0.70 characterized the incremental value of the activity.

Subsequent reviews of individual components—most notably reviews of the wide-ranging literature on feedback—have found highly variable results. For example, in their meta-analysis, Kluger and DeNisi (1996) found a mean effect size for the impact of feedback on performance of .41. However, these investigators also found that 38% of the effects were negative. In a later review, Shute (2008) wrote, "Within this large body of feedback research, there are many conflicting findings and no consistent pattern of results" (p. 153). She noted that "the specific mechanisms relating feedback to learning are still mostly murky, with few (if any) general conclusions" (p. 156). Finally, in his synthesis of many different meta-analyses on a wide variety of educational practices, Hattie (2009) also reported that the effect sizes from 23 meta-analyses of feedback varied considerably but estimated the average effect to be about 0.70.

Of particular note with respect to this first category is that, although the individual components that compose a treatment might be effective, their use in combination might not. It is possible for the elements to interact in ways that magnify or diminish the individual effects. In addition, as Kluger and DeNisi's (1996) analysis suggests, the particular instantiation of an element matters substantially as some approaches produce effects, including negative ones, that are far lower than the average for that element.

A second stream of research on formative assessment concerns studies that go beyond evaluating the effects of individual components to evaluating implementations that assemble components into more coherent treatments. Kingston and Nash (2011) provided an illustration of research movement in this direction with a meta-analysis in which approaches to formative assessment were placed into several categories. In addition to more elemental groupings, their categories included professional development oriented approaches, approaches centered on curriculum-embedded assessment, and approaches that used computer-based systems. Across all types of formative assessment, Kingston and Nash reported a weighted mean effect of 0.20. For approaches based on professional development, the mean effect was 0.30, for curriculum-embedded assessment −0.05, and for computer-based implementations 0.28. In a follow-up commentary, Briggs et al. (2012) noted that the study-exclusion rules used in the Kingston and Nash analysis may have affected their results, with the true effects of studied conditions possibly higher or lower than were reported. Nonetheless, despite the tentative nature of their findings, the Kingston and Nash analysis provides a good illustration of studies that go beyond evaluating the effects of formative elements like feedback to evaluating the impact of more coherent categories of approach. It is to such categorizations that we now turn.

Contemporary Typologies of Formative Assessment

As suggested in the Kingston and Nash (2011) analysis described above, moving toward approaches that assemble elements into describable treatment categories is an advance. However, also critical to advancing the field is creating typologies of approaches that can be distinguished from one another along fundamental dimensions. Such a typology would ideally bring increased coherence to what might now be described as a chaotic collection of ideas, approaches, products and services all sharing the name, formative assessment.

One such typology is that of Shavelson et al. (2008), who describe formative assessment along an informal/formal continuum. In its least formal instantiation—what Shavelson et al. call "on-the-fly" formative assessment—teachers take advantage of a spontaneous "teachable moment" to engage students in a dialogue that generates information about what students know and that provides corrective feedback (p. 300). Shavelson et al. provide an example of this type of formative assessment occurring when a teacher, circulating around a class of students working on a group activity, overhears a student whose statement suggests the presence of a misconception. The teacher then uses the unexpected opportunity to challenge the students' thinking, pose probing questions, and help refine and extend their learning.

In its moderately-formal manifestation—what Shavelson et al. term "planned-for interaction"—the seasoned educator decides in advance to inject critical questions at key junctures in a class activity. The questions posed by the teacher are not superficial, pacing, or simple recall ones, but deliberate questions that, from experience, the teacher knows will help stimulate students to think more deeply, question their own understandings, prompt critical reflection and discussion, and help the teacher gain insights into students' cognitive organization and mastery of concepts.

The most formal type of formative assessment along Shavelson et al.'s (2008) continuum is what they call "embedded-in-the-curriculum formative assessment." This type comes ready-to-use by teachers, and is intentionally and strategically inserted by curriculum developers into instructional guides and materials to aid teachers in discerning whether prerequisite material has been mastered by students, what the status of their current learning is, and what the students still need to master before moving on to a subsequent lesson.

A different typology was proposed by Penuel and his colleagues (see Penuel & Shepard, 2016; Shepard, Penuel, & Davidson, 2017). Their typology includes four categories, among other things differentiated by the extent to which the member formative approaches incorporate theories of learning and the types of theories they draw upon. Their first category, "data-driven decision making," involves setting specific learning goals, using interim assessments to monitor student progress toward those goals, adjusting teaching to address areas of concern, and continuing to evaluate student growth toward the goals over time. This approach, drawn from theories of organizational change described in the business and management literature, uses no theory of learning.

The second category, "strategy-focused formative assessment," is also not grounded in any particular theory of learning but is instead a loose grouping of techniques coming from a variety of theoretical perspectives. Teachers and students use the strategies to assess ongoing work.

"Socio-cognitive formative assessment," the third category, builds on disciplinary theories of learning, such as how students learn mathematics, including both the content and practices that denote growing levels of proficiency in the field. Notably, proficiency is seen as developing in a social context, in essence through a disciplinary community and the job of the student is to progressively take on, not only the knowledge of the members, but also their ways of thinking.

Penuel and colleagues' final category, "socio-cultural formative assessment," adds to the disciplinary theories of socio-cognitive approaches through recognition of the different family and environmental influences that students bring with them to school.

In summary, research and reflection on the nature, critical components, and useful ways of thinking about formative assessment have advanced the theory and practice over the last 20 years. Based on this work, we believe that it is both important and timely to consider a revised definition of formative assessment that, it is hoped, will stimulate further advances in research and practice.

Formative Assessment: A Next-Gen Definition

In this section, we suggest a definition of formative assessment that we offer for broader consideration. As we have argued, an improved definition is necessary in order to foster coherent conditions for educational research, to promote sound educational policy making, to accelerate student learning and achievement and, in general, to advance conceptual clarity in assessment theory and practice. We believe that the definition suggested by Cizek (2010) in the first edition of the *Handbook of Formative Assessment* provides a foundation for a next-generation definition:

> Broadly conceived, formative assessment refers to the collaborative processes engaged in by educators and students for the purpose of understanding the students' learning and conceptual organization, identification of strengths, diagnosis of weaknesses, areas for improvement, and as a source of information that teachers can use in instructional planning, and that students can use in deepening their understandings and improving their achievement.
>
> *(pp. 6–7)*

To that definition, we add four components. First, we incorporate elements of formative assessment that research suggests are effective in themselves: metacognition and self-regulation. Second, it might have been inferred from the earlier definition that formative assessment be conceptualized as a discrete, stand-alone practice. We assert that formative assessment should be considered as one component of a *planned assessment system* (Cizek, 1995)—a comprehensive, purposeful organization of teaching, learning, and assessment activities.

Third, and as this edition of the *Handbook* embodies, we believe that formative assessment should not be conceptualized generically—that is, absent disciplinary substance (Bennett, 2011). Instead, we believe that formative assessment should be conceptualized as an activity that integrates process *and* content; at least one consequence of this conceptualization is that formative assessment takes different forms across various academic areas. Finally, we acknowledge the central role played by inference in all judgments about learning.

To these ends, we propose the following definition that situates formative assessment as one part of a planned assessment ecosystem:

> As part of a planned assessment system, formative assessment supports teachers' and students' inferences about strengths, weaknesses, and opportunities for improvements in learning. It is a source of information that educators can use in instructional planning and students can use in deepening their understandings, improving their achievement, taking responsibility for, and self-regulating, their learning. Formative assessment includes both general principles, and discipline-specific elements that comprise the formal and informal materials, collaborative processes, ways of knowing, and habits of mind particular to a content domain.

The proposed definition explicitly incorporates the notions of inference, self-regulated learning, disciplinary specificity, and being part of a planned assessment system. These elements reflect both established measurement traditions and recent research and advances that are described in greater detail in the following sections.

Formative Assessment as an Inferential Activity

We first note that the preceding definition is grounded in the notion of *inference*—the process of moving from available information to a conclusion as to the meaning of that information. In all assessment contexts, conclusions about student learning are based on incomplete and indirect samples of information from which necessarily tentative conclusions are made. As Wright (1994) has observed:

> I don't want to know which questions you answered correctly. I want to know how much . . . you know. I need to leap from what I know and don't want, to what I want but can't know. That's called inference.

The possible sources of evidence about student learning are many and varied; these sources of evidence must be synthesized to arrive at the judgments that will inform decisions about progress, understanding, next steps, pedagogical choices, and so on (see Bennett, 2011; Chapter 2, this volume). Importantly, all of the sources of evidence should be routinely evaluated themselves as to the quality of information they provide and alternative sources of information should be considered.

For example, in situations where feedback is provided on student work, there is a good argument to concentrate comments on the response rather than on the student himself or herself (Hattie & Timperley, 2007, pp. 90–91; Shute, 2008, p. 177). However, an educator's—or a student's—judgments about the response generally go beyond the response itself, and for good reason. First, the response is an indicator of what the student knows and can do with respect to some task class, and it is that knowledge and capability we want to enhance. Second, what is observed in a student's response must be interpreted in context; that is, the observation is combined with other information about the conditions surrounding that task performance, the student's background, and past performance—evidence that might inform judgments of the student's knowledge and capability related to such tasks. Placed in context, the student's response might lead a teacher to conclude that an observed error on the part of the student was nothing more than a careless mistake, or that it reflected a missing bit of knowledge, or that it represented a deep-seated misconception (Bennett, 2011). The particular inference that is made forms the basis for the (task-focused) feedback given to the student and for the next instructional steps considered.

Formative Assessment and the Self-Regulation of Learning

The proposed definition includes an explicit reference to self-regulated learning. Self-regulated learning (SRL) occurs when learners set goals and then systematically carry out cognitive, affective, and behavioral practices and procedures that move them closer to those goals (Zimmerman & Schunk, 2011). The associations between self-regulated learning and formative assessment have been acknowledged for many years: Black and Wiliam (1998b) described these associations in their early writing on formative assessment; since that time, scholars have since mined the similarities between formative assessment and SRL in terms of their respective forms and functions, and explored the reciprocal support they can provide, under the right conditions (Andrade & Brookhart, 2016, 2019; Nicol & Macfarlane-Dick, 2006).

One of the main similarities in function is related to students' central role in constructing their own learning (Penuel & Shepard, 2016). In the vernacular of assessment, formative assessment can assist students in understanding where they are going, where they are now, and where to go next (Hattie & Timperley, 2007). From the perspective of SRL, formative assessment activates students' cognitive and motivational capacities, focuses them on their learning goals, helps them monitor and reflect on their learning, and provides feedback and strategies they can use to help them reach their goals. In short, formative assessment can help students regulate their learning while also developing important metacognitive and learning management skills (Panadero, Andrade, & Brookhart, 2018).

The theoretical relationship between SRL and formative assessment has been well established: Andrade (2010, 2013) situated scholarship on formative assessment in the literature on self-regulated learning; Allal (2010) expanded the concept of self-regulation via assessment to include assessment by teachers and peers and introduced the term *co-regulation*. Wiliam's (2011) review of formative assessment drew on Boekaerts' (2011) model of SRL, and Clark (2012) provided a theoretical review of the influence of formative feedback on SRL. The left-most column in Table 1.3, entitled Formative Learning Assessment, reflects current conceptions of formative assessment as the regulation of learning (Andrade & Brookhart, 2019) by defining formative assessment using concepts traditionally associated with self-regulated learning, such as goal-setting and metacognition.

Empirical support for the association is recent and incomplete but promising. The trend noted above continues: There is research on elements of formative assessment, such as self-assessment (Panadero, Jonsson, & Botella, 2017), peer assessment (Panadero, Jonsson, & Strijbos, 2016; Reinholz, 2016), or both (Meusen-Beekman, Joosten ten Brinke, & Boshuizen, 2016), as well as research on more comprehensive combinations of elements (Baas et al., 2014; Hawe & Dixon, 2017). Although there is still much to investigate, the evidence for a reciprocal relationship between formative assessment and self-regulated learning is compelling enough to include it in our definition.

Formative Assessment is Discipline-Specific

As others have pointed out (see, e.g., Bennett, 2011; Coffey et al., 2011), conceptualizing formative assessment as a set of generic practices fails to recognize formative assessment as domain dependent. Whereas characteristics such as articulating learning goals, questioning, feedback, peer assessment, and taking ownership of learning are the same at a high level, those process characteristics need to be instantiated in the substance—the content—of the discipline in question. That instantiation will necessarily differ considerably from one discipline to the next. The questions to ask of students; what to look for in and the standards against which to judge their answers; the content of the feedback to supply; what instructional adjustments to make; and what to model for students in terms of the habits of mind that characterize proficient domain performance all vary across disciplines (Bennett, 2011). The characteristic of domain dependency, therefor, not only seems essential to a next-generation definition of formative assessment but, as will be seen in subsequent chapters, has helped frame and organize this *Handbook*.

Conclusions and Directions: The Future of Formative Assessment

Although formative assessment relies on materials and practices, it is *not* the materials and practices themselves that make any assessment event formative. Rather it is the combination of the primary *purpose* to be served by the assessment, the purposeful *design* of the materials and practices, and how the assessment information is actually *used* that distinguishes formative assessment from other types of assessment. For this reason, the next-generation definition presented previously is agnostic as to the *format* of formative assessment. Whereas a formative assessment *might* include next-generation item formats amenable to computer-based administration (aka, technology-enhanced items), constructed-response items, performance tasks, or simulations, it is not a requirement for it to do so—unless particular representations are more common to the essence of disciplinary proficiency than other representations. In writing, for example, it might well be a requirement for formative assessment generally (but not always) to involve productive writing tasks. In other domains, such approaches as multiple-choice items, short answer items, or oral questioning might be employed. The essential point is that effective formative assessment is not characterized by novel features, format, or frequency; rather, formative assessment is an integration of purpose, process, and content, including the ways of knowing that characterize a discipline.

An important consequence of the reconceptualization of formative assessment we have described is that it emphasizes conditions that we assert are not only essential for the effectiveness of formative assessment, but that ought to considerably increase the potential of formative assessment for driving

Formative Assessment

achievement gains. Fostering self-regulation in students, recognizing the role of inference, grounding inference and action deeply in the target disciplines, and designing the overall assessment system so that the formative component works coherently with the summative one results in an approach that, in principle, should add to the positive consequences for learning and instruction described earlier in this chapter.

Quite intentionally, this reconceptualization also distributes responsibility for the success of formative assessment widely under the belief that synergy should produce the maximal impact. Pre-service preparation programs must take responsibility for ensuring that their graduates have the knowledge and skill needed to teach and formatively assess effectively—the disciplinary foundation, an understanding of how to foster self-regulation in the context of that discipline, and a set of basic propositions that help inferentially connect observations from student behavior to instructional actions. School leaders, in turn, must provide the mentoring, in-service, and professional community opportunities that allow their instructional staff to deepen and refine these competencies. Students must rise to the challenge of responsibility for and active participation in the learning process—of becoming formative assessors themselves and engaged members of a disciplinary community. Federal and state policy makers must take responsibility for crafting legislation and regulations that encourage the development of coherent systems of assessment in which formative assessment is a key part. Lastly, curriculum specialists must develop materials that help students become reflective learners and that guide teachers toward knowing what questions are essential to ask, when to ask them, and how to interpret and act upon the results. The best chance of realizing the very considerable effects that formative assessment has to offer will come from all actors working in synchrony from a shared conception. We hope that, in the chapters that follow, the beginnings of such a conception are advanced.

References

American Educational Research Association, American Psychological Association, National Council on Measurement in Education [AERA, APA, NCME]. (2014). *Standards for educational and psychological testing.* Washington, DC: American Psychological Association.

Andrade, H. (2010). Students as the definitive source of formative assessment: Academic self-assessment and the self-regulation of learning. In H. Andrade & G. Cizek (Eds.), *Handbook of formative assessment* (pp. 90–105). New York, NY: Routledge.

Andrade, H. (2013). Classroom assessment in the context of learning theory and research. In J. H. McMillan (Ed.), *SAGE handbook of research on classroom assessment* (pp. 17–34). New York, NY. SAGE.

Andrade, H. & Brookhart, S. M. (2016). The role of classroom assessment in supporting self-regulated learning. In L. Allal & D. Laveault (Eds.), *Assessment for learning: Meeting the challenge of implementation* (pp. 293–309): Springer.

Andrade, H. L., & Brookhart, S. M. (2019). Classroom assessment as the co-regulation of learning. *Assessment in Education: Principles, Policy & Practice.* DOI: 10.1080/0969594X.2019.1571992.

Allal, L. (2010). Assessment and the regulation of learning. In P. Peterson, E. Baker, & B. McGraw (Eds.), *International encyclopedia of education* (Vol. 3, pp. 348–352). Oxford: Elsevier.

Assessment Reform Group. (1999). *Assessment for learning: Beyond the black box.* Cambridge, UK: School of Education, Cambridge University.

Baas, D., Casteliijns, J., Vermeulen, M., Martens, R., & Segers, M. (2014). The relation between Assessment for Learning and elementary students' cognitive and metacognitive strategy use. *British Journal of Educational Psychology, 85*(1), 36–46. doi:10.1111/bjep.12058.

Bennett, R. E. (2011). Formative assessment: A critical review. *Assessment in Education: Principles, Policy and Practice, 18*(1), 5–25. DOI: 10.1080/0969594X.2010.513678.

Bennett, R. E. (2016, June). *Opt out: An examination of issues* (Research Report No. RR-16-13). Princeton, NJ: Educational Testing Service.

Black, P., & Wiliam, D. (2009). Developing the theory of formative assessment. *Educational Assessment Evaluation and Accountability, 21*(1), 5–31.

Black, P., & Wiliam, D. (1998a). Inside the black box: Raising standards through classroom assessment. *Phi Delta Kappan, 80*(2), 139–148.

Black, P., & Wiliam, D. (1998b). Assessment and classroom learning. *Assessment in Education*, *5*(1), 7–74.

Bloom, B. S., Hastings, J. T., & Madaus, G. F. (Eds.) (1971). *Handbook of formative and summative evaluation of student learning*. New York, NY: McGraw-Hill.

Boekaerts, M. (2011). Emotions, emotion regulation, and self-regulation of learning. In B. J. Zimmerman & D. H. Schunk (Eds.), *Handbook of self-regulation of learning and performance* (pp. 408–425). New York: Routledge.

Briggs, D. C., Ruiz-Primo, M. A., Furtak, E., Shepard, L., & Yin, Y. (2012). Meta-analytic methodology and inferences about the efficacy of formative assessment. *Educational Measurement: Issues and Practice*, *31*(4), 13–17. DOI: 10.1111/j.1745-3992.2012.00251.x.

Chappius, J. (2009). *Seven strategies of assessment for learning*. Boston, MA: Allyn & Bacon/Pearson.

Century, J., Rudnick, M., & Freeman, C. (2010). A framework for measuring fidelity of implementation: A foundation for shared language and accumulation of knowledge. *American Journal of Evaluation*, *31*(2), 199–218. DOI: 10.1177/1098214010366173.

Cizek, G. J. (1995). The big picture in assessment and who ought to have it. Phi Delta Kappan, 77(3), 246–249.

Cizek, G. J. (2010). An introduction to formative assessment: History, characteristics, and challenges. In H. L. Andrade & G. J. Cizek (Eds.), *Handbook of formative assessment* (pp. 3–17). New York, NY: Routledge.

Cizek, G. J. (2016). Validating test score meaning and defending test score use: Different aims, different methods. *Assessment in Education: Principles, Policy & Practice*, *23*(2), 212–225. DOI: 10.1080/0969594X.2015.1063479.

Clark, I. (2012). Formative assessment: Assessment is for self-regulated learning. *Educational Psychology Review*, *24*(2), 205–249. DOI: 10.1007/s10648-011-9191-6.

Coffey, J. E., Hammer, D., Levin, D. M, & Grant, T. (2011). The missing disciplinary substance of formative assessment. *Journal of Research in Science Teaching*, *48*, 1109–1136.

Cronbach, L. J. (1963). Education for course improvement. *Teachers College Record*, *64*, 231–248.

Dunn, K. E., & Mulvenon, S. W. (2009). A critical review of research on formative assessment: The limited scientific evidence of the impact of formative assessment in education. *Practical Assessment, Research & Evaluation*, *14*(7).

Every Student Succeeds Act (2015). P.L 114–95, 20 U.S.C. 28.

Gewertz, C. (2015, November 9). Searching for clarity on formative assessment. *Education Week*, *35*(12), p. S2.

Greenstein, L. (2010). *What teachers really need to know about formative assessment*. Alexandria, VA: Association for Supervision and Curriculum Development.

Hattie, J. A. C. (2009). *Visible learning: A synthesis of 800+ meta-analyses on achievement*. Oxford, UK: Routledge.

Hattie, J. & Timperley, H. (2007). The power of feedback. *Review of Educational Research*, *77*, 81–112.

Hawe, E., & Dixon, H. (2017). Assessment for learning: A catalyst for student self-regulation. *Assessment & Evaluation in Higher Education*, *42*(8), 1181–1192. DOI: 10.1080/02602938.2016.1236360.

Heritage, M. (2010). *Formative assessment: Making it happen in the classroom*. Thousand Oaks, CA: Corwin.

Kernan-Schloss, A., & Starr, J. P. (2015). The 47TH annual PDK/Gallup poll of the public's attitudes toward the public schools. *Phi Delta Kappan*, *97*(1), K1–K31.

Kingston, N. & Nash, B. (2011). Formative assessment: A meta-analysis and a call for research. *Educational Measurement: Issues and Practice*, *30*(4), 28–37. DOI: 10.1111/j.1745-3992.2011.00220.x.

Kluger, A. N., & DeNisi, A. S. (1996). The effects of feedback interventions on performance: A historical review, a meta-analysis, and a preliminary feedback intervention theory. *Psychological Bulletin*, *119*(2), 254–284. DOI: 10.1037/0033-2909.119.2.254.

Marzano, R. J. (2010). *Formative assessment and standards-based grading*. Bloomington, IN: Marzano Research Laboratory.

Meusen-Beekman, K. D., Joosten-ten Brinke, D., & Boshuizen, H. P. A. (2016). Effects of formative assessments to develop self-regulation among sixth grade students: Results from a randomized controlled intervention. *Studies in Educational Evaluation*, *51*, 126–136. DOI: 10.1016/j.stueduc.2016.10.008.

Miller, R. L., King, J. A., Mark, M. M., & Caracelli, V. (2016). The oral history of evaluation: The professional development of Robert Stake. *American Journal of Evaluation*, *37*(2), 287–294. DOI: 10.1177/1098214015597314

Moss, C. M. & Brookhart, S. M. (2009). *Advancing formative assessment in every classroom: A guide for instructional leaders*. Alexandria, VA: Association for Supervision and Curriculum Development.

Nicol, D, J. & Macfarlane-Dick, D. (2006), Formative assessment and self-regulated learning: A model and seven principles of good feedback practice. *Studies in Higher Education*, *31*(2), 199–218.

No Child Left Behind Act. (2001). P.L. 107-110. 20 U.S.C. 6301.

Panadero, E., Andrade, H., & Brookhart, S. (2018). Fusing self-regulated learning and formative assessment: A roadmap of where we are, how we got here, and where we are going. *Australian Educational Researcher*, *45*(1), 13–31. DOI: 10.1007/s13384-018-0258-y.

Panadero, E., Jonsson, A., & Strijbos, J. W. (2016). Scaffolding self-regulated learning through self-assessment and peer assessment: Guidelines for classroom implementation. In D. Laveault & L. Allal (Eds.), *Assessment for Learning: Meeting the challenge of implementation* (pp. 311–326). New York, NY: Springer.

Panadero, E., Jonsson, A., & Botella, J. (2017). Effects of self-assessment on self-regulated learning and self-efficacy: Four meta-analyses. *Educational Research Review, 22*, 74–98. DOI: 10.1016/j.edurev.2017.08.004.

Penuel, W. R. & Shepard, L. A. (2016). Assessment and teaching. In D. H. Gitomer & C. B. Bell (Eds.), *Handbook of research on teaching* (5th ed., pp. 787–850). Washington, DC: American Educational Research Association. DOI: 10.3102/978-0-935302-48-6_12.

Popham, W. J. (2008). *Transformative assessment*. Alexandria, VA: Association for Supervision and Curriculum Development.

Popham, W. J. (2011). *Transformative assessment in action*. Alexandria, VA: Association for Supervision and Curriculum Development.

Reinholz, D. L. (2016). The assessment cycle: A model for learning through peer assessment. *Assessment & Evaluation In Higher Education, 41*(2), 301–315. doi:10.1080/02602938.2015.1008982.

Sadler, R. (1989). Formative assessment and the design of instructional assessments. *Instructional Science, 18*, 119–144.

Scriven, M. (1963). *The methodology of evaluation* [Research Report #110]. Lafayette, IN: Purdue University Social Science Education Consortium.

Shavelson, R. J., Young, D. B., Ayala, C. C., Brandon, P. R., Furtak, E. M., Ruiz-Primo, M. A., Tomita, M. K., & Yin, Y. (2008). On the impact of curriculum-embedded formative assessment on learning: A collaboration between curriculum and assessment developers. *Applied Measurement in Education, 21*(4), 295–314. DOI: 10.1080/08957340802347647.

Shute, V. J. (2008). Focus on formative feedback. *Review of Educational Research, 78*(1), 153–189. DOI: 10.3102/0034654307313795.

Shepard, L. A. (2005, October). The future of assessment: *Shaping teaching and learning*. Presentation at the 2005 ETS Invitational Conference, New York, NY.

Shepard, L. A. (2006). Classroom assessment. In R. Brennan (Ed.), *Educational measurement, fourth edition* (pp. 624–646). Westport, CT: Praeger.

Shepard, L. A., Penuel, W. R., & Davidson, K. (2017). Design principles for new assessment systems. *Phi Delta Kappan, 98*(6), 47–52.

Sparks, S. D. (2015, November 9). Types of assessments: A head-to-head comparison. *Education Week, 35*(12), S2.

Stiggins, R. J. (2005). *Student–involved assessment for learning*. New York, NY: Prentice Hall.

Wang, L., Beckett, G. H., & Brown, L. (2006). Controversies of standardized assessment in school accountability reform: A critical synthesis of multidisciplinary research evidence. *Applied Measurement in Education, 19*(4), 305–328.

West, M. R., Henderson, M. B., Peterson, P. E., & Barrows, S. (2018). The 2017 EdNext poll on school reform. *Education Next, 18*(1), 32–52.

Wiliam, D. (2011). What is assessment for learning? *Studies in Educational Evaluation, 37*(1), 3–14. DOI: 10.1016/j.stueduc.2011.03.001.

Wright, B. D. (1994). *Introduction to the Rasch model* [videotape]. University of Chicago: Measurement, Evaluation, Statistics, and Assessment Laboratory.

Zimmerman, B. & Schunk, D. (Eds.). (2011). *Handbook of self-regulation of learning and performances*. New York, NY: Routledge.

2

INTEGRATING MEASUREMENT PRINCIPLES INTO FORMATIVE ASSESSMENT

Randy E. Bennett

In this chapter, I discuss the application of measurement principles to the theory and practice of classroom formative assessment. That measurement principles are important does not suggest that formative assessments should be standardized, quantified, or held to the same standards of technical quality that would be expected of a high-stakes summative test. But it does mean there are fundamental principles that, if ignored, can render the judgments coming from formative assessment—whether by teacher, student, or software—of little value for moving learning forward.

For purposes of the chapter, I describe assessment generally—and formative assessment particularly—from the perspective of evidentiary reasoning. I use that frame because it offers a powerful perspective for making meaning, and taking action, from our observations of student behavior.

Evidentiary Reasoning and Assessment

The development and application of evidentiary reasoning to assessment comes primarily from the work of Mislevy and colleagues on Evidence Centered Design (ECD) (Mislevy, Almond, & Lukas, 2003; Mislevy et al., 2006). The theory and methodology of ECD provides (a) a way of reasoning about assessment design, (b) a way of reasoning about examinee performance, (c) a data framework of reusable assessment components, and (d) a flexible model for test delivery. For purposes of this chapter, the primary interest is in the first two elements, reasoning about design and reasoning about examinee performance. (For a discussion of the remaining two elements, see Mislevy, Almond, & Lukas, 2003.)

Reasoning about assessment design starts with articulating the claims to be made from assessment results about individuals or institutions. Those claims should derive directly from state content standards, cognitive-domain theory, curriculum frameworks, learning objectives, or some combination of these sources. Next, the kinds of evidence required to support those claims are identified. Described last are the tasks that could be used to provide that evidence. Thus, the reasoning proceeds from claims to evidence to tasks.

In contrast to design, reasoning about examinee performance runs in the opposite direction. When a student responds to a single task and provides evidence consistent with a given claim, we can infer with only limited certainty that the claim holds. As the student answers additional questions that provide evidence consistent with the claim, the strength of our inference gets stronger and our level of uncertainty becomes smaller. To the extent that the additional evidence provides an inconsistent picture, uncertainty does not diminish and might even grow.

Integrating Measurement Principles

Notions of uncertainty are of consequence, of course, only if our interest is in characterizing the student. We may, for example, be interested in some attribute that is "latent" or not directly observable (e.g., the student's competency in adding fractions or their level of "grit"); or in the probability that the student will attain an acceptable level of performance in another context (e.g., outside of school, the next grade); or in the likelihood that the student is a member of a particular diagnostic category (e.g., defined as a level in a learning progression or as harboring a particular misconception). If our interest is, on the other hand, simply to gauge a student's performance qua performance—as in a competitive sporting event like the 100-meter dash—then no inference connecting observed evidence to a characterization of the student is required, and no uncertainty exists. That the student achieved a particular ranking, or score (e.g., a time), in the event and won a medal (or didn't) are facts. (See Messick, 1994, for discussion of these two situations in the context of performance assessment.)

To connect observed evidence to characterizations, ECD uses a measurement model. That model weights evidence according to its value, generating a score, a qualitative characterization (e.g., a level in a learning progression, an instructional diagnosis), or both. That measurement model also provides an estimate of the uncertainty associated with that score or characterization. Such models are commonly found in summative assessments but also in some types of formative assessment (e.g., intelligent tutoring systems, educational games like GlassLab's SimCity EDU [Mislevy et al., 2014]).

From an evidentiary reasoning perspective, then, assessment can be viewed as composed of four fundamental acts:

- Engineering opportunities to observe evidence of the competencies we wish to make claims about and then making the relevant observations;
- Inferentially connecting that evidence, with some degree of uncertainty, to meaningful characterizations of individuals, groups, or institutions;
- Acting on those characterizations (including giving feedback, making instructional adjustments and plans); and
- Evaluating the quality and impact of the above.

These four acts apply to the design and use of highly consequential summative tests as well as to the enactment of formative assessment in the classroom, though the rigor, formality, and methodology will differ significantly across these two assessment purposes.

Evidentiary Reasoning as a Design Basis for Formative Assessment

How these four acts are instantiated in formative assessment depends in significant part on the definition of formative assessment to which one subscribes. Penuel and colleagues (Penuel & Shepard, 2016; Shepard, Penuel, & Davidson, 2017) propose a definition that encompasses four categories: data-driven decision making, strategy-focused formative assessment, socio-cognitive formative assessment, and socio-cultural formative assessment. The first category, data-driven decision making, covers approaches grounded in business rather than learning theory. These approaches use data collected from interim assessments and/or electronic learning environments to take instructional action. A distinguishing feature of this category is its attention to quantitative data.

The second category, strategy-focused formative assessment, builds on generic approaches that have roots in different learning theories, without bringing those theories or approaches together into a coherent, principled whole. A distinguishing characteristic of this category is a set of easy-to-learn and easy-to-use, general pedagogical techniques which, individually, have some theoretical basis. These techniques include the use of colored cups by students to quickly signal their level of understanding of work in progress ("traffic lights"), and the teacher drawing from a container of student-labeled popsicle sticks to randomize who gets called to answer questions during class discussion.

The third, or socio-cognitive category, uses a theory of domain proficiency to ground the artifacts and practices of formative assessment. This category is distinctive in its attention to the importance of domain specificity in conceptualizing formative assessment. In other words, how one goes about formative assessment is different depending on domain (e.g., English language arts, science, history) because the nature of what it means to know varies across domains (Bennett, 2011).

The final category, socio-cultural formative assessment, uses cognitive-domain theory but adds to that theory a deep examination and understanding of the culture in which the student lives and learns. The distinguishing feature of this category is, of course, the realization that students are shaped by the cultures from which they come, and instruction and assessment must account for that shaping.

Of note is that these categories of formative assessment can, to varying degrees, be instantiated by teachers, software, or some combination of the two. In the case of data-driven decision making, teachers may use interim, or more finely targeted, assessment results to adjust instruction. At the other end of the spectrum, data gathered through interactions with courseware may be used to automatically make adjustments in real time as students respond (Bienkowski, Feng, & Means, 2012, pp. 17–18). The strategy-focused approach is typically conceived as teacher centered but technological aids can be employed, such as software to pose discussion questions, collect responses, and display them at random on a smart board for the teacher and class to comment upon. With respect to socio-cognitive approaches, a teacher schooled in domain theory in the English language arts, for example, can use that framework to organize instruction, make sense of student responses, and plan next steps. Software, in the form of intelligent tutoring systems (Ritter et al., 2007; van Lehn et al., 2005), as well as some educational games, can in some senses do the same, though in a considerably more structured form and more commonly in domains like mathematics rather than social studies or language arts. Finally, there is much research targeted at incorporating socio-cultural factors into instructional software through personalization based on student background, interests, and levels of engagement (Baker et al., 2010; Gobert, Baker, & Wixon, 2015).

When formative assessment is embedded in educational software, formal measurement models can be employed because student responses can be automatically captured, the responses used in characterizing underlying proficiencies, and those characterizations acted upon to adjust instruction. For example, Mislevy has extensively discussed the application of evidentiary reasoning to the socio-cognitive and socio-cultural formative assessments built into educational games and tutoring systems (Mislevy et al., 2012).

In the case where the teacher or student takes the formative assessment responsibility—in the first instance perhaps through a Socratic dialogue, or in the second by comparing one's work to a checklist—formal modeling is not possible. However, the principles of evidentiary reasoning still apply. It is to the application of these principles that I now turn. The discussion is organized around the four fundamental acts that comprise assessment, concentrating on the implementation of those acts largely from socio-cognitive and socio-cultural perspectives.

Engineering Opportunities to Observe Evidence

The focus of this first assessment act is to *design* situations, activities, tasks, or questions that generate observable *evidence* of the competencies we wish to make claims about (whether we are the teacher or the student monitoring his or her own learning). At least two terms in the description of that act are worth highlighting. The first term is, "design." Design means working intentionally, in ECD fashion, from claims, to the types of evidence required, to the opportunities that will provide that evidence. The work of Wiggins highlights the importance of design in classroom assessment (Wiggins, 1998; Wiggins & McTighe, 2005).

The second term is, "evidence," itself. By its nature, evidentiary reasoning presumes grounding in disciplinary content because one cannot know what constitutes evidence, or value it with respect to some inference, without that disciplinary grounding. Depending on the local context, this grounding might be rooted in state content standards, cognitive-domain theory, or the curriculum frameworks and learning objectives aligned to such standards or theories.

An example of such grounding can be found in Deane's Key Practices, which is a cognitive-domain theory for the English language arts (Deane et al., 2015; Deane & Song, 2015; Deane & Sparks, Chapter 4, this volume; O'Reilly, Deane, & Sabatini, 2015; Sparks & Deane, 2015). A key practice is a bundle of reading, writing, and critical thinking skills required to interact meaningfully with other members of a literate community. Among the key practices are developing and sharing stories and social understandings, building and sharing knowledge, discussing and debating ideas, and research and inquiry. Associated with any given practice are one or more prototypic artifacts. For example, for developing and sharing stories and social understandings, that artifact might be a narrative piece of writing; for building and sharing knowledge, an informational brochure; for discussing and debating ideas, an argumentative essay; and for research and inquiry, a data-based report.

To guide students in learning to create the artifacts that help define the practice, each practice is organized as a series of phases. The phases might initially be carried out sequentially but, over time, become more iterative and interlocking as competency develops. For discussing and debating ideas (or argumentation), the phases are understanding the issue, exploring the subject, considering positions, creating and evaluating arguments, and organizing and presenting arguments (Deane & Song, 2015). Each phase includes questions that students are taught to ask of themselves. For understanding the issue, the questions are:

- Whose opinions about this issue matter?
- What do people who are interested in this issue care about?
- Whom am I trying to convince?
- How will I convince them?
- Whom are others trying to convince?
- How will they convince them?

These questions are critically important from at least two perspectives. First, the questions give the teacher a basis for engineering opportunities to observe evidence of what students know and can do. Second, the questions provide a heuristic for students to employ in attacking an argumentation problem.

The phases that constitute a given key practice can be further decomposed into learning progressions. Following Deane, Sabatini, and O'Reilly (2012), we can generally think of a learning progression as:

> A description of qualitative change in a student's level of sophistication for a key concept, process, strategy, practice, or habit of mind. Change in student standing on such a progression may be due to a variety of factors, including maturation and instruction. Each progression is presumed to be modal—i.e., to hold for most, but not all, students. Finally, it is provisional, subject to empirical verification and theoretical challenge.

Each progression is associated with one or more specific competencies underlying a given phase, such as creating and evaluating arguments. The progressions provide additional grounding for teachers to use in generating opportunities to observe evidence. For creating and evaluating arguments (reasons and evidence), Deane and Song (2015) describe the progression essentially as follows:

1 Understands the idea that positions may need to be supported with reasons that will be convincing to the audience
2 Recognizes, generates, and elaborates on reasons in writing, with some awareness of the need for evidence, and uses one's own argument to counter others' argument in an engaging, familiar context

3 Understands use of evidence and clearly grasps the need to provide evidence and reasons that are directly relevant to and support the main point and that are logically sound
4 Understands the role of critique and rebuttal and is able to reason about and respond to counterevidence and critical questions outside of an immediate oral context
5 Builds systematic mental models of entire debates, and uses these models to frame one's own attempts to build knowledge

To gather evidence with respect to the progression, a teacher might pose an issue such as whether the US should ban advertisements to children under age 12 and then assign brief readings on it. To observe evidence related to student understanding of the relationship between positions and reasons (Level 1), the teacher could pose a series of reasons and ask whether each one fits with a "Ban" or "Allow" position (e.g., the reason, "most people ignore most of the advertisements they see," would fit with an "Allow" position). To generate observations as to student understanding of the connection between reasons and evidence (Level 2), the teacher might display a set of claim-and-evidence pairs, asking if the cited evidence supports, weakens, or is irrelevant to the claim.

One prototypic artifact associated with this key practice is the argumentative essay, which falls at Level 3 of the creating and evaluating arguments progression. Note that, in Deane and colleagues' view, the cognitive-domain theory should make clear to students and teachers the characteristics of quality performance. For that purpose, students are provided with guidelines for the essay that essentially constitute standards for the artifact (Figure 2.1). The guidelines appear as part of formative exercises, as well as on end-or-unit tests. The purpose of repeatedly presenting the guidelines is to get students to internalize them, ideally making them a habit of mind they can call upon in self-monitoring their argumentative writing. In addition, the guidelines make clear for teachers what

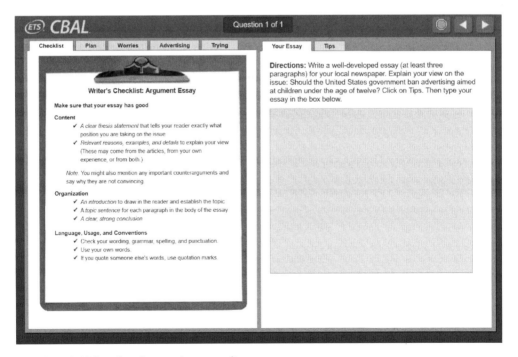

Figure 2.1 Guidelines for what constitutes a quality argument essay.

Note. Copyright © 2017 by ETS. Used by permission.

constitutes evidence of a quality product. For a more in-depth treatment of how to engineer opportunities to observe evidence for discussing and debating ideas, see Deane and Song (2015). For the research and inquiry key practice, see Deane and Sparks (Chapter 4, this volume).

To return to the main points of this section, situations (activities, tasks, or questions) need to be *designed* to reveal evidence concerning the competencies of interest—the competencies that teachers (or students) wish to foster and for which they wish to adjust instruction (or learning). What constitutes *evidence* needs to be grounded in a meaningful conceptualization of the domain, be it content standards, a cognitive-domain theory like the key practices, or a curriculum framework and its associated learning objectives.

Inferentially Connecting Evidence to Characterizations

The goal of a teacher (or a student) in collecting evidence is to use that evidence to make judgments, or characterizations, about what the student knows and can do so that instructional adjustments can be made (or the current instructional plan can be continued as is). Those characterizations of competency—whether they be that the student understands the need in argumentation to back positions with reasons or that the class has mastered isolating variables in algebra—carry with them some degree of uncertainty. In measurement theory, uncertainty is associated with noise, which clouds the underlying signal. Students sometimes misunderstand our questions, feel little connection to the problem situation, or may be momentarily distracted such that their response (or lack thereof) implies a deficiency. Students also sometimes answer correctly for the wrong reasons due, for example, to a lucky guess, an incorrect mathematical algorithm that occasionally generates a satisfactory result, or overhearing the whispered response of a better-informed neighbor.

In more formal measurement contexts like summative assessment, sources of noise are present in test scores and their effects can be estimated via classical test theory methods or through measurement models. Effects can be estimated for the population as a whole, as well as for demographic groups to identify if those groups are being measured more or less precisely than some reference population.

Measurement models can also be used in formative assessments, particularly in the development stages. For example, that modeling can identify cases where authentic-seeming tasks fail to provide the intended evidence, as well as for improving the quality of evidence coming from iterative task revisions (R. Mislevy, personal communication, March 26, 2018). In some instances, such as when formative assessments are embedded in electronic learning environments like games and intelligent tutoring systems (Mislevy et al., 2014), modeling can be incorporated into the learning environment to help determine, for example, if the gathered evidence is sufficient to conclude that a student knows enough to move to the next set of activities.

For teachers engaged in direct interactions with students, the quantification of uncertainty is generally not feasible. All the same, recognizing the existence of noise is important, as are approaches to reducing it, for the same reasons as in electronic learning environments. In both contexts, acting on insufficient information can lead to wrong instructional decisions and, whereas those wrong decisions may be easily reversible, they waste time and effort which could have been spent more productively elsewhere.

How might a teacher reduce uncertainty? One way is to integrate the observed evidence (e.g., what a student wrote on an exit card calling for a reason to back a given position) with what the teacher already knows from past behavior. Does that response agree with what was observed in homework, quizzes, or other classwork on the same topic? How does the response square with what is known of the student's prerequisite, as well as more advanced, knowledge? A wrong response to a question falling at a relatively low level in a learning progression (e.g., pairing reasons with positions) would be unexpected if the student had already provided previous sufficient evidence of a more advanced skill (e.g., being able to evaluate the validity of claim-evidence pairs).

Especially when the observed evidence doesn't agree with past behavior, a sensible strategy is to gather more evidence. In the context of classroom discussion, one might ask questions that probe the same competency more deeply or that attempt to reveal signs of it in a different way. Gathering additional evidence may also be important when prior behavior is consistent with one's current characterizations, simply as a means of confirming those characterizations.

For students learning to self-monitor, the strategy is essentially the same. The proximal goal is reproducibility. Students might be taught to reason as follows: "If I worked a given algebra problem correctly, could I do that again with another problem of the same type? The more problems of a type that I can correctly solve, the greater my confidence that I've mastered that competency." Note that this formative habit of mind not only results in self-monitoring but also deliberate practice, which improves fluency (Ericsson, Krampe, & Tesch-Romer, 1993).

In addition to noise, our characterizations may be affected by systematic biases. Such biases may be borne out of unfamiliarity with the culture, language, or behavior of students from particular demographic groups, as well as from other sources. Research suggests, for example, that teachers' judgments of students' academic competencies may be influenced, unintentionally or not, by such student background characteristics as race, ethnicity, social class, gender, language, and disability status (Bennett et al., 1993; Hurwitz, Elliott, & Braden, 2007; Holder & Kressels, 2017; Meissel et al., 2017; Ready & Wright, 2011). These apparent biases may contribute to consistent under- or overestimates of what students know and can do.

In formal measurement contexts, tools exist to help identify the possible presence of some of these biases. For example, test items sometimes favor or disfavor particular demographic groups because they call for knowledge that is tangential to the competency being measured and not evenly distributed across groups. These items are identified through statistical means but then reviewed by content experts in an attempt to discern the cause. A similar phenomenon could conceivably exist with respect to human raters in their scoring of constructed-response tasks, where some raters might systematically grade the responses of particular groups too low or too high relative to other raters.

In the formative classroom assessment context, such biases can be problematic if they, for example, lead a teacher to misconstrue a poor response to a science question as lack of competency when the cause of that incorrect responding was a construct-irrelevant factor like low English language proficiency or hearing difficulty. That misconstrual, in turn, may lead the teacher to lower expectations inappropriately for some students. It may suggest to those students that they are not progressing as well as they really are, or it may cause instructional time to be spent in unproductive ways.

Teachers can take several steps to reduce the possibility of bias. The first step is to recognize that most individuals have preconceptions about other groups and that these preconceptions can affect how they perceive the behavior of group members. A second step is to develop knowledge of the student groups present in one's classes, especially if they are different from one's own demographic group. This knowledge development is consistent with the socio-cultural perspective on formative assessment, which advocates bringing an understanding of the culture, language, and family background of students to the judgments we as formative assessors make and actions we take (Penuel & Shepard, 2016). A third step, which will facilitate the teacher's knowledge development, is to routinely consult other information sources that might not be subject to the same biases. Colleagues with suitable background and experience with unfamiliar groups may be particularly helpful. Reviewing student work with those colleagues, as well as descriptions of student classroom behavior, can provide invaluable information to be integrated with one's current inferences.

A third consideration in strengthening our characterizations is that of task specificity, which is of particular importance in the characterizations of students that we make from performance tasks like essays, science experiments, or other extended activities. It is well established that how successfully an individual achieves on such a task can vary considerably as a function of topic (Breland et al., 1987; Linn & Burton, 1994). That performance variation occurs because, among other things,

Integrating Measurement Principles

individual students may be more interested in, or knowledgeable about, some topics than other topics. Our characterizations of their argumentative writing skill, for example, may be mistaken because the evidence we observed came from a task concerning the pros and cons of environmental regulation—a topic of little interest or familiarity to a particular student—when they might have argued more effectively about the use of animals in research. An approach sometimes taken is to give students a choice of topics on which to demonstrate competency. Unfortunately, research suggests that students may not always choose well (Bridgeman, Morgan, & Wang, 1996; Powers & Bennett, 1999). Further, in many real-world situations such as some workplace settings, tasks may come with pre-assigned topics, so choice may not exist. From a formative perspective, then, our characterizations will be stronger to the extent that they can be based on tasks drawn from more than one topic. Assigning more than one topic might often not be feasible, in which case it might make sense to condition the characterizations on the topic assigned.

Besides topic, format can also affect the evidence produced by a task. Shavelson, Baxter, and Gao (1993), for example, found that different performance task formats measured different attributes: characterizations of student competency depended on the format taken. More recently, Quellmalz et al. (2013) observed a similar result for science tasks varying in level of interactivity, in this case tasks associated with interactive simulations, dynamic stimuli, and static stimuli. These results argue for teaching and assessing with a variety of task formats. To minimize cost and maximize the chances that students will be familiar with the formats they are presented on high-stakes summative tests, state education departments and their test contractors have typically limited task formats to a very small number. Not surprisingly, teachers have tended to concentrate instruction on those limited formats. Because knowledge is tied to the context in which it is initially learned, it is arguably better for students to be taught and formatively assessed using a variety of task formats (and topics) that help them connect their developing knowledge to conditions of use and to more general problem classes (National Research Council, 2000, pp. 42–44, 62–63).

It should be noted that none of the above considerations should prevent the teacher from giving constructive feedback in response to task performance and, of course, such feedback should be routinely provided. *How* the student performed on a given task is a fact and feedback directed at that particular performance (and only that performance) does not rise to the level of a *characterization* of what the student knows or what the student can do. Task-centered feedback (e.g., does your reason logically support your position?) is generally viewed as having positive effects (Hattie & Timperly, 2007, pp. 90–91; Shute, 2008, p. 177). But giving such feedback is quite different from inferentially characterizing the student (for instructional planning purposes) as not having mastered the relationship between positions and reasons, and therefore needing more work on that competency. It is that type of decision making to which we now turn.

Acting on Characterizations

As suggested above, the actions we take as a result of our initial characterizations can involve integrating prior information with current observations, gathering new information from the student, and consulting colleagues for their input. Each of these actions can reduce our uncertainty as to what the student knows and can do so that a more sensible instructional next step can be taken. That next instructional step also can reduce uncertainty as the student's response to it may confirm or refute our characterization. In that sense, we can think of a characterization as akin to posing what has been termed a "formative hypothesis" (Bennett, 2011, p. 17; Kane, 2006, p. 49; Shepard, 2006, p. 642).

Consider in this regard the distinctions among errors, slips, misconceptions, and lack of understanding. We can think of an error as some difference between a desired response to a problem situation and what it is we observed the student do. That error could have one of several causes. Among other things, it could be a slip, in other words, a procedural mistake that even proficient performers occasionally make because of momentary inattention or a misreading of the problem. Alternatively, the error could be rooted in a misconception—that is, a persistent confusion (or, from another perspective, a naive view that precedes the emergence of more sophisticated views). Finally, the error could be a lack of understanding resulting from a missing bit of conceptual or procedural knowledge, but without any persistent misconception.

Each of these causes implies a different instructional action. If the cause was a slip, the sensible next step would be minimal feedback. Simply pointing out the error or asking the student to look more closely at his or her solution might well suffice. A lack of understanding, in contrast, might suggest re-teaching, perhaps with an elaborated explanation. Correcting a misconception, however, is likely to require the more significant investment associated with engendering a deeper cognitive shift.

It is worth considering that the posing and testing of hypotheses about student understanding will be made stronger if the teacher has a well-developed domain conceptualization. A pedagogically oriented cognitive-domain model, for example, can offer learning progressions in which to locate the gathered evidence. A teacher can use the model to help guide an iterative cycle in which he or she observes behavior, formulates hypotheses about the causes of incorrect responding, takes further action (including the making of instructional adjustments and gathering of new observations), and updates his or her starting hypotheses.

Evaluating Quality and Impact

The previous sections suggest a high-level theory of action for formative assessment, in particular the action mechanisms that explain how and why it should in principle work (Bennett, 2010). That theory might be articulated as follows: We design situations (activities, tasks, questions) to observe evidence of the competencies we wish to make claims about and carry out those observations; make characterizations from our observations as to what students know and can do; and take actions based on those characterizations that are intended to facilitate growth. From that theory of action, we can view the quality of formative assessment as having four components, one related to the situations we engineer; a second to the characterizations of proficiency we take from student behavior in those situations; the third concerning the actions we make based on our judgments or characterizations; and the last about the impact of our actions on achievement.

It should be clear that this theory posits a structure in which the quality of each step depends on the integrity of each of the previous ones. If the situations we design are substandard, they won't reveal meaningful evidence of the competencies of interest. If we base judgments on observations from those situations, those characterizations will most likely be invalid, our actions misguided, and the impact on learning minimal. If the situations we design are aligned to the competencies and designed to probe important distinctions in levels of proficiency, valuable evidence can be obtained. But if our judgments from those observations are biased or too hampered by noise, our actions and their impact are again imperiled. If we have the benefit of well-designed situations and well-founded inferences, then there is a good basis for action. And, finally, presuming those actions are sensible, learning should result.

A second observation from this theory of action is that if learning results but one or more links in the structure are clearly amiss, learning could not have resulted from our attempts at formative assessment. How could it have? More likely is that another source is responsible, perhaps more effective guidance from a parent, tutor, peer, or electronic learning environment.

A third observation is that, if we want our formative assessment to be effective, we need to be deeply attuned to it. Being a teacher (or student) means being self-reflective about one's formative assessment. It means analyzing the situations we design to identify those that work in bringing out useful evidence and those that do not. It means experimenting with new situations and with changes to the ones that didn't work. And it means continuing to deepen one's knowledge of the domain and of the ways in which students typically develop proficiency in it.

Being self-reflective also implies continually reviewing one's judgments and how they compare with those from other sources. Discussing student work with colleagues can be an invaluable mechanism for gaining deeper insight into what features to attend to in evaluating work and how those features might map to levels in a learning progression or other proficiency classification. Comparing one's judgments to standardized test performance can also be helpful, to see if any notable differences are apparent in, for example, performance on groups of items measuring competencies believed to have been mastered vs. ones thought not to have been acquired. Such comparisons need to be made cautiously, of course, because uncertainty exists in both the item performances *and* the teacher's (or student's) judgments of mastery.

Being self-reflective means considering the sensibility of one's instructional decisions. Do those decisions follow logically from the characterizations and from the cognitive-domain theory, content standards, or curriculum and objectives? Would an expert colleague have done something that was materially similar? If not, why not? A very useful device, particularly for less experienced teachers, might be to keep a journal or other record of instructional decisions. It might not be practical to do so for all students, unless that record is a natural byproduct of personalizing instruction through a learning management or other online system. But keeping a record of a sample of instructional decisions made for the class, or for selected students, offers an artifact that facilitates reflection and discussion with colleagues.

Finally, being self-reflective suggests that we integrate all the evidence at our disposal—qualitative as well as quantitative—to come to our best understanding of whether learning has occurred, and whether it can reasonably be connected to the acts we undertook.

Conclusion

This chapter has described how principles from educational measurement and the practice of formative assessment might be brought together. Evidentiary reasoning was employed as a framework for that purpose. This framework helps in designing situations that allow us to observe evidence of the competencies we care about and then in reasoning backward from that evidence to characterizations of proficiency.

Within this reasoning framework, evidence can only be defined in the context of a detailed description of the discipline—content standards, a cognitive-domain theory, or a curriculum framework and learning objectives. The cognitive-domain theory of the English language arts key practices was used to suggest how such a conceptualization can aid the design of situations, the observation of evidence, the characterization of what students know and can do, and the taking of next instructional steps.

Of central importance in the evidentiary reasoning framework is that, although we as formative assessors can and generally should give feedback about task performance, we cannot avoid characterizing students in terms of what they know and can do because those inferences are the basis for next instructional steps. With such characterizations, however, come uncertainty and potential biases, which can reduce the effectiveness and efficiency of our next steps. To minimize uncertainty, we should do our utmost to design situations that pose problems in a variety of topical contexts and that use a diversity of formats consistent with the nature of the domain in question. We should integrate our observations with evidence from other sources. And, we should make special efforts to consult colleagues when we are not familiar with the culture and background of students who are different from us.

Finally, as formative assessors, we should be continually reflecting on the quality and impact of our practice, cultivating in ourselves the same types of self-reflective and self-regulatory behavior we wish our students to develop.

References

Baker, R. S. J. d., D'Mello, S. K., Rodrigo, M. M. T., Graesser, A. C. (2010) Better to be frustrated than bored: The incidence, persistence, and impact of learners' cognitive-affective states during interactions with three different computer-based learning environments. *International Journal of Human-Computer Studies, 68* (4), 223–241.

Bennett, R. E. (2010). Cognitively Based Assessment of, for, and as Learning: A preliminary theory of action for summative and formative assessment. *Measurement: Interdisciplinary Research and Perspectives, 8,* 70–91.

Bennett, R. E. (2011). Formative assessment: A critical review. *Assessment in Education: Principles, Policy and Practice, 18,* 5–25. DOI: 10.1080/0969594X.2010.513678

Bennett, R. E., Gottesman, R. L., Rock, D. A., & Cerullo, F. M. (1993). The influence of behavior and gender on teachers' judgments of students' academic skill. *Journal of Educational Psychology, 85,* 347–356.

Bienkowski, M., Feng, M., & Means, B. (2012). *Enhancing teaching and learning through educational data mining and learning analytics: An issue brief.* Washington, DC: U.S. Department of Education, Office of Educational Technology. Retrieved from https://tech.ed.gov/wp-content/uploads/2014/03/edm-la-brief.pdf.

Breland, H. M., Camp, R., Jones, R. J., Morris, M. M., & Rock, D. A. (1987). *Assessing writing skill.* New York, NY: College Entrance Examination Board.

Bridgeman, B., Morgan, R., & Wang, M. (1996). *Choice among essay topics: Impact on performance and validity* (Research Report No. RR-96-4). Princeton, NJ: Educational Testing Service.

Deane, P., Sabatini, J., Feng, G., Sparks, J.R., Song, Y., Fowles, M., O'Reilly, T. Jueds, K, Krovetz, R, Foley, C. (2015). *Key practices in the English language arts: Linking learning theory, assessment, and instruction* (Research Report No. RR-15-17). Princeton, NJ: Educational Testing Service.

Deane, P. Sabatini, J., & O'Reilly, T. (2012). *The CBAL English language arts competency model and provisional learning progressions: Outline of provisional learning progressions.* Retrieved from http://elalp.cbalwiki.ets.org/Outline+of+Provisional+Learning+Progressions.

Deane, P. & Song, Y. (2015). *The key practice, 'Discuss and debate ideas': Conceptual framework, literature review, and provisional learning progressions for argumentation* (Research Report No. RR-15-33). Princeton, NJ: Educational Testing Service.

Ericsson, K. A., Krampe, R. T., & Tesch-Romer, C. (1993). The role of deliberate practice in the acquisition of expert performance. *Psychological Review, 100,* 363–406.

Gobert, J.D., Baker, R.S., Wixon, M.B. (2015) Operationalizing and detecting disengagement within online science microworlds. *Educational Psychologist, 50* (1), 43–57.

Hattie, J., & Timperly, H. (2007). The power of feedback. *Review of Educational Research, 77,* 81–112.

Holder, K., & Kressels, U. (2017). Gender and ethnic stereotypes in student teachers' judgments: a new look from a shifting standards perspective. *Social Psychology of Education, 20,* 471–490. DOI 10.1007/s11218-017-9384-z

Hurwitz, J. T., Elliott, S. N., & Braden, J. P. (2007). The influence of test familiarity and student disability status upon teachers' judgments of students' test performance. *School Psychology Quarterly, 22,* 115–144. DOI 10.1037/1045-3830.22.2.115.

Kane, M. T. (2006). Validation. In R. L. Brennan (Ed.), *Educational measurement* (4th ed.) (p. 17–64). Westport, CT: American Council on Education/Praeger.

Linn, R. L., & Burton, E. (1994). Performance-based assessment: Implications of task specificity. *Educational Measurement: Issues and Practice, 13*(1), 5–8.

Meissel, K., Meyer, F., Yao, E. S., & Rubie-Davies, C. M. (2017). Subjectivity of teacher judgments: Exploring student characteristics that influence teacher judgments of student ability. *Teaching and Teacher Education, 65,* 48–60. Retrieved from http://www.sciencedirect.com/science/article/pii/S0742051X17303475#bib64.

Messick, S. (1994). The interplay of evidence and consequences in the validation of performance assessments. *Educational Researcher, 23*(2), 13–23.

Mislevy, R. (2018). Personal communication, March 26, 2018.

Mislevy, R. J., Almond, R. G., & Lukas, J. F. (2003). A brief introduction to evidence-centered design (Research Report No. RR-03-16). Princeton, NJ: Educational Testing Service.

Mislevy, R. J., Behrens, J. T., DiCerbo, K. E., & Levy, R. (2012). Design and discovery in educational assessment: Evidence-centered design, psychometrics, and educational data mining. *Journal of Educational Data Mining, 4*(1). Retrieved from http://www.educationaldatamining.org/JEDM/index.php/JEDM/article/view/22/12.

Mislevy, R.J., Steinberg, L.S., Almond, R.G., & Lukas, J.F. (2006). Concepts, terminology, and basic models of evidence-centered design. In D. M. Williamson, I. I. Bejar, & R. J. Mislevy (Eds.), *Automated scoring of complex tasks in computer-based testing* (pp. 15–48). Mahwah, NJ: Erlbaum.

Mislevy, R. J., Oranje, A., Bauer, M. I., von Davier, A., Hao, J., Corrigan, S., Hoffman, E., DiCerbo, K., & John, M. (2014). *Psychometric considerations in game-based assessment.* Redwood City, CA: GlassLab. Retrieved from https://www.envisionexperience.com/~/media/files/blog/glasslab-psychometrics.pdf?la=en.

National Research Council. (2000). *How people learn: Brain, mind, experience, and school* (Expanded ed.). Washington, DC: National Academies Press.

O'Reilly, T., Deane, P., & Sabatini, J. P. (2015). *Building and sharing knowledge key practice: What do you know, what don't you know, what did you learn?* (Research Report No. RR-15-24). Princeton, NJ: Educational Testing Service.

Penuel, W.R. & Shepard, L.A. (2016). Assessment and teaching. In D.H. Gitomer & C.A. Bell, (Eds.), *Handbook of research on teaching* (pp. 787–850). Washington, DC: AERA.

Powers, D. E. & Bennett, R. E. (1999). Effects of allowing examinees to select questions on a test of divergent thinking. *Applied Measurement in Education, 12*, 257–279.

Quellmalz, E. S., Davenport, J. L., Timms, M. J., DeBoer, G. E., Jordan, K. A., Huang, C.-W., & Buckley, B. C. (2013). Next-generation environments for assessing and promoting complex science learning. *Journal of Educational Psychology, 105*, 1100–1114. DOI 10.1037/a0032220.

Ready, D. D. & Wright, D. L. (2011). Accuracy and inaccuracy in teachers' perceptions of young children's cognitive abilities: The role of child background and classroom context. *American Educational Research Journal, 48*, 335–360. DOI 10.3102/0002831210374874.

Ritter, S., Anderson, J. R., Koedinger, K. R., & Corbett, A. (2007) Cognitive tutor: Applied research in mathematics education. *Psychonomic Bulleting & Review, 14*(2), 249–255.

Shavelson, R. J., Baxter, G. P., & Gao, X. (1993). Sampling variability of performance assessments. *Journal of Educational Measurement, 30*, 215–232.

Shepard, L. A. (2006). Classroom assessment. In R. L. Brennan (Ed.), *Educational measurement* (4th ed.) (pp. 623–646). Westport, CT: American Council on Education/Praeger.

Shepard, L. A., Penuel, W. R., & Davidson, K. L. (2017). Design principles for new systems of assessment. *Phi Delta Kappan, 98*(6), 47–52.

Shute, V.J. 2008. Focus on formative feedback. *Review of Educational Research, 78*, 153–189.

Sparks, J. R. & Deane, P. (2015). *Cognitively based assessment of research and inquiry skills: Defining a key practice in the English language arts* (Research Report No. RR-15-35). Princeton, NJ: Educational Testing Service.

van Lehn, K., Lynch, C., Schulze, K., Shapiro, J. A., Shelby, R., Taylor, L., Treacy, D., Weinstein, A., & Wintersgill, M. (2005). The Andes Physics Tutoring System: Lessons learned. *The International Journal of Artificial Intelligence in Education, 15*(3), 147–204.

Wiggins, G. P. (1998). *Educative assessment: Designing assessments to inform and improve student performance.* San Francisco, CA: Jossey-Bass.

Wiggins, G. & McTighe, J. (2005). *Understanding by design* (Second Edition). Alexandria, VA: Association for Supervision & Curriculum Development.

PART II

Intersections of Theory, Research, and Best Practices in Formative Assessment in the Disciplines

3

FORMATIVE ASSESSMENT IN MATHEMATICS

Hugh Burkhardt and Alan Schoenfeld

Our concern in this chapter is *formative assessment for learning mathematics*. This includes what is commonly thought of as formative assessment – the capture by the teacher of information about students' knowledge (including correct understandings and misconceptions) and thought processes, and its use in modifying the course of instruction. Formative assessment *for learning* goes beyond this. It requires a change in classroom roles and culture for both teacher and students, with students opening up their thinking to each other, so that it serves as a resource for everyone's learning.

Formative assessment in mathematics has not been successfully implemented at scale, with one exception – the formative assessment lessons (FALs) produced by the Mathematics Assessment Project (see Burkhardt & Swan, 2017), which have so far had over 7 million lesson downloads. In addition, there has been significant variability in the impact of other attempts that have been documented (Black et al., 2003; Black & Wiliam, 1998; Burkhardt & Schoenfeld, 2018; Wiliam, 2016; Wiliam & Thompson, 2007). This introduction explains why and sets the stage for the rest of the chapter. Our goal is to provide a description of useful tools and techniques by unpacking the following: the specific challenges mathematics teachers face in trying to implement formative assessment, and the reason that standard mechanisms for professional development (PD), such as providing relevant curricula and conducting in-person PD, have not been successful; a research-based vision of the five dimensions of classrooms from which students emerge as mathematically knowledgeable thinkers and problem solvers; a discussion, with exemplification using two FALs, of some principles at the core of formative assessment; a list of design tactics that can be used both by designers and classroom teachers; and a synthesis and discussion of the way forward.

The central premise of this chapter is that formative assessment is an integral part of effective teaching, which is essential in supporting students over the broad range of learning activities central to current learning and performance goals in mathematics. These include mathematical practices such as non-routine problem solving, producing extended chains of mathematical reasoning, modeling real-world situations using mathematical tools and representations, and inquiry.

Engaging in formative assessment is initially difficult for teachers. The challenge is particularly acute for mathematics since, in the US and around the world, teaching has typically addressed a narrow range of learning goals, largely confined to technical skills taught as procedures through show-and-practice (Lappan & Phillips, 2008), so change is decidedly a challenge (see, e.g., Cohen, 1990). Teaching using widely employed imitative methods such as "I do, we do, you do" cannot address the now generally accepted importance of extended autonomous reasoning, including non-routine thinking and problem solving – elements that have long been part of the curriculum in the humanities and to some degree in science. A fundamental issue, then, is how to enable mathematics teachers to acquire the new and challenging pedagogical and mathematical skills needed to implement formative assessment successfully in their classrooms. They face the dual challenge of opening up their pedagogical practices *and* learning to incorporate evidence of student thinking into dynamically evolving lessons.

What is Formative Assessment in Mathematics?

Black and Wiliam's (1998) original use of the term *formative assessment* comprises:

> . . . all those activities undertaken by teachers, and by their students in assessing themselves, which provide information to be used as feedback to modify the teaching and learning activities in which they are engaged. Such assessment becomes "formative assessment" when the evidence is actually used to adapt the teaching work to meet the needs of students.
>
> *(p. 91)*

The late Malcolm Swan, when hearing formative assessment for learning mathematics thus described by Dylan Wiliam, asked, "But isn't this just good teaching?" To the follow-up question from one of us (HB) "Why did you call it *assessment*?" Dylan replied, "We hoped to change the meaning of assessment, but we failed." Our hope is that this book may contribute to remedying that, particularly in mathematics where the nature of so much assessment has *undermined* the learning of real mathematics. Of course, another reason to include "assessment" is that *assessment* is regarded as A Good Thing by the powers that be. But simple tests, beloved of system leaders, encourage simplistic teaching and thus novice-level learning (Mathematics Assessment Project, 2014); formative assessment is the antidote.

Here lies the core challenge: for assessment to be formative the teacher must develop expertise in becoming aware of and adapting to the specific learning needs of students, both when planning lessons and in guiding the moment-by-moment pattern of activity in the classroom. How this can be done in mathematics is the theme of this chapter.

But first, "for the avoidance of doubt" as our legal friends say, we must point out some widely-used interpretations of formative assessment that we will *not* address further, and explain why. Frequent testing of students during and at the end of curriculum units is probably the commonest (mis)interpretation. These tests and the scores they produce have many limitations. The most serious is that they leave the teacher with a lot of information about dozens of individual students who have diverse understandings and misconceptions but give no guidance or support on what to do with this information – apart from reporting it in an essentially summative way.

The typical teacher response to this unreasonable pedagogical design challenge is to re-teach the problematic concepts or skills but much more rapidly than the first time, which had failed. Equally common is to record the scores and simply press on to the next topic. An extreme version of this was experienced by one of us (AS) in an advanced university level mathematics class 50 years ago. The well-intentioned instructor returned an exam on which only one student (not AS) had scored above 40 points out of 100. When he did, he said, "I've taught the content as well as I can, and it obviously didn't help. I don't know how to do anything differently, so I'm just going to proceed with the syllabus." Such honesty is rare; the practice is not.

Above all, this frequent-testing model makes no use of the information that is there every day, minute-by-minute, throughout the sequence of classroom learning activities. Similarly, allowing students to re-take tests after their test papers are returned may have some value as a teaching strategy, but doing so does not in itself contribute to modified classroom practices. The further away information gathering is from informing ongoing instruction, the less it qualifies as formative assessment in the sense we use it in this chapter. The many variants of so-called formative assessment may explain the huge range of gains, and losses, found across the studies that Black and Wiliam (1998) analyzed, with effect sizes from +1.5 to –0.4.

That is, of course, not at all to say that asking students to tackle mathematical tasks unassisted, or to revisit them, is not useful; such practices are integral to the learning process. How useful depends on two main factors: the nature of the tasks and of the follow-up to the students' responses. To begin with, we shall just make two overall remarks on these key elements as they affect the challenge of designing support for formative assessment for learning.

The Importance of a Range of Task Types

The variety of tasks that students are taught to tackle is a central issue in curriculum and assessment design; indeed, we have found that specifying the range of tasks is the clearest way to communicate learning goals. We have argued elsewhere (Balanced Assessment Project, 1999) that, in order to prepare students for mathematics and for life in the outside world, the range of tasks they tackle must include a substantial proportion of non-routine problems that ask students to re-present information, make practical estimates, review and critique arguments, evaluate and recommend options, design, plan, and define concepts, as well as show reliable fluency in technical exercises. This kind of balanced diet, which integrates mathematical concepts and practices, remains rare in classrooms.

However, describing tasks by characterizing their attributes is essentially ambiguous, particularly when such tasks go outside the reader's current experience. For example, the improvements in (intended) mathematics curricula over the last generation are often described as the introduction of, or increased emphasis on, reasoning and problem solving. But both these terms are highly ambiguous: routine subtraction tasks can be claimed to involve reasoning, and typical word problems are actually meant to be routine exercises. Exemplification is essential. A set of exemplar tasks, illustrated with a range of student responses, produces much less ambiguity in interpretation for everyone than a description alone. We shall exploit clarification-through-examples throughout this chapter.

Follow-Up to the Students' Responses

How should teachers modify the teaching and learning activities in which they are engaged in the light of the information they acquire? This is a serious design problem in which the limitations of teacher time are a key design constraint. On average, the teacher has only a minute or two to devote to each individual student during a class period, so individual assessment and treatment by the teacher is functionally impossible. Two possible sources of support for teachers are (a) the literature, which highlights typical student misconceptions and can be used to focus the teacher's attention, and (b) other students, *if* their knowledge and their own partial understandings of what their peers suggest can be harnessed productively. Needless to say, taking advantage of these potential resources is not easy.

This limitation of teacher time makes clear the design challenge. Various groups have tackled it in a variety of ways, mostly through the design of professional development that helps teachers structure lessons to reveal student misunderstandings and make the right kinds of decisions, minute-by-minute, to support learning. These approaches are described, for example, by Dylan Wiliam (2016, particularly Chapter 4.)

Enabling Formative Assessment Through Professional Development

As an introduction to the subject-specific aspects, we shall briefly describe two professional development projects – one in mathematics, one in science – before discussing their likely effectiveness at scale.

Cognitively Guided Instruction

CGI (Carpenter et al., 2014) is built on 30 years of research into elementary school mathematics, its concepts and common misconceptions, and a formative assessment approach to teaching. Based at the University of Wisconsin-Madison, the project developed a genre of research-based instructional sequences that places students' reasoning at the center of teachers' decision making. The focus is on specific detailed misconceptions, which are probed with short tasks. Its outreach is in the form of a professional development program built on teachers' inquiry. An evaluation (Carpenter et al., 2000) points to the challenges of large-scale implementation, emphasizing the need for professional learning communities that provide a supportive environment for teaching of this kind.

The Kings College Professional Development Project

Building on Black and Wiliam's (1998) research review, the group at Kings College ran a professional development project based on intensive collaboration with science teachers in a few schools (Black et al., 2003). Comparison of student scores on school and national tests showed important gains, with effect sizes of 0.3–0.4, and the teachers were happy with the changed approach. However, the changes did not come easily – or at all for some – over the two years of the project. Support from the schools, other teachers, and the project team were seen as essential.

It is clear from these examples – notable among the few successes – that making formative assessment an everyday reality at scale in mathematics classrooms through curriculum or professional development is a prohibitively expensive challenge. To engineer curricular materials such as those used in CGI (a decades-long research and development project) would be a mammoth undertaking – especially since more advanced mathematics is more complex to understand and support than the content addressed to date by CGI. Likewise, going to scale with professional development of the type described by Black et al. (2003) would require many more skilled professional development leaders than currently exist and would, by virtue of the intensity of the work itself, be extraordinarily expensive to conduct at scale. It was in this context that we were led to explore, in our formative assessment lessons, how far appropriately designed teaching materials could enable mathematics teachers to effectively embrace formative assessment. This work and its outcomes are described below.

We focus mainly on materials-supported formative assessment for a number of reasons. First, the approaches that rely on professional development, described in some detail in other chapters, are broadly relevant to mathematics. Our major focus is on mathematics-specific tasks and learning activity sequences. In describing the design of formative assessment lessons for mathematics, the design principles are explicitly set out and illustrated in the exemplar lessons we describe. Typically, this design challenge is – we believe unreasonably – left to the teacher.

Mathematics Teaching with Formative Assessment: A Theoretical Basis

Before looking into the specifics of formative assessment, it is essential to ask: What is formative assessment being used in the service of? The answer seems obvious: improved instruction and student learning, of course. But just what does that mean? In mathematics in particular, the goals of instruction have changed significantly in the past decades, shifting from a content-focused perspective (e.g., students will be able to solve quadratic equations by factoring and using the quadratic formula, and understand the conceptual underpinnings of those procedures) to one that gives equal attention to such content and to practices including reasoning, proving, conjecturing, representing, etc. (National Council of Teachers of Mathematics, 1989; National Research Council, 1989). These, in turn, call for certain mathematical dispositions (to reason, to prove, etc.), which are implicated in

Formative Assessment in Mathematics

the very ways students see themselves mathematically – e.g., do they have a sense of agency, do they see themselves as potential and willing participants in mathematical discourse? A major question is, what are the attributes of classrooms from which students emerge as knowledgeable and resourceful thinkers and problem solvers?

There is a duality in what follows between theory and design. Theory-focused studies provide insights, some general, others more specific; design and development is needed to turn this body of knowledge into effective processes and tools that enable users to realize the potential. This is true across fields. Physics and engineering, for example, have a similar relationship: the laws of physics underlie engineering, which nonetheless has to develop its own principles, strategies, and tactics to turn these into the products we use. There is a similar duality in medicine between understanding the way the body works, or not, and the design of treatments. In all these cases, the design process is not a straightforward deduction from the theory but, if well done, introduces new engineering principles, strategies, and tactics, as well as creativity. It is creative detail that often makes the difference between mediocrity and excellence.

Finally (to complicate the picture) there is a back-and-forth between theory and design. Theoretical ideas are often supported by tools that help people better understand and use the ideas, while new fundamental insights emerge from the engineering, enriching the theoretical basis. We make this point explicitly because, in many studies in STEM education, the design of the treatment seems to receive less attention than the analysis of the results.

We ourselves come from the two sides of the science/engineering duality. In what follows we will try to point out how this duality works in enhancing the overall outcome. We start with the broad theoretical framework (Teaching for Robust Understanding). We move on to describe the more specific diagnostic teaching research that showed the potential power of students learning from mistakes and misconceptions – the heart of formative assessment. We then move to the engineering – the design and development process that has turned these insights into tools and processes that actually enable typical teachers to make formative assessment in mathematics a reality in their classrooms.

Teaching for Robust Understanding

The Teaching for Robust Understanding (TRU) Framework (Schoenfeld 2013, 2014, 2015, 2017; Schoenfeld and the Teaching for Robust Understanding Project, 2016) represents an empirically validated distillation of the properties of classrooms from which students emerge as mathematically knowledgeable and resourceful reasoners and problem solvers. Table 3.1, from Schoenfeld and the Teaching for Robust Understanding Project (2016), provides a terse description of the five key aspects (dimensions) of mathematically powerful classrooms. TRU provides a strategic framework for quality in classroom activities that we shall use throughout, within which formative assessment plays its key role.

These five aspects of mathematics instruction have been seen to be necessary and sufficient: if any are missing, instruction is compromised, and if all are present to a substantial degree, then students learn a significant amount (Schoenfeld, 2013, 2014). A high-quality balanced curriculum may be viewed as a direct product of these five dimensions of classroom activity with the range of task types outlined in the previous section. These enlarge on the mathematics – the first dimension of TRU – as does the rest of this chapter on the other dimensions as elements in formative assessment.

The core idea is that the quality of instruction is primarily determined by *what the students are doing* in the sequence of learning activities the teacher instigates and manages, and not on the teacher's performance per se. In what follows we briefly describe the rationale for the claim that these five dimensions are both necessary and sufficient, the implications for teaching and professional development, and the key role that formative assessment plays.

Table 3.1 The TRU Framework: The Five Dimensions of Powerful Mathematics Classrooms

The Five Dimensions of Powerful Mathematics Classrooms

1. The Mathematics	2. Cognitive Demand	3. Equitable Access to Mathematics	4. Agency, Ownership, and Identity	5. Formative Assessment
The extent to which classroom activity structures provide opportunities for students to become knowledgeable, flexible, and resourceful mathematical thinkers. Discussions are focused and coherent, providing opportunities to learn mathematical ideas, techniques, and perspectives, make connections, and develop productive mathematical habits of mind.	The extent to which students have opportunities to grapple with and make sense of important mathematical ideas and their use. Students learn best when they are challenged in ways that provide room and support for growth, with task difficulty ranging from moderate to demanding. The level of challenge should be conducive to what has been called "productive struggle."	The extent to which classroom activity structures invite and support the active engagement of all of the students in the classroom with the core mathematical content being addressed by the class. Classrooms in which a small number of students get most of the "air time" are not equitable, no matter how rich the content: all students need to be involved in meaningful ways.	The extent to which students are provided opportunities to "walk the walk and talk the talk" – to contribute to conversations about mathematical ideas, to build on others' ideas and have others build on theirs – in ways that contribute to their development of agency (the willingness to engage), their ownership over the content, and the development of positive identities as thinkers and learners.	The extent to which classroom activities elicit student thinking and subsequent interactions respond to those ideas, building on productive beginnings and addressing emerging misunderstandings. Powerful instruction "meets students where they are" and gives them opportunities to deepen their understandings.

As described in Schoenfeld (2013, 2018), the TRU framework was created by conducting a broad literature review that identified as many productive classroom practices as could be found, and distilling them into classes of similar activities. Concurrently and then subsequently, videotapes of classroom practices were scored, using a TRU rubric (Schoenfeld, Floden, & the Algebra Teaching Study and Mathematics Assessment Project, 2014), according to their performance on the resulting five TRU dimensions. Scores were then compared with the performance of students from those classrooms on measures of mathematical thinking and problem solving. Classrooms that did well on the rubric did well on the mathematics measures; classrooms that scored poorly did not.

The TRU Toolkit

A key feature of TRU is that its focus is on the student's classroom experience. That experience is orchestrated by the teacher, of course, but the student is the person doing the learning! How does one assess how a specific classroom activity reflects the values of TRU? To be useful in practice, the broad statement above needs tools that help users answer that question. Table 3.2, taken from a professional development tool known as the TRU Observation Guide (Schoenfeld & the Teaching for Robust Understanding Project, 2016), frames the question of what instruction looks like from the student's point of view. That is, it poses the question, what are the affordances of the lesson for student learning? This is an example of a tool to facilitate and enrich readers' understanding of TRU.

These being the central issues for the consumers of instruction, they can now be framed from the teacher's perspective; the question is, what can the teacher consider in order to make the answers to the questions posed in Table 3.2 increasingly rich and productive? Table 3.3 offers a summary set of questions, taken from a professional development tool known as the TRU Conversation Guide (Baldinger, Louie, & the Algebra Teaching Study and Mathematics Assessment Project, 2016), that teachers (individually, collectively, and in conversations with coaches and specialists) use both for planning and reflection.

The five dimensions of TRU represent what has been referred to as a nearly decomposable system. By way of analogy, think of human physiology: A functional way to analyze the human body is to consider the circulatory system, respiratory system, nervous system, skeletal system, muscular system, digestive system, etc. Each can be examined profitably on its own terms, but of course they

Table 3.2 The Five Dimensions of Powerful Mathematics Classrooms From the Student Perspective

Observe the Lesson Through a Student's Eyes	
The Content	• What's the big idea in this lesson?
	• How does it connect to what I already know?
Cognitive Demand	• How long am I given to think, and to make sense of things?
	• What happens when I get stuck?
	• Am I invited to explain things, or just give answers?
Equitable Access to Content	• Do I get to participate in meaningful math learning?
	• Can I hide or be ignored? In what ways am I kept engaged?
Agency, Ownership, and Identity	• What opportunities do I have to explain my ideas? In what ways are they built on?
	• How am I recognized as being capable and able to contribute?
Formative Assessment	• How is my thinking included in classroom discussions?
	• Does instruction respond to my ideas and help me think more deeply?

Table 3.3 Key Questions for Planning and Reflection

Framing Questions for Planning and Reflection	
The Mathematics	How do mathematical ideas from this unit/course develop in this lesson/lesson sequence? How can we create more meaningful connections?
Cognitive Demand	What opportunities do students have to make their own sense of mathematical ideas? To work through authentic challenges? How can we create more opportunities?
Equitable Access to Content	Who does and does not participate in the mathematical work of the class, and how? How can we create more opportunities for each student to participate meaningfully?
Agency, Ownership, and Identity	What opportunities do students have to see themselves and each other as powerful mathematical thinkers? How can we create more of these opportunities?
Formative Assessment	What do we know about each student's current mathematical thinking? How can they and we build on it?

interact when the body functions as a whole. Similarly, each of the five TRU dimensions can be considered on its own, but they function in interaction. A mathematical task may be enriched, for example, by having students view the task using a range of representations and compare the insights gained by using different representations. When one does so, one may well broaden access to the core mathematics of the task without scaffolding away the difficulty of the task, a major challenge with regard to cognitive demand or productive struggle. The idea here is that students learn best when actively engaged in sense making; when discussing the mathematics with and explaining it to each other, students also have opportunities to develop a deeper sense of agency, ownership of the mathematics (they made sense of it rather than having it handed to them), and more productive mathematical identities (Engle, 2011; Engle & Conant, 2002).

Finally, we note that the five dimensions of TRU serve as a set of broad design principles: The goal when designing instruction is to make the affordances along each dimension as powerful as possible. That is, one wants the mathematics that students encounter to be rich, connected, and conceptually grounded; one wants to maximize opportunities for productive struggle; and so on. The sections on design, below, illustrate how these ideas play out.

Formative Assessment and TRU

Formative assessment plays a special role in this mix. If a task is too easy, for example, there is no productive struggle; but struggle is also likely to be unproductive if the task is too challenging (Dimension 2 of TRU). Formative assessment (Dimension 5) gets student thinking out in the open so that challenges of both types are revealed, and adjustments can be made. Such adjustments, or changes in classroom discourse structures (e.g., suggesting "why don't you discuss this in small groups for a few minutes" when an idea doesn't seem to take hold) can open up the space of ideas, and allow for more sense making (Dimension 2), thus enhancing access (Dimension 3) and agency (Dimension 4). Hearing what students find problematic can help the teacher locate the core issues that need attention – whether the ways in which those issues are attended to are led by the teacher, perhaps with careful scaffolding, or turned back to the students for explicit discussion. Looked at in the right way, each of the key questions listed in Table 3.3 represents an aspect of formative assessment. So formative assessment can be seen as the glue that holds the dimensions of a mathematically powerful classroom together (Figure 3.1).

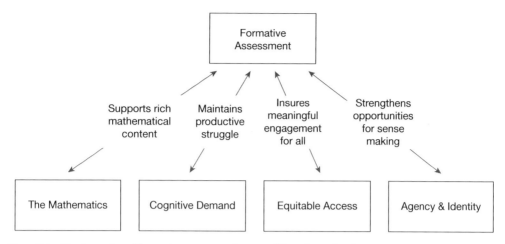

Figure 3.1 The key roles of formative assessment in powerful mathematics classrooms.

Discipline Specificity

Finally, we note that although the themes described in this section can be seen as domain-general – issues of content, cognitive demand, access, agency and identity, and formative assessment arise in all classrooms – their instantiation in the mathematics classroom is clearly domain-specific. The content, in this case mathematics, matters a great deal.

The reasons for this are two-fold. The first concerns the discipline itself. The importance of multiple representations and connections between them, for example, is much more central to mathematics than to other disciplines, as are the relationships between procedures and their conceptual underpinnings, the role of proof, and so on. Moreover, as discussed briefly above (see Burkhardt & Schoenfeld, 2018, for more detail), disciplinary standards have evolved significantly in recent decades, demanding student proficiency in mathematical practices as well as knowledge of concepts and procedures. This puts increased pressure on mathematics teachers. The specifics of what students are to learn make a fundamental difference.

Second, a significant way in which this plays out in any classroom depends on the pedagogical content knowledge (PCK) of the teacher (see, e.g., Shulman, 1986, 1987). After a year or two of teaching algebra, for example, virtually every mathematics teacher knows that some of their class will convert the expression $(a + b)^2$ to the expression $a^2 + b^2$ instead of $a^2 + 2ab + b^2$. Those who have developed some PCK will know to anticipate this error and be ready to problematize the issue for students, perhaps by asking them to check their expression with convenient numbers such as $a = 3$, $b = 4$. Those who have developed yet more PCK will have a number of different approaches (e.g., algebraic and pictorial) in their back pockets to address the misconception – the adaptive expertise (Hatano & Inagaki, 1986) that is an essential part of formative assessment. Formative assessment goes beyond that, of course. It involves crafting learning environments that are responsive to student thinking in an ongoing, organic way, including shaping classroom interactions so that students serve as resources for each other.

This latter point underscores the challenge of preparing mathematics teachers for implementing formative assessment in their classrooms. Implementing formative assessment is a matter of inclination and knowledge. The teacher who has learned to listen to and support student thinking in, say, Cognitively Guided Instruction, may have that inclination in a geometry or algebra class but he or she would still have to develop, or be supported in, the specific kind of PCK described in the previous paragraph in order to be truly effective at employing formative assessment in those courses. Just as progress in ELA may be viewed as writing and analyzing increasingly sophisticated texts using increasingly sophisticated methods, we see progress in mathematics in similar terms – with *texts* replaced by *tasks*. We find comparisons between subjects to be very useful.

The Diagnostic Teaching Approach to Formative Assessment: The Research Base

We now turn from the general theoretical framework to the specific research that underpins the design phase described below. The approach is based on a 30-year program of Shell Centre research on diagnostic teaching (Bell, 1993; Burkhardt & Swan, 2017; Swan, 2006, 2017; Swan & Burkhardt, 2014). The program's formal title, Teaching for Long-term Learning (TLL), rightly suggests that this approach is consonant with TRU. It promotes learning through structured, task-based activities that lead students to recognize their misconceptions and subsequently resolve them together through structured discussion – the essence of formative assessment for learning. Schoenfeld's work and the Shell Centre's have been parallel and productively intertwined for decades, with the Shell Centre's work more focused on design. Both bodies of work have been consistent with the core ideas in TRU, as has the teaching of the best teachers of mathematics. In this, one is reminded of Moliere's *Bourgeois Gentilhomme*, who was surprised to discover that he had been speaking "prose" all his life.

Research-based design should be based on principles that have well-established domains of validity. Individual studies rarely provide the body of evidence on the generalizability and limits of validity that design needs (Burkhardt, 2013; Schoenfeld, 2001). This needs coherent programs, each studying the same specific principles applied across a well-planned range of the important variables: students, teachers, topics, etc. (Burkhardt & Schoenfeld, 2003). This section outlines such a program – one that provided the research basis for the design and development program that culminated in the concept development lessons of the Mathematics Assessment Project.

Led initially by Alan Bell and taken forward by Malcolm Swan, the team first explored in a sequence of small-scale studies the validity of the approach across three key variables: students, mathematical topics, and different designers of the experimental teaching material (Bell, 1993). Later, the research moved on to the key teacher variables, focusing on more typical teachers and showing that collaborative discussion materials can be effective when used appropriately, even with low attaining students (Swan, 2006). The research program also offered insights into the ways in which teachers' beliefs about mathematics, teaching, and learning affect the ways in which they use teaching materials and, conversely, the ways in which the materials can be designed to change beliefs and practices – a crucial aspect of formative assessment. First, we describe two of the challenges that arose in the research.

Eliciting Student Thinking

A fundamental element in formative assessment is the surfacing of each student's understandings and misconceptions. A student's errors in mathematics are rarely random; as research dating back decades in mathematics documents (e.g., Brown & Burton, 1978), and contemporary work on learning progressions (see http://ime.math.arizona.edu/progressions/) attempts to address, they often arise from misunderstandings of previous mathematical experience. Research on learning mathematics (for example, Hart, 1981; Higgins et al., 2002) makes it clear that students' conceptual difficulties are often caused by over-generalization, where students transfer prior knowledge to new domains. For example, students often generalize from their experiences with natural numbers that "numbers with more digits are larger in value," "multiplication makes things bigger," or that "when multiplying by 10, you add a zero." Such sensible generalizations may become misconceptions when applied to new domains, such as decimals and fractions. Similarly, standard restricted paradigmatic examples presented in textbooks lead students to generalize that "you always divide the larger number by the smaller" or "the smaller the area, the shorter the perimeter." A carefully designed formative assessment lesson brings out such misconceptions, which might otherwise go unnoticed or unaddressed.

We note here that misconceptions that arise from overgeneralizations of observed patterns, while not a uniquely mathematical phenomenon, are certainly a distinctively domain-specific one. There is a vast literature on student misconceptions in mathematics and science: See Ay (2017) and Confrey (1990) for reviews.

Interactions That Respond to Student Thinking

The second key challenge of formative assessment for the teacher is how to respond constructively to evidence from student performance during the lesson. The normal, indeed obvious, response is for the teacher to "clear up" a student's misunderstandings by quickly re-teaching the topic: "No, with decimals, adding a zero doesn't multiply the number by ten; you move the decimal point a place to the right," perhaps adding, "This makes units tens and so on." Unsurprisingly, for most students this approach is confusing rather than effective: They misunderstood it when it was taught much more slowly before, *and* the misconceptions are deeply engrained – malknowledge can't simply be replaced with the correct knowledge. (For an early discussion of this issue with a focus on arithmetic and fractions learning, see Maurer, 1987.)

For the reasons discussed in the previous section, the more powerful alternative is for the teacher to structure a sequence of learning activities so that the *students*, individually and with their peers, resolve the misconceptions. This is challenging for a teacher to do well. The Shell Centre's goal in this program was to develop, with examples, a set of principles to guide an effective lesson design process in which group debugging happens naturally.

The Classroom Contract

A basic misapprehension about formative assessment is that the teacher is responsible for setting all the students straight. That misunderstanding places an impossible burden on the teacher who, after all, has only a minute or two per student in each lesson. Rather, the idea of using students as resources for each other (and thus themselves) is central. It is elaborated and exemplified below. In every classroom, there is a contract (Brousseau, 1997) that defines, usually implicitly, the respective activities and roles that teachers and students will perform. Formative assessment for learning involves a change in this classroom contract, with students taking more responsibility for their and their peers' learning in a way summarized in the Agency, Ownership and Identity dimension of TRU.

Evidence From the Studies

The studies of this approach to formative assessment, when compared with the standard direct instruction approach of the time, showed a common pattern of much improved long-term learning, illustrated by Figure 3.2. In this case, the students were ages 12–13 and the mathematical topic was Reflections. Each line in the diagrams connects an individual student's score on a pre-test, a post-test at the end of the unit, and a delayed test about six months later. Note in the right-hand graph the subsequent loss, so familiar to teachers, of most of the gains made during the teaching of the unit through direct instruction; this did not occur with the diagnostic teaching approach to formative assessment.

This key result was stable across the sequence of parallel studies (Bell, 1993; Swan, 2006); together they represent empirical evidence of generalizability – that the design principles set out below are indeed principles, not simply features of a specific treatment. From these studies it was observed that the power of diagnostic teaching appears to lie in the extent to which it values the intuitive methods

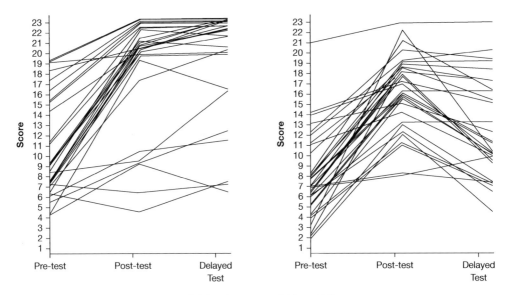

Figure 3.2   Mean scores on pre, post and delayed post-tests (Birks, 1987).

and ideas that students bring to each lesson, offers experiences that create inter- and intra-personal conflicts of ideas, and creates opportunities for students to reflect on and examine inconsistencies in their interpretations. Note as well the high-level cognitive demand and the role of the teacher and materials in adjusting it – addressing TRU Dimension 2, cognitive demand.

While this program provided the key elements of design, materials that motivate students and teachers call for a mixture of insight, creative design, and systematic iterative development in classrooms – the essence of good engineering research (Burkhardt, 2006). The current apotheosis of this long research-based design and development program is the 100 formative assessment lessons of the Mathematics Assessment Project (MAP), designed and developed to support teachers and students in the implementation of the US Common Core State Standards. We describe these lessons in what follows, providing detailed exemplification of dialogic structures that focus students on thinking within their own zones of proximal development (a fundamental aim of formative assessment), and that support reflection. The role of carefully selected tasks, with examples of student responses, in promoting self- and peer assessment is one of the design tactics that will be examined.

Formative Assessment in Mathematics: Moving from Theory to Design

TRU provides our strategic framework, setting out goals against which specific instantiations are judged, along with some tools to check how well each of the five dimensions is covered. The diagnostic teaching studies show the potential of learning through mistakes and misconceptions that are revealed through activities that generate cognitive conflict and then enable students to resolve it through discussion. The goal then was to enrich theoretical understanding of the diagnostic teaching approach to formative assessment, adding to the body of theory in this area. But, in the course of the work, a set of broad design principles was formulated. These are set out in Table 3.4 (Swan, 2014; Swan & Burkhardt, 2014). While derived from a specific approach, we believe that these principles are a strong guide to the design of any type of formative assessment in mathematics.

We will enrich the meaning of these briefly-stated principles through a few examples of tasks and learning activities that have been developed by the team over the last 35 years. Many of these early materials are available for free download from www.mathshell.com. The examples that follow aim to

Table 3.4 Principles for the Design of Formative Assessment in Mathematics

Teaching is More Effective When it . . .

Builds on the knowledge learners already have	This means developing formative assessment techniques and adapting our teaching to accommodate individual learning needs.
Exposes and discusses common misconceptions and other Surprising phenomena	Learning activities should expose current thinking, create "tensions" by confronting learners with inconsistencies and surprises, and allow opportunities for their resolution through discussion.
Uses higher-order questions	Questioning is more effective when it promotes explanation, application and synthesis rather than mere recall.
Makes appropriate use of class interactive teaching, individual work and cooperative small work group	Collaborative group work is more effective after learners have been given an opportunity for individual reflection. Activities are more effective when they encourage critical, constructive discussion, rather than either argument or uncritical acceptance. Shared goals and group accountability are important.
Creates connections between topics both within and beyond mathematics and with the real world	Often, learners are more concerned with what they have "done" than with what they have learned. It is better to aim for depth than for superficial "coverage," even though this takes time.
Encourages reasoning rather than answer-getting	Learners often find it difficult to generalize and transfer their learning to other topics and contexts. Related concepts (such as division, fraction and ratio) remain unconnected. Effective teachers build bridges between ideas.
Uses rich, collaborative tasks	The tasks we use should be accessible, extendable, encourage decision making, promote discussion, encourage creativity, encourage "what if" and "what if not?" questions.
Confronts difficulties rather than seeks to avoid or pre-empt them	Effective teaching challenges learners and has high expectations of them. It does not seek to "smooth the path" but creates realistic obstacles to be overcome. Confidence, persistence and learning are not attained through repeating successes, but by the productive struggle with difficulties.
Develops mathematical language through communicative activities	Mathematics is a language that enables us to describe and model situations, think logically, frame and sustain arguments and communicate ideas with precision. Learners do not know mathematics until they can "speak" it. Effective teaching, therefore, focuses on the communicative aspects of mathematics by developing oral and written mathematical language.
Recognizes both what has been learned and how it has been	What is to be learned cannot always be stated prior to the learning experience. After a learning event, however, it is important to reflect on the learning that has taken place, making this as explicit and memorable as possible. Effective teachers will also reflect on the ways in which learning has taken place, so that learners develop their own capacity to learn.
Uses resources, including computer-based technologies, in creative and appropriate ways	ICT offers new ways to engage with mathematics. At its best it is dynamic and visual: relationships become more tangible. ICT can provide feedback on actions and enhance interactivity and learner autonomy. Through its connectivity, ICT offers the means to access and share resources and – even more powerfully – the means by which learners can share their ideas within and across classrooms.

give the reader a feeling for the richness and variety of classroom activity that the principles demand. We choose examples of what two of the statements in Table 3.4 mean. We encourage the reader to look for places in what follows where other principles are in action.

Exposes and Discusses Common Misconceptions and Other Surprising Phenomena

The second principle, surfacing misconceptions, is the focus of the first task in Figure 3.3, from *The Language of Functions and Graphs* (Swan et al., 1985).[1] It gets students involved in a discussion that brings out the common *graph as picture* misconception – the motion goes up and down because the graph does – which misses the fact that the graph represents speed, not height, against time. If a group does not resolve the question, the teacher can ask a student to explain his or her thinking (a core example of the principle, *uses higher level questions*), then perhaps point to the axis labels. We address the central issue of questioning in some detail in the next section.

Complementing this is the task from "Be a Paper Engineer," a module from the *Numeracy through problem solving* project (Shell Centre, 1988). This module enables students to explore the geometrical principles used in making pop-up cards and gift boxes, then to go on to use these to create and make new designs themselves. The second task in Figure 3.3 sets students the challenge of designing a pop-up card, and discovering in the process that there are principles (of parallelogram geometry in this case) for the positioning of fold and cut lines so that the tower does not crease in the wrong place or protrude when the card is closed. Later the students explore possibilities where the folds are not all parallel – there is challenging mathematics at all levels. When working on this task, a student engages in the principles related to creating connections between topics and with the real world. Both tasks encourage reasoning, not just answer-getting.

Each task leads to revealing student errors and, because the activity and the context are rich enough, supports discussions in pairs or small groups – peer assessment through which the misconceptions

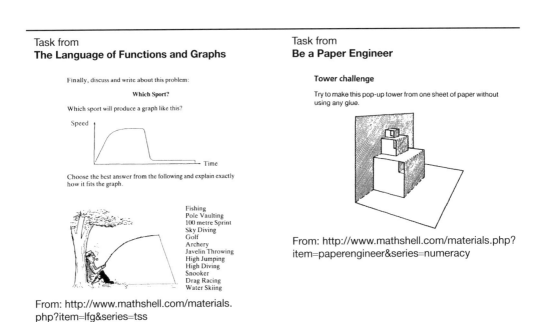

Figure 3.3 Tasks designed to promote the surfacing and subsequent resolution of misconceptions.

are recognized and corrected. It does, that is, provided that the teacher develops a classroom culture in which there is time and support for this to happen. Arguing one's position may be common in a literature or history class, but the classroom contract in traditional show-and-practice mathematics classrooms needs to be modified significantly for these activities to have a central place.

Both these modules, from different projects, also contained professional development materials to support the changing pedagogy, along with examples of assessment questions to show the variety of tasks to be expected in the associated examinations. Many rich task types have been devised in pure mathematics as well, although embedding deep mathematics in real-world contexts often helps support student comprehension and motivation.

Uses Rich, Collaborative Tasks

A design principle derived from Dimension 1 (The Mathematics) of TRU is that all practice should be embedded in rich tasks that are extendible, generalizable, and make connections. The examples in Figure 3.4 below illustrate two specific genres of activity that Malcolm Swan devised (e.g., Swan, 2006). The first is a *conjecture, justify, and prove* activity. In the second, students are given a number of statements, such as the one shown on connections between areas, perimeters and functions; they are then asked to either justify why it is *always* or *never* true, or to identify all the cases where it is *sometimes* true. The card below the statement is given only to students that become completely stuck. Such differentiation through support is an example of the fourth dimension of TRU, encouraging student agency and ownership.

Checking back to the strategic framework of TRU, these tasks involve serious mathematics and substantial cognitive demand that involves the mathematical practices; the group work helps the teacher ensure all students are actively involved, and that together each group creates and owns its explanations. The activities involved are designed to provide formative feedback throughout, enhanced by the teacher where support is needed.

Possible and impossible shapes
Plot points on the Perimeter-Area grid that represent squares, then other classes of shapes. Find a shape that would be plotted at (12, 4), then (4, 12).
Find which points on the grid represent possible shapes and which do not – and why.

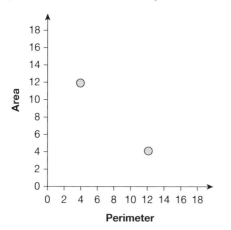

Always, sometimes or never true?
Is this statement always, sometimes or never true? Justify your answer, giving examples and counterexamples.
"When you cut a piece off a shape, you reduce its area and perimeter."

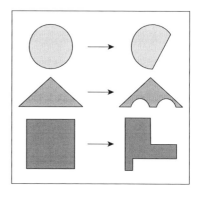

Figure 3.4 Two genres of learning activity.

Formative Assessment Lessons From the Mathematics Assessment Project

We now move onto the core of design: how to turn these principles into tools and processes that work well in typical classrooms. Each of us long ago pointed out, in the different contexts of mathematical problem solving and of modeling (Burkhardt, 1981; Burkhardt et al., 1986; Schoenfeld. 1985), that strategic principles are not enough: domain-specific tactics are needed at every level. The same applies here; design *is* problem solving.

Here we use examples of formative assessment lessons from the Mathematics Assessment Project, entitled Classroom Challenges, to illuminate the challenges that must be faced in designing tasks and learning activity sequences that will stimulate learning mathematics through formative assessment. One hundred FALs, including these, may be downloaded free from map. mathshell.org. These have had some impact at scale: More than 7 million lessons have been downloaded from this site alone, with downloads continuing at about one-third the rate at the launch four years ago.

To summarize Table 3.4 and the last section, MAP concept-focused lessons are designed with *three complementary objectives*:

1   reveal to the teacher, and the student, each student's current understanding and misunderstandings of the central concept – as in all well designed diagnostic and formative assessment.

2   move the student's understanding forward by a process of debugging through discussion, in pairs, small groups, and with the class as a whole, thus integrating diagnosis and treatment.

3   build connections between different conceptual strands. The linear sequence of lesson-by-lesson teaching naturally develops *strands* of learning – strands that, for most students, have weaknesses and breaks in them. But mathematics content is best understood as a connected *network* of concepts and skills. As in other networks, the connections reinforce the strands.

To illustrate these and the design principles of the last section, we describe in some detail two formative assessment lessons. These exemplify the two main types of formative assessment lessons (FALs): concept development lessons, and non-routine problem solving lessons. They focus on, respectively, the content and practices of the US Common Core State Standards for Mathematics (CCSSM), though both content and practices are integral to both types of lesson. We analyze the implementation of the design principles of the last section in the design of these lessons and outline evidence on outcomes and impact. Swan and Burkhardt (2014) give a fuller discussion.

The performance goals of the FALs are in close harmony with the following broad overview of mathematical expertise, taken from an early CCSSM draft (personal communication from Phil Daro, 2010)

> Proficient students expect mathematics to make sense. They take an active stance in solving mathematical problems. When faced with a non-routine problem, they have the courage to plunge in and try something, and they have the procedural and conceptual tools to carry through. They are experimenters and inventors, and can adapt known strategies to new problems. They think strategically.

The contrast with learning through imitative *show-and-practice* is stark.

Finally, we note that, in design, the details matter. Mozart's *Marriage of Figaro* and The Beatles' *Yesterday* use the same rules of melody, harmony, and counterpoint as lesser works; the difference lies in a mixture of tactical skill and creative ingenuity that fine design in education also embodies. In this case, the examples illustrate something of the essential *variety* and *creativity* – missing in so many classrooms – of tasks and learning activities, and suggest answers to such questions as: What else should the teacher ask students about this problem and about their solutions? Should he or she ask if the answer given here is the only correct answer and why? Should he or she present the same problem in different forms to ensure that students have internalized the concept and can generalize it? The answer in each case is "Yes," but there is more to it than that.

The Design of the MAP Concept Development Lessons

The challenge in concept development lessons is to build on prior research on concept learning (see, e.g., Ay, 2017; Bell, 1993; Confrey, 1990; Hart, 1981; Swan, 2006) by designing lessons that uncover students' existing ways of thinking, then create cognitive conflicts, or disturbances, that lead students to realize and confront inconsistencies. The lessons must then help to resolve these conflicts through student-student and student-teacher discussion, in pairs or small groups, and then across the class as a whole.

The design principles in Table 3.4, and many years of experimental design and development research, guided the design of the activity sequence of a typical MAP concept development lesson. The tactical design is set out in Text Box 3.1 (Swan, 2006). We shall illustrate this structure, using the FAL *Increasing and decreasing quantities by a percent* (see Figure 3.5, and http://map.mathshell.org/lessons. php?unit=7100&collection=8).

Text Box 3.1

Tactical design of a formative assessment lesson for concept development

A   *Before teaching, explore existing conceptual frameworks through a pre-assessment.* Students' intuitive interpretations or methods are identified through a written test. The teacher surveys, but does not score, the responses looking for patterns of misconceptions. This feedback gives the teacher "a picture of the class."

B   *Make existing concepts and methods explicit in the classroom.* An initial activity is designed with the purpose of making students aware of their own intuitive interpretations and methods. At the beginning of a lesson, for example, students are asked to attempt a task individually, with no help from the teacher. No attempt is made, at this stage, to teach anything new or even make students aware that errors have been made. The purpose here is to expose pre-existing ways of thinking.

C   *Provoke and share cognitive conflicts.* Feedback to the students is given in one of three ways:

–   by asking students to compare their responses with those made by other students;
–   by asking students to repeat the task using alternative methods;
–   by using tasks which contain some form of inbuilt check.

This feedback produces cognitive conflict when students begin to realize and confront the inconsistencies in their own interpretations and methods. Time is spent reflecting on and discussing the nature of this conflict. Students are asked to write down the inconsistencies and possible causes of error. This typically involves both small group and whole-class discussion.

D   *Resolve conflict through discussion and formulate new concepts and methods.* A whole-class discussion is held in order to resolve a conflict. Students are encouraged to articulate conflicting points of view and reformulate ideas. At this point, the teacher suggests, with reasons, a mathematician's viewpoint.

(continued)

(continued)

E   *Consolidate learning by using the new concepts and methods for further problems.* New learning is utilized and consolidated by:

- offering further practice questions;
- inviting students to create and solve their own problems within given constraints;
- asking students to analyze completed work and to diagnose causes of errors for themselves.

To give the teacher time to get a view of the class's existing knowledge, the lesson begins with a pre-assessment, shown in Figure 3.5. The pre-assessment is tackled over 20 minutes – nothing tactically unusual there, though the detailed design of the tasks, not demanding calculation, is novel. What *is* tactically novel is the Common Issues table in Figure 3.6. The table describes misconceptions that teachers are likely to see and, equally important, questions they can use to stimulate further thought without telling the students the answer.

Percent Changes

One month Rob spent $8.02 on his phone. The next month he spent $6.00. To work out the average amount Rob spends over the two months, you could press the calculator keys:

1. Tom usually earns $40.85 per hour.
   He has just heard that he has had a 6% pay raise.
   He wants to work out his new pay on this calculator.
   It does not have a percent button.

   Which keys must he press on his calculator?
   Write down the keys in the correct order.
   (You do not have to do the calculation.)

2. Maria sees a dress in a sale. The dress is normally priced at $56.99.
   The ticket says that there is 45% off.
   She wants to use her calculator to work out how much the dress will cost.
   It does not have a percent button.

   Which keys must she press on her calculator?
   Write down the keys in the correct order.
   (You do not have to do the calculation.)
   ....

3. Last year, the price of an item was $350. This year it is $450.
   Lena wants to know what the percentage change is.
   Write down the calculation she will need to do to get the correct answer.
   (You do not have to do the calculation.)
   ....

4. In a sale, the prices in a shop were all decreased by 20%.
   After the sale they were all increased by 25%. What was the overall effect on the shop prices?
   Explain how you know.
   ....
   ....
   ....

Student materials   Increasing and Decreasing Quantities by a Percent © 2015 MARS,   S-1
                     Shell Center, University of Nottingham

Figure 3.5   Pre-assessment for percent changes.

Common issues:	Suggested questions and prompts:
Makes the incorrect assumption that a percent increase/decrease means the calculation must include an addition/subtraction For example: 40.85 + 0.6 or 40.85 + 1.6 (Q1). *A single multiplication by 1.06 is enough.* Or: 56.99 − 0.45 or 56.99 − 1.45 (Q2). *A single multiplication by 0.55 is enough.*	• Does your answer make sense? Can you check that it is correct? • "Compared to last year 50% more people attended the festival." What does this mean? Describe in words how you can work out how many people attended the festival this year. Give me an example. • In a sale an item is marked "50% off." What does this mean? Describe in words how you calculate the price of an item in the sale. Give me an example. • Can you express the increase/decrease as a single multiplication?
Converts the percent to a decimal incorrectly For example: 40.85 × 0.6 (Q1).	• How can you write 50% as a decimal? • How can you write 5% as a decimal?
Uses an inefficient method For example: The student calculates 1%, then multiplies by 6 to find 6% and then adds this answer on: (40.85 ÷ 100) × 6 + 40.85 (Q1). Or: 56.99 × 0.45 = ANS, then 56.99 − ANS (Q2). *A single multiplication is enough.*	• Can you think of a method that reduces the number of calculator key presses? • How can you show your calculation with just one step?
Is unable to calculate percent change For example: 450 − 350 = 100% (Q3). Or: The difference is calculated, then the student does not know how to proceed or he/she divides by 450 (Q3). *The calculation (450 − 350) ÷ 350 × 100 is correct.*	• Are you calculating the percent change to the amount $350 or to the amount $450? • If the price of a t-shirt increased by $6, describe in words how you could calculate the percent change. Give me an example. Use the same method in Q3.
Subtracts percents For example: 25 − 20 = 5% (Q4) *Because we are combining multipliers: 0.8 × 1.25 = 1, there is no overall change in prices.*	• Make up the price of an item and check to see if your answer is correct.
Fails to use brackets in the calculation For example: 450 − 350 ÷ 350 × 100 (Q4). **Misinterprets what needs to be included in the answer** For example: The answer is just operator symbols.	• In your problem, what operation will the calculation carry out first? • If you just entered these symbols into your calculator would you get the correct answer?

Teacher guide   Increasing and Decreasing   T-3
Quantities by a Percent

Figure 3.6   Common Issues table for percent changes.

This concise summary of pedagogical content knowledge scaffolds formative assessment on the part of the teacher in two critically important ways:

(1) It draws upon the misconceptions literature and extensive field-testing to highlight likely challenges the students will face. This codifies for use PCK that the teacher might well not have, and might otherwise have to try to develop informally.
(2) It suggests *ways that maintain cognitive demand* to respond to student misconceptions – a major pedagogical challenge being that teachers tend to make things *easier* for students (often too easy) by telling them what to do when they run into difficulty (see, e.g., Henningsen & Stein, 1997; Stein et al., 2008; Stein, Grover & Henningsen, 1996.)

In the main lesson, for activities B and C of Table 3.5, the students are given four cards with carefully chosen numbers (100, 150, 200, 160) for the corners of a poster, and ten arrow cards. Eight of the arrow cards contain expressions like "increase by 50%" or "decrease by 25%"; two are blank. The students' task, working in pairs or threes, is to place the arrow cards that correctly indicate the relationships between the four numbers. They have calculators.

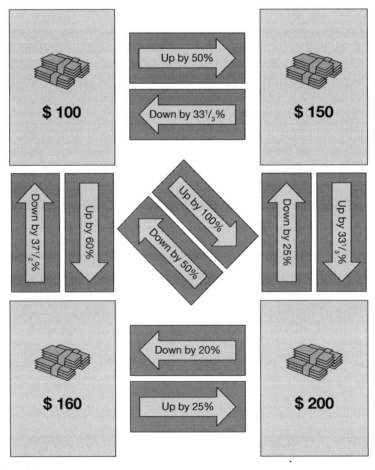

Figure 3.7 Up and down percentage.

Formative Assessment in Mathematics

In practice, standard misconceptions rapidly appear: placing the "increase by 50%" arrow between 100 and 150 is straightforward, but many students place the reverse, "decrease by 50%," between 150 and 100. They then discover they need that arrow to connect 200 to 100. Gradually, over about 15 minutes, the groups mostly get all ten correct, occasionally prompted by questions (not explanations) from the teacher. The result, shown in Figure 3.7, realizes objectives 1 and 2 from the summary at the beginning of this section: to reveal misconceptions and then to resolve them through discussion.

A structured whole-class discussion, representing activity D in Table 3.5 (resolve conflict through discussion and formulate new concepts and methods), provides the opportunity to iron out remaining difficulties.

This sequence is repeated twice to develop the link with decimals and fractions, emphasizing at the same time that percentage change is a fundamentally (but well concealed) multiplicative process. Two further sets of arrow cards are distributed, and placed in a similar way: first multiplications by decimals (x 1.5, etc.) and then multiplication by fractions (x 3/2, with x 2/3 for the inverse – a key insight for proportional reasoning). The fractions are particularly powerful at providing opportunities

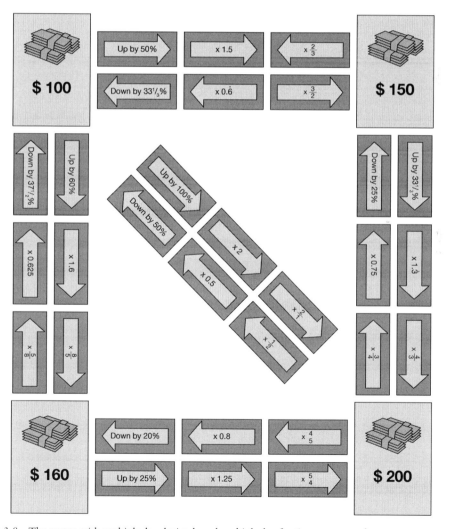

Figure 3.8 The poster with multiply-by-decimals and multiply-by-fractions arrow cards.

for students to explain links between each percent change and its inverse. Throughout this complex process, students are encouraged to explain connections to one another and make generalizations.

The final result, shown in Figure 3.8, exemplifies this third objective, linking topics that are initially taught separately in most classrooms. Note that the links between 150 and 160 were not included in the arrow sets but left as an option for the teacher of a high performing class or group to suggest. Fine design includes leaving good things out. Although this lesson is aimed at 12–13-year-old students, it also provides a valuable tool for testing of understanding in later grades – one that is challenging to many students.

Comparing the Formative Assessment Lesson to the TRU Framework

How does this lesson, as an exemplar of the corpus of FALs, fit with the principles from the TRU framework? First, Dimension 1, The Math: the mathematics in this lesson represents central curricular content, highlighting key mathematical ideas that students find difficult. Second, Dimension 2, Cognitive Demand: in working on these tasks collaboratively, the students are actively engaged in productive struggle aimed at sense making. They get feedback both from the computations and from each other; so they are working at a productive level of cognitive demand. While we note that no materials themselves can guarantee equitable access, working in small groups helps to involve all students (Dimension 3) and the creation of a group product, the poster, helps students to develop aspects of agency, ownership, and productive mathematical identities (Dimension 4); the classroom norms and climate established by the teacher are the context within which students can take advantage of those opportunities. Further, in providing multiple points of access (going from 100 to 200 is easy; from 160 to 200 and back somewhat more challenging), the task opens up opportunities for students to enter into the conversations at levels with which they feel comfortable. As for Dimension 5, Formative Assessment, the Common Issues questions in the teacher guide scaffold the teacher in providing appropriate support to the students but not telling them what to do, and the student–student discourse facilitated by the lesson makes students resources for each other. Such differentiation by support is another design tactic that is a powerful feature of formative assessment. In sum, this kind of design scores well on the dimensions of TRU.

The review of Black and Wiliam (1998) and subsequent work shows that formative assessment, when done well, is a powerful way to advance student learning. TRU provides a framework that describes well done. The FALs, products of the Shell Centre diagnostic teaching research and development program, fit that framework, which was developed in parallel. The next question is whether there is evidence of the kinds of student learning gains that these prior studies, individually and collectively, would predict.

The Design of the MAP Problem Solving Lessons

The strategic design of problem solving FALs is based on students developing multiple solutions, comparing, critiquing, and improving them through discussion in small groups and in the class as a whole. The structure of a typical problem solving lesson is illustrated using the FAL: *Maximizing profits: selling boomerangs* (Figure 3.9; see http://map.mathshell.org/lessons.php?unit=7100&collection=8).

This optimization problem (maximizing an outcome, given certain constraints) is not yet a typical curriculum task in the US, so it provides opportunities for students to frame the task and make sense of how to analyze it. Such problems focus largely on the mathematical practices aspects of the Common Core (problem solving, reasoning, modeling), rather than the content aspects. The outcome is the profit made; the constraints include the total time of 24 hours and the maximum number of ten boomerangs in all; the time to carve small or large boomerangs and the profit each yields differ. So, this is a complex problem, but one that works well in the classroom, often to the surprise of teachers who are new to this kind of problem and doubt their students could make much progress with them. The strategic challenge for the student is to find a systematic way to handle the complexity. The challenge for the teacher is to support them in this endeavor without telling them how to do it.

Boomerangs

Phil and Cath make and sell boomerangs for a school event. The money they raise will go to charity.

- They plan to make them in two sizes: small and large.
- Phil will carve them from wood. The small boomerang takes 2 hours to carve and the large one takes 3 hours to carve.
- Phil has a total of 24 hours available for carving.
- Cath will decorate them. She only has time to decorate 10 boomerangs of either size.
- The small boomerang will make $8 for charity.
- The large boomerang will make $10 for charity.

They want to make as much money for charity as they can.

How many small and large boomerangs should they make?

How much money will they then make?

Figure 3.9   The task from the boomerangs lesson.

Common issues:	Suggested questions and prompts:
Has difficulty getting started	• What do you know?
	• What do you need to find out?
Makes an incorrect interpretation of the constraints and variables	• What figures in the task are fixed?
	• What can you vary?
For example: The student has applied just one constraint, such as 'Phil has only 24 hours to make the boomerangs' or 'Cath can only make 10 boomerangs.'	• What is the greatest number of small/large boomerangs they can make?
	• Have you used any unnecessary restrictions on the number of small and large boomerangs to be made?
Or: The student has calculated the profit for making just one type of boomerang.	• Why can't they make 50 boomerangs?
Works unsystematically	• Can you organize the numbers of large and small boomerangs made in a systematic way?
For example: The student shows three or four seemingly unconnected combinations, such as 5 small and 5 large boomerangs, then 10 large.	• What would be sensible values to try? Why?
	• How can you check that you remember all the constraints?
	• Do you cover all possible combinations? If not, why not?
	• How do you know for sure your answer is the best option?
	• Can you organize your work in a table?

Figure 3.10   The first part of the Common Issues table for boomerangs.

Unlike the diagnostic tests in the content-oriented FALs, the problem solving pre-assessment asks the students to tackle the core task, in this case boomerangs, on their own, typically for about 15 minutes. Again, the teacher reviews the responses looking for different approaches and patterns of misunderstanding. Figure 3.10 shows an excerpt from the Common Issues table that supports the teacher in this, suggesting feedback to give to the class or, when time allows, to individual students. This begins to surface misunderstanding; the first objective set out at the beginning of this section.

In the main lesson, the students review the teacher's feedback and their own solution. They then move into small groups and, setting aside what they have done, work together to construct a solution in the form of a poster. The teacher observes, intervening where necessary in the form of questions like those in the Common Issues table. This begins to meet the second objective – moving students' reasoning forward through discussion.

Students Critiquing Student Work Examples

The next phase asks the students to critique carefully selected (or designed) examples of student work, first in small groups then in a whole-class discussion. Figure 3.11 shows three of the examples from this lesson. The lesson also includes Tanya's graphical solution, not shown here.

The students' task is to understand each sample solution, to work out its strengths and limitations (none is correct and complete), and to be prepared to explain their critiques in the class discussion. To unpack the mathematics just a bit:

- Alex uses the two constraints successively, starting with Phil's and taking the extreme cases only, then using Cath's constraint to choose between them. His calculations are correct but he has not fully explored the space of possibilities.
- Danny has tried to explore in a systematic way but he has not used either constraint systematically. He gave up, perhaps because the profit seems to be going down, just before the optimum: six small and four large.
- Jeremiah uses algebra and produces a correct solution to the two equations, but the equations should be inequalities. He does not calculate the profit.

---

a) Phil can only make 12 small or 8 large boomerangs in 24 hours
12 small makes $96
8 large makes $80
Cath only has time to make 10, so $96 is impossible.
She could make 10 small boomerangs which will make $80.
So she ether makes 8 large or 10 small boomerangs
and makes $80

b)

No of small S	S×8	No of large	l×10	Profit
0	0	8	80	80
1	8	8̶ 7	70	78
2	16	6	60	76
3	24	5	50	74
4	32	5	50	82 ←
5	40	4	40	80
6	48	3	30	78

The most profit is $82

c) Small boomerangs = x
Large boomerangs = y
Time to carve 2x+3y = 24   ①
Only 10 can be decorated x+y =10   ②
   2x+2y = 20   ③
① - ③   y = 4   x = 6
So make 4 large boomerangs
6 small boomerangs.

Figure 3.11   Sample student work by Alex (a), Danny (b) and Jeremiah (c).

Formative Assessment in Mathematics

This phase of work on the boomerangs task addresses objective 3 above, building connections by linking different mathematical models of the situation. Note that there are no calculation errors: field trials showed these familiar concerns distracted students from attending to the methods. Finally, each student reflects on their own solution in the light of the discussion.

One can analyze this lesson, dimension by dimension, using the TRU framework. In brief: The mathematics is rich and challenging, focusing on key mathematical practices (Dimension 1); the multiple approaches to the problem demonstrated in Figure 3.10 provide access but a good cognitive challenge for all students (Dimensions 2 and 3); the opportunities to discuss and explain their thinking provide opportunities for agency, ownership, and identity (Dimension 4); and both discussions and written work shape teacher moves and student thinking, making this fundamentally a formative assessment lesson (Dimension 5).

Evaluations of the FALs in Action

The funders of the Mathematics Assessment Project, the Bill and Melinda Gates Foundation, supported a series of independent evaluations of FAL implementation entitled Mathematics Development Collaborative, or MDC. These were conducted by UCLA's National Center for Research on Evaluation, Standards, and Student Testing (CRESST) and by the research group Research for Action. A report from CRESST on the impact on ninth-grade algebra students in Kentucky provides the following information (Herman et al., 2014).

CRESST created a measure of algebraic growth based on Kentucky's statewide mathematics assessment, called PLAN. The summary results were:

> For MDC, participating teachers were expected to implement between four and six Classroom Challenges [FALs], meaning that students were so engaged only 8–12 days of the school year. [CRESST] used recently developed methodology to convert the observed effect size for MDC into a gross indicator of the number of months of learning it represents (see Hill et al., 2007). Relative to typical growth in mathematics from ninth to tenth grade, the effect size for MDC represents 4.6 months of schooling.
>
> *(pp. 9–10)*

That is, the average learning gains as a result of 8–12 days of instruction using FALs were 4.6 months. A close examination of all the evidence suggests that the explanation for these large gains has two elements: the deeper understanding of the content that the FALs produced, and the professional development teachers experienced during FAL implementation, with partial transfer of the pedagogical approach of the FALs to the teachers' other lessons (Kim, 2017). This is backed up by data from Research for Action (2015), summarizing the impact of the FALs on teachers:

> Almost all [98%] participating teachers indicated that the role of teacher as instructional "facilitator" or "coach," which is embodied in the [FALs], supports increasing students' mathematical understanding. Compared to providing direct instruction, coaching enables students to take on a more active learning role.
>
> The vast majority (91%) of MDC teachers reported that the lessons provided them with effective strategies for teaching math and strengthening mathematical discourse in their classrooms.
>
> "The students actually talk about math and they are actually having debates and they are debating between who is correct. Before, without this type of teaching, they never talked about math. It was always the teacher talking and they never got into good discussions or justify their answers, and they were never responsible for understanding what other people were thinking as well." – High school math teacher

In addition, teachers reported that MDC practices were affecting their instruction, even when they weren't using the challenges. At least three-quarters of MDC teachers said that the lessons had become important to their instructional practice and that they were infusing strategies from the Classroom Challenges into their ongoing instruction.

(pp. 3–5)

In addition, the Inverness Research Associates' (2014) MAP project portfolio and feedback from other users of the FALs describe them as tools for professional development as well as powerful enhancements of the curriculum.

Design Tactics for Formative Assessment in Mathematics

We have described a set of design principles for formative assessment lessons, which were illustrated in some detail by the examples in the last section. But principles alone do not guarantee effective products. *Strategic design* and *tactical design* (Burkhardt, 2009) are critically important. On strategic design, the ways in which a curriculum innovation relates to the school system at each level (classroom, school, district), and the roles it plays, we shall simply say that this is critical to its impact. Many potentially excellent innovations fail through poor strategic design. For the FALs, the over 7 million lesson downloads so far reflect the way they were introduced as the core of a coherent program: the Gates Foundation's College and Career Readiness program.

We now describe a collection of *design tactics* that have been shown to be useful. All of these tactics can be found in the Mathematics Assessment Project's FALs, but the point is that they can be usefully employed in almost all instruction. We begin with tactics exemplified in the last section and then move to others.

Posters

Getting the students to use poster-size paper and thick pens has three strengths: 1) It promotes a common effort in group work on the poster, where otherwise the small size of individual note books makes it hard to collaborate; 2) It allows teachers to observe group work without physically inserting themselves into the group, which is always disruptive; and 3) It creates a product for which the group is the responsible author, which can be shared with other groups, displayed and discussed, thereby enhancing the ownership dimension of TRU. The poster and its easy visibility create an environment in which peer assessment and formative feedback happen easily and naturally.

Sorting and Matching

Sorting and matching cards or arrows represents a valuable intermediate level of challenge, requiring *understanding* and *critical thinking* but not *creating*. Imagine, for example, in the Percent Change lesson above (Figure 3.7), if all the arrows were blank and the students had to write the appropriate phrase in each case; the misconceptions and contradictions that stimulate the debugging process would not be revealed in the way they are through the matching process. In this way, the structure naturally provides formative feedback, as peer feedback within each group and through the class discussion that follows.

Critiquing Sample Student Work

Critiquing sample student work, as in the boomerangs lesson, has similar strengths. It again gives the students something specific to think through, relating it to their own solutions. For this purpose, it is clear that the work must be carefully chosen to illustrate alternative approaches. This tactic also helps overcome a common criticism of problem solving tasks, which is that the math is not up to grade level, by showing higher level solutions that would rarely appear in most classrooms. Critiquing is clearly a higher-order skill, involving both analysis and the production of extended chains of reasoning in response to the sample work – putting students into a teacher role. This develops peer assessment skills that carry back into their own and their peer's work.

Some teachers select work from their own class for comment by other students. This introduces a social dimension that can work well, or can be awkward. Classroom norms are important (cf. TRU Dimensions 3 and 4) and, if the teacher wants some clever or non-standard approach to a problem to be discussed, it is useful to have that example in a back pocket. The key here is to engineer situations in which students reflect critically (and collaboratively!) on various aspects of the mathematics – not distracted by interpersonal relationships.

Role Shifting

As we have seen, the classroom contract needed for formative assessment involves students moving into roles that are traditional for teachers. The MAP team's theoretical understanding of role shifting as a powerful design tactic was based on Shell Centre research by Phillips et al. (1988). We outline this research here because introducing role shifting is a powerful design tactic that is general. The study found that role shifting, which involves critiquing and explaining, leads to higher level discussions in the classroom, encompassing strategic as well as technical issues.

In this study middle-school teachers taught lessons using software developed by the *Investigations on Teaching with Microcomputers as an Aid* project (ITMA, National Archive of Educational Computing, 2018). An example is given in Figure 3.12.

Each lesson was observed using SCAN, a Systematic Classroom Analysis Notation (Beeby, Burkhardt, & Fraser, 1979) that focuses on the nature of the classroom dialogue. From these observations, the team developed a roles analysis, initially identifying over 30 roles, grouped into six categories (Table 3.5). The names are self-explanatory except for *Resource*, which refers to a person who supplies information but only when asked.

The analysis of the lesson reports showed that most teachers naturally moved from their traditional directive roles into facilitative roles – a well-known and elusive objective, essential for teaching non-routine problem solving. In response students became *explainers* and minor *task setters*,

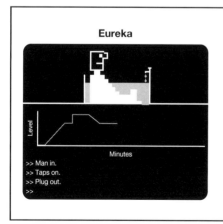

Figure 3.12 The ITMA microworld, Eureka.

Table 3.5 Roles of Teacher and Students in the Classroom

Directive roles	Facilitative roles
• Manager	• Counselor
• Explainer	• Fellow student
• Task-setter	• Resource

asking questions of themselves and their group peers. This shift was exemplified in the teacher questioning, which moved from the usual focus on long teacher explanations and short student answers to questions demanding student explanations of reasoning, and of new insights.

What are the implications here? Self- and peer assessment, so central to formative assessment, involves students moving into teacher roles – notably *explainer* and *questioner/task-setter* – while enriching the facilitative roles through peer-peer discussion. This role shifting is a process that teachers need to facilitate rather than direct in detail. The design or choice of tasks that encourage thinking and reasoning is crucial in encouraging this shift of roles, and of the classroom culture toward the inquiry-rich formative assessment approach embodied in TRU.

Design Tactics for Teachers

We have so far emphasized principles and tactics for the design of formative assessment in mathematics, viewed from our own perspective as professional educational engineers. We conclude with a guide to tactics that teachers can employ in the course of their regular teaching insofar as outside constraints, such as a required textbook or (worse) a district pacing plan, allow. Together these tactics will help teachers to enhance their students' performance in mathematics and feelings of worth as mathematicians, and change the minds of the many students who think math is boring and irrelevant to their lives.

Make Space to Reflect on and Respond to Student Thinking

In the heat of the classroom, teachers often find it difficult to spend enough time listening and responding helpfully to student explanations. A student's thinking can take some time to make sense of! That is a main reason for the use of pre-assessments in the FALs, given a few days before the main lesson. With time to reflect on what students reveal about their understandings, there is a better chance that the lesson will meet the students where they are. We note that it is a common practice in Japanese classrooms for students to write short end-of-lesson reflections, which the teacher reads. The teacher then has a richer sense of what has been *understood* (as opposed to what has been *taught*) in order to plan the next day's lesson. Slower can be quicker. This practice is related to the use of exit tickets, but specifically focused on revealing student thinking, above and beyond seeing how well students are picking up the material.

Give Formative, Qualitative Feedback to Students

Given the clear result from the research on formative assessment that shows the destructive effect of scoring (Black & Wiliam, 1998), how can one ensure that students attend to the constructive guidance the teacher offers? It helps to work out in advance the issues that are likely to arise (as in the Common Issues tables in the FALs), devising specific, appropriate, *qualitative* feedback related to each issue that might be helpful for students. This feedback, usually in the form of open questions, lifts the otherwise heavy load from the teacher during the lesson.

Provide Support to Students Without Taking Over

Teachers' use of thought-provoking *questions*, rather than explanations or direct instruction, is key: offer questions linked to each common issue and also suggest key questions at significant points in the lesson plan that will encourage students to think more deeply. *Teachers ask questions, students explain* encapsulates the basic shift of roles that is needed.

Adapt Teaching to Students with a Range of Difficulties

Try to use "differentiation by support," tailored to the difficulties and capabilities (revealed not assumed) of each student or group. Collaborative activities that encourage student self- and peer assessment are at the heart of formative assessment (Andrade, 2010; Black & Wiliam, 1998). This gives students a more responsible role, lightening the load on the teacher and building the students' sense of responsibility for their own work. It requires the creation of tasks that may be shared and mechanisms for sharing, i.e., use of shared resources and group-generated products, such as posters. The idea is *not* to offer students different tasks related to some pre-determined notion of ability, but rather to offer all students tasks that are sufficiently rich that, with multiple entry points, students can access the core mathematics at their own level, then work through different approaches and understandings.

Allow Students Autonomy, Yet Confront Them with Powerful Methods

Students will tackle rich tasks in many different ways; one should surely encourage this diversity. Yet many students will adopt inefficient or unproductive methods and are unlikely to choose to deploy mathematical concepts and methods with which they are not fully comfortable. Classroom discussions will compare and contrast methods; given two different methods, the teacher can ask which method is preferable, and why. As discussed above, the use of handwritten sample work from another class for critique is a powerful tactic for this purpose.

Find and Choose Rich Tasks

Finding appropriately rich, group-worthy tasks (Lotan, 2003) that provide students with opportunities to engage with central mathematical content and practices is, to put it mildly, a challenge. But the variety of tasks is critical to both motivation and performance. The nature and various roles of tasks in learning mathematics has become a focus of attention in recent years (MAP, 2014; Watson & Ohtani, 2015). It may be most helpful here to communicate through examples: the lessons and tasks at map. mathshell.org provide a rich and varied source. Note the detailed engineering of the lessons, analyzed above, which is a key factor in the quality of the learning activities.

While the *principles* set out here are, we believe, essential to the design of formative assessment, designers and teachers will, of course, need to adapt these *tactics* to their own circumstances. Again, in the design of teaching the details matter.

The Challenges of Designing for Others

The tactics described in this section can be used by individual teachers or, better, by teacher learning communities. With an eye toward the future, we end this section with comments on the additional challenges in the design of teaching materials for others to use. This requires more than an effective learning activity sequence; the design has to communicate to teacher-users so that they understand what is intended and, as with any tool, so that it fits both their capabilities and the job in hand. The process of systematic development through iterative trials, observation and revision is key. The aim is to learn more on questions including:

- Do the teacher and students understand the materials?
- How closely does the teacher follow the lesson plan?
- Are any of the variations damaging to the purpose of the lesson?
- What features of the lesson proved awkward for the teacher or the students?
- What unanticipated opportunities arose that might be included on revision?

This approach, although standard in product development generally, is much more expensive than the authorship model so often used in education: produce a draft, gather comments, revise, then publish. However, methodology is not the focus here, so we shall simply note the development process is where much of the effort and cost of engineering research arises. For a description of the multiple design cycles that gave rise to the FALs described above, see Burkhardt (2006, 2013) and Swan and Burkhardt (2014).

Discussion

As noted in the introduction, it has been difficult for formative assessment in mathematics to take hold, especially at scale. Given disciplinary traditions, this should not be surprising. In literature classes, sharing drafts with peers as well as the teacher is a common and natural practice; multiple revision cycles are understood to be necessary to make a complex argument. Thus, well-established conditions for looking at work in progress, along with well-established heuristics for supporting writing, provide a rich context within which formative assessment can more easily flourish. In mathematics, however, teachers need to overcome an answer-oriented tradition, show-and-practice pedagogies, and the need for a wide range of pedagogical content knowledge (different at each grade level) to be able to implement formative assessment with success. Even if there were enough expertise to carry out the work, the costs of K–12 curriculum development that would provide effective support for teachers in formative assessment is often seen as prohibitive, as is the cost of in-person professional development on the timescale required. Given this fact, it is understandable that the Mathematics Assessment Project's formative assessment lessons are, as far as we are aware, the only teacher support mechanism for formative assessment in mathematics that has worked at scale.

This chapter has unpacked the theoretical framework, the specific research basis, the design principles, strategies, and tactics that were the foundation for the FALs, in order both to explain why they work and to provide a basis for moving forward. The tactics discussed in the last section can be used by individual teachers in planning their own lessons, and by designers who hope to construct materials that will work well for others. The principles are general.

There is a chance that readers, having examined the principles, strategies, and tactics described above, will respond in a way similar to Malcolm Swan: "But isn't this just good teaching?" Well, yes. The point is that there is now a usable analytic framework that characterizes good teaching along the five dimensions of the Teaching for Robust Understanding framework. Such teaching is much more likely to produce knowledgeable, resourceful, and flexible thinkers and problem solvers than students who do not learn in classrooms that reflect the TRU Dimensions. The alignment between the FALs and TRU is no accident: The FALs stand as an embodiment of the kinds of classroom practices valorized in TRU.

What, then, is the way forward? Large-scale development of materials such as the FALs is still to be desired (Burkhardt, 2015), but securing funding for such efforts is a challenge in the current climate. In the meantime, the tactics and strategies described in this paper do work, at the individual teacher, teacher-coach, and teacher learning community levels. An example of professional development models addressing the spectrum of issues discussed above can be found at http://www.bowlandmaths.org.uk/pd/index.html. A growing set of TRU-related tools, including the TRU *Conversation Guide* and the TRU *Observation Guide* discussed in Section 2, is available in the TRU Math Suite at http://map.mathshell.org/trumath.php and at http://truframework.org. Over time, as the implementation of high standards – including the mathematical practices – becomes more widespread, there may be increased opportunities for professional development using tools such as these. However, our research over 35 years suggests that more detailed and specific support, when well-engineered, enables more teachers to achieve challenging teaching goals.

Note

1 Often called "The Red Box," this module from the Shell Centre's *Teaching Strategic Skills* project was one of the first examples of teaching material in mathematics that focus on the interpretation of line graphs of real-life situations. Later its lead designer, Malcolm Swan, was the first recipient of the "Eddie," the prize for excellence in design of the International Society for Design and Development in Education (ISDDE), for this module.

References

Andrade, H. (2010). Students as the definitive source of formative assessment: Academic self-assessment and the self-regulation of learning. In H. Andrade & G. Cizek (Eds.), *Handbook of formative assessment*, (pp. 90–105). New York: Routledge.

Ay, Y. (2017). A review of research on the misconceptions in mathematics education. *Education Research Highlights in Mathematics, Science and Technology 2017, 12*(1) 21–31.

Balanced Assessment Project. (1999). *High school assessment package*. White Plains, NY: Dale Seymour Publications.

Baldinger, E., Louie, N., & the Algebra Teaching Study and Mathematics Assessment Project. (2016). *TRU Math conversation guide: A tool for teacher learning and growth (mathematics version)*. Berkeley, CA & E. Lansing, MI: Graduate School of Education, University of California, Berkeley and College of Education, Michigan State University. Retrieved from http://map.mathshell.org/materials/pd.php.

Beeby, T., Burkhardt, H., & Fraser, R. E. (1979). *SCAN: A systematic classroom analysis notation for mathematics classrooms*. Nottingham, England: Shell Centre for Mathematical Education.

Bell, A. (1993). Some experiments in diagnostic teaching. *Educational Studies in Mathematics, 24*, 115–137.

Birks, D. (1987). *Reflections: A diagnostic teaching experiment*. University of Nottingham: Shell Centre.

Black, P. J. & Wiliam, D. (1998). Assessment and classroom learning. *Assessment in Education 5*, 7–74.

Black, P., Harrison, C., Lee, C., Marshall, B., & Wiliam, D. (2003). *Assessment for learning: Putting it into practice*. Buckingham, England: Open University Press.

Brousseau, G. (1997). *Theory of didactical situations in mathematics: Didactique des mathematiques, 1970–1990*. Dordrecht, the Netherlands: Kluwer.

Brown, J. S. & Burton, R. R. (1978). Diagnostic models for procedural bugs in basic mathematical skills. *Cognitive Science, 2*, 155–192.

Burkhardt, H. (1981). *The real world and mathematics*. Glasgow, Scotland: Blackie.

Burkhardt, H. (2006). From design research to large-scale impact: Engineering research in education. In J. Van den Akker, K. Gravemeijer, S. McKenney, & N. Nieveen (Eds.), *Educational design research* (pp. 121–150). London: Routledge.

Burkhardt, H. (2009) On strategic design. *Educational Designer, 1*(3). Retrieved from http://www.education aldesigner.org/ed/volume1/issue3/article9.

Burkhardt, H. (2013). Methodological issues in research and development. In Y. Li & J. N. Moschkovich (Eds.), *Proficiency and beliefs in learning and teaching mathematics – Learning from Alan Schoenfeld and Günter Törner*. Rotterdam, the Netherlands: Sense Publishers.

Burkhardt, H. (2015). Mathematics education research: a strategic view. In English, L & Kirshner D. (Eds.), *Handbook of international research in mathematics education, 3rd ed*. (pp. 689–712). London: Taylor and Francis.

Burkhardt, H., Groves, S., Schoenfeld, A., & Stacey, K. (Eds). (1986). *Problem solving – a world view*. Nottingham, England: Shell Centre for Mathematical Education.

Burkhardt, H. & Schoenfeld, A. H. (2003). Improving educational research: towards a more useful, more influential and better funded enterprise. *Educational Researcher, 32*, 3–14.

Burkhardt, H. & Schoenfeld, A. H. (2018). Assessment in the service of learning: Challenges and opportunities. In G. Nortvedt & N. Buchholtz (Eds.), *Assessment in mathematics education: Responding to issues regarding methodology, policy and equity, a special issue of ZDM*, DOI: 10.1007/s11858-018-0937-1.

Burkhardt, H. & Swan, M. (2017). Design and development for large-scale improvement. Emma Castelnuovo Award lecture. in G. Kaiser (Ed.) Proceedings of the 13th International Congress on Mathematical Education (pp. 177–200). Berlin: Springer.

Carpenter, T., Fennema, E., Franke, M., L. Levi, & Empson, S. (2000). *Cognitively guided instruction: A research-based teacher professional development program for elementary school mathematics.* Madison, WI: National Center for Improving Student Learning and Achievement In Mathematics and Science.

Carpenter, T., Fennema, E., Franke, M., L. Levi, & S. Empson. (2014). *Children's mathematics, cognitively guided instruction* (2nd edition). Portsmouth, NH: Heinemann.

Cohen, D. K. (1990). A revolution in one classroom: The case of Mrs. Oublier. *Educational Evaluation and Policy Analysis, 12,* 311–330.

Confrey, J. (1990). A review of the research on student conceptions in mathematics, science, and programming. *Review of Research in Education, 16,* 3–56.

Daro, P. (2010). Personal communication.

Engle, R. A. & Conant, F. R. (2002). Guiding principles for fostering productive disciplinary engagement: Explaining an emergent argument in a community of learners classroom. *Cognition and Instruction, 20*(4), 399–483.

Engle, R. A. (2011). The productive disciplinary engagement framework: Origins, key concepts, and continuing developments. In D. Y. Dai (Ed.), *Design research on learning and thinking in educational settings: Enhancing intellectual growth and functioning* (pp. 161–200). London: Taylor & Francis.

Hart, K. (Ed.). (1981) *Childrens' understanding of mathematics 11–16.* London: John Murray

Hatano, G. & Inagaki, K. (1986). Two courses of expertise. In H. W. Stevenson, H. Azuma & K. Hakuta (Eds.), *Child development and education in Japan* (pp. 262–272). New York, NY: W H Freeman/Times Books/ Henry Holt & Co.

Henningsen, M. & Stein, M. K. (1997). Mathematical tasks and student cognition: classroom-based factors that support and inhibit high-level mathematical thinking and reasoning. *Journal for Research in Mathematics Education, 28*(5), 524–549.

Herman, J., Epstein, S., Leon, S., La Torre Matrundola, D., Reber, S., & Choi, K. (2014). *Implementation and effects of LDC and MDC in Kentucky districts (CRESST Policy Brief No. 13).* Los Angeles: University of California, National Center for Research on Evaluation, Standards, and Student Testing (CRESST).

Higgins, S., Ryan, J., Swan, M., & Williams, J. (2002). Learning from mistakes, misunderstandings and misconceptions in mathematics. In I. Thompson (ed.), *National Numeracy and Key Stage 3 Strategies.* (pp. 102–126). London: Department for Education and Skills.

Hill, C., Bloom, H., Black, A. R., & Lipsey, M. W. (2007). *Empirical benchmarks for interpreting effect sizes in research* (Working Paper). New York: MDRC.

Inverness Research Associates (2014) MAP Project Portfolio. Retrieved from http://inverness-research.org/mars_map/index.html.

Kim, H-j. (2017). Teacher learning opportunities provided by implementing formative assessment lessons: Becoming responsive to student mathematical thinking. *Int. J. Sci & Math Ed., 17*(2). DOI: 10.1007/s10763-017-9866-7.

Lappan, G., & Phillips, E. (2008). Challenges in US Mathematics education through a curriculum developer lens. *Educational Designer, 1*(2). Retrieved from http://www.educationaldesigner.org/ed/volume1/issue3/article11/index.htm.

Lotan, R. (2003, March). Group-worthy tasks. *Educational Leadership, 60*(6), 72–75.

Mathematics Assessment Project (MAP) (2014) Summative assessment. Retrieved from http://map.mathshell.org/background.php?subpage=summative

Maurer, S. (1987). New knowledge about errors and new views about learners: What they mean to educators and what educators would like to know. In A. Schoenfeld (Ed.), *Cognitive science and mathematics education* (pp. 165–187). Mahwah, NJ: Erlbaum.

National Archive of Educational Computing (2018). Micros in the mathematics classroom. Retrieved from http://www.naec.org.uk/artefacts/software/micros-in-the-mathematics-classroom.

National Council of Teachers of Mathematics. (1989). *Curriculum and evaluation standards for school mathematics.* Reston, VA: NCTM.

National Research Council. (1989). *Everybody counts: A report to the nation on the future of mathematics education.* Washington DC: National Academy Press.

Phillips, R., Burkhardt, H., Fraser, R., Coupland, J., Pimm, D., & Ridgway, J. (1988). Learning activities and classroom roles with and without the microcomputer. *Journal of Mathematical Behavior, 6,* 305–338.

Research for Action (2015). *MDC's Influence on Teaching and Learning.* Philadelphia, PA: Author. Retrieved from https://www.researchforaction.org/publications/mdcs-influence-on-teaching-and-learning/

Schoenfeld, A. H. (1985). *Mathematical problem solving.* Orlando, FL: Academic Press.

Schoenfeld, A. H. (2001). Purposes and methods of research in mathematics education. In Holton, D., Artigue, M., Kirchgraber, U, Hillel, J., Niss, M. and Schoenfeld, H. (Eds.) *The teaching and learning of mathematics at the University Level* (pp. 221–236). Dordrecht, the Netherlands: Kluwer.

Schoenfeld, A. H. (2013). Classroom observations in theory and practice. *ZDM, the International Journal of Mathematics Education, 45,* 607–621. DOI 10.1007/s11858-012-0483-1.

Schoenfeld, A. H. (2014, November). What makes for powerful classrooms, and how can we support teachers in creating them? *Educational Researcher, 43*(8), 404–412. DOI: 10.3102/0013189X1455

Schoenfeld, A.H. (2015). Thoughts on scale. *ZDM, the international journal of mathematics education, 47,* 161–169. DOI: 10.1007/s11858-014-0662-3.

Schoenfeld, A. H. (2017). Teaching for robust understanding of essential mathematics. In T. McDougal, (Ed.), *Essential Mathematics for the Next Generation: What and How Students Should Learn* (pp. 104–129). Tokyo, Japan: Tokyo Gagukei University.

Schoenfeld, A. H. (2018) Uses of Video in Understanding and Improving Mathematical Thinking and Teaching. *Journal of Mathematics Teacher Education,* 415–432. DOI 10.1007/s10857-017-9381-3.

Schoenfeld, A. H. & the Teaching for Robust Understanding Project. (2016). *The Teaching for Robust Understanding (TRU) observation guide for mathematics: A tool for teachers, coaches, administrators, and professional learning communities.* Berkeley, CA: Graduate School of Education, University of California, Berkeley. Retrieved from http://TRUframework.org.

Schoenfeld, A. H., Floden, R. E., & the Algebra Teaching Study and Mathematics Assessment Project. (2014). The TRU Math Scoring Rubric. Berkeley, CA & E. Lansing, MI: Graduate School of Education, University of California, Berkeley & College of Education, Michigan State University. Retrieved from http://map.mathshell.org/trumath/tru_math_rubric_alpha_20140731.pdf.

Shell Centre. (1988). *Be a Paper Engineer.* Retrieved from http://www.mathshell.com/materials.php?item=paperengineerandseries=numeracy.

Shulman, L. (1986). Those who understand: Knowledge growth in teaching. *Educational Researcher, 15*(2), 4–14.

Shulman, L. (1987). Knowledge and Teaching: Foundations of the New Reform. *Harvard Educational Review, 57*(1), 1–23.

Stein, M. K., Engle, R. A., Smith, M. S. & Hughes, E. K. (2008). Orchestrating Productive Mathematical Discussions: Five Practices for Helping Teachers Move Beyond Show and Tell. *Mathematical Thinking and Learning, 10*(4), 313–340.

Stein, M. K., Grover, B., & Henningsen, M. (1996). Building student capacity for mathematical thinking and reasoning: An analysis of mathematical tasks used in reform classrooms. *American Educational Research Journal, 33*(2), 455–488.

Swan, M. (2006). *Collaborative Learning in Mathematics: A Challenge to our Beliefs and Practices.* London: National Institute for Advanced and Continuing Education (NIACE) for the National Research and Development Centre for Adult Literacy and Numeracy (NRDC).

Swan, M. (2014). *Improving the alignment between values, principles and classroom realities.* In Y. Li & G. Lappan (Eds.), Mathematics Curriculum in School Education: Springer.

Swan, M., Pitts, J., Fraser, R., Burkhardt, H., & the Shell Centre team (1985). *The language of functions and graphs,* Manchester, U.K.: Joint Matriculation Board and Shell Centre for Mathematical Education, Retrieved from http://www.mathshell.com.

Swan, M. & Burkhardt, H. (2014) Lesson design for formative assessment. *Educational Designer, 2*(7). Retrieved from: http://www.educationaldesigner.org/ed/volume2/issue7/article24.

Swan, M. (2017). Towards a task-based curriculum: Frameworks for task design and pedagogy. In T. McDougal (Ed.), *Essential mathematics for the next generation* (pp. 29–60). Tokyo: Tokyo Gakugei University Press.

Watson, A. & Ohtani, M. (Eds.) (2015) *Task Design In Mathematics Education: ICMI study 22,* Berlin: Springer.

Wiliam, D. (2016). *Leadership for teacher learning: Creating a culture where all teachers improve so that all learners succeed.* West Palm Beach, FL: Learning Sciences International.

Wiliam, D. & Thompson, M. (2007). Integrating assessment with instruction: What will it take to make it work? In C. A. Dwyer (Ed.) *The future of assessment: shaping teaching and learning* (pp. 53–82). Mahwah, NJ: Erlbaum.

4

SCENARIO-BASED FORMATIVE ASSESSMENT OF KEY PRACTICES IN THE ENGLISH LANGUAGE ARTS

Paul Deane and Jesse R. Sparks

Formative Assessment Principles

The concept of formative assessment arises from the recognition that effective learning is a process in which both teachers and students must play active roles. This is particularly true in the case of complex skills, where effective performance requires a clear understanding of the goals to be achieved, effective strategies for achieving those goals, the ability to monitor and evaluate one's own progress (which requires learners to internalize evaluation criteria that may not be self-evident or easily learned or applied), and the self-awareness to modify subgoals and select alternative strategies as needed (Sadler, 1983, 1989, 1998, 2010). This emphasis on reflection, internalization, and self-regulation is consistent with learning sciences theories highlighting the centrality of metacognitive knowledge and skills in fostering students' learning of complex skills like inquiry (cf. Collins, Brown, & Newman, 1988; Resnick, 1987; White & Frederiksen, 1998). Effective learning of such complex concepts is facilitated by assessment practices that create a closed feedback loop that helps teachers elicit evidence of students' current learning and meet students' current needs with the design or selection of the most effective instruction for their students. This assessment-driven feedback loop also helps students engage with, and internalize, the goals, evaluation criteria, and strategies that they need to learn (Black, 2015; Black & Wiliam, 1998, 2010). Major strategies by which teachers can enact formative assessment include the following (Andrade & Heritage, 2017; Black & Wiliam, 2009; Wiliam & Thompson, 2007):

- explicitly communicating what students are expected to learn and the criteria for successful performance;
- structuring classroom discussion and other interactions to provide evidence of student learning;
- providing feedback that helps students internalize the success criteria and identify ways to improve their performance;
- using classroom structures and strategies that facilitate students in supporting one another's learning (for instance, by having them collaborate on projects or by providing peer feedback on individual work); and
- getting students to take responsibility for their own learning through a variety of strategies including self-evaluation and revision after feedback (i.e., fostering self-regulation skills).

However, a number of recent analyses have raised critical issues about the nature, and efficacy, of formative assessment. In particular, Bennett (2011) discusses:

- Concerns that claims about the effectiveness of formative assessment have been exaggerated. Bennett's concern is reinforced by the meta-analysis performed by Kingston and Nash (2011), who found a mean effect size for formative assessment of 0.20, in contrast to claims commonly repeated in the literature that indicated effect sizes between 0.40 and 0.70. However, Briggs at al. (2012) contend that methodological issues in Kingston and Nash's study precluded the use of their estimate as a baseline for the effectiveness of formative assessment.

- Concerns about a lack of clarity in how formative assessment has been defined. This issue is related to another issue that Bennett raises, namely the way formative assessment interacts with a larger assessment system. To the extent that systemic pressures privilege formal instruments separated from classroom practice, and other practices that do not integrate well with formative assessment practice, there is the risk that formative assessment will be conceptualized and implemented in distorted ways or not at all.

- Concerns about how effectively teacher professional development based upon formative assessment methods will work if not all teachers have associated critical competencies, including well-developed pedagogical content knowledge (Shulman, 1986, 1987) and an understanding of educational measurement principles. A related issue is that teachers may have difficulty in creating formative assessment tasks that are well-aligned to relevant standards, particularly if those standards reflect skills that are not regularly taught or practiced, or for which the teacher lacks pedagogical content knowledge or has had little professional development. The resulting formative assessments may inadequately prepare students for the kinds of performances required on summative tests.

- Concerns about the validity of the inferences that some teachers may draw as they incorporate formative assessment in their classroom practice. In particular, teachers' formative inferences may be influenced by (possibly unconscious) subjective biases and uncertainty (i.e., measurement error) that can impact their instructional usefulness.

- Concerns about the potential fragility of the causal mechanisms underlying effective formative assessment if domain dependencies are ignored. According to the theory of action outlined in Black and Wiliam (2009), effective formative assessment requires teachers to make detailed inferences about what students know and can do on the basis of classroom interactions and make carefully tailored adjustments to instruction on the basis of that information. The efficacy of the inferences and adjustments that teachers make is likely to be very sensitive to the quality of their pedagogical content knowledge, which may not be fully developed in preservice settings and may need to be refined further through professional development over the course of their careers. Bennett's concern is echoed elsewhere in the literature. For instance, Coffey et al. (2011) question the use of general formative assessment techniques unless those techniques are closely integrated with disciplinary thinking, a perspective echoed by Cowie and Moreland (2015), who contend that formative assessment may be particularly effective when it is embedded in experiences that emulate common disciplinary practices.

In practice, these concerns interact. If different people mean different things by formative assessment, it will be enacted differently across contexts. If formative assessment (however it is understood) is implemented at varying levels of fidelity, and interpreted differently by teachers with more or less teaching experience, and if the inferences teachers draw are more or less meaningful (depending on the domain and their level of knowledge), the effects of formative assessment on learning may be highly inconsistent. In this paper, however, we are concerned primarily with the relationships among formative assessment, disciplinary practice, and the domain of instruction.

We would contend that domain integration is critical for many reasons: not only for those identified by Bennett (2011), but because teachers themselves may vary in pedagogical content knowledge (Shulman, 1986, 1987), in their understanding of formative assessment (Heritage, 2007), and especially in their ability to integrate the two (Heritage et al., 2009). One of the greatest potential benefits of a system that explicitly integrates domain knowledge with formative assessment (and models how to use formative assessment information to make classroom instructional decisions) may lie in its effects on teacher professional development.

In what follows, we articulate our approach to the design and development of cognitively based models and assessment tasks intended to support a form of discipline-specific formative assessment practice and support teachers in their efforts to enact that practice. First, we discuss our approach to domain analysis, articulating the importance of two critical concepts for our model: learning progressions and key literacy practices. Next, we discuss our approach to task analysis, which suggests particular task designs grounded in the structure of relevant key practices and learning progressions. The second half of this chapter presents an illustration of this approach using assessments of research skills (i.e., evaluating sources), including descriptions of the domain analysis, task analysis, and sample task designs. We then articulate our vision for how such materials could be integrated into teachers' formative assessment practice and the potential benefits that could result from using this cognitively based disciplinary approach.

Domain Analysis

The considerations we have previously cited suggest that formative assessment can be strengthened by framing it in the context of a well-thought-out domain analysis which identifies the knowledge and skills that are central to the domain and describes how novices can progressively master the domain. We primarily organize this analysis in terms of two critical concepts: *learning progressions*, and *key literacy practices*, as follows.

Learning Progressions: Linking Formative Assessment With Pedagogical Content Knowledge

The recent literature suggests a model for integrating domain knowledge with formative assessment that builds upon the concept of learning progressions (cf. Sztajn et al., 2012 for a discussion of this approach in the context of mathematics). Learning progressions are hypotheses that describe qualitative shifts in the sophistication of a skill that develops over time with appropriate instruction (Corcoran, Mosher, & Rogat, 2009; Duncan & Hmelo-Silver, 2009; Heritage, 2008; Wilson, 2009). Based on available empirical research and developmental theory in the cognitive and learning sciences, learning progressions detail provisional claims (subject to validation) about how skills or strategies progress from novice to expert-level performances (Corcoran, Mosher, & Rogat 2009). Learning progressions function, in effect, as systems that organize pedagogical content knowledge within a domain.

Importantly, learning progressions can support the formative assessment process (Bennett, 2011; Popham, 2008) in that they provide teachers and students with an overarching framework that integrates specific instructional targets with high-level academic and professional outcomes (e.g., writing and publishing a research report to share one's findings). Learning progressions serve to make implicit knowledge explicit for students and teachers who may not have the relevant domain knowledge to help them meaningfully organize the various skills and strategies they practice in the classroom, particularly as those skills and strategies relate to and support real-world communicative purposes in academic and workplace contexts. Learning progressions also help define cognitive targets for formative assessment tasks; students' performance on such tasks can reveal critical information about students' current levels of proficiency with particular subskills. This analysis can inform instructional next steps, such as points where students may need additional practice or reteaching, or suggesting tasks which may pose the next level of challenge for students who already appear to have mastered a particular skill level.

A system that integrates learning progressions with formative assessment would include the following elements (Black, Wilson, & Yao, 2011; Furtak, Morrison, & Kroog, 2014; Shavelson et al., 2006):

- An explicit learning progression (i.e., a road map for learning a set of core domain concepts)
- A battery of tasks designed to identify students' specific conceptual gaps or misconceptions
- A psychometric model that uses student performance patterns to place students at specific levels in the learning progression
- Recommendations for instructional next steps, depending upon where students are placed on the learning progression.

Note that these elements do not suffice, by themselves, to create an assessment system that supports formative assessment in the sense advocated by Black and Wiliam (2009). That support depends on the nature of the tasks and the ways that teachers integrate those tasks into classroom practice. It is also worth noting that each of these elements may individually contribute to and support teachers' formative assessment practice in the absence of the other elements (e.g., teachers may examine student work to make formative inferences about students' strengths and weaknesses without the aid of a psychometric model). But with appropriate classroom implementation, this kind of design cohesively links an explicit domain model with concrete, cognitively based recommendations for formative assessment practice.

There is, however, a problem with applying the concept of learning progressions to a skill-based domain like the English Language Arts (ELA). Most existing efforts to articulate learning progressions have taken place in mathematics (Daro, Mosher, & Corcoran, 2011; Graf & Arieli-Attali, 2015) and science (Alonzo & Gotwals, 2012; Corcoran, Mosher, & Rogat 2009), and have focused on mapping the development of curricular concepts (e.g., linear functions, control-for-variables strategy), rather than skills. But in the ELA domain, the skills of reading and writing are central, and literacy tasks typically involve complex performances that require the functional coordination of a variety of skills, ranging from simple reading literacy tasks like scanning for keywords to complex critical thinking tasks, such as evaluating an argument (Applebee & Langer, 1983). If learning progressions are framed concretely enough to provide specific feedback about skills students need to learn, it may be necessary to specify dozens of learning progressions, even though (for most students) these skills are acquired together as part of integrated performances, and must ultimately be applied in that way.

Mosher and Heritage (2017) outline some of the knowledge and skills that enter into literacy learning and review some of the efforts that have been made to develop literacy learning progressions. They argue that in the literacy domain, the complexity of the skills involved means that any practical approach to learning progressions will be closely tied to decisions about teaching strategies and curricular scope and sequence, such as the progressions proposed for reading and writing by the Teachers College Reading and Writing Project (Calkins, 2015; Calkins, Hohne, & Robb, 2015), or the literacy learning progressions developed by the New Zealand Ministry of Education (Ministry of Education, 2010). Mosher and Heritage emphasize the importance of core literacy skills (such as knowledge of the orthographic code and orthography) but acknowledge the importance of these skills being integrated to support literate communication. Their review highlights the complexity of the skills that must be mastered even if attention is focused only on fundamental aspects of literacy. However, if we consider the ELA domain more broadly, as more recent standards documents such as the Common Core State Standards (CCSS) do, it becomes even more urgent that students learn how to integrate literacy skills in ways that enable them to do well on complex performance tasks (National Governors Association Center for Best Practices & Council of Chief State School Officers, 2010).

Key Practices: Analyzing Integrated Skills

The problem of teaching complex performance skills underlies many of Sadler's (1983, 1989) concerns about traditional approaches to classroom assessment. When students must learn a complex performance task that involves the integration of many different skills (and thus the application of multiple standards of evaluation), it is difficult to characterize student progress by focusing on a single learning progression (or standard for evaluation). The strategies that enable students to coordinate the skills they have are at least as important as their ability to apply component skills successfully in isolation. As a result, we contend that domain analysis will best support ELA formative assessment by addressing what we term key practices that define the end goals of literacy instruction (Deane et al., 2015).

A *practice* is a coordinated set of behaviors undertaken by individuals within a social structure (with associated norms and expectations for participant behaviors) aimed at achieving particular goals that are valued within a social group, such as discussing and debating ideas (argumentation), publishing professional documents, or conducting research and inquiry. For example, professional scientists working within a discipline have shared norms, values, and expectations for participation that must be learned in order for new members to achieve full participation in the practices of the group (Lave & Wenger, 1991). Norms for locating and evaluating evidentiary sources, for conducting original investigations, and for communicating the results of one's work with members of one's discipline – or the broader public – guide participation in these practices; thus, disciplinary practices coordinate individual and collaborative activities linked by a common purpose or goal that is valued within a particular social context (Brown, Collins, & Duguid, 1989).

Following Deane et al. (2015), we define a *key practice* as "a class of literacy activities that use similar methods to accomplish similar goals" (p. 2). We contend that standards documents and curricular frameworks can fruitfully be interpreted by considering what practices they define as end goals for K–12 education and, therefore, privilege. For instance, the Common Core State Standards prioritize such practices as the rhetorical interpretation of texts, the construction, and evaluation of arguments, and the gathering and sharing of information through research. Viewing the ELA construct through this lens, Deane et al. (2015) identified eight key practices that jointly define major curricular goals in the English Language Arts, and classified them at three levels: *fundamental literacy practices* (supported by speaking and listening, reading, and writing skills which enable literate communication without any specialized disciplinary knowledge); *model-building practices* (supported by metacognitive awareness of reading and writing processes, and knowledge of text structure); and *applied practices* (supported by the specialized reading and writing skills needed to participate in key disciplinary activities, such as building and justifying interpretations, analyzing writer's craft, discussing and debating ideas, constructing arguments, and supporting collaborative, project-based work).

This approach has been applied to several key practices, including informational reading and writing (O'Reilly, Deane, & Sabatini, 2015), argumentation (Deane & Song, 2014; van Rijn, Graf, & Deane, 2014), and research skills (Sparks & Deane, 2015). There are two major benefits that can be obtained by using key practices to organize the ELA domain. First, it can help to define priorities for instruction and assessment. Once we know what key practice is being taught or assessed, we can identify and target the specific cognitive abilities that are most important to achieving the communicative goals central to that practice. Second, it can help students (and preservice or less-experienced teachers) see how the targeted skills are related. In contrast to componential approaches which often generate disordered inventories of skills to be learned and assessed, we use the goal-driven nature of key practices to organize component skills into functionally-related sets.

Ultimately, one of the goals of formative assessment is to encourage deep learning while facilitating the development of students' self-regulation skills (Clark, 2012; Tay, 2015) which in the ELA context means learning how to manage literate communication practices. One of the most effective strategies for teaching process management is the use of scripts that communicate to students which skills they need to use under what conditions (Panadero, Alonso-Tapia, & Reche, 2013; Panadero, Tapia, & Huertas, 2012). Domain analysis should, therefore, identify the major goals and subtasks that are critical to success in a specific practice and clarify exactly how each targeted skill contributes to effective strategies for achieving those goals.

In summary, as part of the domain analysis, we expect to develop learning progressions for each targeted skill, but those skills must also fit together functionally, so that teachers will be able to give their students effective scripts to follow. This kind of domain analysis can serve several purposes. It can be used to provide the foundation for curriculum design, as a method for specifying the targets for assessment, as the basis for teacher professional development, or as the basis for developing exemplary formative assessment tasks (or, preferably, for all of these purposes). But we would contend, in particular, that domain analysis is a critical first step toward making ELA pedagogical content knowledge explicit and more easily communicated both to students and in teachers' professional development.

Task Analysis

The kind of domain analysis we have just described is best viewed as a precursor to what is called *task analysis* in some theories of assessment development, such as Evidence-Centered Design (Mislevy et al., 2017). Task analysis involves the consideration of the types of tasks and environments that are best suited to elicit relevant evidence of student learning in the target domain, as defined in the domain analysis. In addition, given the focus on formative assessment, task analysis should also consider the extent to which the design of candidate assessment tasks can provide students with effective feedback, activate fellow students as instructional resources, and encourage students to take ownership of their learning.

Experience in the design of summative assessments suggests that task analysis is not a trivial matter since it requires a careful consideration of the nature of the task, the ways that students may attempt to perform the task, and the construction of an evidentiary argument that details how the task will provide evidence of the targeted skill (Zieky, 2014). Teachers generally do not have the expertise, or the time, to do this kind of task construction and analysis on a regular basis during instruction. Yet the potential value of the tasks embedded in a formative assessment will depend critically on the quality of the preceding task analysis, regardless of whether that analysis was conducted as part of curriculum development or as part of the development of a targeted battery of formative assessment tasks.

Challenges With Performance Tasks

These kinds of task design issues are particularly important when we consider the problem of drawing appropriate inferences about what students know and can do from their behavior on complex performance tasks, which implicitly require students to successfully complete a variety of preliminary steps. It is common for teachers to assign such tasks during regular schoolwork and for them to appear as standalone tasks in a summative assessment as well. For example, students may be assigned writing tasks that require them to read and comprehend multiple passages, evaluate the reliability of information contained in those passages, extract information that is relevant to an argument or issue discussed across the passages, and write an extended argumentative essay defending one's conclusion or claim about the issue, incorporating evidence from the source materials. There are a variety of such tasks on summative assessments, such as on the Collegiate Learning Assessment (CLA+) and its K-12 counterpart, the College and Work Readiness Assessment (CWRA+; Council for Aid to Education, 2016; Zahner, 2013), or in the Smarter Balanced and PARCC CCSS assessments (Herman & Linn, 2013). However, it is often the case that only the final written product is evaluated and little attention is given to the foundational reading comprehension and critical evaluation and analysis skills required to achieve a successful result. Thus, such assessments may yield little instructionally-relevant information about possible weaknesses or breakdowns in students' component skills that could be fruitfully targeted for subsequent instruction.

Similar observations apply to the classroom. If less-experienced teachers are not provided with models that show them how to collect formative assessment evidence about the wide variety of skills that contribute to successful performance, they may only observe global patterns of success and failure, missing potentially important process differences in the ways students address the complexities of the task. Some students may fare poorly because of unclear or excessively broad directions and attempt to complete the task using inappropriate strategies borrowed from some other task with which they are more familiar. Even if the directions are clear, there is a risk with complex performance tasks that weaker students may not attempt some aspects of the task that more skilled students can do. If less skilled students do attempt all the major subtasks, the teacher may not have structured classroom assessments in ways that will provide her with clear evidence about patterns of student strengths and weaknesses in component skills that contribute to the overall product.

These features of complex performance tasks are linked to the way we have conceptualized key literacy practices. Achieving high-level communicative goals requires the strategic, fluent coordination of a variety of cognitive and socio-cognitive skills in complex activities that may involve a whole hierarchy of goals and subgoals. Thus, there is a need to develop explicit models for teaching and assessing performance tasks that not only make each of the moving parts visible (e.g., comprehend the text; evaluate its reliability; compare its information with other available, reliable sources), but also clarifies for students (and, where appropriate, teachers) why these steps are necessary for achieving larger goals (e.g., writing a source-based research essay). The resulting sequence of activities, if well designed, may provide multiple opportunities for formative assessment, and enable teachers to more effectively identify where less-capable students need the most support and instruction.

Scenario-based Tasks (SBTs)

The task design that results from the analysis described above is what we term a *scenario-based task*. SBTs engage students in reading, writing, and critical thinking activities in the context of a specific, simulated social context or scenario; these scenarios provide students with an overarching goal (often involving a culminating writing task) and an overarching purpose for engaging with the stimulus materials provided. We have applied these principles to design scenario-based summative and interim assessments, where similar considerations apply – when it is well-constructed, a scenario-based task makes it possible to identify patterns of strengths and weaknesses on the complex array of skills needed to achieve success on the performance task as a whole (Bennett, Deane, & van Rijn, 2016; Sabatini et al., 2014; Sheehan & O'Reilly, 2012).

SBTs provide an approach to assessment design that helps to scaffold strategies for overall, integrated performances through a sequenced, targeted series of assessment tasks tapping into component skills. By providing an overarching social context and goal, SBTs are purpose driven, providing a meaningful framework to organize the component skills in a way that highlights for students and teachers the contribution of those skills to the overall aim. SBTs also help to define occasions where additional in-depth formative assessment for specific skills may be appropriate; for example, students may need to engage in additional practice to overcome weaknesses in component skills identified through results from a scenario-based assessment. This approach supports individualized instruction, since results from SBTs can identify which students need additional support for which parts of the task, and which students can work independently. This approach can support teachers in developing a gradual release of agency, as students move toward increasingly independent performance, with less intervention or scaffolding needed.

Scenario-Based Formative Assessment

Formative Task Models Aligned To Learning Progression Levels

Critical to the conception we have just sketched is the idea that a scenario-based task may require students to demonstrate several different, but functionally related, skills linked to a specific key practice. In our framework, there are learning progressions for each targeted skill. As teachers walk students through a scenario during class, they may discover that some of their students find a particular task challenging. The teacher may then want to follow up with the collection of additional evidence to support or refine this initial hypothesis about student skill levels.

We envision developing additional formative assessment tasks aligned to the learning progressions, which can be deployed by teachers to gain additional, just-in-time insights into students' proficiency with particular skills and strategies beyond the information yielded from completion of the scenario-based tasks. Tasks targeting the same learning progressions at the same/lower/higher levels can be administered as needed to help students further develop weak skills or to help them stretch to achieve more challenging levels of performance.

Note that the approach we have just described can be viewed either as an abstract structure or as a concrete model of practice. The task analysis should identify a replicable structure that could be instantiated across a wide range of specific contexts. But when that structure is embodied in a specific set of tasks and texts focused on a given topic, the result is a concrete model that can illustrate how to perform formative assessment while taking students through the steps needed to complete a complex performance task. Additionally, the key practice, learning progressions, and illustrative tasks can serve (if the connections are made explicit) to help teachers deepen their content knowledge for teaching. We believe that this kind of concrete illustration may be extremely useful in teacher professional development.

Developing Model Research and Inquiry Tasks

All the points we have made so far are programmatic. They describe a strategy for building teachers' pedagogical content knowledge, while helping them link that knowledge with effective formative assessment. We have been engaged for some time in instantiating this approach in selected domains as part of the CBAL™ (Cognitively Based Assessment of, for, and as Learning) tools being developed at ETS. These tools emanate from a theory of action in which formative assessment plays a central role (Bennett, 2010; Bennett & Gitomer, 2009). Thus far, we have made the greatest progress with argumentation (the key practice, *Discuss and Debate Ideas*). In that subdomain, we have developed scenario-based summative and interim assessments (Deane et al., 2015; Deane & Song, 2014; van Rijn et al., 2014), explored why students perform well or poorly on particular argumentation writing tasks (Song, Deane, & Fowles, 2014, 2017), supported efforts to provide formative assessment of argumentation skill in game-based formats (Bauer et al., 2017; Bertling et al., 2015; Song & Sparks, 2017), and developed formative assessment materials that have become part of the Smarter Balanced Formative Task Library (see: http://www.smarterbalanced.org/educators/the-digital-library/).

In the following sections, we illustrate the notions of domain and task analysis described above, and demonstrate how these analyses inform the design of assessment tasks intended for use as part of a domain-specific approach to formative assessment focusing on the key practice of *Conducting Research and Inquiry* (Sparks & Deane, 2015). We chose this focus for two reasons. First, this key practice represents a complex skill that is prioritized by the Common Core State Standards for ELA, with relevant competencies highlighted in the reading standards (e.g., RI.6, RI.9) and writing anchor standards (e.g., W.7, W.8), as well as in the overall design principles that emphasize the need to conduct research across all aspects of the curriculum (National Governors Association Center for Best Practices & Council of Chief State School Officers, 2010). Second, since this practice (or particular aspects of it) may be unfamiliar to many ELA teachers, we describe a model of cognition and learning for research and inquiry, and how assessment tasks can be designed from that model.

It is our hope that this description will help teachers develop pedagogical content knowledge for this subject. The work we describe is just beginning to move from design and development to usability and pilot testing in schools, and we expect in the future to be able to present more detailed empirical results about the implementation of these tasks as classroom-based formative assessments. In advance of classroom implementations, however, the work we describe is useful as an exercise in thinking through the connection between formative assessment, pedagogical content knowledge, and the need to design concrete tasks that can be integrated effectively into a language arts curriculum.

From Domain and Task Analysis to Assessment Development

Any domain analysis begins with a consideration of the primary goals of the domain, and the necessary knowledge, skills, strategies, and processes required for success in that domain. With respect to the domain of English Language Arts, where the acquisition of literacy is the ultimate goal, the CBAL framework conceptualizes ELA proficiency as requiring the skillful coordination of multiple types of cognitive representations (social, conceptual, discourse, verbal, and print), across three modes of cognitive processing (interpretive, expressive, and deliberative, which correspond roughly to reading, writing, and critical thinking processes; see Deane et al., 2015). Specifically, the CBAL framework suggests that the acquisition of literacy skills requires coordination of cognitive processes across various levels of representation, with skills becoming increasingly routinized, automatic, and fluent as learners approach higher levels of expertise.

Defining the Key Practice

The practice *Conducting Research and Inquiry*, as articulated previously, is part of a set of applied practices (Deane et al., 2015) which also includes discussing and debating ideas (argumentation); building and justifying interpretations, analyzing craft and literary elements; and proposing, reviewing, recommending, and evaluating texts as part of a process of publication and peer review. The shift from more foundational to more applied practices is consistent with Chall's (1983) distinction among learning to read, reading to learn, and reading to do. Thus, research, argumentation, publishing, and conducting literary analysis and interpretation represent the high-level literacy practices in which learners should be able to participate if they are to be prepared for participation in college coursework or in careers which emphasize literate communication to achieve shared goals. Facility with applied practices presupposes fluency with fundamental literacy and model-building practices.

In its most basic instantiation, *Conducting Research and Inquiry* as a key literacy practice requires reading comprehension, critical analysis and evaluation, and written synthesis of multiple documents in order to answer research questions or evaluate the validity of knowledge claims (cf. Britt, Rouet, & Durik, 2017; Perfetti, Rouet, & Britt, 1999). Building on extant research on multiple-document comprehension from the cognitive and learning sciences (Britt et al., 2017; Goldman et al., 2012, 2016; Goldman, Lawless, & Manning, 2013; Kuiper, Volman, & Terwel, 2005; Walraven, Brand-Gruwel, & Boshuizen, 2008; Wiley et al., 2009), CBAL research defines this key practice as involving the

> mastery of the knowledge, skills, and strategies needed to participate in a research community, including the abilities to gather, evaluate, and synthesize information from multiple sources, to plan and conduct inquiry and experimentation to answer driving questions or solve problems, and to present information one has learned in appropriate forms and formats.
>
> *(Sparks & Deane, 2015, pp. 3–4)*

In the service of conducting inquiry, readers must go beyond basic understanding of text content (i.e., the focus of the key practice *Building and Sharing Knowledge*) to make informed judgments about the relative usefulness or applicability of information obtained from reliable sources for addressing specific questions or issues that are of interest to a particular research community or to the broader public. Thus, comparative evaluation and deep, coherent synthesis of multiple, reliable sources in an effort to continually advance one's thinking about a subject (cf. Scardamalia & Bereiter, 2006) are central in our model of research and inquiry as a key literacy practice.

We conceptualize *Research and Inquiry* as involving three phases or subgoals, namely: (a) *Inquiry and Information Gathering*, which entails skills and strategies for planning, monitoring, and carrying out information gathering or data collection activities; (b) *Analysis, Evaluation, and Synthesis*, which includes strategies for comprehending, critically evaluating, and consolidating information from multiple documents; and (c) *Communication and Presentation of Results*, which involves activities related to organizing and disseminating information from sources in one's own written products, including documenting sources. These subgoals may be pursued in any order or configuration and are not confined to a strictly linear sequence of actions; while inquiry often starts with a question and proceeds to location, evaluation, and synthesis of sources, new questions or conceptualizations of the subject matter may emerge over time as learners accumulate additional evidence, views, or interpretations, thereby expanding their knowledge base. Within each phase, we define a set of hypothesized learning progressions for skills that support achieving that subgoal.

Learning Progressions

Based on available literature from the cognitive and learning sciences, we defined a set of nine hypothesized learning progressions for the key practice of Conducting Research and Inquiry (see Sparks & Deane, 2015). Grouped within the three phases we just defined, the learning progressions describe qualitative shifts in sophistication for the following skills: Asking Guiding Questions; Testing Hypotheses; Locating Sources; Evaluating Sources; Reconciling Perspectives; Integrating Multiple Formats; Comparing, Contrasting, and Organizing; Synthesizing Research Results; and Citing and Using Sources (see Table 4.1).

As an example, consider the skill of Evaluating Sources, within the *Analysis, Evaluation, and Synthesis* phase of this practice. Proficiency with evaluating sources involves attention to and critical consideration of information as a function of the characteristics of its source (i.e., author, creator, or publisher) as well as judgments of task relevance, reliability, and credibility. The learning progression for *Evaluating Sources* defines a set of five levels of performance from Level 1 (Preliminary) to Level 5 (Advanced), where the lowest level reflects novice proficiency and the highest level reflects college-level or even expert-level performance of the skill. A brief description

Table 4.1 Learning Progressions and Phases for Key Practice: Research and Inquiry.

Phase	Learning Progressions
Inquiry and Information Gathering	Asking Guiding Questions
	Testing Hypotheses
	Locating Sources
Analysis, Evaluation, and Synthesis	Evaluating Sources
	Reconciling Perspectives
	Integrating Multiple Formats
	Comparing, Contrasting, and Organizing
Communication and Presentation of Results	Synthesizing Research Results
	Citing and Using Sources

Paul Deane and Jesse R. Sparks

Table 4.2 High-Level Description of Learning Progression for Evaluating Sources

Level	High-Level Description
1	Can evaluate sources based on simple evaluations of their information content, including judgments of informational quantity (i.e., how much information does the source provide) and judgments of accuracy (i.e., obvious violations of prior knowledge or lived experiences).
2	Can evaluate sources based on their relevance to a specific topic or focus (i.e., whether the source is "about" a particular subject) and based on whether they provide additional, "new" information relative to prior knowledge or other given sources. At this level, students also begin to make comparative evaluations between pairs of sources, making judgments of relative (versus absolute) accuracy or identifying consistencies and discrepancies in the information between two sources.
3	Can evaluate sources based on judgments of reliability and credibility (including author expertise, possible biases, and the timeliness of information) and can apply ranking strategies to evaluate a set of multiple sources with regard to content relevance and factors bearing on reliability.
4	Can use instrumental goals as a primary criterion for evaluating sources in order to evaluate the applicability of sources to support their own specific purposes (including considerations of relevance and reliability).
5	Includes disciplinary considerations as a part of the evaluative criteria learners are expected to apply to multiple sources; these considerations include disciplinary standards of evidence, centrality of the document to the theoretical or empirical roots of the field, or other relevant aspects as a function of the domain-specific lens through which sources should be considered before their contents are used to support one's own efforts to build and share new research-based knowledge and insights about subjects of interest.

of the hypothesized progression for source evaluation skills appears in Table 4.2 (see Sparks & Deane, 2015 for more detail).

The learning progressions for Evaluating Sources and other skills provide specific targets for assessment and instruction that are linked both to empirical cognitive research and to educational standards which reflect high-level curricular goals. Thus, the learning progressions provide a detailed roadmap for how students can develop (and teachers can deepen) proficiency with the critical aspects of conducting research from multiple sources, in order to better achieve the high-level intended outcome of becoming critical consumers of research who can conduct and disseminate the results of their own research projects.

To date, we have taken two approaches to the development of assessment tasks based on the learning progressions for *Conducting Research and Inquiry*. This development includes an extended, scenario-based task set designed to engage students in a simulated version of a research project that spans the entire scope of the key practice from question generation to composition of an extended research-based report; as well as a battery of independent tasks aligned to specific learn-ing progressions (for diagnostic assessment or for targeted practice of specific skills at particular learning progression [LP] levels). We briefly describe examples of these two approaches and articulate how the approaches fit within our vision of domain-specific formative assessment to support ELA instruction.

Scenario-Based Task Model (Roman Meal)

We developed *A Meal in Ancient Rome* (*Roman Meal*) with the aim of creating an SBT that would engage students in all phases of the *Conducting Research and Inquiry* key practice and would be suitable for implementation within the classroom context for use as a tool to support formative assessment while developing students' research skills. Designed for use with students in fifth through eighth grades, the task set is delivered online via interactive computer-based activities; a back-end database records all student responses for review and evaluation by the teacher.

In the scenario-based *Roman Meal* task set, students participate in a historical research project in the context of an upcoming (fictional) presentation at a school event called "Living History Day," in which students work to recreate a day in the life of the Ancient Romans (see Figure 4.1). Students are assigned the topic of Ancient Roman food and are asked to investigate two driving questions: *What was a meal in ancient Rome really like? How do we know?* Within the scenario introduction, it is noted that students are expected to share the results of their research with peers and with social studies teachers, who will be evaluating the historical accuracy and completeness of the research. This fictional scenario is intended to provide an overarching purpose for reading the texts and engaging in the assessment tasks. Avatars represent a simulated teacher and peer group within the activities (see Figure 4.2); these avatars provide necessary instruction and guidance to students, in addition to creating a simulated social context and structure for participation in the research-related activities within the task set. Teachers and students can also create their own Living History Day events in conjunction with or subsequent to using the *Roman Meal* task set in the classroom, giving students a real opportunity to share the results of their research with fellow students, teachers, or parents.

The *Roman Meal* scenario is organized into three main sections (see Figure 4.2):

- Ask good questions and search for useful sources of information
- Evaluate, organize, and compare different sources of information
- Use what you've learned to answer your research questions

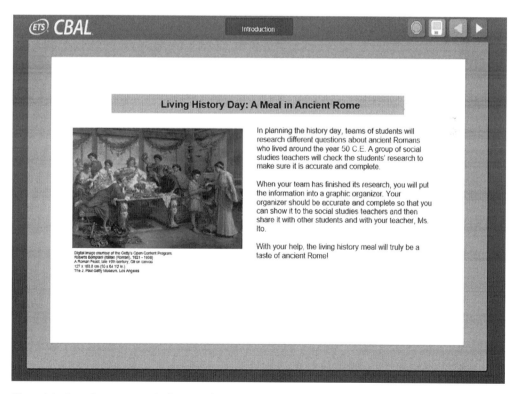

Figure 4.1 Introductory scenario for *A Meal in Ancient Rome*.

Copyright © 2017 by Educational Testing Service.

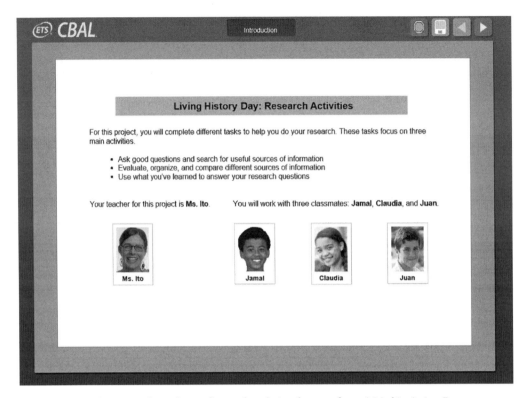

Figure 4.2 Introduction to three phases of research and virtual avatars from *A Meal in Ancient Rome*.
Copyright © 2017 by Educational Testing Service. "Ms. Ito" © sjharmon / iStockPhoto #20736164; "Jamal" © Educational Testing Service; "Claudia" © Steve Debenport / iStockPhoto #28338978; "Juan" / "Marco" © Juanmonino / iStockPhoto #35514700.

These sections correspond to the three phases of the Research and Inquiry key practice. Across these three phases, the activities in *Roman Meal* are divided into a series of nine tasks (see Table 4.3), with each task aligned to one or more of the Research and Inquiry learning progressions (see Table 4.1 for the learning progressions organized by the three phrases in the key practice). The tasks mainly target Level 2 performance, which is appropriate for the upper elementary/early middle-school level toward which the task is targeted, but include items measuring the Interpretive, Expressive, and Deliberative cognitive processes (i.e., reading, writing, and critical thinking skills) spanning from Levels 1 to 3 across the set of activities. Each task presents between 4 and 20 items; the items include a combination of traditional multiple-choice, short constructed-response, extended constructed-response, and technology-enhanced item types (i.e., click-and-click, matching, inline choice, timeline). We next briefly describe the design of each task.

The first activity, Task 1, involves planning one's inquiry and building necessary background knowledge about the broader subject of ancient Rome (i.e., When did the Roman Empire exist? Where was it located on a map? What are some basic facts about the people and culture of ancient Rome?). In Task 2, students delve into identifying more detailed research questions (e.g., Who was at the meal and what were their customs? What foods were available?), classifying background sources according to their relevance to those research questions, and creating a graphic organizer to provide an overarching structure for the research project. Task 2 focuses specifically on the learning progression for *Asking Guiding Questions*. In Task 3, students engage in *Hypothesis Testing* by making predictions about what an Ancient Roman meal might have been like and generating

Scenario-Based Formative Assessment

Table 4.3 Task Descriptions for "A Meal in Ancient Rome" Assessment

Phase	Task	Task Name	Learning Progression: Level	#of Items
Inquiry and Information Gathering	1	Setting the Scene and Clarifying Goals	*Asking Guiding Questions*: 1E, 1D	4
	2	Asking Good Questions	*Asking Guiding Questions*: 1E, 1I, 2I, 2E, 2D Compare, Contrast, Organize: 1D	14
	3	Making and Checking Predictions	*Testing Hypotheses*: 2E, 2D Asking Guiding Questions: 1E	6
	4	Locating Useful Sources	*Locating Sources*: 2D, 3I Asking Guiding Questions: 1E	5
Analysis, Evaluation, and Synthesis	5	Evaluating Different Sources of Information	*Evaluating Sources*: 2I, 2E, 2D, 3I Asking Guiding Questions: 2I, 3E Compare, Contrast, Organize: 1D	8
	6	Comparing and Contrasting Sources	*Reconciling Perspectives*: 1I, 2I, 2E, 2D Asking Guiding Questions: 1E, 1D, 2I Compare, Contrast, Organize: 1D, 2E	20
	7	Combining Different Kinds of Sources	*Integrating Multiple Formats*: 1D, 2I, 2E, 2D Asking Guiding Questions: 1E, 2I Compare, Contrast, Organize: 1D	16
Communication and Presentation of Results	8	Making Sure our Research is Complete	*Synthesizing Research Results*: 1E *Citing and Using Sources*: 1E, 1D Asking Guiding Questions: 1E, 2I Locating Sources: 1I, 2D Compare, Contrast, Organize: 1D	8
	9	Presenting our Research Results	*Synthesizing Research Results*: 2E, 3E, 3D *Citing and Using Sources*: 1E, 2E, 3E, 1D Asking Guiding Questions: 2E, 3E	6

Note. Learning progressions in italics in Learning Progression Level column represent the primary focus of the task. I=Interpretive (Reading), E=Expressive (Writing), D=Deliberative (Critical Thinking).

ideas for how to test whether those predictions are correct (i.e., locate a source describing what foods were commonly eaten, use a timeline to determine whether an ingredient or cooking method would have been available to Ancient Romans at the time). Task 4 engages students in locating sources that might yield useful information, including selecting useful search terms, and choosing relevant sources within simulated digital (i.e., web search results) and print (i.e., table of contents) contexts. Task 5 engages students in evaluating sources, including judgments of topical relevance, novelty of information, and considerations of sources' expertise and reliability (including comparative evaluation of two sources discussing the same subject). Task 6 engages students more deeply in multiple-source comparisons, including an analysis of primary and secondary sources, identification of authors' perspectives and motivations for writing, and analysis and explanation of agreements and disagreements (and similarities and differences) among sets of sources. This task also provides students with an initial opportunity to address the research questions in their graphic organizer using the sources they have accumulated in the previous task sections (i.e., "what we already know"), and/or to identify areas of research where further investigation is needed (i.e., "need to know more"). Task 7 engages students in considering the added value of illustrations, photographs, and diagrams in multimodal texts for enriching their understanding of Ancient Roman dining customs and settings. Task 8 asks students to consider and to identify sources that help to address any remaining research questions and evaluate the accuracy of their initial predictions generated during Task 3 using available historical evidence.

Finally, Task 9 presents a culminating activity in which students first work to develop brief answers to all the research questions in their graphic organizer, using available sources to support their answers, and ultimately, to compose a multi-paragraph essay addressing the two driving questions regarding what an Ancient Roman meal would have been like and how we know (i.e., what historical evidence supports the conclusions). Thus, the culminating activity presents a scaffolded approach to measuring research-based writing in that students are first asked to work through answering the individual research questions in their graphic organizer one-by-one, identifying the source material that supports each response, prior to tackling the integrated performance expected in the final essay. Indeed, given that the scenario-based context is informed by the key practice model, items included in Tasks 1 through 8 are intended to provide teachers and students with useful information about the potential strengths and weaknesses in students' research and inquiry skills in order to prepare them for completing the final essay or to further elucidate the locus of specific challenges students may experience in producing that essay. The aim of the *Roman Meal* task set is to provide a comprehensive picture of how students are progressing in each of the nine key proficiencies that are required for successful inquiry.

We have also developed a teacher handbook to accompany the *Roman Meal* tasks; in addition to providing answer keys, essay scoring rubrics, and sample responses for short constructed-response items, this handbook aims to provide teachers with strategic support for integrating the assessment tasks into the classroom within a unit on research skills, ancient civilizations, or some combination of these two subjects. In particular, learning targets, learning intentions, success criteria, and alignment to Common Core State Standards for ELA are provided for each task, along with mappings to the relevant learning progressions (as shown in Table 4.1). This introductory material is intended to make the learning goals and alignment to curricular standards of the task set and its constituent activities explicit to both teachers and students in order to facilitate the integration of the tasks into existing curriculum, to illustrate how a teacher might use particular tasks within the set in conjunction with ongoing instruction over a period of time, and to illustrate how the individual tasks work together to support the high-level goal of training students to thoughtfully consume and produce research. Thus, learning targets and success criteria can be shared directly with students in order to support them in understanding the research process, and understanding how specific steps contribute to the outcomes of an overall research project. Threaded throughout the task descriptions, we also provide suggestions for implementation (i.e., in terms of individual, small-group, or whole-class activities). For example, teachers might introduce some activities as small-group work, then project the screens to the whole class in order to facilitate the sharing of ideas and encouraging class discussion. In particular, the implementation suggestions include ideas for using a variety of formative assessment techniques (e.g., Think-Pair-Share, Exit Ticket; cf. Lyon, Mavronikolas, and Wylie, 2011; Wiliam and Thompson, 2007) to elicit additional information about students' progress toward the learning targets. An appendix provides teachers with a glossary describing a number of such techniques, which can be used flexibly as specific instructional needs require. While these techniques are described as domain general (consistent with our previous discussion), specific suggestions within the assessment activities support teachers in connecting these techniques to ELA-specific learning targets. Taken together, the key features of the *Roman Meal* task set and companion handbook are designed to make the key practice of research and inquiry explicit to teachers and students, to illustrate how the component skills work together to support integrated performances and provide specific guidance for integrating the tasks as part of formative assessment in ELA.

Independent Learning Progression Tasks

In contrast to extended, scenario-based task sets, we have also developed a number of standalone, independent tasks aligned to specific levels of the ELA learning progressions. These LP-based tasks are intended for just-in-time use by teachers who are interested in eliciting additional information about students' understanding and/or strengths and weaknesses with respect to a particular aspect of the research process. These tasks can also provide students with targeted practice with specific skills at appropriate levels of difficulty, given their current skill development.

As an example, for the practice of *Conducting Research and Inquiry*, we have developed a set of 25 brief tasks aligned to different levels of the learning progression for Evaluating Sources, as described above. Specifically, we developed six or seven tasks at each learning progression level (from Levels 1 to 4), covering all three cognitive processing modes of reading/interpretive, writing/expressive, and critical thinking/deliberative (see Table 4.4 for titles and descriptions of the LP tasks). The tasks are designed to take fewer than 10 minutes to complete. Each task introduces a research topic (from the natural or social sciences) and a specific focus, and provides students with guidelines articulating the relevant criteria to be used in evaluating sources that may (or may not) provide useful and reliable information about the topic. These guidelines are specifically aligned with the primary emphasis of the target learning progression level within a given task (e.g., Level 1: simple judgments of information accuracy and quantity; Level 2: judgments of relevance, novelty, and relative accuracy; Level 3: judgments of source credibility, including expertise, bias, and currency, in addition to considerations of topical relevance; Level 4: instrumental usefulness in achieving one's specific goals). Items within each task engage students in the analysis and evaluation of source materials (i.e., text-based documents) using a combination of selected-response (including innovative item types like matching and inline choice), constructed-response, and extended constructed-response formats.

Students could be assigned any number or combination of LP tasks that teachers deem appropriate in order to yield a specific, detailed picture of their proficiency with the target skills that are required for successful performances of the overall key practice. It would be difficult to imagine a context in which a teacher would use all 25 of these tasks with a single class, so they are designed to permit flexible implementation. Results from these LP tasks are intended to give teachers and students information about the extent to which a student has mastered evaluating sources in light of specific criteria and for which criteria students may require additional practice. For example, a student or group of students may demonstrate proficiency with determining the relevance of information sources to a specific topic (i.e., whether a source is truly "about" a given topic), yet experience difficulty in evaluating evidence of sources' credibility (i.e., cues to author expertise, such as education or experience or cues to the biased presentation of information, such as presenting only one-sided information or evidence of financial conflicts, which might affect the conclusions reached). This finding would suggest that students are currently at Level 2 and that additional practice may be needed with the evaluative criteria emphasized in Level 3 tasks. In this way, results from LP tasks can inform instructional next steps, since the learning progression serves as a road map for how skills develop over time.

While the *Evaluating Sources* LP tasks described above have not yet been used in classrooms as a part of formative assessment, we conducted a pilot study with a sample of 360 middle-school students in grades 6, 7, and 8 ($n = 120$ per grade) in which students completed two of four possible online test forms, each comprised of six tasks from Table 4.4 selected to represent all four LP levels within each form (see Sparks, van Rijn, & Deane, 2018). Note that one Level 4 task (Food Allergies) was not included in the pilot study (although the parallel task about Acid Rain was included). In addition to LP task performance, we also collected measures of ELA proficiency levels, including ELA grades and state test scores. Preliminary results revealed that performance on the LP tasks was generally correlated with students' ELA proficiency levels from standardized state assessment scores (median

Paul Deane and Jesse R. Sparks

Table 4.4 Task Descriptions for Evaluating Sources Learning Progression Tasks

LP Level	Task Name	Task Type	Task Mode	Evaluation Criteria
1	Bees	SR	D	Accuracy (vs. Background Knowledge)
	Pandas	Both	D	Accuracy (vs. Background Knowledge)
	Giant Squid (A)*	Both	E	Quantity & Accuracy (vs. 2nd Source)
	Video Games*	Both	E	Quantity & Accuracy (vs. 2nd Source)
	Giant Squid (B)[x]	SR	I	Quantity & Accuracy (vs. 2nd Source), Date
	Electric Cars[x]	SR	I	Quantity & Accuracy (vs. 2nd Source), Date
2	Dogs	SR	I	Relevance
	Pet Turtles[†]	SR	D	Relevance (Topics in Print Sources)
	Cinco De Mayo[†]	SR	D	Relevance (Topics in Web site Sources)
	Georgia O'Keeffe[‡]	Both	E	Relevance & Novelty (vs. Given Topics)
	Language Immersion[‡]	Both	E	Relevance & Novelty (vs. Given Topics)
	Redwoods~	SR	I	Relevance & Novelty (vs. Given Topics)
	The Arctic~	SR	I	Relevance & Novelty (vs. Given Topics)
3	New Zealand°	Both	I	Relevance, Expertise, Bias, Date
	Clouds°	Both	I	Relevance, Expertise, Bias, Date
	Coral Reefs	Both	D	Usefulness, Relevance, Expertise, Bias, Date
	Greenhouse Effect	Both	D	Relevance, Expertise, Bias, Date
	Invite an Expert	CR	E	Expertise and Bias
	Ancient Greece	Both	E	Expertise and Bias
4	Composting[¶]	Both	D	Usefulness (vs. Specific Goal)
	Helping Honeybees[¶]	Both	D	Usefulness (vs. Specific Goal)
	P.T. Barnum	SR	I	Usefulness, Relevance (vs. Specific Topics)
	Title IX	Both	I	Usefulness (vs. Specific Goal), Relevance (vs. Specific Topics)
	Acid Rain+	CR	E	Usefulness, Relevance, Expertise, Bias, Date
	Food Allergies+	CR	E	Usefulness, Relevance, Expertise, Bias, Date

Note. Tasks with matching symbols following their names have parallel or similar designs.
I=Interpretive (Reading), E=Expressive (Writing), D=Deliberative (Critical Thinking).

form-level $r = 0.59$; range: 0.32 to 0.69 across forms and grade levels) and ELA grades (median form-level $r = 0.52$; range: 0.25 to 0.63 across forms and grade levels). At the level of individual tasks, correlations with the ELA state test proficiency levels ranged from $r = 0.06$ to 0.72 across tasks; all but three tasks had correlations above 0.25 with this proficiency level, suggesting that the majority of LP tasks for Evaluating Sources were meaningfully associated with an estimate of students' literacy skills derived from a summative assessment aligned to state-level standards. Further, results of an IRT-based model used to assign tasks to LP levels based on the pilot data revealed that several items which combined selected-response and constructed-response formats were unexpectedly challenging relative to their hypothesized LP level. This finding is in part likely due to the tasks' design (e.g., insufficient scaffolding) and in part due to the use of rather stringent scoring criteria (e.g., students were required to make a correct judgment in the selected-response item to earn credit for the associated constructed-response item that explained the student's judgment). These issues have been addressed in subsequent revisions to the items and tasks; the effects of these revisions on student performance remain to be examined in future research with larger student samples.

Ultimately, statistical modeling approaches can be used to assign students to LP levels based on their performance on LP tasks (see van Rijn et al., 2014), so that an estimate of a student's current level could be reported as an indicator of what they can and cannot do. Knowledge of a student's

Scenario-Based Formative Assessment

current standing on a given learning progression (based on which tasks the student can and cannot successfully complete) can aid teachers in choosing relevant assessments and instructional activities that are tailored to the developmental needs of their students, in order to individualize instruction and help students further develop their skills.

Integrating Model Tasks into the Formative Assessment Cycle

To illustrate how we envision our tasks supporting formative assessment (and teacher professional development), we will provide a sketch using a single CBAL *Evaluating Sources* LP task called *Clouds* (see Table 4.3), which focuses on one part of the research process: the process of evaluating search results and selecting appropriate sources from the phase *Analysis, Evaluation, and Synthesis*. The task we present focuses on a specific research topic (the nature of clouds) and on a small pool of pre-selected sources. This task is designed to measure Level 3 of the Evaluating Sources LP and emphasizes evaluating sources with respect to the criteria of relevance, expertise, bias, and currency. The activity is designed so that it could be completed individually, in which case it would function as a mini-tutorial, as a review of key ideas, or else used as the basis for classroom formative assessment activities. In this section, we will explore how a resource like the *Clouds* task could be used to support formative assessment and to deepen teachers' pedagogical content knowledge.

In a typical cycle of informal, classroom formative assessment, the classroom may move through several activities during a single lesson. Formative assessment techniques can be applied throughout this cycle, helping the teacher evaluate how well the students are doing, while also helping students understand and communicate their learning needs to the teacher.

Consider, for example, the screen shown in Figure 4.3. In the online version of this activity, this screen functions to introduce the task and provide necessary context for evaluating sources. But the information it provides is also a natural launching point for a lesson. If a teacher was to display this screen to the class and pose the question, "How will I know which sources I should use in this research project?" it could serve as the basis for self-reflection (helping students to make their current research practices explicit) or as the stimulus for group or whole-class discussion focused on eliciting various standards to use in evaluating sources. If the teacher is alert to what students say during discussion or express as a result of self-reflection, the teacher may be able to identify gaps in students' conceptual understanding and/or their misconceptions about research (based on how student responses do or do not align to the expectations based on the relevant learning progression descriptors; see Table 4.2). This analysis can help the teacher determine which parts of the lesson, at its outset, might be most important for this particular group of students.

Figure 4.4 shows the next screen from the *Clouds* task, which is intended to identify the key criteria that students must learn to address during source evaluation based on our domain analysis (Sparks & Deane, 2015). These criteria are used to judge *relevance* (whether the information helps address the informational needs defined by the research project), *expertise* (whether the person providing the information is a credible authority on the topic being researched), *bias* (whether the person providing the information has any motivation to favor one side or the other), and *currency* (whether the information is recent enough to reflect current knowledge of the topic). The ability to make accurate judgments of relevance comes earlier in our learning progression (Level 2) than the ability to evaluate source credibility by examining expertise, lack of bias, and currency (Level 3). This ordering is consistent with prior research showing that students who are more proficient in source evaluation consider topical relevance prior to making judgments based on factors affecting credibility (Braasch et al., 2009). Making the learning progression explicit to teachers can support more attuned listening and attention to the nuances in student responses on the part of the teacher, thus resulting in more finely honed questions to probe students' thinking on this issue in light of the major developmental milestones embodied by the learning progression.

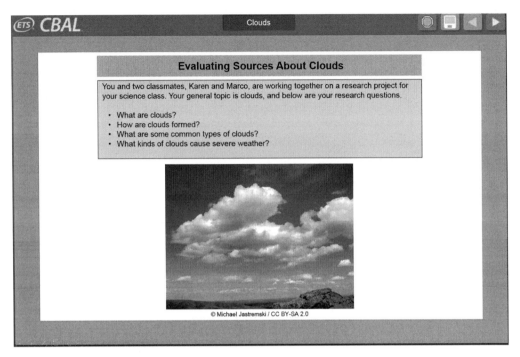

Figure 4.3 Opening screen from the task, "Evaluating Sources about Clouds."
Copyright © 2017 by Educational Testing Service.

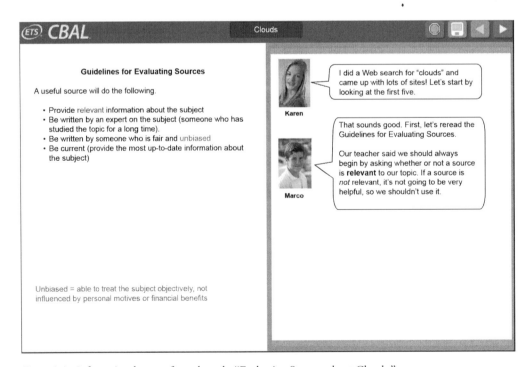

Figure 4.4 Informational screen from the task, "Evaluating Sources about Clouds."
Copyright © 2017 by Educational Testing Service. "Karen" © Pamela Moore/ iStock #42528538.

Scenario-Based Formative Assessment

The right side of the screen in Figure 4.4 models some of the guidance we would like teachers to give to students about the context in which source evaluation is practiced. Evaluating sources evaluation is part of a regular practice of critical evaluation that students need to internalize, in which researchers habitually evaluate the sources they consider against various criteria that indicate the likely quality of the information provided by the source. Therefore, these guidelines recur across related tasks and teachers are encouraged to make use of them outside of the tasks themselves in order to support students in monitoring and regulating their own learning. The practice of conducting research includes other skills, such as how to make predictions about the possible contents of a source and the ability to extract the most useful information for one's task, which would be addressed in other model tasks aligned to other learning progressions (with their own corresponding sets of guidelines or evaluative criteria).

The left side of the screen in Figure 4.4 is intended as a simplified presentation that describes the criteria in a form that could be posted in a classroom as a poster or provided as a rubric for students to use during source evaluation tasks. To make this kind of task fully support formative assessment, we have developed handbook materials for other task sets that define the learning intentions and success criteria teachers should use when introducing domain concepts to students. These materials contain notes that identify characteristic patterns of behavior that may be observed when students have not yet mastered one of the targeted source evaluation skills. As noted earlier, we have already developed this kind of handbook for the Roman Meal scenario task set and intend to develop a similar set of supporting materials for the other learning progression tasks we describe in this paper, including *Clouds*.

As an example of the kind of support we can give students, we know from the literature that students who have not yet reached LP Level 1 on Evaluating Sources may understand relevance in very shallow ways (such as the presence of explicit keyword matches in the source; Rouet et al., 2011), rather than evaluating the text in terms of its utility for answering pertinent research questions. We have not yet developed lesson plan outlines that would help teachers conceptualize how these concepts might be effectively communicated during the early stages of a lesson. Such a lesson plan would explicitly define learning intentions for the teacher to articulate in this introductory part of the task.

The success criteria for this task emphasize the accuracy with which students can make judgments of relevance, expertise, lack of bias, and currency. To enable teacher formative assessment of student performance on these skills, we provide screens like that shown in Figure 4.5, where students are prompted (in this case) to make an initial classification of several sources as likely to be relevant (or irrelevant) given the research questions that have been posed.

Note that the left side of the screen repeats the research questions we gave in the opening screen of the task to help students keep their research goals in mind. Implicit in the screen, but explicit in the teacher support that we are developing, is the idea that *relevance is relative to purpose*. In the case of a research project, source evaluation requires judgments of how useful sources are for the purpose of answering research questions that have already been defined before students begin narrowing their lists of sources.

The items on the right side of the screen (Figure 4.5) capture only the students' final judgments – to accept a source as relevant or to reject it as irrelevant. In this case, given the relatively small number of sources students are asked to classify, the screen is likely to be much more useful to teachers as the jumping-off point for formative assessment than administered to students individually. Teachers need to understand the reasoning students are applying in making their judgments in order to gauge how much further instruction and practice they need to provide before students are able to satisfy the success criteria (which in this case, would mean that they recognize that *Clouds for Kids, Wild Weather Facts,* and *Beginners' Cloud Guide* are probably relevant, while *Clouds* and *Cloudy or Clear* are not).

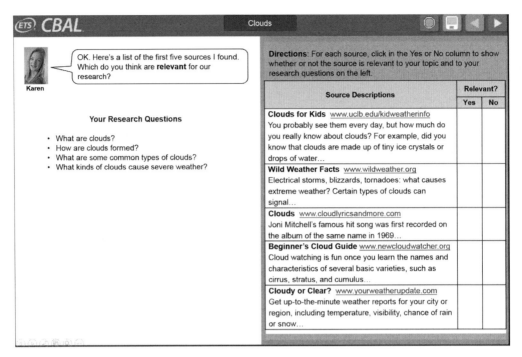

Figure 4.5 Relevance item screen from the task, "Evaluating Sources about Clouds."

Copyright © 2017 by Educational Testing Service.

Thus, our recommendation for teachers to make formative use of tasks like this screen from *Clouds* might include a whole-class discussion with polling (where the teacher asks for a show of hands to find out which students think a particular source is relevant, followed by teacher questioning to ask students to articulate how they reached their conclusions), or small-group discussions where each group records their decisions about individual sources and their reasons for the choice, and then reports back to the whole class.

This kind of formative assessment practice presupposes that teachers understand in depth why each source is (or is not) relevant and know when to release students to work independently. There are obvious pitfalls in teaching students more advanced skills (such as evaluating the credibility of a source) if more fundamental skills, such as their relevance judgments, are not yet accurate (cf. Braasch et al., 2009). And yet it is often necessary to proceed to address more advanced aspects of a skill, even if some students may not have fully mastered some of the prerequisite skills. We can address these kinds of issues in two ways. First, it may be useful to provide detailed notes for teachers about the justification for each choice in Figure 4.5. Second, we can build scaffolding into the scenario sequence. For instance, we can move to the screen shown in Figure 4.6, which reveals which items are relevant and refocuses students' attention on the credibility of the three relevant sources. The task, therefore, models several aspects of a recommended teaching process: (a) teaching relevance before credibility; (b) scaffolding students through credibility judgments by providing them with examples of relevant texts that may not be credible; and (c) modeling a research strategy that starts with a search for sources but narrows down the results of that search by adding successive filters, first for relevance and second for credibility (i.e., expertise, lack of bias, and currency).

Once again, the scaffolded sequence of screens is designed for use in a formative assessment context (though it could also be used to gather information about individuals in an interim or

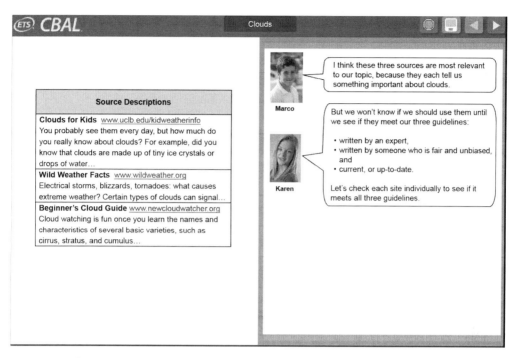

Figure 4.6 Informational screen from the task, "Evaluating Sources about Clouds."

Copyright © 2017 by Educational Testing Service.

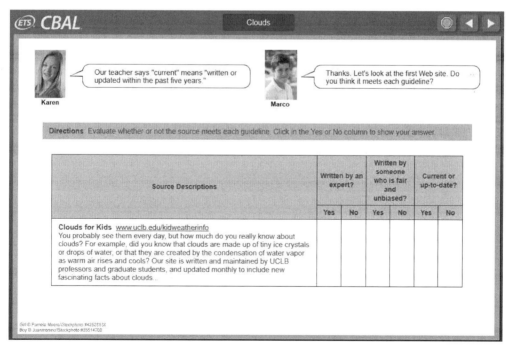

Figure 4.7 Credibility item screen from the task, "Evaluating Sources about Clouds."

Copyright © 2017 by Educational Testing Service.

summative context). A screen like that shown in Figure 4.6 could be used as the launching point for class or group discussion, eliciting from students what they would look for if they examined each source more closely to judge its credibility (e.g., what are some ways we can tell that a source's author is an expert in a subject?). Various other kinds of scaffolded follow-ups are possible. For instance, Figure 4.7 gives the information a student might find if they took a closer look at a source that asks them to make credibility judgments on all three criteria – which is, once again, most likely to be useful to the teacher for formative assessment purposes as a launching point for teacher questioning and class discussion

Figure 4.8 and Figure 4.9 illustrate other ways source materials can be used to provide stimuli for scaffolded formative assessment. Since students may not be accurate in their credibility judgments, we adopt the scaffolding strategy of revealing what is wrong with a source (that it is biased or not written by an expert) and then asking students to judge what information in the source description supports that conclusion. Figure 4.8 provides a list of explanations in the form of a multiple-choice item which would lend itself to a questioning strategy in which students are quickly polled to see who supports each option, and then asked about their reasoning. This strategy can function as a quick check on students' understanding of the notion of bias. Figure 4.9 illustrates a more challenging item, since it requires students to generate and explicitly state their justification for the conclusion that the source is not credible.

Finally, Figure 4.10 shows the final justification for determining which of the sources are both relevant and credible, and thereby models the overall search strategy (search, filter by relevance, filter by credibility, select useful sources). The sequence of screens in the *Clouds* task thus has several benefits. First, it directly elicits evidence of whether students can satisfy the success criteria. Second, it provides opportunities for formative assessment that would give the teacher rich information about how students are currently approaching the problem of judging the value of sources for their research.

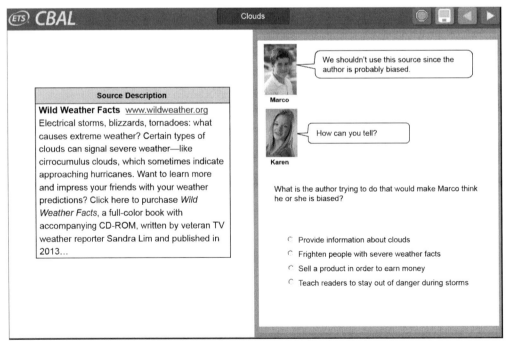

Figure 4.8 Bias item screen from the task, "Evaluating Sources about Clouds."

Copyright © 2017 by Educational Testing Service.

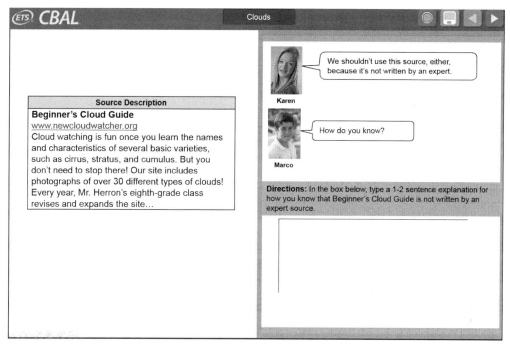

Figure 4.9 Expertise item screen from the task, "Evaluating Sources about Clouds."
Copyright © 2017 by Educational Testing Service.

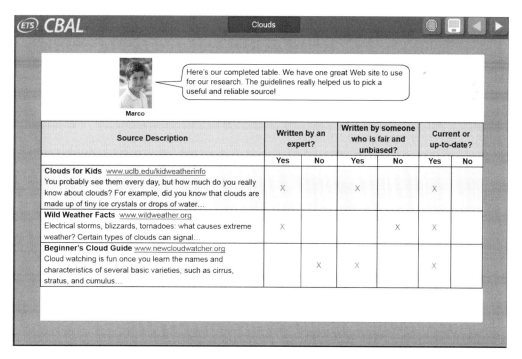

Figure 4.10 Screen showing final classification of relevant sources from the task, "Evaluating Sources about Clouds."
Copyright © 2017 by Educational Testing Service.

Third, it models for students and teachers a strategy commonly used by experts, in which a broad initial search is used to collect a list of possible sources that are then examined in greater depth and filtered to eliminate irrelevant or unreliable sources, given one's specific research questions. Fourth, it models for teachers the way in which a task can illuminate an aspect of student understanding represented in the learning progression, and (with explicit supporting materials) can aid teachers in deepening their knowledge of how student understanding develops in this domain.

Note that the value of this screen, and of the entire task, lies in the potential for using it as a model from which to generalize. Embedded in a series of lessons with rich formative assessment opportunities, the task could be used to support teaching and learning directly. But embedded in a teacher professional development course or supported by a school-based teacher learning community, this task, together with the concepts of learning progressions and key practices, could be used to enrich teachers' pedagogical content knowledge about research skills. One of the primary issues for teacher professional development, especially for preservice and early-career professionals, is creating an awareness of the kinds of tasks that will give evidence about student learning for specific learning targets, the kinds of follow-up questions and probes that will help identify student weaknesses and misconceptions, and the kinds of instructional interventions that will help get students to the next level of development. The materials we have created illustrate a strategy for addressing this need. Such materials can also help teachers plan how to incorporate the same kinds of scaffolding and formative assessment into other tasks and topics they may be using to instruct students on this particular skill of source evaluation or on the broader subject of conducting research and inquiry from multiple sources.

Conclusion

The project we have described illustrates a domain analysis and task development effort that closely integrates pedagogical content knowledge with concrete models for formative assessment from a disciplinary perspective. The assessment tasks provide students with an explicit model of the research and inquiry process, helping them to internalize relevant skills and evaluative criteria to apply in self- or peer-evaluation (i.e., supporting metacognition and self-regulation). As such, this work provides a useful example of an Evidence-Centered Design approach to formative assessment in an ELA content domain, which could potentially be extended to other content domains or disciplinary-based approaches to assessment development.

This work is necessarily preliminary. It reflects a transition between an initial stage in which we have focused on developing a collection of tasks that could effectively support formative assessment of research and inquiry skills. In future work, we will focus on improving teachers' pedagogical content knowledge via explicit cognitive models and teacher support materials. These models and materials will be intended to help teachers interpret the standards in light of the key literacy practices that those standards privilege. Future work will also investigate models for building effective teacher learning opportunities that help educators integrate formative assessment with specific domain content.

The approach described in this paper is intended to be an example of a generally applicable strategy; we are in fact working to develop similar models in a number of related domains. The approach illustrates principles that we believe are central to formative assessment in the disciplines. In particular, we believe that formative assessment will be most effective when it:

- is closely coordinated with curricular design and teacher professional development,
- builds upon a detailed domain analysis that identifies not only the targets for learning, but also learning progressions that can be used to chart student progress on the skills that support a specific literacy practice, and
- provides exemplary tasks that can be used to place students at specific levels on each learning progression.

References

Alonzo, A. C. & Gotwals, A. W. (Eds.). (2012). *Learning Progressions in Science*. Rotterdam: SensePublishers.

Andrade, H. L. & Heritage, M. (2017). *Using Formative Assessment to Enhance Learning, Achievement, and Academic Self-Regulation*. New York, NY: Routledge.

Applebee, A. N. & Langer, J. A. (1983). Instructional Scaffolding: Reading and Writing as Natural Language Activities. *Language Arts, 60*(2), 168–175. Retrieved from https://www.jstor.org/stable/41961447.

Bauer, M., Wylie, C., Jackson, T., Mislevy, B., Hoffman-John, E., John, M., & Corrigan, S. (2017). Why video games can be a good fit for formative assessment. *Journal of Applied Testing Technology, 18*(S1), 19–31.

Bennett, R. E. (2010). Cognitively based assessment of, for, and as learning (CBAL): A preliminary theory of action for summative and formative assessment. *Measurement, 8*(2–3), 70–91. DOI: 10.1080/15366367.2010.508686.

Bennett, R. E. (2011). Formative assessment: a critical review. *Assessment in Education: Principles, Policy & Practice, 18*(1), 5–25. DOI: 10.1080/0969594X.2010.513678.

Bennett, R. E., Deane, P., & van Rijn, P. W. (2016). From cognitive-domain theory to assessment practice. *Educational Psychologist, 51*(1), 82–107. DOI: 10.1080/00461520.2016.1141683.

Bennett, R. E. & Gitomer, D. H. (2009). Transforming K-12 assessment: Integrating accountability testing, formative assessment and professional support. In C. Wyatt-Smith & J. Cumming (Eds.), *Educational assessment in the 21st century* (pp. 43–61). New York, NY: Springer.

Bertling, M., Jackson, G. T., Oranje, A., & Owen, V. E. (2015). *Measuring argumentation skills with game-based assessments: Evidence for incremental validity and learning*. Paper presented at the International Conference on Artificial Intelligence in Education.

Black, P. (2015). Formative assessment – an optimistic but incomplete vision. *Assessment in Education: Principles, Policy & Practice, 22*(1), 161–177. DOI: 10.1080/0969594X.2014.999643.

Black, P. & Wiliam, D. (1998). Assessment and Classroom Learning. *Assessment in Education: Principles, Policy & Practice, 5*(1), 7–74. DOI: 10.1080/0969595980050102.

Black, P. & Wiliam, D. (2009). Developing the theory of formative assessment. *Educational Assessment, Evaluation and Accountability(formerly: Journal of Personnel Evaluation in Education), 21*(1). DOI: 10.1007/s11092-008-9068-5.

Black, P. & Wiliam, D. (2010). Inside the Black Box: Raising Standards through Classroom Assessment. *Phi Delta Kappan, 92*(1), 81–90. DOI: 10.1177/003172171009200119.

Black, P., Wilson, M., & Yao, S.Y. (2011). Road Maps for Learning: A Guide to the Navigation of Learning Progressions. *Measurement: Interdisciplinary Research and Perspectives, 9*(2–3), 71–123. DOI: 10.1080/15366367.2011.591654.

Braasch, J. L., Lawless, K. A., Goldman, S. R., Manning, F. H., Gomez, K. W., & Macleod, S. M. (2009). Evaluating search results: An empirical analysis of middle school students' use of source attributes to select useful sources. *Journal of Educational Computing Research, 41*(1), 63–82.

Briggs, D. C., Ruiz-Primo, M. A., Furtak, E., Shepard, L., & Yin, Y. (2012). Meta-Analytic Methodology and Inferences About the Efficacy of Formative Assessment. *Educational Measurement: Issues and Practice, 31*(4), 13–17. DOI: 10.1111/j.1745-3992.2012.00251.x.

Britt, M. A., Rouet, J.F., & Durik, A. M. (2017). *Literacy beyond text comprehension: A theory of purposeful reading*. New York: Routledge.

Brown, J. S., Collins, A., & Duguid, P. (1989). Situated cognition and the culture of learning. *Educational Researcher, 18*(1), 32–42. DOI: 10.3102/0013189X018001032.

Council for Aid to Education (2016). *CWRA+ National Results, 2015–16*. Retrieved from New York: Council for Aid to Education. Retrieved from http://cae.org/images/uploads/pdf/CWRA_National_Results_2015-16.pdf.

Calkins, L. (2015). *Reading Pathways, performance assessments and learning progressions: Grades 3–5*. Portsmouth, NH: Heinemann.

Calkins, L., Hohne, K. B., & Robb, A. K. (2015). *Writing pathways: Performance assessments and learning progressions, grades K-8*. Portsmouth, NH: Heinemann.

Chall, J. S. (1983). *Learning to read: The great debate*. New York, NY: McGraw-Hill.

Clark, I. (2012). Formative Assessment: Assessment Is for Self-regulated Learning. *Educational Psychology Review, 24*, 205–249. DOI: 10.1007/s10648-011-9191-6

Coffey, J. E., Hammer, D., Levin, D. M., & Grant, T. (2011). The missing disciplinary substance of formative assessment. *Journal of Research in Science Teaching, 48*(10), 1109–1136. DOI: 10.1002/tea.20440.

Collins, A., Brown, J. S., & Newman, S. E. (1988). Cognitive apprenticeship: Teaching the craft of reading, writing and mathematics. *Thinking: The Journal of Philosophy for Children, 8*(1), 2–10. DOI: 10.5840/thinking19888129.

Corcoran, T., Mosher, F. A., & Rogat, A. (2009). *Learning progressions in science: An evidence-based approach to reform*. Philadelphia, PA: Consortium for Policy Research and Education. DOI: 10.12698/cpre.2009.rr63.

Cowie, B. & Moreland, J. (2015). Leveraging disciplinary practices to support students' active participation in formative assessment. *Assessment in Education: Principles, Policy & Practice, 22*(2), 247–264. DOI: 10.1080/0969594X.2015.1015960.

Daro, P., Mosher, F. A., & Corcoran, T. B. (2011). *Learning Trajectories in Mathematics: A Foundation for Standards, Curriculum, Assessment, and Instruction*. Philadelphia, PA: Consortium for Policy Research in Education. DOI: 10.12698/cpre.2011.rr68.

Deane, P., Sabatini, J., Feng, G., Sparks, J. R., Song, Y., Fowles, M.,O'Reilly, T., Jueds, K., Krovetz, R., & Foley, C. (2015). Key practices in the English Language Arts (ELA): Linking learning theory, assessment, and instruction. *ETS Research Report Series, 2015*(2), 1–29. Princeton, NJ: Educational Testing Service.

Deane, P. & Song, Y. (2014). A Case Study in Principled Assessment Design: Designing Assessments to Measure and Support the Development of Argumentative Reading and Writing Skills. *Educativa Psicologia, 20*(2), 99–108. DOI: 10.1016/j.pse.2014.05.006.

Duncan, R. G. & Hmelo-Silver, C. E. (2009). Learning progressions: Aligning curriculum, instruction, and assessment. *Journal of Research in Science Teaching, 46*(6), 606–609. DOI: 10.1002/tea.20316.

Furtak, E. M., Morrison, D. E. B., & Kroog, H. (2014). Investigating the Link Between Learning Progressions and Classroom Assessment. *Science Education, 98*(4), 640–673. DOI: 10.1002/sce.21122.

Goldman, S. R., Braasch, J. L. G., Wiley, J., Graesser, A. C., & Brodowinska, K. M. (2012). Comprehending and learning from Internet sources: Processing patterns of better and poorer learners. *Reading Research Quarterly, 47*(4), 356–381. DOI: 10.1002/RRQ.027.

Goldman, S. R., Britt, M. A., Brown, W., Cribb, G., George, M. A., Greenleaf, C., Lee, C. D., Shanahan, C., & Project READI. (2016). Disciplinary literacies and learning to read for understanding: A conceptual framework for disciplinary literacy. *Educational Psychologist, 51*(2), 219–246. DOI 10.1080/00461520.2016.1168741.

Goldman, S. R., Lawless, K., & Manning, F. (2013). Research and development of multiple source comprehension assessment. In M. A. Britt, S. Goldman, & J. F. Rouet (Eds.), *Reading from words to multiple texts*. New York: Routledge.

Graf, E. A. & Arieli-Attali, M. (2015). Designing and developing assessments of complex thinking in mathematics for the middle grades. *Theory Into Practice, 54*(3), 195–202. DOI: 10.1080/00405841.2015.1044365.

Heritage, M. (2007). Formative assessment: What do teachers need to know and do? *Phi Delta Kappan, 89*(2), 140–145.

Heritage, M. (2008). *Learning progressions: Supporting instruction and formative assessment*. Paper presented at the Meeting on Advancing Research on Adaptive Instruction and Formative Assessment, Philadelphia, PA.

Heritage, M., Kim, J., Vendlinski, T., & Herman, J. (2009). From Evidence to Action: A Seamless Process in Formative Assessment? *Educational Measurement: Issues and Practice, 28*(3), 24–31. DOI: 10.1111/j.1745-3992.2009.00151.x.

Herman, J. & Linn, R. (2013). On the Road to Assessing Deeper Learning: The Status of Smarter Balanced and PARCC Assessment Consortia. CRESST Report 823. *National Center for Research on Evaluation, Standards, and Student Testing (CRESST)*.

Kingston, N. & Nash, B. (2011). Formative Assessment: A Meta-Analysis and a Call for Research. *Educational Measurement: Issues and Practice, 30*(4), 28–37. DOI: 10.1111/j.1745-3992.2011.00220.x.

Kuiper, E., Volman, M., & Terwel, J. (2005). The Web as an information resource in K-12 education: Strategies for supporting students in searching and processing information. *Review of Educational Research, 75*, 285–328. DOI: 10.3102/00346543075003285.

Lave, J. & Wenger, E. (1991). *Situated learning: Legitimate peripheral participation*. Cambridge, UK: Cambridge University Press.

Lyon, C. J., Mavronikolas, E., & Wylie, E. C. (2011). *Using Assessment to Help Students Succeed: A Report on the Implementation and Impact of the Keeping Learning on Track Program*. Unpublished manuscript for the GATES Foundation.

Ministry of Education. (2010). *The literacy learning progressions: Meeting the reading and writing demands of the curriculum*. Wellington, NZ: Learning Media Limited.

Mislevy, R. J., Haertel, G., Riconscente, M., Rutstein, D. W., & Ziker, C. (2017). Evidence-centered assessment design. *Assessing Model-Based Reasoning using Evidence-Centered Design* (pp. 19–24). New York, NY: Springer.

Mosher, F. & Heritage, M. (2017). *A Hitchhiker's Guide to Thinking about Literacy, Learning Progressions, and Instruction*. Philadelphia, PA: Consortium for Policy Research in Education.

National Governors Association Center for Best Practics & Council of Chief State School Officers. (2010). *Common Core State Standards for English language arts and literacy in history/social studies, science, and technical subjects*. Retrieved from www.corestandards.org/the-standards/ELA-Literacy

O'Reilly, T., Deane, P., & Sabatini, J. (2015). Building and Sharing Knowledge Key Practice: What Do You Know, What Don't You Know, What Did You Learn? *ETS Research Report Series, 2* (1). Princeton, NJ: Wiley. DOI 10.1002/ets2.12074.

Panadero, E., Alonso-Tapia, J., & Reche, E. (2013). Rubrics vs. self-assessment scripts effect on self-regulation, performance and self-efficacy in pre-service teachers. *Studies in Educational Evaluation, 39*(3), 125–132. DOI: 10.1016/j.stueduc.2013.04.001.

Panadero, E., Tapia, J. A., & Huertas, J. A. (2012). Rubrics and self-assessment scripts effects on self-regulation, learning and self-efficacy in secondary education. *Learning and Individual Differences, 22*(6), 806–813. DOI: 10.1016/j.lindif.2012.04.007.

Perfetti, C. A., Rouet, J. F., & Britt, M. A. (1999). Toward a theory of documents representation. In H. Van Oostendorp & S. R. Goldman (Eds.), *The construction of mental representation during reading* (pp. 99–122). Mahwah, NJ: Erlbaum.

Popham, W. J. (2008). *Transformative assessment.* Alexandria, VA: Association for Supervision and Curriculum Development.

Resnick, L. (1987). *Education and learning to think.* Washington, DC: National Academy Press.

Rouet, J. F., Ros, C., Goumi, A., Macedo-Rouet, M., & Dinet, J. (2011). The influence of surface and deep cues on primary and secondary school students' assessment of relevance in Web menus. *Learning and Instruction, 21*(2), 205–219. DOI: 10.1016/j.learninstruc.2010.02.007.

Sabatini, J. P., O'Reilly, T., Halderman, L., & Bruce, K. (2014). Broadening the scope of reading comprehension using scenario-based assessments: Preliminary findings and challenges. *L'Année psychologique, 114*(04), 693–723. DOI: 10.4074/S0003503314004059.

Sadler, D. R. (1983). Evaluation and the Improvement of Academic Learning. *The Journal of Higher Education, 54*(1), 60–79. DOI :10.1080/00221546.1983.11778152.

Sadler, D. R. (1989). Formative assessment and the design of instructional systems. *Instructional Science, 18*(2), 119–144. DOI: 10.1007/BF00117714.

Sadler, D. R. (1998). Formative assessment: Revisiting the territory. *Assessment in Education: Principles, Policy & Practice, 5*(1), 77–84.

Sadler, D. R. (2010). Beyond feedback: developing student capability in complex appraisal. *Assessment & Evaluation in Higher Education, 35*(5), 535–550. DOI: 10.1080/0969595980050104.

Scardamalia, M. & Bereiter, C. (2006). Knowledge building: Theory, pedagogy, and technology. In R. K. Sawyer (Ed.), *Cambridge handbook of the learning sciences* (pp. 97–115). New York, NY: Cambridge Univ. Press.

Shavelson, R. J., Yuan, K., Alonzo, A. C., Klingberg, T., & Andersson, M. (2006). *On the integration of formative assessment in teaching and learning with implications for teacher education.* Paper prepared for the Stanford Education Assessment Laboratory and the University of Hawaii Curriculum Research and Development Group. Retrieved from http://www.stanford.edu/dept/SUSE/SEAL

Sheehan, K. & O'Reilly, T. (2012). The case for scenario-based assessments of reading competency. In J. P. Sabatini, T. O'Reilly, & E. R. Albro (Eds.), *Reaching an understanding: Innovations in how we view reading assessment* (pp. 19–33). Lanham, New York, Toronto, and Plymouth, UK: Rowman & Littlefield.

Shulman, L. S. (1986). Those who understand: Knowledge growth in teaching. *Educational Researcher, 15*(2), 4–14. DOI 10.3102/0013189X015002004.

Shulman, L. S. (1987). Knowledge and teaching: Foundations of the new reform. *Harvard Educational Review, 57*(1), 1–22. DOI 10.17763/haer.57.1.j463w79r56455411.

Song, Y., Deane, P., & Fowles, M. (2017). Examining students' ability to critique arguments and exploring the implications for assessment and instruction. *ETS Research Report Series 17*(1).

Song, Y., Deane, P., & Fowles, M. E. (2014). Assessing students' ability to summarize arguments: A multistate reading and writing test. In P. J. Dunston, S. K. Fullerton, M. W. Cole, D. Herro, J. A. Malloy, P. M. Wilder, & K. N. Headley (Eds.), *63rd yearbook of the Literacy Research Association* (pp. 127–140). Altamonte Springs, FL: Literacy Research Association.

Song, Y. & Sparks, J. R. (2017). Measuring Argumentation Skills Through a Game-Enhanced Scenario-Based Assessment. *Journal of Educational Computing Research.* DOI 10.1177/0735633117740605.

Sparks, J. R. & Deane, P. (2015). Cognitively based assessment of research and inquiry skills: Defining a key practice in the English language arts. *ETS Research Report Series, 2015*(2). Princeton, NJ: Educational Testing Service

Sparks, J. R., van Rijn, P. W., & Deane, P. (2018). *Assessing source evaluation skills of middle school students using learning progressions.* Manuscript submitted for publication.

Sztajn, P., Confrey, J., Wilson, P. H., & Edgington, C.. (2012). Learning Trajectory Based Instruction: Toward a Theory of Teaching. *Educational Researcher, 41*(5), 147–156. DOI10.3102/0013189X12442801.

Tay, H. Y. (2015). Setting formative assessments in real-world contexts to facilitate self-regulated learning. *Educational Research for Policy and Practice, 14*(2), 169–187. doi:10.1007/s10671-015-9172-5.

van Rijn, P. W., Graf, E. A., & Deane, P. (2014). Empirical Recovery of Argumentation Learning Progressions in Scenario-Based Assessments of English Language Arts. *Educative Psicologia*, *20*(2), 109–115. DOI: /10.1016/j.pse.2014.11.004.

Walraven, A., Brand-Gruwel, S., & Boshuizen, H. P. A. (2008). Information-problem solving: A review of problems students encounter and instructional solutions. *Computers in Human Behavior*, *24*, 623–648. DOI 10.1016/j.chb.2007.01.030.

White, B. Y. & Frederiksen, J. R. (1998). Inquiry, modeling, and metacognition: Making science accessible to all students. *Cognition and instruction*, *16*(1), 3–118. DOI 10.1207/s1532690xci1601_2.

Wiley, J., Goldman, S. R., Graesser, A. C., Sanchez, C. A., Ash, I. K., & Hemmerich, J. A. (2009). Source evaluation, comprehension, and learning in Internet science inquiry tasks. *American Educational Research Journal*, *46*(4), 1060–1106. DOI 10.3102%2F0002831209333183.

Wiliam, D. & Thompson, M. (2007). Integrating assessment with instruction: What will it take to make it work? In C. A. Dwyer (Ed.), *The future of assessment: Shaping teaching and learning* (pp. 53–82). Mahwah, NJ: Erlbaum.

Wilson, M. (2009). Measuring progressions: Assessment structures underlying a learning progression. *Journal of Research in Science Teaching*, *46*(6), 716–730. DOI 10.1002/tea.20318.

Zahner, D. (2013). Reliability and validity – CLA+. *New York, NY: Council for Aid to Education. Retrieved from http://cae.org/images/uploads/pdf/Reliability_and_Validity_of_CLA_Plus.pdf.*

Zieky, M. J. (2014). An introduction to the use of evidence-centered design in test development. *Psicología Educativa*, *20*(2), 79–87. DOI 10.1016/j.pse.2014.11.003.

5

FORMATIVE ASSESSMENT IN SCIENCE EDUCATION

Mapping a Shifting Terrain

Erin Marie Furtak, Sara C. Heredia, and Deb Morrison

Science, as a discipline, encompasses both the body of knowledge which represents the current state of understanding of the natural world, as well as the processes and practices by which that body of knowledge is continuously built, refined, and extended (National Research Council [NRC], 2007). For decades, the science education community has been concerned with supporting students in understanding this body of knowledge, as well engaging in these processes and practices to build conceptual understanding (e.g., Schwab, 1962; NRC, 1996; Duschl, 2008). Historically, formative assessment in science education has been mapped onto these categories and has focused upon eliciting student thinking (e.g., Bell & Cowie, 2001), diagnosing and providing feedback to move students away from misconceptions (e.g., Thissen-Roe, Hunt, & Minstrell, 2004), confronting and replacing student ideas (e.g., White & Gunstone, 1992), and providing space for students to demonstrate their understanding of inquiry (e.g., Duschl & Gitomer, 1997).

Enactment of formative assessment in science has been widely promoted in education policy documents (NRC, 2001), curriculum materials (Draney & Wilson, 1997), and professional development approaches (Gotwals, 2018), but has proven difficult for science teachers to enact, even with support (Atkin et al., 2005; Furtak et al., 2008; Sezen-Barrie & Kelly, 2017). In this context, Black and Wiliam's (1998) contention that formative assessment has the potential to narrow achievement gaps between lower- and higher-achieving students has not yet been realized.

Developments in science education in the past 10 years have represented a significant change in the ways that the vision for science education is articulated and enacted. This shift is embodied by publication of the US policy document, *A Framework for K-12 Science Education* (*Framework*; Board on Science Education [BOSE], 2012), which re-oriented the focus of science education toward a three-dimensional vision that combined disciplinary core ideas with science and engineering practices and crosscutting concepts. The *Framework* also emphasizes the importance of anchoring students' science learning experiences in contextualized, engaging phenomena. This change repositions the ways that assessment is designed and conducted in science classrooms (NRC, 2014; 2017) and is consistent with international moves that have pushed science learning toward a focus on engagement in practice (Ford & Forman, 2006; OECD, 2017).

In this chapter, we map the shifting terrain of formative assessment in the field of science education over the last decade. We begin by connecting formative assessment as it has been traditionally defined in science education by domain-general studies. Then, we describe shifts in theoretical perspectives in educational research in recent years, focusing on how reframing goals for science learning has begun to change ways that formative assessment activity is defined and enacted in science classrooms, and the resultant influence these changes have had on conceptualizations of formative assessment classroom practice. On the basis of these theoretical shifts, we propose a framework for formative assessment in science education, which we then apply to a review of published studies of formative assessment over the past 10 years, examining trends in formative assessment task design, pre-service and in-service teacher education, and technological supports. Finally, we propose a new agenda for formative assessment research in science education.

Formative Assessment in Science Education: Domain-General Origins

Definitions of formative assessment in science education have historically been rooted in domain-general research. As has been the case in other disciplines, Black and Wiliam's review (1998) and other studies (Black & Wiliam, 2009; Wiliam, 2007) have been foundational for science education researchers, and are frequently cited as rationales for conducting formative assessment in science classrooms. In the US, the National Research Council (2001) included formative assessment as part of the *National Science Education Standards'* vision for science teaching and learning, and articulated a widely-cited three-step process to inform instruction: *Where are you trying to go?*, *Where are you now?*, and *How can you get there?* The first question can be used to define the goal or objective of learning, the second can be used to define the prior knowledge and practices that students bring to the learning space that would support learning toward the goal, and the final question can be used to center the actions of all participants on what would be needed to work toward the goal given current understandings. At its foundation, this process of formative assessment in science education has focused upon making student ideas explicit so that teachers and students can together take action to move toward learning goals.

Conceptualizing Goals for Science Teaching and Learning and Their Implications for Formative Assessment

It is difficult to conceive of formative assessment without first discussing the ways in which the goals or outcomes of science education have been conceptualized. We embed our discussion of these goals in the context of larger shifts in the way learning has been conceptualized, and the resulting implications for educational assessment. Historically, classroom assessment has been informed by behavioral and cognitive theoretical perspectives on learning which focus on individual acquisition of atomized bits of knowledge and skills, emphasize that learning should be sequenced in particular ways or is hierarchical, and claim that transfer is limited and all content should be explicitly taught (Shepard, 2000).

In science education, efforts have been made to broaden ways of thinking about what we want students to learn, differentiating between the ways of knowing – the epistemic process of science (aka scientific inquiry), and the product of science – the scientific knowledge or concepts (Schwab, 1962). Assessment in science has similarly focused on these domains, seeking to assess both the process by which students build knowledge, or what some have called scientific procedures, and the scientific concepts students build by engaging in those procedures. For example, Li et al. (2006) made the distinction between procedural knowledge, or students' abilities to engage in processes of inquiry; declarative knowledge, or knowledge of *what*; schematic knowledge, or knowledge of *why* something happens; and strategic knowledge, or knowledge of *how* something happens.

In recent years, sociocultural learning perspectives have shaped the ways in which assessment in general, and formative assessment in particular, is positioned in science classrooms (Shepard, 2000). Sociocultural learning perspectives include a variety of frameworks derived from Vygotsky (1978) that articulate learning as a social process that happens in activity and is mediated by a collection of tools and practices endemic to particular communities (e.g., Cole, 1996; Lave & Wenger, 1991; Greeno, 2006). We can see this turn toward social aspects of student science learning in Duschl's (2003) three-part framework that included conceptual, epistemic, and social domains for student science learning. The conceptual domain illuminates the understandings of "structures and cognitive processes used when reasoning scientifically" (p. 42). The epistemic domain goes deeply into the assessment of how students develop and evaluate scientific knowledge, and the social domain provides insight into the "processes and forums that shape how knowledge is communicated, represented, argued, and debated" (p. 42) within science.

In recent reform efforts, the field of science education has worked to articulate the social nature of science learning as a set of scientific practices (BOSE, 2012). This *practice turn* (Ford & Forman, 2006) extends Duschl's epistemic and social domains to articulate the ways in which scientists, and in turn students, engage in scientific activity. Ford and Forman (2006) identified three ways to conceive of disciplinary practices in science based on perspectives of learning as a social process and social science literature on disciplinary practices. First, they suggested attending to the social aspect of scientific practice such as the norms and means of the activity. Second, they suggested attending to the material aspect of scientific practice such as the way in which nature is measured, modeled or otherwise quantified. Third, they viewed scientific practice as the interplay of roles, arguing that those involved in the scientific enterprise are making claims and critiquing others' claims. It is this interplay of roles that collectively provides disciplinary authority.

This articulation of science learning as consisting of both engagement in a disciplinary practice and demonstrating understanding of a body of knowledge can thus form a different way of thinking about goals for students' science learning that would then be the object of a formative assessment. As an example, we can consider an example from the IQWST middle school curriculum (Krajcik et al., 2008), *What's Happening to My Body?*

> Inspector Bio wants to know what you have figured out about the oxygen that is missing from the air that you exhale. Explain to her where the oxygen goes, what uses it, and why. Write a scientific explanation, a claim, sufficient evidence, and reasoning.
>
> *(NRC, 2014, p. 42)*

This embedded assessment task, while simple in design, combines a deep disciplinary focus, asking students to explain what happens to oxygen when it enters the body while also engaging in a scientific practice with a particular scaffold of a claim, evidence, and reasoning style of explanation (McNeill et al., 2006). The task thus provides students an opportunity to not only explain the science, but to construct an argument for why their perspective makes sense, and to provide evidence for the strength of that argument (NRC, 2014).

Defining Formative Assessment in Science Education: Tools, Practices, and Participants

Informed by the *practice turn* in educational theory (Ford & Forman, 2006), we use a sociocultural perspective to define formative assessment. While prior definitions of formative assessment have delineated it as a series of steps in which a teacher elicits and responds to student thinking (e.g., NRC, 2001), in this review we use the practice turn in science education as an occasion to reframe formative assessment as an activity engaged in by groups of individuals. We build on Bennett's (2011) definition of formative assessment framing it as a network of *participants* engaging in *practices* organized and coordinated by a set of *tools* within a specific context (Furtak & Heredia, 2014; Furtak, Morrison, & Kroog, 2014). We explicate each of these elements and provide examples in the sections below.

Erin Marie Furtak et al.

Formative Assessment Tools

Tools are used within the activity of science formative assessment to elicit and make sense of student learning around specific goals and may take a variety of forms. The most recognizable form of tools for student and teacher formative assessment activity are tasks – specific tools that organize activity to create opportunities for students to share their thinking with their teacher and peers (Bennett, 2011). Examples of tasks include a set of open-ended questions, a free write, a clicker question, or some other object or artifact embedded within an activity in which students and teachers participate and in which student ideas are shared. In the past, the most ubiquitous example of formative assessment tools in science classroom have been tasks such as Paige Keeley's (2005) formative assessment probes. An example of a task that addresses both disciplinary ideas and engages students in scientific practices as it elicits student ideas about a scientific phenomenon is illustrated in Figure 5.1. This task, similar to a version developed by a group of high school biology teachers as part of a research project (Furtak, 2018), was developed to connect with students' lived experiences in observing red foxes in the communities around their homes, and create an opportunity for students to speculate about the conditions under which these foxes might have developed the particular set of adaptations to their environment (Evans et al., 2010). The task uses a common format for formative assessment, one in which students respond to a small number of related, open-ended questions tied to a common scenario. The task then leaves space for students to draw upon their understanding of variation within members of a population, differential survival and reproduction to predict what might happen were the environmental conditions to change in the habitat of this particular red fox population. Finally, the last question asks students to design an experiment to determine what they might need to do to determine if their prediction was correct (Palma et al., 2015).

Adaptation

There is a population of red foxes living together in the foothills of Denver, Colorado where there is a large variety of habitats ranging from open woodlands, pasture, agricultural areas, rivers, and streams. Red foxes can also be seen on the edges of urban areas.

Red foxes, despite their name, vary in coloration across their lifespan. They are born black or brown and develop reddish orange and white fur with black ears and feet when they are about 2-3 months old. However, the color of fur varies, with foxes also occasionally having black, silver, or mixed-color fur with a long dark stripe running down its back.

Imagine that there is a major fire in the area that a population of red foxes lived. Now there are fewer trees in the area.

1. Predict which of the fox populations would be more successful in surviving in order to reproduce under these new conditions.

2. Explain your reasoning.

3. What could we do to find out if your prediction was correct?

Figure 5.1 Example formative assessment tool: The red fox task.

Note: Information about red foxes adapted from Colorado Parks and Wildlife (n.d.)

Formative Assessment in Science Education

Formative assessment tools extend beyond the tasks themselves that organize student activity. Tools also include protocols that teachers use to guide their interpretations of samples of student work according to a rubric or learning progression related to science content or practices to plan for next instructional steps (e.g., Furtak, Morrison, & Kroog, 2014). In this instance, the student work, the protocol for sorting that work, and the learning progression all might be considered formative assessment tools. In the science classroom, one might see students engaging with clickers or post-it notes to respond to a teacher's questioning prompt. These examples illuminate the idea that a formative assessment tool can be any artifact or object that is used for the purpose of gaining information about student learning, making sense of student thinking, or modifying classroom instruction.

Formative assessment tools help to foster student learning in key ways. Formative assessment tools that organize tasks or objects are of interest in so far as they either promote insight into student thinking or facilitate student understanding toward a learning objective (Thompson, Braaten, & Windschitl, 2009). These tools may move back and forth from the classroom to spaces of teacher learning communities as boundary objects (Star, 2010), facilitating both student and teacher learning. For example, a question such as "How do species change over time?" asked within a formative assessment tool such as an exit ticket may elicit student thinking on a wide range of ideas related to natural selection, which can have cultural or everyday meanings outside the science classroom, or even the content area of science. Formative assessment tools may facilitate the systematic collection of data on the range of student thinking, provide a focal point for teacher talk about student thinking, and inform the next steps in the classroom.

Formative Assessment Practices

Practices are the actions in which teachers and students engage. These include discourse practices or what are often called "talk moves" (e.g., Michaels & O'Connor, 2012) including making ideas explicit, listening to each other's ideas, probing each other's thinking, pressing for a specificity of reasoning and providing informational feedback to advance learning (Ruiz-Primo & Furtak, 2007). Classroom participation structures that facilitate the sharing of student ideas, such as think–pair–shares and whole-class conversations (also called "assessment conversations," see Duschl & Gitomer, 1997) fit into this category as well.

Formative assessment practices also include instances during which criteria for quality work are articulated and negotiated between teachers and students (Coffey, 2003; Sadler, 1989). In addition, formative assessment practices include those actions taken by the teacher between class sessions as they read and respond to students' written work, providing written feedback (e.g., Butler, 1987; Ruiz-Primo & Li, 2004) and also planning subsequent instructional activities on the basis of what they have inferred about student performance from student work (Cowie & Bell, 1999). These practices may be enacted at different time scales including micro interactions in the classroom, daily routines of checking in on student learning, or longer weekly or unit level assessment timelines (Wiliam, 2007). As the teacher and students' progress through units of instruction, ongoing formative assessment across these varied timescales can help to connect student understandings with learning goals, and suggest next steps in instruction.

Formative assessment practices involve the way in which learning is organized and thus reflect particular perspectives about what is being learned and what constitutes learning. For example, students may be arranged in groups and assigned a particular assessment task that they discuss in a structured talk format (Lemke, 1990). The teacher then moves around the room, probing student thinking as needed or listening and taking notes about the conceptual learning of students as well as the scientific practices they may be engaging in, such as evidence-based argumentation. In addition, the teacher may also be supporting academic and/or scientific language development in on-the-fly questions or feedback moments.

The following classroom excerpt shows the ways in which an exchange between a teacher and a student in whole-class assessment conversation (Duschl & Gitomer, 1997) can be conceived of as formative assessment practice. The teacher, Ms. Schafer, had participated in a research project that supported her use of formative assessment embedded in a unit supporting students' density-based explanations of sinking and floating in middle school (Furtak et al., 2008). Ms. Schafer had been leading a whole-class discussion about students' developing explanations for the question, "*Why do things sink and float?*" and heard a student use the word "density." Rather than accepting the student's use of this word at face-value, Ms. Schafer seized the opportunity to unpack what Cole meant by this word and engaged him with a series of questions to press him to explain what he meant.

Ms. Schafer:	That was an interesting word you used, Cole. You used the word density. That was an interesting word. What did you mean by that?
Cole:	I meant like, it might have been a lot thicker with the mass, you know, like there could be . . . You know, like if you had a piece of bread. You know it's got like holes in it? Kind of?
Ms. Schafer:	Uh-huh. A piece of bread has holes in it.
Cole:	And then you get like a stack of paper. You get 'em at like both the same mass, about, the same size, actually.
Ms. Schafer:	The same size.
Cole:	Yeah.
Ms. Schafer:	So I'll make my bread like this [gestures with hands].
Cole:	The paper would have thicker density. Thicker mass.
Ms. Schafer:	Okay. And he's saying that if we had papers that are about the same size, this would have more mass, are you saying?
Cole:	Yeah. Well, the papers might.
Ms. Schafer:	Are they the same size? That's important, right? They're the same size.
Cole:	Yes.
Ms. Schafer:	But instead of a piece of bread with holes in it, over here you have a stack of papers.
Cole:	It's really solid, like . . .
Ms. Schafer:	Solid. I hear the word solid. I hear more mass.

In this exchange, Ms. Schafer engaged in several practices associated with formative assessment, including asking open-ended questions (Cazden, 2001), re-voicing Cole's ideas (O'Connor & Michaels, 1993), and attending to the substance of his ideas (Coffey et al., 2011). Cole has expanded on his ideas, made his thinking explicit (Windschitl et al., 2012), and engaged in science disciplinary practices (Engle & Conant, 2002). By drawing out an example of a stack of bread, which has a lot of empty space in it because it has holes, and comparing to a stack of paper of the same size which does not have holes in it, Cole created an analogy that showed that these two substances, while taking up the same amount of space, will not have the same density because of the amount of matter in the same amount of space. Cole interspersed his account with both everyday words like "thicker" and scientific words like "mass," weaving an explanation that connected his lived experiences with what he was learning in science class. This example extends the sociocultural perspective that can be instantiated in formative assessment practices by illustrating how students' everyday ideas and language can be leveraged by the teacher.

Formative Assessment Participants

The primary *participants* in formative assessment are the teacher and students, and the activity of formative assessment, consisting of practices organized by tools, cannot be fully considered without

Formative Assessment in Science Education

incorporating the actors. Historical participation structures in classrooms foreground the teacher as the central participant, asking questions, selecting and administering formative assessment tools, interpreting student responses, and providing feedback (e.g., Cazden, 2001). However, a more complete perspective on formative assessment also integrates the role of students as active participants in this process, engaging in self- and peer-assessment (e.g., Coffey, 2003; Sadler, 1989; Sato, Wei, & Darling-Hammond, 2008). This process may be scaffolded through the use of tools such as rubrics and checklists (Kang, Thompson, & Windschitl, 2014) and other resources that support classroom routines and make learning criteria explicit. In such a context, both teacher and students ask questions to make ideas public (Engle & Conant, 2002), make inferences about that thinking (Pellegrino, Chudowsky, & Glaser, 2001), and provide appropriate feedback. Students then use this information about their thinking or practices to improve their learning.

From a broader perspective, formative assessment participants may expand beyond the participants in a single classroom. For example, if teachers are working to develop and enact common formative assessment tools (Ainsworth & Viegut, 2006), there may be multiple, collaborating teachers supporting each other in reflecting on student work and in identifying next steps for instruction (Furtak & Heredia, 2014; Furtak, Morrison, & Kroog, 2014). In other settings, formative assessment data might be shared in rapid cycles within research-practice partnerships in order to improve teaching and learning in quick and nimble cycles at scale (Bryk et al., 2015).

Complex Interactions Among Practices, Participants, and Tools

Although existing studies often foreground certain of the preceding elements, in our framing, formative assessment is a complex interaction of participants, practices, and tools. For example, a high school biology teacher interested in what her students know about matter and energy cycling in ecosystems might ask students to draw a model of how energy and matter transfer across organisms in a given environment. She could hand this task out as an exit ticket at the end of class, and flip through student work at the end of the day. In looking at students' models, she may quickly see that students have represented energy as transferring between levels with no heat lost, indicating that students need support in thinking about energy dissipation and conservation (Neumann et al., 2013). She may also note how some students included the Sun in their models, indicating the original source of energy, while others did not. From this information, the teacher may plan instruction with specific ideas about feedback to move students forward to draw on experiences from their daily life (e.g., thinking about energy as coming from the Sun, thinking about the number of producers versus consumers in the environment, as well as different learning experiences that could engage students directly in these experiences).

From our conceptual framework of formative assessment tools, practices, and participants, we can view this instance of formative assessment to encompass the ways in which tools organize the practices of participants into routines and participation structures. This more complex framing not only capitalizes on the richness of our understanding about the discursive moves that support science learning in the classroom, but also builds on research into the scaffolds and structures of instruments and formative assessment tools that best draw out the nature and quality of student thinking (Kang, Thompson, & Windschitl, 2014). Furthermore, this framing helps us to foreground the ways in which tools can help teachers learn about student thinking. To further illustrate applications of this conceptual framework to studies of formative assessment in science education, we analyze two examples: one from the classroom, and one from teacher professional development.

Example from the Classroom: Ambitious Science Teaching Tools

For a classroom-facing example, we turn to the published work of Kang and colleagues, who have examined the ways in which formative assessment tasks are scaffolded (Kang,

Thompson, & Windschitl, 2014) as well as the ways in which tasks are launched and enacted by teachers with students in science classrooms. Our framework for tools, practices, and participants helps us to see a complete picture of the interrelationship between these three elements as formative assessment is conducted.

In this study, we see instances in which teachers work with tools from the Ambitious Science Teaching set of resources (ambitiousscienceteaching.org) that are explicitly designed to support particular sets of formative assessment practices or routines in the classroom. As an example, we can examine a task from a seventh-grade earth science unit (Kang, Thompson, & Windschitl, 2014). This task contextualizes the general phenomenon of the seasons into the specific geographic locations of Seattle and Samoa, asks students to take multiple variables into account (e.g., the distance from these locations to the Sun, penetration of light into the atmosphere, the angle of the Sun as it intersects with the surface of the earth), and then asks students to write a claim and provide evidence for that claim to explain why countries near the equator, like Samoa, don't have seasons like Seattle. Students were then given options of choosing another country near the equator, such as Kenya or Cambodia (Kang and colleagues note that the teacher was aware that many of her students were from immigrant populations whose families had come from these parts of the world).

We can take the example of this task and envision how it could function as a tool that organizes the engagement of students and teacher into a set of routines and practices in the classroom around surfacing, sharing, attending, and responding to each other's ideas. The task was provided to students with a rubric that supported them in deciding what information to include in their explanation, inviting them to engage in a high level of intellectual work, and also embedding opportunities for self-assessment as they completed the formative assessment themselves.

Kang and colleagues note significant progress made by students in their responses to these questions when they returned to them later in the unit, indicating the efficacy of the approach of the sentence frames in the task, the rubric, and the feedback provided by the teacher. Our conceptual framing highlights the routines organized by the *tools* (the task and the rubric); the lived histories being brought into play by the design of the assessment by the teacher (the *participants*) that engaged students in learning about the phenomenon of the seasons through modeling, argumentation, and explanation; and the *formative assessment practices* in which the students were engaging (sharing their ideas with each other, attending and responding to each other's ideas).

Example from Teacher Professional Development: Formative Assessment Design Cycle

Our conceptual framework also helps us trace formative assessment with a community of teachers as they design, enact, and reflect upon formative assessment tasks to organize their classroom practices. In a series of studies, Furtak and colleagues (Furtak, 2012; Furtak & Heredia, 2014; Furtak, Morrison, & Kroog, 2014; Furtak et al., 2016) have developed and studied the *Formative Assessment Design Cycle*, shown in Figure 5.2.

In this iterative cycle, discipline-specific groups of science teachers gather together in successive meetings to *explore student thinking* as a basis for setting learning goals or formative assessment targets, *design formative assessment tools* to organize routines and participation structures in their classrooms, and *practice using those tools* with each other, rehearsing routines and envisioning how the tools will organize classroom activity with their students. They bring the tools into their classroom spaces, collecting evidence of enactment and also drawing upon the conversations they had with their colleagues to inform in-the-moment responses and feedback to student ideas in the course of classroom practice. Finally, teachers return together, *reflect on enactment*, and plan feedback and next steps for instruction.

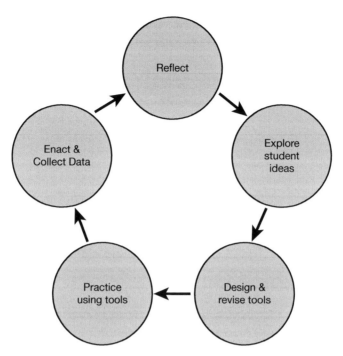

Figure 5.2 Formative Assessment Design Cycle.

From the perspective of our framework, we can envision the ways in which *tools*, the focal point of the design cycle, serve to organize not only the *practices* of the teacher *participants* in the professional learning community meetings, but also migrate (Kazemi & Hubbard, 2008) as boundary objects maintaining flexible meaning across contexts (Star & Griesemer, 1989) into classroom spaces. Once in these classroom spaces, these *tools* organize the routines and *practices* of the teacher and student *participants*.

Formative Assessment in Science Education: Emergent Themes in Recent Literature

In the preceding sections, we have presented both the goal of science education based upon students learning the big ideas of science by engaging in the practices of science, as well as a reframing of science learning inspired by the practice turn in sociocultural theory now embodied in science standards in the US (BOSE, 2012) and in international assessment frameworks (OECD, 2017). We have also developed a framework for unpacking the phrase "formative assessment" into tools, practices, and participants. In the next section, we turn to a review and summary of recent articles in the science education literature that have studied formative assessment innovations.

To perform the review, we conducted a systematic literature search extending back to 2007, the year that the watershed report, *Taking Science to School* (NRC, 2007), which included a thorough review of the literature on formative assessment in science education, was published. This timeframe also corresponds with the timing of the last edition of the *Handbook of Formative Assessment*. Without attempting to exhaustively review all of the published articles in this domain, we nevertheless developed a set of search terms to help us locate published studies conducted in K-12 classrooms in formal school contexts. After eliminating the studies that were not about formative assessment, we read the abstracts of the remaining papers and then, through conversation among the three authors, identified key themes or "bins" of major areas of research represented by these articles. We then systematically read each of the abstracts and sorted each of the articles into those bins. We use those bins to organize the sections of major areas of research below, and also inform our writing of these sections with our knowledge of the literature. In the sections that follow, we summarize and synthesize the research that has been performed in each area, highlighting the tools, practices, and participants in each.

Curriculum-Embedded Formative Assessment

Given the role that materials play in teachers communicating lesson ideas with each other in the teaching profession (Grossman, Smagorinsky, & Valencia, 1999), it is perhaps not surprising that tasks or tools constitute the most recognizable form of formative assessment in science education. Among science teachers, the most commonly recognized science formative assessment tasks in the past 10 years are those published in multiple books and articles written by Paige Keeley and colleagues, who have produced a large number of formative assessment "probes" tailored to specific ideas in the different content areas and for different levels of science teaching (e.g., Keeley, Eberle, & Farrin, 2005a). These tasks rely upon a variety of formats and are deliberately designed to draw out common student prior ideas; for example, the probe *Going Through a Phase* (Keeley, Eberle, & Farrin, 2005a) asks students to share their ideas about what causes the different phases of the Moon, and then provides students with a set of possible explanations beside student names, including the following choices:

Mona: The Moon lights up in different parts at different times of the month.
Sofia: Parts of the Moon reflect light depending on the position of the Earth in relation to the Sun and Moon.
Trey: Different planets cast a shadow on the Moon as they revolve around the Sun.

(p. 183)

Students are asked to select a response they agree with, and then to explain why they selected that choice. Probes like this one, which are easily printed off and used in classrooms, allow students to provide information that is quickly interpretable with respect to standards (Keeley, Eberle, & Farrin, 2005b).

Curriculum-embedded formative assessments are tools that are designed specifically to be placed within pre-existing units of instruction. Embedded assessments are commonly placed at what are sometimes described as turns, "bends" (Penuel et al., 2018a) or "joints" (Brandon et al., 2008) in units of instruction at which mastery of particular ideas or practices is necessary before moving on. Such turns offer opportunities for students and teachers to pause to check for understanding. In contrast to domain-independent strategies that might work at any point during a unit, or, for that matter, in any content area, curriculum-embedded assessments are specific to particular places in disciplinary curricular units.

Smaller scale studies have investigated the ways in which researchers might partner with individual teachers to embed tasks in curriculum materials. Atkin and colleagues (2005), in the CAPITAL project, found that the teachers' trajectories of development were deeply personalized. Across these cases, we see science teachers making sense of what formative assessment means in their classrooms and developing curriculum-embedded activities and tailored feedback experiences for their students around these activities, with the support of the researchers with whom they were partnered. Similarly, Yin and Buck (2015) studied how a Chinese chemistry teacher worked to integrate formative assessment activities into his curriculum materials. These studies indicate the depth of partnership, support, and effort necessary – nearly on a one-to-one-basis – to realize full enactment of curriculum-embedded formative assessment in these classrooms.

Formative Assessment in Science Education

A separate line of research has explored the ways in which researchers might partner with school district leaders and teachers in processes of co-design and principled adaptation to develop formative assessment activities as part of replacement units to support science teaching and learning activities (Penuel et al., 2018a). In an ongoing research-practice partnership, Penuel and colleagues have developed three-dimensional units of science instruction and, as part of that design process, embedded formative assessments at "bends" in the curriculum storylines.

Embedded assessments need not focus only on concepts as they unfold across units, but also may be used to support students' developing engagement in scientific practices across the arc of an unfolding instructional unit (Kang, Thompson, & Windschitl, 2014; Windschitl et al., 2012). For example, students might draw a model to illustrate their initial explanations of a phenomenon, like a collapsing oil tanker, or a man flipping over by running up the side of a building, at the beginning of a unit. The embedded formative assessment takes the form of the teacher returning and asking students to revise the models after important learning activities (Windschitl et al., 2012), using various scaffolds to elicit and support ongoing changes in student thinking (Kang, Thompson, & Windschitl, 2014). Curriculum-embedded formative assessment tools can also support the bridging of students' everyday lived experiences with classroom science learning. Terrazas-Arellanes, Knox, and Rivas (2013) illustrated this bridging by building, in a Mexico–USA partnership, a culturally and linguistically relevant science curriculum that included embedded formative assessment tasks as part of its design.

While these curriculum-embedded tasks have been developed by researchers in partnership with curriculum developers (Brandon et al., 2008), teachers (Atkin et al., 2005), and district leadership (Penuel et al., 2018a), a smaller subset of studies have examined the effect of the enactment of these tasks on student learning. In a quasi-experimental study, Shavelson and colleagues (2008) developed a set of formative assessments to support the development of students' understanding of a density-based explanation of sinking and floating (Ayala et al., 2008) in the Foundational Approaches to Science Teaching Curriculum (Pottenger & Young, 1992). Results indicated that teachers' implementations varied significantly in their effects on student motivation, achievement, and conceptual change (Yin et al., 2008). A follow-up study with one teacher implementing both the control and experimental conditions found the hypothesized, positive effect of the curriculum-embedded assessments on student learning (Yin, Tomita, & Shavelson, 2013).

Both Shavelson and colleagues' (2008) and Hondrich and colleagues' (2016) studies found that the implementation of embedded formative assessment was key to understanding its relation to student learning gains. In the original Yin et al. (2008) findings, an implementation study revealed a large degree of variation in the enactment of the formative assessment tasks, and teachers who enacted the formative assessments with higher fidelity to the intended treatment had students with higher learning gains in the quasi-experimental study (Furtak et al., 2008). Hondrich and colleagues (2016) found that teachers participating in a direct application approach to professional development had higher fidelity to enacting curriculum-embedded tasks.

Studies of Teachers' Formative Assessment Practices

Several studies developed and applied frameworks for science formative assessment practice to understand the development of teachers' practice over time, or to examine the fidelity of teachers' implementations of formative assessment tools. Research on identifying and defining formative assessment practices focused on breaking down these practices into different dimensions (Gotwals et al., 2015; Sato, Wei, & Darling-Hammond, 2008) or strategies (Wylie & Lyon, 2015). Investigators then measured teachers' proficiency along a continuum (Gotwals et al., 2015), changes over time within each practice dimension (Sato, Wei, & Darling-Hammond, 2008), or the degree to which different strategies were used (Wylie & Lyon, 2015). While there was certainly overlap within and between the categories each research group developed, the field might consider how to come to a consensus on formative assessment practices in science to both better support science teacher education and compare formative assessment practices across research studies.

Wylie and Lyon (2015) showed that teachers varied in their use of five strategies for formative assessment: 1) identifying learning goals, 2) designing tasks, 3) providing feedback that moves student learning forward, 4) student responsibility over their learning, and 5) students as resources for each other's learning. They found the strategies most used by teachers in their study were developing tasks and activating students to be resources to one another. They found that teachers' strategies for providing feedback were the weakest of the five and that teachers used more grades-based feedback rather than actionable, task-centered feedback that could move students' forward. Lastly, they found that there was little integration of the strategies.

Similarly, Gotwals et al. (2015) recognized that teachers who fell more toward the expert end of the continuum showed a stronger integration of formative assessment into their instructional practices. These investigators employed three practice dimensions: setting learning goals, recognizing where students were in relation to those goals, and closing the gap between what students currently understood and the learning goals set for the students. Then, through the use of classroom video, they rated teachers along a continuum of novice to expert and articulated dimensions of each practice along a progression. Their research suggests that, as teachers become more expert in their practice, formative assessment becomes more integrated and seamless rather than a set of strategies used intermittently in the classroom.

Research has focused on the characteristics of science teachers in relation to their formative assessment practice and the ways in which practices can be categorized and understood. One common finding among the articles reviewed suggests challenges science teachers have in relation to feedback in formative assessment. Teachers relied on general teaching practices, rather than specific curricular materials, and on grades rather than qualitative descriptions. As such, their practice did little to move student learning forward. In addition, the studies suggest that teachers need discipline-specific supports to help them integrate formative assessment practices into their regular curriculum and instruction.

Supporting Teacher Professional Learning for Formative Assessment Practice

A second group of studies examined the ways in which researchers have created and/or studied professional learning experiences related to assessment, inquiry-based teaching, or curriculum implementation. These studies foregrounded, to differing degrees, formative assessment practices, tools, or participants. A small portion of studies examined teachers' formative assessment practices naturalistically and not in relation to a particular classroom intervention (Ateh, 2015; Box, Skoog, & Dabbs, 2015; Edwards & Edwards, 2017; Gotwals et al., 2015). In the following sections, we describe relevant findings within each of the categories of formative assessment activity, as it relates to in-service science teachers.

A subset of papers examined characteristics of the teachers themselves and the relationships between these characteristics and formative assessment, including teachers' understanding of science (Forbes, Sabel, & Biggers, 2015), pedagogical content knowledge (Falk, 2012), beliefs about student learning (Box, Skoog, & Dabbs, 2015; Buck & Trauth-Nare, 2009), and experience as science learners (Edwards & Edwards, 2017). For example, Box, Skoog, and Dabbs (2015) developed personal practice assessment theory (PPAT) profiles for the three teachers in their study and looked at how PPAT related to teachers' formative assessment activities in the classroom. They found that all three teachers' internal constructs about how students learn in science and external pressures to cover content mattered for the ways in which the teachers were able to translate ideas about formative assessment into classroom practice. Specifically, the two teachers that had tightly held constructive

Formative Assessment in Science Education

beliefs about student learning made more room for formative assessment as part of the learning process, whereas the teacher that held beliefs on science instruction consistent with rote memorization and teacher transmission of knowledge focused more on summative assessment. Their findings support recommendations from another study finding that purposeful attention to and eliciting of a teacher's beliefs about assessment in professional development are key to shifting her focus from summative to formative assessment (Buck & Trauth-Nare, 2009).

Researchers have also sought to relate science teachers' content knowledge and pedagogical content knowledge (Shulman, 1986) to formative assessment. Forbes, Sabel, and Biggers (2015) found that there was no correlation between a group of elementary teachers' content knowledge and productive formative assessment activity in the classroom, although collaborating with colleagues on formative assessment was related to increases in the teachers' understanding of students' development of conceptual understanding in science.

Studies that looked at different facets of elementary teachers' knowledge when engaging with formative assessment found issues in relation to teacher feedback within formative assessment. For example, professional development in formative assessment showed no impact on teachers' pedagogical content knowledge related to feedback from formative assessment (Falk, 2012). The teachers showed little to no gain in how to provide specific, meaningful feedback to student ideas. This result relates to a similar finding in Forbes, Sabel, and Biggers (2015), who found that teachers relied heavily on general teaching practices in cycles of feedback, rather than content-specific curricular choices to inform feedback (Forbes, Sabel, & Biggers, 2015). Together, these studies suggest a need for research and professional development centered on feedback that is specific to the content teachers are teaching and the ideas students bring to the classroom.

Several studies focused on larger structures or tools to organize teacher learning in professional development settings (Avramides et al., 2015; Furtak & Heredia, 2014; Harrison, 2014; Panizzon & Pegg, 2008). These tools include models of assessment for inquiry (Harrison, 2014), models of cognitive development (Avramides et al., 2015; Furtak & Heredia, 2014), or tools that organized teachers' collective work on formative assessment (Panizzon & Pegg, 2008). Each of these studies found that these tools supported science teachers' learning about formative assessment and growth in conceptions of assessment (Panizzon & Pegg, 2008), seeing their students as resourceful and creative (Harrison, 2014), and how students ideas or skills developed over time (Furtak & Heredia, 2014; Harrison, 2014).

Trauth-Nare and Buck (2011) surfaced differences between a middle school science teacher and researchers' definitions of formative assessment, as well as students' initial resistance to participating in formative assessment. Through reflective practice, the researchers and the collaborating teacher came to shift their definitions of formative assessment and came to new understandings of how it could support teaching and learning in the classroom. This study underscores the importance of discussing meanings of formative assessment during professional learning sessions, and of researchers approaching collaborations with teachers with learning orientations.

Each of these studies demonstrated that teacher agency over assessment processes was key to their use of the tools and the development of their assessment practices. For example, Panizzon and Pegg (2008) supported math and science teachers to not only determine what the content focus of their conceptual model was like, but also the structure of their professional learning time dedicated to this work. Similarly, in Harrison's (2008) research, teachers chose the inquiry activities that would be implemented and their assessment activity based on the assessment model provided in the project. This research strongly suggests the importance of teacher choice and input into the focus of their formative assessment activity.

Resources for Enacting Formative Assessment in the Classroom

A subset of researchers has been exploring different types of resources to help scaffold the enactment of formative assessment in classrooms. These investigators were motivated by research indicating the challenges facing science teachers as they enact formative assessment. We identified three emergent categories: studies examining (1) how learning progressions could support teachers in enacting formative assessment, (2) different types of formative assessment task formats, and (3) technology resources for supporting formative assessments.

Learning Progressions

Learning progressions have been defined as representations of the progressive ways that student ideas develop over time, usually in response to a curriculum (Corcoran, Mosher, & Rogat, 2009), and have been the focus of much development work in science education in recent years (NRC, 2007). As summaries of student ideas, learning progressions have served as guides for assessment development and curriculum design (Alonzo & Gotwals, 2012), and also as frameworks for curriculum-embedded assessment (Ayala et al., 2008). As such, these progressions can be employed by teachers as tools in recognizing and responding to student ideas during instruction (Bennett, 2011; Furtak, 2012; Heritage et al., 2009). A cluster of research articles has examined this contention.

In several connected studies, Furtak and colleagues have studied the ways in which learning progressions might serve as the centerpiece of a professional learning experience in which teachers iteratively design, enact, and reflect upon formative assessments. Evidence suggests that repeated use of a learning progression in recognizing and responding to student ideas during classroom discussions organized around formative assessment tasks is effective (Furtak, 2012; Furtak et al., 2016), although in some cases this use also helped teachers recognize and label students' ideas as incorrect or as "misconceptions" (Furtak, 2012).

Jin and colleagues (2017), in the process of developing a learning progression for matter and energy cycling in socio-ecological systems, examined how the learning progression framework that underlay a plant unit, which included embedded assessment activities, supported discourse strategies that involved encouraging students to talk about the "how" and "why" behind their answers. The teacher who most successfully used these types of discourse frames, and who was most influenced by the learning progression framework, had students with higher learning gains as compared to other teachers.

Task Formats

Task formats are structures for formative assessment tools that help students to make their ideas explicit to teachers (Cowie, Jones, & Otrel-Cass, 2011). Multiple scholars have examined different types of formative assessment task formats (e.g., Furtak & Ruiz-Primo, 2008; Kang, Thompson, & Windschitl, 2014; Merrill, 2013; Won et al., 2017). Findings indicate that not all formative assessment task formats are equal in eliciting the nature and quality of student thinking, nor are they equally capable of being scorable by teachers. Kang and colleagues (2014) suggest a variety of scaffolds can help to make student thinking explicit, including checklists, rubrics, sentence frames, and contextualized phenomena. Checklists can support students as they engage in self-assessment to be sure that they are, for example, including both observable and not directly observable elements of phenomena. Checklists can also remind students to make keys to explain symbology in models and drawings so others can understand their thinking. Sentence frames can help students learn to construct explanations, starting students off with phrases such as "What I saw was . . ." Such frames can focus students on the phenomenon at hand, or prompt them to provide evidence, as in "I know this because" (p. 13). Rubrics can help students focus on required elements in their responses, and support and encourage self-assessment.

Furtak and Ruiz-Primo (2008) found that open-outcome space prompts may be better at helping students share what they know, whereas constrained prompts may be better at helping to focus classroom conversations on a smaller universe of possibilities for teachers. Concept maps have also been found to be useful formative assessment formats (Won et al., 2017) that can help make student thinking explicit in ways that only marginally correlate with traditional, multiple-choice assessments, and that can still be evaluated consistently by teachers. Concept maps can also encourage students to connect their experiences from outside school to what they are learning in school (Merrill, 2013).

Holmeier and colleagues (2018) examined the ways in which specifically-designed formative assessment tools could support teacher feedback for students during inquiry-based science lessons, and in turn, the effect of using those tools on the quality of teacher feedback and student adjustment of their work. The work was carried out in multiple countries with slight variations in the tools used. Included was a "feedback journal" in secondary chemistry lessons in Germany, which reminded students of the learning goal, and then included space for teachers to tell students their current state of learning, as well as next steps for what they should change in planning and carrying out future experiments. Findings indicated that the tool supported teachers in giving students specific feedback for next instructional steps, although students used the feedback in a variety of ways that was not necessarily consistent with the specific guidance provided by teachers in the feedback. In Denmark, in a lower secondary school lesson, teachers used a "progression step" template and assigned students to specific levels of learning objectives achieved, provided justifications for these levels, and provided suggestions for what students should consider on their next assignments. The tool supported teachers in providing criteria for denoting what learning objectives were achieved, as well as some guidance in selecting the next steps for learning.

Technology

Another subset of studies has explored the ways in which technological tools have facilitated formative assessment. We group these studies into two broad categories: (1) those technologies that gather and aggregate student response information, often anonymously, and provide it to teachers so that they might take instructional action on the basis of that information, and (2) technologies that integrate some form of diagnosis, feedback, or intelligent tutoring.

The first category of studies examined how a wide range of technologies has allowed student responses or votes to be quickly collected by teachers. These technologies are often called student response systems or "clickers." Recent studies have explored the ways in which these technologies affect student learning (Ruiz-Primo et al., 2011), and how studies of how they influence student learning in higher education (e.g., Abrahamson, 2006) might extend to K-12 science classrooms.

For example, Beatty and Gerace (2009), and Beatty et al. (2008), have explored classroom response systems in a model they call "technology-enhanced formative assessment." This perspective emphasizes that the clickers alone are not a sufficient intervention to improve student learning. Rather, the clickers can be viewed as tools that mediate particular kinds of practices and participation structures that include motivating and focusing student learning with question-driven instruction, developing students' understanding and scientific fluency with dialogical discourse, informing and adjusting teaching and learning decisions through formative assessment, and helping students to develop meta-cognitive skills and to cooperate with each other. The authors articulate a cycle in which a question is posed to students, students wrestle with the question, either alone or in groups, students share their responses via the response system and the teacher displays the aggregated responses, and then the teacher elicits reasons and justifications for different types of responses from the whole class. Then, the teacher develops a student discussion of those justifications and reasons, supporting students' developing understanding, and then providing a summary and closure.

Some of these technologies are accessible through websites or smartphone apps (e.g., Socrativ or Mentimeter), or also desktop software (e.g., Group Scribbles, Chen & Looi, 2011). Shirley and colleagues (2011) found that although science teachers encountered initial challenges in learning to use these types of technologies, they were more likely to be successful when they were implemented with the support of school administrators and colleagues.

A second subset of studies builds technologies and systems that move beyond aggregating student responses and which move toward interactive systems that provide feedback for teachers and students in real-time to inform teaching and learning. Minstrell's DIAGNOSER software (Thissen-Roe, Hunt, & Minstrell, 2004) was built on his extensive prior studies (e.g., Minstrell, 2001) and has been followed by new systems which hybridize the aggregating of student response data described in the previous section along with his sets of "facets" and "facet clusters." These new systems provide teacher reports that give a diagnostic profile for students and classes, and also offer suggested feedback activities teachers might use to further support student learning (Minstrell, Anderson, & Li, 2016). In this approach, the technology has been built to take the extra step of diagnosing student thinking and then suggesting the next steps for the teacher.

However, given new algorithms and voice and text recognition through semantic frames, formative assessment technologies are also being developed as intelligent tutors that interactively collect responses from students, interpret response patterns, provide real-time feedback in text or writing, and adjust instruction accordingly (e.g., Koedinger, McLaughlin, & Heffernan, 2010). Ward et al. (2011) describe "My Science Tutor," a program for elementary level in which students interact in spoken dialogues with scaffolding to learn science concepts linked to lessons embedded in the Full Option Science System [FOSS]. A system architecture has been built whereby initial questions are asked of students, the system receives and interprets student responses, and then creates follow-up queries. The system asks aloud for elaboration, connections to other ideas, or explanation. A majority of students working with the system enjoyed it and were excited to learn about science. Teachers said they would recommend it to other teachers and wanted to use it with more of their students.

A new resource emerging in the past several years is the STEM Teaching Tools website (stemteachingtools.org), which provides multiple resources for practitioners to engage in formative assessment activity using research-based tools. In 2014, the University of Washington launched this website in an effort to "bridge that gap by offering STEM educators tools that leverage the best knowledge from both research and practice" (Bell & Wunderlich, 2014). The STEM Teaching Tools on designing three-dimensional assessment (tool #29), integrating science practices into tasks (tool #30), and prompts for integrating crosscutting concepts into assessment and instruction (tool #41) are frequently-downloaded resources for facilitating three-dimensional formative assessment task development (Penuel et al., 2018a).

Supporting Pre-Service Teacher Learning of Formative Assessment

Similar to the scholarship on science teacher learning about formative assessment, the literature on pre-service teacher learning focused on characteristics of the pre-service teachers and their formative assessment practice, the development of their formative assessment practices over the course of their education, or how particular tools supported their development of formative assessment activity. There is also research on how a focus on formative assessment can develop science teachers' content knowledge, especially with pre-service elementary teachers.

An important place to start when considering pre-service teachers' understanding of formative assessment is concerned with what their initial ideas are about formative assessment (Otero & Nathan, 2008). Not surprisingly, new teachers have little understanding of formative assessment prior to their education courses (Yaşar, 2017). Otero and Nathan (2008) invited pre-service teachers to view their students' early conceptions of formative assessment as a starting point. They categorized four patterns of pre-service teachers' views about their own students' prior conceptions, how teachers' views related to their formative assessment practices, and how their conceptions about student learning and their formative assessment practices grew over the course of their teacher education experience. The investigators noted that as teachers developed their understanding, they moved through a hybrid space where they began to elicit and recognize that students' experience-based conceptions were important resources for student learning.

The majority of the research on pre-service science teachers focused on the development of formative assessment practices over the course of their pre-service teacher education (Aydeniz & Dogan, 2016; Cartwright, 2012; Gotwals & Birmingham, 2016; Buck, Trauth-Nare, & Kaftan, 2010; Lyon, 2012; 2013; Weiland, Hudson, & Amador, 2014; Talanquer, Tomanek, & Novodvorsky, 2013). These studies highlight features of the education courses that engaged pre-service teachers with formative assessment and then measured the impact on their practice during internship through such methods as looking at classroom artifacts, like video (Gotwals & Birmingham, 2016), or at interviews of students (Weiland, Hudson, & Amador, 2014).

An emergent finding from this body of research is that formative assessment interventions in education courses help pre-service teachers notice and recognize variation in student ideas. All the same, teachers' feedback practices and how to move students forward based on what they observe remains challenging. For example, Buck, Trauth-Nare, and Kaftan (2010) redesigned their elementary science methods course to focus on student/teacher interaction in formative assessment. They found that while pre/post measures showed gains in understanding of student roles in formative assessment and connections to planning for instruction, the pre-service teachers found it difficult to use information elicited from embedded ongoing formative assessment to shift and inform their instructional practice.

Similarly, Aydeniz and Dogan (2016) noted that pre-service teachers could locate errors and mistakes in student thinking, but lacked strategies to elaborate on those mistakes and to think about how students' preconceptions might be productive starting points for student learning in science. The investigators also found that the majority of the instructional strategies pre-service teachers suggested did not attend to the particular conceptual issue that students were exhibiting. Rather, pre-service teachers suggested more general instructional strategies such as inquiry-based lessons, reading the book, or homework problems to move student thinking forward. Multiple studies showed that while pre-service teachers were able to develop their noticing and eliciting practices, they held naive conceptions about student ideas (Gotwals & Birmingham, 2016) or about formative assessments as strings of mini-summative assessments (Buck, Trauth-Nare, & Kaftan, 2010).

Not all interventions focused on the development of formative assessment practice. Some research has focused on formative assessment as a way to develop pre-service teachers' content knowledge in their education coursework (Brower, 2012; Sabel, Forbes, & Zangori, 2015). In a newly designed pre-service science course for elementary teachers, Sabel, Forbes, and Zangori (2015) focused on developing pre-service teachers' life science content knowledge through formative assessment practices. These investigators looked at the relationship between pre-service teachers' developing content knowledge and various formative assessment practices, which included eliciting and evaluating student thinking, and planning for next steps. They found that pre-service teachers' content understanding did develop over the course of the semester, along with their ability to elicit and anticipate student ideas in the content domain. However, there was no significant impact on pre-service teachers' ability to plan next steps, again a common theme among other research on pre-service teachers' formative assessment development.

There were few published studies of pre-service teacher learning focused on tool development in pre-service courses. An exception (Kang & Anderson, 2015) describes how pre-service teachers developed their formative assessment capacity through an iterative development and use of formative assessment tasks. They found that high-quality assessment tasks that provided students the space to share their ideas prompted the pre-service teachers to have more in-depth and nuanced reflections on student ideas. These investigators noted that pre-service teachers' epistemic framing of student learning related to the quality of the tasks that the teachers chose to use. The authors suggested that high-quality formative assessment tasks and opportunities to discuss student ideas supported the development of the teachers' formative assessment practices.

Lastly, an important and emerging focus is examining the ways in which pre-service candidates develop equitable teaching practices in the context of formative assessment (Lyon, 2012, 2013). Lyon (2012) developed a framework for science formative assessment consisting of three elements: constructing cohesive assessments to elicit student thinking, using the assessments to support student learning, and equitably assessing English Language Learners (CUE). In this framework, the formative assessments include not only eliciting and attending to students' science concept development but also their language development. In a case study of one pre-service physics teacher, Lyon (2013) found that the teacher's capacity to engage in equitable assessment practices lagged behind his understanding of the role of language in ELLs' learning. The pre-service teacher did develop and change his classroom practice to attend to ELLs' language needs but only focused on language needs in relation to the students' conceptual development. The teacher showed little attention to students' use of language in science more broadly, for example, their use of language to communicate effectively or using evidence in their explanations. Lyon (2013) suggests that focused attention on assessment activities, and time to practice and reflect on assessment activities with culturally and linguistically diverse students, might support pre-service teachers' development of more equitable teaching practices.

The research on pre-service science teacher learning of formative assessment demonstrates the ways in which teacher educators can support their development of this important classroom practice. A focus on formative assessment supports pre-service teachers to develop content understanding (Sabel, Forbes, & Zangori, 2015), to shift their beliefs about the role of student prior conceptions and everyday ideas (Kang & Anderson, 2015; Otero & Nathan, 2008), and to understand the role of language in student science learning (Lyon, 2013). Similar to in-service teachers, researchers have found that content-specific feedback and shifts to instructional next steps as a result of formative assessment are challenging for pre-service teachers (Buck, Trauth-Nare, & Kaftan, 2010; Gotwals & Birmingham, 2016).

Sensemaking of Student Ideas

A key area of research in formative assessment in the past 10 years has focused on the ways in which teachers make sense of student ideas. From this perspective, formative assessment is viewed as a fundamental process going beyond providing feedback to move learners forward in their thinking. Instead, from the sensemaking perspective, formative assessment is viewed as a process where teachers listen and attend to student ideas, not simply to compare those ideas to some standard, but to understand the nature, substance, and quality of student thinking.

This perspective is perhaps best exemplified by Coffey and colleagues' 2011 paper which noted that previous studies of formative assessment in science education had not attended to the *disciplinary substance* of student thinking in formative assessment but instead had focused on general formative assessment strategies and talk moves. Rather than foregrounding the general formative assessment strategies, Coffey and colleagues argued that formative assessment should have as its centerpiece attention to student disciplinary ideas, with teachers making sense of what students are trying to explain. They write, "Conceptualizing assessment as attention [to student ideas] . . . formative assessment should be understood and presented as nothing other than genuine engagement with [disciplinary] ideas, which includes being responsive to them and using them to inform next moves" (p. 1129). This perspective on formative assessment highlights the ways in which teachers listen to and make sense of the various ideas and lived experiences students bring to the classroom, and then, in turn, use those ideas to inform their classroom instruction.

This view of formative assessment is different from the perspectives held by some in the late 1980's and early 1990's that explicitly designed tasks around what were termed "misconceptions" and sought to elicit, confront and replace students' prior ideas with correct explanations (e.g. Posner et al., 1982; White & Gunstone, 1992). The language of misconceptions, which has been criticized because it reinforces a "get it or don't" perspective about students' scientific ideas (e.g., Otero & Nathan, 2008), has to a certain degree been replaced by conversations around students' lived experiences and everyday ideas. These terms help to reposition thinking about student ideas as beneficial to instruction in association with what they have learned outside of school, and not as separate from what they are learning in school. Furthermore, the sensemaking perspective on formative assessment foregrounds teachers' comprehending students' understanding, and students being held accountable for probing one another's understandings (Engle & Conant, 2002), using these multiple understandings as resources to inform instruction; in essence, the approach encourages asset-based perspectives, rather than deficit-based perspectives, on student thinking.

The example of Ms. Schafer above, in which the teacher doesn't end a line of inquiry with a student's use of the word "density," but rather probes with multiple questions before encouraging the student to leverage everyday ideas about thickness and to use examples of stacks of paper and stacks of bread, is an excellent illustration of this principle: by pausing to draw out students' ideas, by being genuinely curious about what students know and how they describe their understandings, we actually become more informed about what they know. A simple, parroted definition of *density as mass divided by volume* contains much less information than a description of the amount of stuff contained in an amount of space, or contrasting a stack of paper to a stack of bread that has holes in it.

A wide range of studies has examined sensemaking as it applies to teachers' ability to conduct formative assessment in science classrooms. Many of these studies have focused on the vital role that teachers' knowledge, writ broadly, plays in their ability to listen to and interpret students' ideas in this manner. For example, Herman and colleagues (2015) examined the quality and relationship of elementary teachers' science pedagogical knowledge and assessment practice, and found that teachers' formative assessment practices were positively related to student learning, despite overall weaknesses in teachers' pedagogical and formative assessment knowledge. Sadler and colleagues (2013), in a large study of middle school physical science teachers, found that teachers' ability to identify the most commonly selected incorrect answer on multiple-choice items – which Sadler and colleagues called misconceptions – was positively related to students' learning gains.

A separate set of studies has examined, from a sociocultural perspective, how teachers draw on students' lived experiences and discourses and leverage these as resources or "funds of knowledge" for students' science learning (e.g., Stears & Gopal, 2010; Calabrese Barton & Tan, 2010; Rivet & Krajcik, 2008). In fact, some have argued, in the era of the NGSS in the US, that constructing tasks with students' lived experiences in mind is a fundamental principle that should underlie all formative assessment tasks (Mislevy & Durán, 2014). Although these studies are not always necessarily labeled as "formative assessment," we recognize them in this section as they do attend to the ways in which teachers listen and attend to student ideas and draw upon them to inform instruction. Discursive practices are used to co-construct meaning in these assessment settings (Reis & Barwell, 2013). Through talk formats, including pastiche, or collecting and compiling multiple representations for consideration by others (as an example, the stacks of paper, bread, mud, and water could all be considered a pastiche for thinking about density), teachers may help to assemble ways of representing student thinking that make the ideas more understandable not only to the teacher, but also to other students, a fundamentally important process in formative assessment (Olander & Ingerman, 2011; Renshaw & Brown, 2007; Sharma, 2008).

Power, Culture, and Identity

The preceding articles that emphasize the ways in which teachers listen and attend to student ideas through processes of sensemaking are part of a larger push in education to not only bring students' lived experiences (Warren et al., 2001) and funds of knowledge (Moll et al., 1992) into the science classroom, but to leverage these experiences as essential elements for supporting students' science learning. As the studies above show, the complex linguistic realities of multilingual students suggest that if we limit students to speaking only the dominant language, and to using only scientific terms to describe what they are learning, we are unlikely to reveal the true depths of what they know (De Backer, Van Avermaet, & Slembrouck, 2017).

Critical perspectives on science learning take this argument further and emphasize that the discourses learned in science education classrooms privilege predominantly White, western ways of knowing in science and thus bring students to understand these viewpoints asymmetrically with their own cultural backgrounds and identities. Instead, the critical perspective posits that science education has the potential to change what is valued as science in school settings (Philip & Azevedo, 2017), as well as to encourage students to use scientific practices to challenge and problematize societal systems and structures (Calabrese Barton, 1998). Classroom communities that use task structures to draw out student ideas and engage in formative assessment practices such as discipline-specific discourse moves have the potential to afford greater participation and equity for students as they learn and engage in science (Morrison, 2015).

A key argument from this perspective is to create science learning environments in which students simultaneously have access to scaffolds to reach full participation in science, while also leveraging and responding to their own lived experiences relevant to their cultures and home languages. This perspective goes beyond defining equity as an increase in achievement, arguing that the language of "achievement gap" frames students as having certain deficits they need to overcome (Carlone, Haun-Frank, & Webb, 2011). A small subset of articles in our literature review have explored the ways in which formative assessment tools and practices broaden the participation of students from historically marginalized populations in science learning, measuring outcomes that extend beyond science conceptual learning and engagement in practices, such as affective outcomes like motivation, identity development, and empowerment. As Cowie, Jones, and Otrel-Cass (2011) emphasize, assessments have the potential to make a powerful contribution to students' science identities.

Brown (2008) conducted an ethnography of a high school biology classroom and connected formative assessment to "teachable moments" as follows:

> Teachable moments are occasions that arise as teachers use formative assessment to identify students' understanding of phenomena. These moments are fruitful for instruction because they provide opportunities for teachers to build instruction on students' cultural understandings and pre-existing knowledge. In many cases, teachable moments occur as students are made aware of discrepancies in their understanding or come to understand the intrinsic value of the ideas involved in classroom discussion. These connections to what students know and how students see themselves provide opportunities for identity construction that is commensurate with learning science.
>
> *(p. 2119)*

Brown emphasized that using formative assessment as a lens helps to foreground that these teachable moments can be built into the course of classroom instruction, rather than arising serendipitously. In a year-long study, Brown examined the ways in which these moments of formative assessment helped a teacher to create space for classroom discourse around students' conceptual understandings of phenomena presented in class. Furthermore, Brown identified the ways in which, through orchestrating classroom discourse in these moments of formative assessment, the teacher was able to support students' thinking across their use of scientific discourse, their epistemic positions, and their conceptual understandings as they gained access to and facility with multiple forms of testing, such as analyzing charts and graphs, using multiple-choice items, and reading and interpreting problems.

For example, Stears and Gopal (2010) used student interactive assessments designed to honor the ways in which individual learners construct reality in South African classrooms. They found that levels of participation were high when learners were able to demonstrate their practical knowledge.

Donnelly, McGarr, and O'Reilly (2014) studied the ways in which inquiry-based science education interacted with power structures in two Irish science classrooms, performing an analysis of the discourses in which teachers and students engaged during inquiry-based activities (that included, from our framing, formative assessment practices). The authors found that there was a focus on "doing" versus "understanding" and that there was a culture of "monitoring and surveillance" as students engaged in inquiry-based learning, suggesting that the framing or launch (Kang et al., 2016) of these activities was essential to reposition the roles and routines in which students were engaging. These findings of surveillance culture in inquiry-based settings runs counter to the culture of trust that has been shown to be an essential element of effective formative assessment settings (Cowie, Jones, & Otrel-Cass, 2011). The study related to other arguments as to whose voices have power and authority in classrooms (Michaels et al., 2010), themes explored in science education research that addresses the extent to which students from marginalized backgrounds are assigned and/or afforded epistemic agency to co/construct their own understandings in these kinds of learning environments (Keifert et al., 2018; Krist & Suárez, 2018).

The take-away from a formative assessment perspective in the context of science education is that, from the point of view of power, culture, and identity, students and their ideas need to be repositioned (e.g., Engle & Conant, 2002). This does not mean that teachers surrender all of their agency; Trauth-Nare (2012) found that multiple positional identities were claimed, assigned, and negotiated by a middle school science teacher and her students when engaging in formative assessment. While the teacher positioned herself as an authority during these interactions, students were also able to influence the direction of the formative assessment activities in which they engaged, suggesting the active and negotiated participation of both teacher and students in formative assessment.

Summary

Our review of recent studies of formative assessment in science education has revealed an uneven emphasis on areas of research when mapped onto the framework of participants, practices, and tools. In the following sections, we summarize across the different areas that emerged in the literature review, and also identify persistent questions and continuing conversations in each area of research.

Tools

Our review of the literature illustrates that, by and large, research on formative assessment remains focused on the design and use of formative assessment tools. Clearly, the research on curriculum-embedded tasks foregrounds tools, as does the research on learning progressions and other resources to support classroom enactment of formative assessment. A sociocultural perspective on formative assessment broadens the focus on tools to include the ways those tools mediate the ways that participants engage in certain sets of practices. If we view formative assessment tools as objects that have flexible meanings across contexts – that is, as they travel, they are subject to differential interpretations by the teachers who implement them, as the research clearly indicates – then these tools may be viewed, from a sociocultural perspective, as boundary objects (Star, 2010; Star & Griesemer, 1989). The potential issue with tools as the primary carriers of meaning in the dissemination of formative assessment as a reform to improve the quality of classroom teaching and learning, then, follows directly from this framing: tools viewed in isolation will not retain their intended function as they move from one context to another.

Practices

Clearly, formative assessment practices are also subject to local interpretation, and various frameworks identified in this review illustrate the wide variations in classroom practice observed by teachers enacting formative assessment in a range of classroom contexts. We identified separate strands of research that focused on formative assessment practices. Research in some instances has been able to disaggregate formative assessment practices from tools, as we saw in the Furtak et al. (2008) and Hondrich et al. (2016) implementation studies, as well as the Kang et al. (2016) study, lending empirical weight to the disaggregation of formative assessment and tools. Teacher education programs and professional development approaches alike focus on the development of teacher practices to support classroom enactment of formative assessment. In addition, the more recent emphasis on sensemaking of student ideas – the resources perspective – rather than confront-and-replace approaches to student ideas in the misconceptions literature, places a strong emphasis on teachers' ability to use classroom discursive moves, routines, and organization structures to support formative assessment in the classroom.

Participants

The majority of studies included a focus on the student and the teacher, although to differing degrees. Many studies focused more on the teacher and student, and few studies involved explorations of self- and peer- assessment. Studies on sensemaking, as well as power, identity, and culture explicitly attend to who the students are, their lived histories, and their ideas in the context of science. In addition, studies attended to the multiple ways that students' ideas may be leveraged as resources to help them learn science. Our framework helps us to identify the ways in which the interactions of participants could be structured by tools in professional learning contexts to make students' thinking explicit, and in turn to structure the feedback provided between teachers and students.

Future Research Directions: Toward an Emphasis on Equity in Science Learning Through Formative Assessment

We conclude our review by asserting that future research on formative assessment in science would be strengthened by explicit attention to equity. In making this argument, we reference Rodriguez's (2016) definition:

> *Equity* refers to the enactment of specific policies and practices that ensure equitable access and opportunities for success for everyone . . . in order to be equitable, we cannot treat everyone the same. To be equitable, we must treat individuals according to their needs and provide multiple opportunities for success.
>
> *(p. 243)*

The majority of studies reviewed in this chapter do not address equity; this fact applies not only to science education, but to research on formative assessment more broadly (Penuel & Shepard, 2016). An example of a study that did noticeably attend to issues of equity was that of Kang et al. (2016). As mentioned above, the researchers made themselves aware of the variations in lived experiences of the students with which they were engaged. They then leveraged this knowledge to design a formative assessment tool which drew upon those lived experiences (varied national origins or connections to other countries). In doing so, the researchers invited in students who may have otherwise lacked opportunities to connect with the science learning content: they engaged the students by bridging their personal and academic lives. This type of attention to the micro aspects of students' interests and identities as they participate in school-based learning is critical to ensuring "equitable access and opportunities," centering participants' lived experiences in the activity of formative assessment tool use within the science classroom.

We argue that future research should consider the largely unrealized potential of formative assessment to broaden participation in science learning through consideration of sociocultural lenses on research. Those lenses center differences in participants' experiences as they pertain to formative assessment tool design and use, and practices engaged in the classroom. In this way, and similar to Mislevy and Durán (2014), we argue that formative assessment tools, practices, and participation structures should be constructed in ways that learners – in particular, those who have been historically marginalized in science – can meaningfully engage and benefit from them, not in ways that will further maintain or magnify existing inequities in science classrooms.

We also note that the studies that have taken an explicit lens focusing on culture, equity, and power in science formative assessment open up many possibilities in terms of future research questions. For example, how can professional development programs be designed to support teachers who often come from dominant communities to value and attend to the ideas their students bring, and to navigate and negotiate the complex discursive spaces in which those ideas are developed through feedback? What kinds of tools and resources best support those practices? How can students be viewed as integral participants in the formative assessment process, being assigned greater agency in their own learning progresses?

More broadly, and maintaining this focus on equity, we also note several other themes that have emerged from this review. For example, several frameworks granularize teachers' formative assessment practices, while others capture a broad-strokes summary of these approaches. Which perspectives have greater benefits for teacher learning of formative assessment? Some interventions focus on building teacher disciplinary knowledge, while others foreground attention to student thinking. What is the intersection of these two perspectives, how do they mutually interact and support each other, and how can the field come to the perspective that, as we learn to better listen to and understand student thinking, we open up fruitful avenues to problematize and build the knowledge teachers need to navigate unstructured classroom learning environments?

Many studies point to the importance of teachers working within larger systems that support their learning, innovation, and access to professional learning opportunities and resources. Future studies can also examine how organizational supports around systems of assessment in districts and states play out in terms of equity for educators, such as vertical coherence of equity within systems of assessment (Heredia, 2015). For example, the ACESSE project – a research-practice partnership between the Council of State Science Supervisors (CSSS), the University of Colorado at Boulder and the University of Washington at Seattle – began a coordinated effort in 2016 to research the equity and coherence of state science education systems with respect to the implementation of the new *Framework* vision of science education (CSSS, 2016; Penuel et. al., 2018b). A central lever within this project is the use of formative assessment development to support teacher learning and implementation of the *Framework* vision. Tools being developed from the ACESSE project include resources to help educators consider both the defined three dimensions of science learning outlined in Chapter 2 of the *Framework* as well as dimensions of equity outlined in Chapter 11 of the *Framework* (Board on Science Education [BOSE], 2012). The ACESSE resources operate as tools that can move from national meetings into state and local professional development settings and back again through the involvement of state science educators who act as brokers across diverse boundaries within the state educational system (Honig, 2006; Wenger, 1998). These partnerships are well-positioned to maximize the potential of formative assessment to engage students in science learning as they focus on multiple participants in the formative assessment process, integrate tools and resources to support teacher learning, and attend to the development of formative assessment practices in the service of equity.

References

Abrahamson, L.A. (2006). A brief history of networked classrooms: Effects, cases, pedagogy, and implications. In Banks, D.A. (Ed.), *Audience response systems in higher education: Applications and cases, pp 1–25.* Hershey, PA: Idea Group Inc.

Ainsworth, L. & Viegut, D. (2006). *Common formative assessments: How to connect standards-based instruction and assessment.* Thousand Oaks, CA: Corwin Press.

Alonzo, A. C. & Gotwals, A. W. (2012). *Learning progressions in science.* A. C. Alonzo & A. W. Gotwals (Eds.). Rotterdam, The Netherlands: Sense Publishing.

Ateh, C. M. (2015). Science teachers' elicitation practices: Insights for formative assessment. *Educational Assessment, 20*(2), 112–131.

Atkin, J. M., Coffey, J. E., Moorthy, S., Sato, M., & Thibeault, M. (2005). *Designing Everyday Assessment in the Science Classroom.* New York, NY: Teachers College Press.

Avramides, K., Hunter, J., Oliver, M., & Luckin, R. (2015). A method for teacher inquiry in cross-curricular projects: Lessons from a case study. *British Journal of Educational Technology, 46*(2), 249–264.

Ayala, C. C., Shavelson, R. J., Araceli Ruiz-Primo, M., Brandon, P. R., Yin, Y., Furtak, E. M., Young, D. B., Tomita, M. K. (2008). From formal embedded assessments to reflective lessons: The development of formative assessment studies. *Applied Measurement in Education, 21*(4), 315–334.

Aydeniz, M. & Dogan, A. (2016). Exploring pre-service science teachers' pedagogical capacity for formative assessment through analyses of student answers. *Research in Science & Technological Education, 34*(2), 125–141.

Beatty, I.D., Feldman, A., Leonard, W.J., Gerace, W.J., St Cyr, K., Lee, H., & Harris, R. (2008). Teacher learning of technology-enhanced formative assessment. Paper Presented at the Annual Conference of the National Association for Research in Science Teaching, Baltimore, MD.

Beatty, I. D. & Gerace, W. J. (2009). Technology-enhanced formative assessment: A research-based pedagogy for teaching science with classroom response technology. *Educational Technology, 18*(2) 146–162.

Bell, B. & Cowie, B. (2001). *Formative Assessment and Science Education.* Dordrecht, Netherlands: Kluwer Academic Publishers.

Bell, P. & Wunderlich, D. (2014). New website offers tools for improved STEM teaching. Oct 20 2014. Retrieved from https://education.uw.edu/news/new-website-offers-tools-improved-stem-teaching.

Bennett, R. E. (2011). Formative assessment: A critical review. *Assessment in Education: Principles, Policy and Practice, 18*, 5–25.

Black, P. & Wiliam, D. (1998). Assessment and classroom learning. *Assessment in Education: Principles, Policy & Practice, 5*(1), 7–74.

Black, P. & Wiliam, D. (2009). Developing the theory of formative assessment. *Educational Assessment, Evaluation and Accountability, 21*, 5–31.

Board on Science Education. (2012). *A Framework for K-12 Science Education: Practices, Crosscutting Concepts, and Core Ideas.* Washington DC: National Academies Press.

Box, C., Skoog, G., & Dabbs, J. M. (2015). A case study of teacher personal practice assessment theories and complexities of implementing formative assessment. *American Educational Research Journal, 52*(5), 956–983.

Brandon, P., Young, D. B., Shavelson, R. J., Jones, R., Ayala, C. C., Ruiz-Primo, M. A., Furtak, E. M. (2008). Lessons learned from the process of curriculum developers' and assessment developers' collaboration on the development of embedded formative assessments. *Applied Measurement in Education, 21*(4), 390–402.

Brower, D. J. (2012). *Incorporating formative assessment and science content into elementary science methods: a case study.* Doctoral dissertation, Montana State University-Bozeman, College of Education, Health & Human Development.

Brown, B. A. (2008). Assessment and academic identity : Using embedded assessment as an instrument for academic socialization in science education. *Teachers College Record, 110*(10), 2116–2147.

Bryk, A. S., Gomez, L. M., Grunow, A., & LeMahieu, P. G. (2015). *Learning to Improve: How America's Schools Can Get Better at Getting Better.* Cambridge, MA: Harvard University Press.

Buck, G. A. & Trauth-Nare, A. E. (2009). Preparing teachers to make the formative assessment process integral to science teaching and learning. *Journal of Science Teacher Education, 20*(5), 475–494.

Buck, G. A., Trauth-Nare, A., & Kaftan, J. (2010). Making formative assessment discernable to pre-service teachers of science. *Journal of Research in Science Teaching, 47*(4), 402–421.

Butler, R. (1987). Task-involving and ego-involving properties of evaluation: Effects of different feedback conditions on motivational perceptions, interest, and per- formance. *Journal of Educational Psychology, 79*(4), 474–482.

Calabrese Barton, A. (1998). Reframing "Science for all" through the politics of poverty. *Educational Policy, 12*(5), 525–541.

Calabrese Barton, A. & Tan, E. (2010). Journal of the learning we be burnin'! Agency, identity, and science learning. *Journal of the Learning Sciences*, (January 2012), 37–41.

Carlone, H. B., Haun-Frank, J., & Webb, A. (2011). Assessing equity beyond knowledge- and skills-based outcomes: A comparative ethnography of two fourth-grade reform-based science classrooms. *Journal of Research in Science Teaching*, *48*(5), 459–485.

Cartwright, T. J. (2012). Science talk: Preservice teachers facilitating science learning in diverse afterschool environments. *School Science and Mathematics*, *112*(6), 384–391.

Cazden, C. B. (2001). *Classroom discourse: The language of teaching and learning*. Portsmouth, NH: Heinemann.

Chen, W. & Looi, C. K. (2011). Active classroom participation in a Group Scribbles primary science classroom. *British Journal of Educational Technology*, *42*(4), 676–686.

Coffey, J. (2003). Involving Students in Assessment. In J. M. Atkin & J.E.Coffey (Eds.), *Everyday assessment in the science classroom* (pp. 75–87). NSTA Press: Arlington, VA.

Coffey, J. E., Hammer, D., Levin, D. M., & Grant, T. (2011). The missing disciplinary substance of formative assessment. *Journal of Research in Science Teaching*, *48*(10), 1109–1136.

Cole, M. (1996). *Cultural psychology: A once and future discipline*. Cambridge, MA: Belknap.

Colorado Parks and Wildlife. (n.d.). Red Foxes. Retrieved from https://cpw.state.co.us/fox [Accessed March 6, 2019].

Corcoran, T., Mosher, F. A., & Rogat, A. (2009). Learning Progressions in Science: An Evidence-Based Approach to Reform. Philadelphia, PA: Consortium for Policy Research in Education.

Council of State Science Supervisors (CSSS). (2016). Advancing coherent and equitable systems of science education (ACESSE). Retrieved from http://cosss.org/ACESSE.

Cowie, B. & Bell, B. (1999). A Model of Formative Assessment in Science Education. *Assessment in Education: Principles, Policy & Practice*, *6*(1), 101–116.

Cowie, B., Jones, A., & Otrel-Cass, K. (2011). Re-engaging students in science: Issues of assessment, funds of knowledge and sites for learning. *International Journal of Science and Mathematics Education*, *9*(2), 347–366. DOI: .1007/s10763-010-9229-0.

De Backer, F., Van Avermaet, P., & Slembrouck, S. (2017). Schools as laboratories for exploring multilingual assessment policies and practices. *Language and Education*, *31*(3), 217–230.

Donnelly, D. F., McGarr, O., & O'Reilly, J. (2014). "Just Be Quiet and Listen to Exactly What He's Saying": Conceptualising power relations in inquiry-oriented classrooms. *International Journal of Science Education*, *36*(12), 2029–2054.

Draney, K. & Wilson, M. (1997, July). Mapping student progress with embedded assessments: The challenge of making evaluation meaningful. Paper presented at the National Evaluation Institute Workshop, Indianapolis, IN.

Duschl, R. A. (2003). Assessment of inquiry. In J. M. Atkin and J. Coffey (Eds.), *Everyday assessment in the science classroom* (Chapter 4, pp. 41–60). Arlington, VA: NSTA Press.

Duschl, R. A. (2008). Science education in three-part harmony: Balancing conceptual, epistemic, and social learning Goals. *Review of Research in Education*, *32*(1), 268–291.

Duschl, R. A. & Gitomer, D. H. (1997). Strategies and challenges to changing the focus of assessment and instruction in science classrooms. *Educational Assessment*, *4*(1), 37–73. DOI: 10.1207/s15326977ea0401.

Edwards, F. C. E. & Edwards, R. J. (2017). A story of culture and teaching: the complexity of teacher identity formation. *The Curriculum Journal*, *28*(2), 190–211.

Engle, R. A. & Conant, F. R. (2002). Guiding principles for fostering productive disciplinary engagement: Explaining an emergent argument in a community of learners classroom. *Cognition and Instruction*, *20*(4), 399–483.

Evans, E. M., Spiegel, A. N., Gram, W., Frazier, B. N., Tare, M., Thompson, S., & Diamond, J. (2010). A conceptual guide to natural history museum visitors' understanding of evolution. *Journal of Research in Science Teaching*, *47*(3), 326–353.

Falk, A. (2012). Teachers learning from professional development in elementary science: Reciprocal relations between formative assessment and pedagogical content knowledge. *Science Education*, *96*(2), 265–290.

Forbes, C. T., Sabel, J. L., & Biggers, M. (2015). Elementary teachers' use of formative assessment to support students' learning about interactions between the hydrosphere and geosphere. *Journal of Geoscience Education*, *63*(3), 210–221.

Ford, M. J. & Forman, E. A. (2006). Redefining disciplinary learning in classroom contexts. *Review of Research in Education*, *30*(1), 1–32.

Furtak, E. M. & Ruiz-Primo, M. A. (2008). Making students' thinking explicit in writing and discussion: An analysis of formative assessment prompts. *Science Education*, *92*, 799–824.

Furtak, E. M., Ruiz-Primo, M. A., Shemwell, J. T., Ayala, C. C., Brandon, P. R., Shavelson, R. J., & Yin, Y. (2008). On the fidelity of implementing embedded formative assessments and its relation to student learning. *Applied Measurement in Education*, *21*(4), 360–389.

Furtak, E. M. (2012). Linking a learning progression for natural selection to teachers' enactment of formative assessment. *Journal of Research in Science Teaching, 49*(9), 1181–1210. DOI: 10.1002/tea.21054.

Furtak, E. M., Kiemer, K., Circi, R. K., Swanson, R., de León, V., Morrison, D., & Heredia, S. C. (2016). Teachers' formative assessment abilities and their relationship to student learning: findings from a four-year intervention study. *Instructional Science, 44*(3), 267–291.

Furtak, E. M. & Heredia, S. (2014). Exploring the influence of learning progressions in two teacher communities. *Journal of Research in Science Teaching, 51*(8), 982–1020.

Furtak, E. M., Morrison, D. L., & Kroog, H. (2014). Investigating the link between learning progressions and classroom assessment. *Science Education, 98*, 640–673.

Furtak, E.M. (2018). *Supporting Teachers' Formative Assessment Practice with Learning Progressions*. New York, NY: Routledge.

Gotwals, A. W., Philhower, J., Cisterna, D., & Bennett, S. (2015). Using video to examine formative assessment practices as measures of expertise for mathematics and science teachers. *International Journal of Science and Mathematics Education, 13*(2), 405–423.

Gotwals, A. W. & Birmingham, D. (2016). Eliciting, identifying, interpreting, and responding to students' ideas: Teacher candidates' growth in formative assessment practices. *Research in Science Education, 46*(3), 365–388.

Gotwals, A. W. (2018). Applied measurement in education where are we now ? Learning progressions and formative assessment. *Applied Measurement in Education, 31*(2), 157–164.

Greeno, J. G. (2006). Learning in Activity. In R. K. Sawyer (Ed.), *The Cambridge Handbook of the Learning Sciences* (pp. 79–96). Cambridge: Cambridge University Press.

Grossman, P. L., Smagorinsky, P., & Valencia, S. (1999). Tools for teaching English : A theoretical framework for research on learning to teach. *American Journal of Education, 108*(1), 1–29.

Harrison, C. (2014). Assessment of inquiry skills in the SAILS project. *Science Education International, 25*(1), 112–122.

Heredia, S.C. (2015). *Dilemmas of Reform: Science Teachers' Collective Sensemaking of Formative Assessment Practices*. University of Colorado BO, Unpublished doctoral dissertation.

Heritage, M., Kim, J., Vendlinski, T., & Herman, J. (2009). From evidence to action: A seamless process in formative assessment? *Educational Measurement: Issues and Practice, 28*(3), 24–31.

Herman, J., Osmundson, E., Dai, Y., Ringstaff, C., & Timms, M. (2015). Investigating the dynamics of formative assessment: relationships between teacher knowledge, assessment practice and learning. *Assessment in Education: Principles, Policy & Practice, 22*(3), 344–367. DOI: 10.1080/0969594X.2015.1006521.

Holmeier, M., Grob, R., Nielsen, J. A., Rönnebeck, S., & Ropohl, M. (2018). Written teacher feedback: Aspects of quality, benefits and challenges. In *Transforming Assessment: Contributions from Science Education Research* (Vol. 4, pp. 175–208). Dordrecht, the Netherlands: Springer International Publishing. DOI: 10.1007/978-3-319-63248-3.

Hondrich, A. L., Hertel, S., Adl-Amini, K., & Klieme, E. (2016). Implementing curriculum-embedded formative assessment in primary school science classrooms. *Assessment in Education: Principles, Policy & Practice, 23*(3), 353–376.

Honig, M. I. (2006). Street-level bureaucracy revisited: Frontline district central-office administrators as boundary spanners in education policy implementation. *Educational Evaluation and Policy Analysis, 28*(4), 357–383.

Jin, H., Johnson, M. E., Shin, H. J., & Anderson, C. W. (2017). Promoting student progressions in science classrooms: A video study. *Journal of Research in Science Teaching, 54*(7), 852–883.

Kang, H., Thompson, J., & Windschitl, M. (2014). Creating opportunities for students to show what they know: The role of scaffolding in assessment tasks. *Science Education, 98*(4), 674–704.

Kang, H. & Anderson, C. W. (2015). Supporting preservice science teachers' ability to attend and respond to student thinking by design. *Science Education, 99*(5), 863–895.

Kang, H., Windschitl, M., Stroupe, D., & Thompson, J. (2016). Designing, launching, and implementing high quality learning opportunities for students that advance scientific thinking. *Journal of Research in Science Teaching, 53*(9), 1316–1340.

Kazemi, E. & Hubbard, A. (2008). New directions for the design and study of professional development: Attending to the coevolution of teachers' participation across contexts. *Journal of Teacher Education, 59*(5), 428–441.

Keeley, P. (2005). *Uncovering student ideas in science, Volume 1: 25 Formative Assessment Probes*. Arlington, VA: National Science Teachers' Association Press.

Keeley, P., Eberle, F., & Farrin, L. (2005a). *Assessment probes: Uncovering students' ideas in science*. Arlington, VA: NSTA Press.

Keeley, P., Eberle, F., & Farrin, L. (2005b). Formative assessment probes. *Science Scope*, (January), 18–21.

Keifert, D., Krist, C., Phillips, A. M., & Scipio, D. A. (2018). Epistemic agency as a members' experience. Proceedings of the 13th International Conference of the Learning Sciences, June 23–27, 2018, London.

Krajcik, J., McNeill, K.L. and Reiser, B. (2008). Learning-goals-driven design model: Curriculum materials that align with national standards and incorporate project-based pedagogy. *Science Education, 92*(1), 1–32.

Krist, C. & Suárez, E. (2018). Doing science with fidelity to persons: Instantiations of caring participation in science practices. Proceedings of the 13th International Conference of the Learning Sciences, June 23–27, 2018. London.

Koedinger, K. R., McLaughlin, E. A., & Heffernan, N. T. (2010). A Quasi-experimental evaluation of an on-line formative assessment and tutoring system. *Journal of Educational Computing Research, 43*(4), 489–510.

Lave, J. & Wenger, E. (1991). *Situated Learning: Legitimate Peripheral Participation.* Cambridge: University of Cambridge Press.

Lemke, J. L. (1990). *Talking Science: Language, Learning, and Values.* Norwood, N.J.: Ablex Publishing Corporation.

Li, M., Ruiz-Primo, M. A., & Shavelson, R. J. (2006). Towards a science achievement framework: The case of TIMSS-R study. In T. Plomp & S. Howie (Eds.), *Contexts of learning mathematics and science: Lessons learned from TIMSS* (pp. 291–312). New York, NY: Routledge.

Lyon, E. G. (2012). *Unraveling the complex: Changes in secondary science preservice teachers' assessment expertise.* Unpublished doctoral dissertation, University of California, Santa Cruz.

Lyon, E. G. (2013). "Assessment as Discourse": A pre-service physics teacher's evolving capacity to support an equitable pedagogy. *Education Sciences, 3*(3), 279–299.

McNeill, K. L., Lizotte, D. J., Krajcik, J., & Marx, R. W. (2006). Supporting Students' Construction of Scientific Explanations by Fading Scaffolds in Instructional Materials. *The Journal of the Learning Sciences, 15*(2), 153–191.

Merrill, M.L. (2013). The nature of third grade students' experiences with concept maps to support learning of science concepts. Concept Maps: Theory, Methodology, Technology Proc. of the Fifth Int. Conference on Concept Mapping, Valletta, Malta, 2012.

Michaels, S. & O'Connor, C. (2012). *Talk science primer.* Cambridge, MA: TERC. Retrieved from https://inquiryproject.terc.edu/shared/pd/TalkScience_Primer.pdf

Michaels, S., O'Connor, M. C., Hall, M. W., & Resnick, L. B. (2010). *Accountable talk sourcebook.* Pittsburg, PA: Institute for Learning University of Pittsburgh.

Minstrell, J. (2001). Facets of students' thinking: designing to cross the gap from research to standards-based practice. In *Designing for science: Implications from everyday, classroom, and professional settings.* Mahwah, NJ: Lawrence Erlbaum Associates.

Minstrell, J., Anderson, R., & Li, M. (2016). Diagnostic instruction: Toward an integrated system for classroom assessment. In R. A. Duschl & A. S. Bismack (Eds.), *Reconceptualizing STEM education: The central role of practices* (pp. 49–67). New York: Routledge.

Mislevy, R. J. & Durán, R. P. (2014). A sociocognitive perspective on assessing EL students in the age of common core and next generation science standards. *TESOL Quarterly, 48*(3), 560–585.

Moll, L., Amanti, C., Neff, C. & Gonzalez, N. (1992). Funds of knowledge for teaching: Using a qualitative approach to connect homes and classrooms. *Theory into Practice, 31*(2), 132–41.

Morrison, D. (2015). *Formative assessment and equity: An exploration of opportunities for eliciting, recognizing, and responding within science classroom conversations.* School of Education Graduate Theses & Dissertations. Proquest published doctoral dissertation. Retrieved from https://scholar.colorado.edu/educ_gradetds/54.

National Research Council. (1996). *National science education standards.* Washington, DC: National Academies Press.

National Research Council. (2001). *Classroom assessment and the national science education standards.* Washington, DC: National Academies Press.

National Research Council. (2007). *Taking science to school: Learning and teaching science in Grades K-8.* Washington, DC: National Academies Press.

National Research Council. (2014). *Developing Assessments for the next generation science standards.* Washington DC: National Academies Press.

National Research Council. (2017). *Seeing students learn science: Integrating assessment and instruction in the classroom.* Washington, DC: National Academies Press.

Neumann, K., Viering, T., Boone, W. J., & Fischer, H. E. (2013). Towards a learning progression of energy. *Journal of Research in Science Teaching, 50*(2), 162–188.

O'Connor, M. C. & Michaels, S. (1993). Aligning academic task and participation status through revoicing: Analysis of a classroom discourse strategy. *Anthropology and Education Quarterly, 24*(4), 318–335.

OECD. (2017). *PISA assessment and analytical framework: Science, reading, mathematics, financial literacy and problem solving.* Paris: OECD Publishing.

Olander, C. & Ingerman, Å. (2011). Towards an inter-language of talking science: Exploring students' argumentation in relation to authentic language. *Journal of Biological Education, 45*(3), 158–164.

Otero, V. K. & Nathan, M. J. (2008). Preservice elementary teachers' views of their students' prior knowledge of science. *Journal of Research in Science Teaching, 45*(4), 497–523.

Palma, C., Plummer, J., Ghent, C., Gleason, T., Ong, Y. S., & McDonald, S. (2015). Have astronauts visited Neptune? Student ideas about how astronomers study the solar system. *National Association of Research on Science Teaching, 4*(1), 63–74.

Panizzon, D. & Pegg, J. (2008). Assessment practices: Empowering mathematics and science teachers in rural secondary schools to enhance student learning. *International Journal of Science and Mathematics Education, 6*, 417–436.

Pellegrino, J. W., Chudowsky, N., & Glaser, R. (2001). *Knowing what students know: the science and design of educational assessment*. Washington DC: National Academies Press.

Penuel, W.R., Reiser, B., Novak, M., McGill, T., Frumin, K., van Horne, K., Sumner, T. & Watkins, D.A. (2018a). Using co-design to test and refine a model for three-dimensional science curriculum. Paper presented at the Annual Meeting of the American Educational Research Association, New York, NY.

Penuel, W. R., Bell, P., Pierre, S. D., Hopkins, M., & Farrell, C. C. (2018b). building a networked improvement community to promote equitable, coherent systems of science education: How a state-level team can support district-level change efforts. Editorial Review Board, 2018, 30.

Penuel, W. R. & Shepard, L. A. (2016). Social models of learning and assessment. In A. A. Rupp and J. P. Leighton (Eds), *The Wiley handbook of cognition and assessment: Frameworks, methodologies, and applications* (Chapter 7, pp.146–173). Chichester, UK: John Wiley & Sons.

Philip, T. M. & Azevedo, F. S. (2017). Everyday science learning and equity: Mapping the contested terrain. *Science Education, 101*(4), 526–532.

Posner, G., Strike, K. A., Hewson, P., & Gertzog, W. (1982). Accommodation of a scientific conception: Toward a theory of conceptual change. *Science Education, 66*(2), 211–227.

Pottenger, F. M. & Young, D. B. (1992). *The local environment teacher's guide* (2nd Edition). Honolulu: Curriculum Research and Development Group.

Reis, G. & Barwell, R. (2013). the interactional accomplishment of not knowing in elementary school science and mathematics: Implications for classroom performance assessment practices. *International Journal of Science and Mathematics Education, 11*(5), 1067–1085.

Renshaw, P. & Brown, R. A. J. (2007). Formats of classroom talk for integrating everyday and scientific discourse: Replacement, interweaving, contextual privileging and pastiche. *Language and Education, 21*(6), 531–549.

Rivet, A. E. & Krajcik, J. S. (2008). Contextualizing instruction: Leveraging students' prior knowledge and experiences to foster understanding of middle school science. *Journal of Research in Science Teaching, 45*(1), 79–100.

Rodriguez, A. J. (2016). For whom do we do equity and social justice work? Recasting the discourse about the Other to effect transformative change. In N. M. Joseph, C. Haynes, and F. Cobb (Eds.), *Interrogating whiteness and relinquishing power: White faculty's commitment to racial consciousness in STEM classrooms* (pp.241–252). New York, NY: Peter Lang.

Ruiz-Primo, M. A. & Li, M. (2004). On the use of students' science notebooks as an assessment tool. *Studies in Educational Evaluations in Educational Evaluation, 30*, 61–85.

Ruiz-Primo, M. A. & Furtak, E. M. (2007). Exploring teachers' informal formative assessment practices and students' understanding in the context of scientific inquiry. *Journal of Research in Science Teaching, 44*(1), 57–84.

Ruiz-Primo, M. A., Briggs, D. C., Iverson, H., Talbot, R. M., & Shepard, L. (2011). Impact of undergraduate science course innovations on learning. *Science, 331*(6022), 1269–1270.

Sabel, J. L., Forbes, C. T., & Zangori, L. (2015). Promoting prospective elementary teachers' learning to use formative assessment for life science instruction. *Journal of Science Teacher Education, 26*(4), 419–445.

Sadler, D. R. (1989). Formative assessment and the design of instructional systems. *Instructional Science, 18*, 119–144.

Sadler, P. M., Sonnert, G., Coyle, H. P., Cook-Smith, N., & Miller, J. L. (2013). The Influence of teachers' knowledge on student learning in middle school physical science classrooms. *American Educational Research Journal, 50*(5), 1020–1049.

Sato, M., Wei, R. C., & Darling-Hammond, L. (2008). Improving teachers' assessment practices through professional development: The case of national board certification. *American Educational Research Journal, 45*(3), 669–700.

Schwab, J. J. (1962). *The Teaching of Science as Enquiry*. Cambridge, MA: Harvard University Press.

Sezen-Barrie, A. & Kelly, G. J. (2017). From the teacher's eyes: facilitating teachers noticings on informal formative assessments (IFAs) and exploring the challenges to effective implementation. *International Journal of Science Education*, 1–32.

Sharma, A. (2008). Portrait of a science teacher as a bricoleur: A case study from India. *Cultural Studies of Science Education, 3*(4), 811–841.

Shavelson, R. J., Young, D. B., Ayala, C. C., Brandon, P. R., Furtak, E. M., Ruiz-Primo, M. A., Tomita , M.K., Yin, Y. (2008). On the impact of curriculum-embedded formative assessment on learning: A collaboration between curriculum and assessment developers. *Applied Measurement in Education, 21*(4), 295–314.

Shepard, L. A. (2000). The role of assessment in a learning culture. *Educational Researcher, 29*(7), 4–14.

Shirley, M. L., Irving, K. E., Sanalan, V. A., Pape, S. J., & Owens, D. T. (2011). The practicality of implementing connected classroom technology in secondary mathematics and science classrooms. *International Journal of Science and Mathematics Education, 9*(2), 459–481.

Shulman, L. S. (1986). Those Who Understand: Knowledge growth in teaching. *Educational Researcher, 15*(2), 4–14.

Star, S. L. (2010). This is not a boundary object: Reflections on the origin of a concept. *Science, Technology & Human Values, 35*(5), 601–617.

Star, S. L. & Griesemer, J. R. (1989). Institutional ecology, "translations" and boundary objects: Amateurs and professionals in Berkeley's museum of vertebrate zoology. *Sage Social Studies of Science, 19*(3), 387–420.

Stears, M. & Gopal, N. (2010). Exploring alternative assessment strategies in science classrooms. *South African Journal of Education, 30*, 591–604.

Thissen-Roe, A., Hunt, E., & Minstrell, J. (2004). The DIAGNOSER project: Combining assessment and learning. *Behavior Research Methods, Instruments, and Computers, 36*(2), 234–240.

Thompson, J., Braaten, M., & Windschitl, M. (2009). Learning progressions as vision tools for advancing novice teachers' pedagogical performance. Learning Progressions in Science Conference. Iowa City, IA.

Talanquer, V., Tomanek, D., & Novodvorsky, I. (2013). Assessing students' understanding of inquiry: What do prospective science teachers notice?. *Journal of Research in Science Teaching, 50*(2), 189–208.

Terrazas-Arellanes, F. E., Knox, C., & Rivas, C. (2013). Collaborative online projects for English language learners in science. *Cultural Studies of Science Education, 8*(4), 953–971.

Trauth-Nare, A. (2012). *The influence of relational formative discourse on students' positional identities in a middle school science classroom.* Unpublished doctoral dissertation, Indiana University.

Trauth-Nare, A., & Buck, G. (2011). Using reflective practice to incorporate formative assessment in a middle school science classroom: A participatory action research study. *Educational Action Research, 19*(3), 379–398.

Vygotsky, L. S. (1978). *Mind in society: The development of higher mental processes.* Cambridge, MA: Harvard University Press.

Ward, W., Cole, R., Bolaños, D., Buchenroth-Martin, C., Svirsky, E., Vuuren, S. Van, . . . Becker, L. (2011). My science tutor. *ACM Transactions on Speech and Language Processing, 7*(4), 1–29.

Warren, B., Ballenger, C., Ogonowski, M., Rosebery, A. S., & Hudicourt-Barnes, J. (2001). Rethinking diversity in learning science: The logic of everyday sense-making. *Journal of research in science teaching, 38*(5), 529–552.

Wenger, E. (1998). *Communities of practice: Learning, meaning, and identity.* Cambridge University Press.

White, R. & Gunstone, R. (1992). *Probing Understanding.* New York: Falmer.

Weiland, I. S., Hudson, R. A., & Amador, J. M. (2014). Preservice formative assessment interviews: The development of competent questioning. *International Journal of Science and Mathematics Education, 12*(2), 329–352.

Wiliam, D. (2007). Keeping learning on track: Classroom assessment and the regulation of learning. In J. F. K. Lester (Ed.), *Second handbook of mathematics teaching and learning* (pp. 1053–1098). Greenwich, CT: Information Age Publishing.

Windschitl, M., Thompson, J., Braaten, M., & Stroupe, D. (2012). Proposing a core set of instructional practices and tools for teachers of science. *Science Education, 96*(5), 878–903.

Won, M., Krabbe, H., Ley, S. L., Treagust, D. F., & Fischer, H. E. (2017). Science teachers' use of a concept map marking guide as a formative assessment tool for the concept of energy. *Educational Assessment, 22*(2), 95–110.

Wylie, E. C. & Lyon, C. J. (2015). The fidelity of formative assessment implementation: issues of breadth and quality. *Assessment in Education: Principles, Policy & Practice, 22*(1), 140–160.

Yin, X., & Buck, G. A. (2015). There is another choice: an exploration of integrating formative assessment in a Chinese high school chemistry classroom through collaborative action research. *Cultural Studies of Science Education, 10*(3), 719–752.

Yin, Y., Shavelson, R. J., Ayala, C. C., Ruiz-Primo, M. A., Brandon, P. R., Furtak, E. M., Tomita, M. & Young, D. B. (2008). On the impact of formative assessment on student motivation, achievement, and conceptual change. *Applied Measurement in Education, 21*(4), 335–359. DOI: 10.1080/08957340802347845.

Yin, Y., Tomita, M. K., & Shavelson, R. J. (2013). Using formal embedded formative assessments aligned with a short-term learning progression to promote conceptual change and achievement in science. *International Journal of Science Education*, (December), 1–22.

Yaşar, M. D. (2017). Prospective science teachers' perception related to formative assessment approaches in Turkey. *Journal of Education and Training Studies, 5*(4), 29–43.

6
FORMATIVE ASSESSMENT
IN THE ARTS

Heidi L. Andrade, Joanna Hefferen, and Maria E. Palma

[In arts education] the desire is to enable students to do something that is distinctive [or] . . . inventive. Put another way, surprise rather than predictability is the aim. This, of course, creates certain problems, or at least challenges, for assessors.

(Eisner, 2007, p. 425)

This chapter is about adapting formative assessment to the context of arts education while preserving the core features of each. Informed by a decade of work with hundreds of dance, theater, visual arts, and music teachers in New York City, the chapter illustrates how formative assessment in arts classrooms must navigate the tension between pre-determined standards for craft and the elements of the creative process, such as experimentation and risk-taking.

The nature of the tension lies in the conflict between the goals of the artist and the goals of arts *education*. Professional artists' goals are their own, artistic choice and creative personal expression are central, and feedback is just feedback, not a mandate to change one's work. Although arts education supports these goals, a conflict can arise when pre-determined learning goals (i.e., content standards in an arts curriculum) must still be met. In this chapter, we illustrate how arts educators have navigated this tension through the thoughtful application of formative assessment techniques.

We subscribe to the definition of formative assessment presented in the opening chapter of this book: Formative assessment is "a source of information that educators can use in instructional planning and students can use in deepening their understandings, improving their achievement, taking responsibility for, and self-regulating their learning" (Cizek, Andrade, & Bennett, Chapter 1, this volume, p. X). In broad stroke, this definition accommodates arts education's emphasis on the creative process, which involves making decisions, evaluating, and revising (Hetland et al., 2013). In fact, in many ways, formative assessment is an authentic and essential part of the creative process. In theater, for example, formative assessment occurs during the rehearsal process. A rehearsal is more than reciting memorized lines and moving about the stage: It is a collaborative process of exploration, discovery, feedback, and revision. The director has a vision for the work, observes the actors, and gives feedback that they apply in their interpretation of the characters. Actors come to rehearsal with targets for their day's work—*today I want to explore my relationship with the other characters*, or *I want to explore the objects in the scene and my character's relationship to these things*. The actors' goals are noted, progress toward them is assessed, and the goals are revised or reapplied in the next rehearsal, which involves revision—*let's run that piece again with an adjustment*. As this example illustrates, a core feature of formative assessment—feedback—is a fundamental aspect of every theater teacher's work (Schonmann, 2007). This is also true for dance, music, and visual arts education.

Professional artists have internalized the formative feedback process as the way they work. The arts educator's task is to scaffold the process for students and engage them in protocols that make feedback accessible and actionable. So far, so good—formative assessment can be applied to arts education with at least one of its core features—feedback—intact. The devil is in the details, however. Consider, for example, the following description of formative assessment written by the Council of Chief State School Officers' (CCSSO) (2008), which includes a number of attributes of formative assessment in addition to feedback:

> Formative assessment is a process used by teachers and students during instruction that provides feedback to adjust ongoing teaching and learning to improve students' achievements of intended instructional outcomes. The attributes below have been identified as critical features of effective formative assessment:
>
> - Learning Progressions. Learning progressions should clearly articulate the sub-goals of the ultimate learning goal.
> - Learning Goals and Criteria for Success. Learning goals and criteria for success should be clearly identified and communicated to students.
> - Evidence of Learning. Evidence of learning is elicited during instruction.
> - Descriptive Feedback. Students should be provided with evidence-based feedback that is linked to the intended instructional outcomes and criteria for success.
> - Self- and Peer Assessment. Both self- and peer assessment are important for providing students with an opportunity to think metacognitively about their learning.
> - Collaboration. A classroom culture in which teachers and students are partners in learning should be established.

Like most models of formative assessment (e.g., Andrade & Heritage, 2017; Cizek, 2010; Moss & Brookhart, 2012; Penuel & Shepard, 2016; Wiliam & Thompson, 2007), the CCSSO's description has a prominent place for learning goals (or intentions) and success criteria. As a result, feedback "permits the comparison of actual performance with some established standard of performance" (Shute, 2008, p. 175). Thus, the first point at which the aforementioned tension arises is when a teacher takes the fundamental step in the formative assessment process of articulating the learning goals. Those goals could focus on skill development (e.g., learn to use a particular technique in a traditional way) or creativity (develop your own technique or use the traditional one in a new way) or both, but if it is both, the tension is unresolved. The tension surfaces again at the point at which students receive feedback on their works in progress: Should the feedback be tied to the success criteria regarding traditional technique and direct students to make revisions that indicate mastery of those disciplinary standards, or be open-ended in order to favor creativity and artistic choice? Is *both* a viable option?

This conflict between evaluative standards for technique and creative processes is at the center of a controversy about assessment in arts education (Colwell, 2004). Some argue that artistry cannot be objectively assessed (Hernandez, 2012), while others acknowledge the importance of assessment in classrooms where students direct their own learning about composition, technique, and rehearsal (Englebright & Mahoney, 2012; Harding, 2012). Feedback, however, is generally seen as an integral part of creation and performance (Warburton, 2009). Good arts educators continually monitor and assess the progression of learning by their students as it happens (Eisner, 2007; Kempe & Ashwell, 2002). Summative evaluation of the products of arts education is still problematic, with little agreement about the standards and their application, but summative assessment of art, happily, is not the subject of this chapter.

Rubric-referenced assessment is a similarly polarizing issue. Some educators argue that rubrics can actually "hurt kids," replace professional decision making by attempting to standardize creative processes (Wilson, 2006, back board), and undermine learning by focusing only on the most quantifiable and least important qualities of student work (Kohn, 2006). This is probably true of poorly written rubrics, but there is no evidence that technically sound rubrics (see Brookhart, 2013) will damage students or limit their opportunities for creative expression. In fact, research on writing has shown that formative self-assessment with rubrics that emphasize qualities of writing typically considered to be highly subjective and difficult to teach, such as ideas and voice, are associated with meaningful improvements in students' handling of those qualities in their writing (Andrade, Du, & Mycek, 2010; Andrade, Du, & Wang, 2008). This positive effect is especially true when students are involved in creating the rubrics and use them to provide feedback on their own and each other's work (Andrade, 2010).

The tension between disciplinary standards and creativity is not just intellectual. Because "school art is a blend of educational and artistic expectations, where the agenda of schools and their expectations seems to be dominant" (Bresler, 2002, p. 182), arts educators wrestle with it every day. When we began talking with art, dance, theater, and music teachers about formative assessment, many of them objected on the grounds that assessing children's art-making would inhibit their creativity. Yet their daily lessons tended to target technique and skill development because, as one elementary music teacher put it, *they don't even know where to put their fingers on the keyboard yet.*

Those of you who do know where to put your fingers on the keyboard, or how to blend colors, do a plié, or write stage instructions probably have an intuitive sense of how the tension between criteria and creativity is resolved in effective arts instruction:

> What is required is a dynamic relationship between the freedom of imagination and the constraints of tradition. Skills and knowledge must be developed, but in a manner that also encourages questioning and criticism, the development of critical judgment, and the personal appropriation of the tradition by each individual student.
>
> *(Bailin, 2015, p. 10)*

Resolving the tension requires embracing it, and designing instruction that balances the teaching of traditional technique with support for experimentation and innovation. Bailin calls such an approach *critical inquiry*:

> Disciplinary skills must be learned in the context of this type of inquiry approach. Skills are not merely habits; they adapt to changing circumstances and involve critical judgments. Thus, skills should be taught as flexible abilities that are applied in a variety of circumstances. Also, the ends to which they are applied need not always be fixed in advance but may change in the course of the inquiry. And the ends may sometimes be chosen by the students themselves as opposed to being set by others. In addition, skills must be understood within the broad context of the discipline as a whole. It is important to develop the ability to see beyond the specific problem or issue with which one is dealing and to have a real understanding of the methods and procedures of the discipline, and the principles and goals that lie behind them.
>
> Creative achievement is best fostered, then, through an understanding of the critical and creative nature of disciplinary inquiry, and through participating in the dynamics of the discipline in a way that is personally meaningful. The disciplines must be seen as modes of inquiry, exploration, experimentation, and expression.
>
> *(pp. 10–11).*

Skills are not static: Wielded well, they are techniques that flex to meet the demands of whatever problem an artist (or scientist, engineer, mathematician, physician, writer, or whoever) is trying to solve. Goals can change and can be determined by the student-artist. Knowledge, skill, and confidence allow young artists to make informed creative decisions and choices that express their personal artistic vision. Nonetheless, the originality of interpretation and the formality of structure is a point of tension that arts teachers must navigate.

A Theory of Action

Formative assessment in an arts classroom must be part of the dynamic relationship between the freedom of imagination and the constraints of tradition called for by Bailin (2015), where the constraints of tradition include prescribed educational standards, learning goals, and success criteria. Such a relationship requires a theory of action that reflects the values underlying the learning goals because learning goals are

> informed by implicit and explicit values and are framed in terms of what learners should learn and what kinds of persons they should become . . . and may be justified in terms of what the society values, what experts in a domain agree is important to learn, or what the research indicates is a good sequence of learning goals to promote development over time . . . Justifications such as these are necessary because learning goals are often an object of deliberation and debate in education [especially arts education].
>
> *(Penuel & Shepard, 2016, p. 791)*

Current theories of action for formative assessment tend to be informed by Sadler's (1989) list of three elements of assessment needed to promote student learning: 1) a clear view of the learning targets, 2) information about the present state of the learner, and 3) action to close the gap between the present level of competence and the target. As a result, many theories of action (e.g., Andrade & Heritage, 2017; Bennett, 2011) frontload standards, learning goals, and success criteria at the beginning of the learning process, as in Figure 6.1:

Figure 6.1 Typical theory of action for formative assessment.

This rudimentary theory of action assumes a more or less straight line from standards to goals through criteria to performance, but that straight line is not universally accepted by arts educators, who sometimes want students to muck around, in an exploratory kind of way, before subjecting their creations to criteria-referenced critiques. Such a theory of action looks something like Figure 6.2:

Figure 6.2 Theory of action with no explicit reference to standards or criteria.

Note that this theory of action makes no explicit reference to standards or criteria. But of course, teachers of dance, theater, art, and (perhaps especially) music recognize the need for technique. Honoring both kinds of learning goals—the creative process and traditional technique—demands

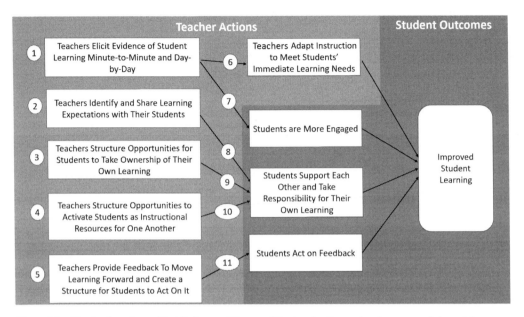

Figure 6.3 *Keeping Learning on Track® Program* Theory of Action for Formative Assessment (adapted from ETS, 2009).

a flexible theory of action. An adaptation of ETS's model (2009, as cited in Bennett, 2011; see Figure 6.3) can meet this demand, since the expectations introduced in box 2 (Teachers identify and share learning expectations, which are derived from standards, with their students) can take nearly any form, from exploration to technique.

If a teacher has designed instruction that targets skills-based learning goals, perhaps with the longer-term goal of enabling students to use particular skills in innovative ways, she is likely to identify and share task-specific standards, learning goals, and success criteria with her students. The success criteria might be articulated in rubrics or checklists. If, in contrast, the teacher wants to support students in exploration and experimentation in the art form, she might indicate to students that those are her learning expectations and withhold specific success criteria, either in the short run or indefinitely—this is where the dynamic interplay between the freedom of imagination and the constraints of tradition comes in.

There is still an issue with this theory of action, however, that limits its relevance to arts education: It does not explicitly represent the student-artist's voice and choice. One of the highest aspirations of many arts educators is to instill an artistic vision in their students. Such a vision involves having a voice in decisions about the goals for their art-making, as well as having a choice about whether or not feedback is incorporated into their work (the notion of feedback as feedback, not a mandate, has special meaning in the arts). The theory of action in Figure 6.4, where the revisions to the original model are bolded for visual accessibility, represents student voice in box 3, which creates a place for students to set goals for their learning and their work, perhaps as the result of interactions between the student-artist, teacher, and materials. Student choice is represented by the two dashed lines to box 10, which is where students decide whether or not to take the suggestions they receive from their teachers and peers, depending on their goals for their work.

Boxes 4 and 5 are where students serve as useful sources of feedback through self- and peer assessment. Because this is a model of formative, not summative, assessment, peer and self-assessment do not involve students in grading or scoring their own or their neighbor's work: Rather, they are processes

Formative Assessment in the Arts

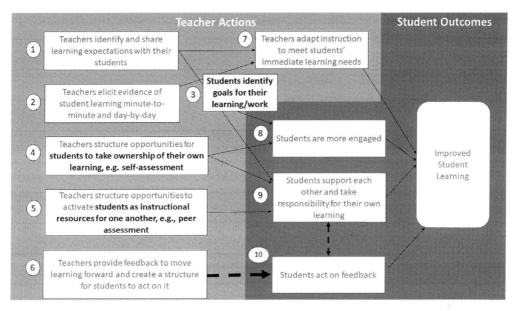

Figure 6.4 Theory of Action for Formative Assessment in Arts Education (adapted from ETS, 2009).

during which students reflect on the quality of their own or their classmate's work, compare it to either the success criteria and/or the student's personal goals, and make suggestions for revision and improvement (Andrade, 2010; Hale & Green, 2009; Parkes, 2010).

Formative Assessment Practices in Arts Classrooms

The theory of action represented by Figure 6.4 contains the core features of formative assessment while also honoring the essence of the arts, which is a generative interplay between traditional forms with established techniques, structures, and constraints, and the pursuit of creative interpretations and extensions of those forms. How can teachers apply this dynamic interplay between disciplinary standards and the creative process to classroom instruction in the arts? One way is through the thoughtful application of formative assessment practices. In this section of the chapter, we will introduce examples of practice and discuss how they address the need to provide criteria-referenced feedback to students while also aiming for the artistic goal of thinking and acting in original ways.

Our work with arts educators began in 2008 with a project called Artful Learning Communities: Assessing Learning in the Arts (ALC), a partnership between the New York City Department of Education and ArtsConnection, a U.S. Department of Education-recognized model arts education organization. This initial project was supported by a professional development grant from the U.S. Department of Education.

The goals of the ALC were to 1) strengthen the capacity of elementary and middle school arts educators to assess standards-based learning in the arts, 2) promote increased student achievement in the arts through ongoing classroom assessment, and 3) develop the ability of educators to define, systematize and communicate their assessment strategies and tools to local and national audiences. The third goal is being met, in part, through the Arts Assessment for Learning website, where dozens of examples of formative assessment practices can be found: http://artsassessmentforlearning.org/

At the time of writing, we have worked with over 300 arts educators, but the examples of practice shared in this chapter began with our work with 96 visual art, music, dance and theater specialists and their 48,000 students in grades 3 through 8 at high-poverty schools in Brooklyn, New York. The teachers engaged in action research focused on collaborative inquiry into the relationship between formative assessment and student achievement, and worked in professional learning communities that regularly brought them together across schools.

Our first challenge was to convince some of our new collaborators, the arts educators, of the value of assessment in arts education. Early on, we were politely told that the arts cannot be assessed and, furthermore, we should not assess children's art-making because so doing could threaten their self-esteem and diminish their motivation to engage in art-making. Recognizing in this argument the lack of distinction between evaluation and assessment, we presented theory and research on the distinctions between summative and formative assessment, and stressed the ways in which ongoing, informal feedback from the teacher and from the students themselves can deepen students' understanding of important concepts and skills (Hattie & Timperley, 2007). We presented evidence that students benefit from Sadler's (1989) three elements of formative assessment: 1) An understanding of the criteria for successful performance, 2) feedback on the gap between the standards represented by those criteria and the students' current work, and 3) knowing how to close the gap through revision.

Reconceptualizing assessment as a moment of learning (Zessoules & Gardner, 1991) allowed the teachers to see it in terms of authentic artistic processes such as setting goals, critiquing one's own and each other's work, and revising—processes that are inherent to any creative endeavor that involves rehearsal, revision, redoing. In the remainder of this section, we describe the teachers' work in terms of the theory of action in Figure 6.4.

Teachers Identify and Share Learning Expectations (Box 1, Figure 6.4)

As is clear from the first goal of the ALC ("to strengthen the capacity of elementary and middle school arts educators to assess standards-based learning in the art"), our work began with an explicit emphasis on standards, which in this case were the New York City Department of Education's (2015) *Blueprints for Teaching and Learning in the Arts*. The *Blueprints* describe what PreK-12 children, including students with disabilities and English language learners, should know, understand, and be able to do in the arts in Grades 2, 5, 8, and 12. Naturally, the *Blueprints* address both technique/skills and the creative process. For example, note how these guidelines for fifth-grade painting target discrete skills such as mixing colors, as well as creativity in terms of inventive problem solving:

- observation of detail and inventive solutions to design problems
- mixing tints, shades, and tones of primary and secondary colors
- expressive use of paint media such as tempera
- use of large and medium brushes to make a variety of marks such as dabbing and dry brush
- basic organization of space such as foreground and background

(p. 16)

The *Blueprints* are a useful resource for arts educators. They guide the development of curriculum, learning goals, and even task-specific success criteria. The teachers with whom we work often use them to sketch out criteria for a task in preparation for co-creating criteria with their students. The co-creation process typically involves sharing samples of the task (e.g., sculptures, choreographies, songs, or tableaus) with a class, asking them to identify what works about each sample, and then brainstorming a list of qualities of effective pieces. The brainstormed list is then condensed into a checklist or expanded into a rubric and shared with students.

Student involvement, with or without rubrics, is a key component of the assessment process in arts classrooms like those described in this chapter, where students actively participate in giving and receiving feedback and meaningfully engage in rethinking and revising performances. An innovative example of co-creating criteria was developed by Jason Rondinelli and Emily Maddy for their middle school visual arts classes. They asked students to design cars that were biomorphic, or inspired by shapes found in nature. The learning goals for the project included:

- awareness of light, value and contrast
- observation of detail
- use of monochromatic color gradation
- understanding of form follows function relationships

As students worked on their drawings, Jason and Emily noted that many of them needed additional instruction in gradation, which is a matter of teachers eliciting evidence of student learning (box 2), and then adapting instruction to meet students' immediate learning needs (box 7). After reviewing the concept of gradation and how it could be used in the project, they showed students a visual gradation rubric (Figure 6.5) created from other, anonymous artwork. The visual rubric illustrated how to categorize drawings in terms of the use of gradation only—not other aspects of the car such as shape, color, design, or use of detail.

Jason and Emily asked students to use it to write a narrative gradation rubric that described progressively more sophisticated uses of gradation. In groups, students defined one level of the rubric (4, 3, 2, or 1) by describing the positive and negative uses of gradation in each of the examples, and listing five or more descriptions for their rubric level. Once the students had defined and described their level, they combined their ideas into the rubric in Table 6.1, which was then used to scaffold self-assessment and revision.

This excerpt from Jason and Emily's biomorphic car project (see Andrade, Hefferen, & Palma, 2014, for more information) is a good illustration of the interplay between sharing learning expectations with students (box 1), eliciting evidence of learning (box 2) and adapting instruction to meet

Gradation Rubric

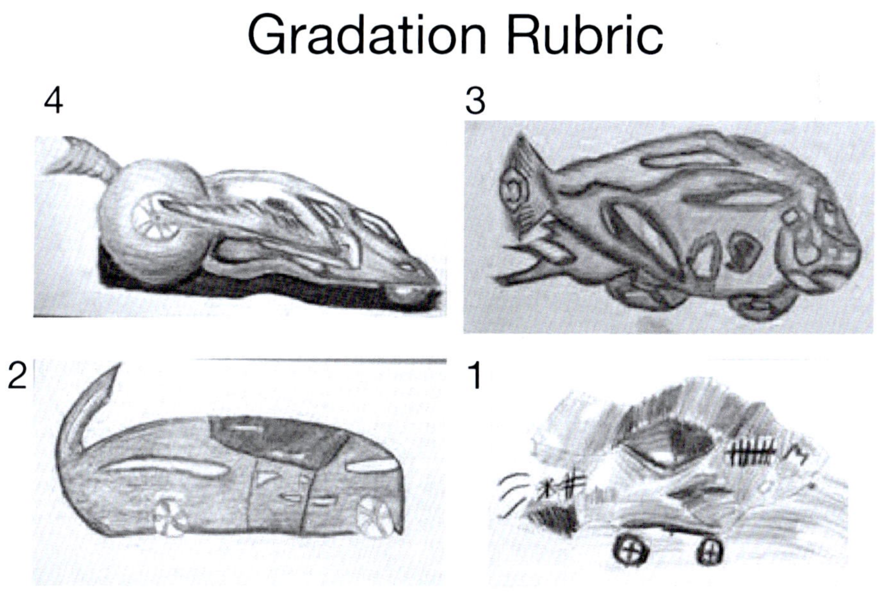

Figure 6.5 Visual gradation rubric.

Reproduced from Andrade, Hefferen, and Palma (2014), used with permission.

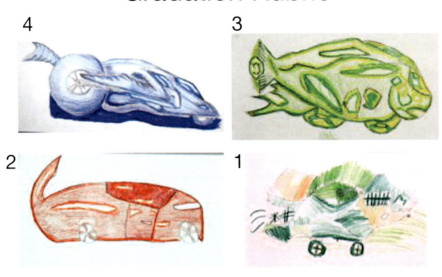

Plate 1 Visual gradation rubric. Reproduced from Andrade, Hefferen, and Palma (2014), used with permission.

Plate 2 Peer feedback about a self-portrait. Reproduced from Andrade, Hefferen, and Palma (2014), used with permission.

Plate 3 Result of revision after peer feedback. Reproduced from Andrade, Hefferen, and Palma (2014), used with permission.

Heidi L. Andrade et al.

Table 6.1 Narrative Gradation Rubric Written by Students Based on the Visual Rubric

4 Yes	3 Yes and . . .	2 No, but . . .	1 No
+	+	+	+
It has a cast shadow. It has gradation on the bottom. It has a light source. It goes from light to dark very clearly. Light colors blend in with dark. The way the artist colored the car showed where the light source was coming from.	It has shine marks. Artist shows good use of dark and light values. The picture shows gradual shades in the car. Used light values. Used shadows.	There is gradation on the bottom of the door.	The rims are shaded darkly. The car looks 3-D.
	−	−	−
−	Needs more gradual value. Give wheels lighter gradation or darker shade. The direction of the light is not perfectly directed. Has an outline. Has more dark value than light values. The wheels are too light.	The car is outlined. There is no shadow. It's not shaded from light to dark. The windows have no shine marks. The wheels do not look 3-D.	The gradation starts wrong. Some spots are not well shaded. The shadow is not shaded correctly.
It has an outline. Cast shadow is too dark. Doesn't go from light to dark. Doesn't have enough gradation. Outlined some body parts. Cast shadow is really straight.			

students' needs (box 7). Although the project as a whole facilitated creative design processes, the focus on gradation techniques in the lesson described here places the lesson squarely in the realm of tradition: Students were to master a disciplinary standard found in the *Blueprint*.

As noted above, however, teachers sometimes want to discourage a focus on specific techniques or goals in order to encourage exploration and experimentation, and/or honor students' own goal setting for their work. In such a case, a different approach is needed. We have recently begun to experiment with Liz Lerman's Critical Response Process and Mutual Coaching Strategy (Borstel, Franz, & Johnson, 2011; Lerman & Borstel, 2003), which explicitly encourage artists to think and act in original ways and focuses feedback on the goals of the artist, which is Box 3 in Figure 6.4.

Students Identify Goals for Their Learning and Work (Box 3)

The Mutual Coaching Strategy is informed by an awareness of the powerful role of judgment in art-making, and when judgment is and is not useful:

> The judgmental mechanisms have to be silenced at the inspiration and generation phases of the creative act, and successful artists often have developed particular habits of mind that enable them to achieve this silencing. But we must be ready to reengage that capacity of judgment when we get to other stages of the creative process, those where we take the raw material we've generated, and do the sorting, sifting, and amending that inform a rigorously crafted piece of work. In the creative process itself, it is essential to be able to both engage and suspend judgment depending on the particular task at hand, with generative acts, for instance, benefitting from suspended judgment, and planning and assessment acts benefitting from engaged judgment.
>
> *(Borstel, Franz, & Johnson, 2011, pp. 16–17)*

Formative Assessment in the Arts

The Mutual Coaching Strategy (Text Box 6.1) is used by teachers to suspend judgment in terms of disciplinary standards and instructional goals in favor of conversations about the artist's intentions for and puzzles about works in progress. The conversation starts not with criteria but with the work itself and the artist's goals for it (box 3 of Figure 6.4).

Text Box 6.1

Mutual Coaching Strategy

Round 1

1   Artist shows work: Participating artists/students form pairs. One ("artist") performs/shows the material while the other ("coach") watches/listens.
2   Coach comments: The watching/listening partner offers a few comments on aspects of the performance that worked well or were effective, striking, or meaningful.

Round 2

1   Artist states area of focus: The artist now invites feedback about a specific aspect of his/her presentation. A dancer might say: "I'm working on my transitions," a storyteller: "I'm trying to differentiate my voice as narrator from the characters who speak in the story," or a pianist: "I want the right hand to play lyrically while I keep the left hand percussive." The artist then repeats the passage.
2   Coach responds: The coaching partner attends to the repeat and gives feedback on the focus area the artist has identified.

Round 3

1   Coach offers an additional focus area: The coach now names another area for the performer to work on, "Think about keeping your movement more fluid across the shoulders"; "Try varying the loudness and softness of your speaking"; "See what results you get if you use the pedal a little more sparingly."
2   Debrief: After a final performance of the material, partners debrief to assess the progress that was observed, share insights gained, or consider future steps.

From the Top

Switch and repeat: Participants reverse roles and repeat the process.

(Borstel, Franz, & Johnson, 2011: Reproduced with permission of the first author.)

The Mutual Coaching Strategy is a variation on another protocol called the Critical Response Process (Text Box 6.2), which also scaffolds feedback focused on the artist's intent. Because "to be mindful and agile with judgment takes technique" (Borstel, Franz, & Johnson, 2011, p. 17), these protocols, and all like them, must be taught. This chapter is not the place to describe effective instruction in the use of protocols, but it is important to stress that they must be carefully taught in order to enable the outcome in box 9 in Figure 6.4: Students support each other and take responsibility for their own learning.

Text Box 6.2

Liz Lerman's Critical Response Process

The Roles

- The *artist* offers a work-in-progress for review and is prepared to question that work in a dialogue with other people.
- One, a few, or many *responders*—committed to the artist's intent to make excellent work—engage in the dialogue with the artist.
- The *facilitator* initiates each step, keeps the process on track, and works to help the artist and responders use the process to frame useful questions and responses.

The Process

The Critical Response Process takes place after a presentation of artistic work. Work can be short or long, large or small, and at any stage in its development.

The Core Steps

1 *Statements of Meaning*: Responders state what was meaningful, evocative, interesting, exciting, striking in the work they have just witnessed. Discomforts, doubts, and negative opinions are withheld until the appropriate opportunities later in the Process.

2 *Artist as Questioner*: The artist asks questions about the work. Responders answer being mindful to stay on topic with the question. Responders may express opinions if they are in direct response to the question asked and do not contain suggestions for changes.

3 *Neutral Questions*: Responders ask neutral questions about the work. The artist responds. Questions are *neutral* when they do *not* have an opinion couched in them. For example, if you are discussing the lighting of a scene, "Why was it so dark?" is not a neutral question. "What ideas guided your choices about lighting?" is.

4 *Opinion Time*: Responders state opinions, subject to permission from the artist. The usual form is "I have an opinion about _____, would you like to hear it?" The artist has the option to say no.

(Lerman & Borstel, 2003. Reproduced with permission of authors.)

Students Take Ownership of Their Own Learning, and Serve as Instructional Resources for One Another (Boxes 4 and 5)

Whether their goals are their own, their teacher's, or a combination of the two, students are able to support each other and take responsibility for their own learning by using carefully applied formative assessment strategies. The arts teachers we work with frequently employ student self- and peer assessment. Feedback from peers can be mostly or entirely untethered to disciplinary standards, as in the critique protocols described above, or it can be grounded in explicitly stated criteria, as in the example from the biomorphic car project. Jason and Emily asked students to self-assess by referring to the co-created rubric in Table 6.1 when writing answers to these questions: 1) Based on the gradation rubric, what is the rubric level of your car? 2) What will you do to improve the gradation of your car? After thinking about the quality of their work and the ways in which it could be improved,

Formative Assessment in the Arts

the students revised their drawings. Finally, they did some reflection by writing their responses to these questions: 1) Did you reach your goals? 2) Did you improve the gradation in your cars? Have you reached a higher rubric level?

Peers are a plentiful and, under the right conditions, useful source of feedback (Topping, 2013) in arts classrooms. For peer feedback to be useful, however, it is important that students deliver it in a constructive manner. The Mutual Coaching Process is an example of a constructive critique protocol. Another protocol that is popular with teachers is called the Ladder of Feedback (Figure 6.6; Perkins, 2003). The Ladder of Feedback protocol has four steps of equal importance: 1) the deliverer of the feedback first asks questions of clarification about the other student's work, then 2) identifies strengths and other aspects of the work that he or she values, 3) raises concerns about the work, and finally 4) offers suggestions for ways in which the work can be improved. The Ladder is often used with a checklist or rubric in order to ensure that peer feedback is focused on relevant success criteria.

Jason and Emily found that students were remarkably able to serve as instructional resources for one another, and applied peer assessment strategies across their curriculum. While working on self-portraits, for instance, students gave each other feedback on their value scales using the template in Figure 6.7 and words from a word bank.

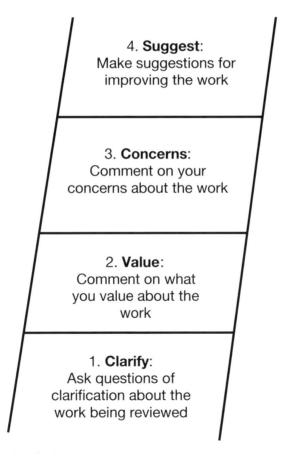

Figure 6.6 The Ladder of Feedback.
From Perkins, D. (2003). *King Arthur's round table: How collaborative conversations create smart organizations.* Hoboken, NJ: John Wiley & Sons, Inc.

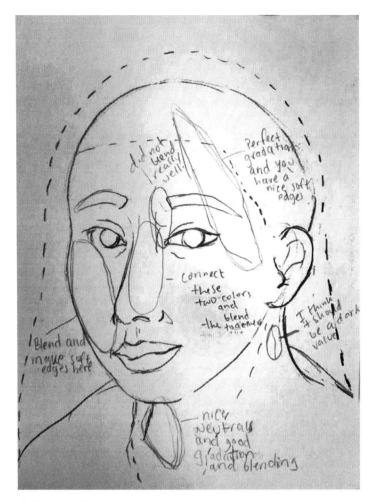

Figure 6.7 Peer feedback template.
Reproduced from Andrade, Hefferen, and Palma (2014), used with permission.

Figure 6.7 includes the feedback given about the self-portrait in progress found in Figure 6.8: *Perfect gradation and you have a nice soft edge; Connect these two colors and blend them together*, and so on. After receiving feedback, the student-artists in their classes reflected on the degree to which they agreed with the feedback, planned next steps, and continued to work on the self-portraits. Figure 6.9 reveals how one student's mastery of gradation (among other things) improved.

Jason and Emily report that their students were articulate in their discussions, used art vocabulary they had rarely used before, and addressed specific areas of each other's artwork during the peer assessment process (see videos that include interviews of each of them at https://studentsatthecenterhub.org/resource/student-centered-assessment-video-suite/). Many students improved their work after getting feedback, although some chose not to follow the advice given to them by their peers. This decision to disregard some or all of their peers' suggestions was considered a natural part of the process of art-making: Each artist must make decisions about his or her own work.

Figure 6.8 Peer feedback about a self-portrait.
Reproduced from Andrade, Hefferen, and Palma (2014), used with permission.

Figure 6.9 Result of revision after peer feedback.
Reproduced from Andrade, Hefferen, and Palma (2014), used with permission.

The Ladder of Feedback

To _____
From _____

4. Suggest:
Make suggestions for improving the work

Have you considered..........?
I have an opinion.
Would you like to hear it?

3. Concerns:
Comment on your concerns about the work

I wonder.........?

2. Value:
Comment on the strengths of the work

I really like........!

1. Clarify:
Ask questions of clarification about the work being
reviewed

How did you.....?
What were you thinking about
When you.........?

Figure 6.10   Peer feedback scaffolding used by Angela Fremont, elementary visual arts.

Perkins, D. (2003)

Several of the teachers with whom we worked have combined elements of the Ladder of Feedback and Critical Response Process in order to support peer feedback (Figure 6.10).

As a result, Angela Fremont's third-grade artists were able to write thoughtful reflections. For example, one student wrote this:

My partner said how I can draw the patterns with color. My partner said I need to add details.

I saw that I can add more colors and patterns and crops. The rubric said to fill the page with large and small houses.

My partner had some drawing problems with patterns and crops. I had a chance to help her with it.

When I did the painting longer, I painted more things. I made improvements when I got to paint longer.

They were crops and patterns. It is also the houses.

Managing the Dynamic Relationship Between Criteria and Artistic Vision

At the beginning of this chapter, we introduced the tension between success criteria for a task and students' artistic vision and asked if *both* was a viable option. It appears that it is. A skillful teacher in the arts can approach box 1 in Figure 6.4 by selecting standards related to technique and then write related learning goals and criteria for student work, or by selecting standards and learning goals related to the creative process and withholding task-specific criteria. Students can approach box 3 by adopting their teacher's goals and criteria, or inventing their own.

It is not that simple, of course. The boxes in Figure 6.4 are phenomena that interact in sometimes messy ways that are hard to capture in a stripped-down model. Yet, this theory of action plays out in hundreds of arts educator's classrooms every day, with measurable influences on student learning. Those classrooms provide compelling anecdotal evidence of the relationship between formative assessment and learning in the arts. In the next section, we present empirical evidence of the effectiveness of formative assessment in arts education.

Research on the Effects of Formative Assessment on Student Learning in the Arts

Schonmann observed in 2007 that we do not have any data in the arts that indicate the strengths and weaknesses of particular assessment methods. This is almost still true today, especially for studies of formative assessment. Two exceptions (Chen et al., 2017; Mastrorilli, Harnett, & Zhu, 2014) are studies of a project called *Arts Achieve: Impacting Student Success in the Arts*, which was a collaboration between the authors of this chapter, the New York City Department of Education, and five arts organizations. The Arts Achieve project was funded by a U.S. Department of Education Investing in Innovation (i3) grant and an Arts in Education Model Development and Dissemination (AEMDD) grant.

Starting in the 2011–2012 school year, Arts Achieve provided two years of professional development on the use of formative assessment. The participating dance, theater, music, and visual arts teachers, some of whom had already participated in the Artful Learning Communities work introduced earlier, attended workshops, formed professional learning communities, conducted action research, attended inter-visitations in each other's classrooms, and consulted with facilitators from the partner arts organizations. The workshops were designed to help teachers articulate success criteria (box 1 in Figure 4), with an emphasis on co-creating checklists and rubrics with students, as well as to learn how to scaffold student self-assessment (box 4), use constructive critique protocols like the Ladder of Feedback for peer assessment (box 5), and provide time and support as students revised their work (box 10).

Arts Achieve was evaluated by colleagues at Metis Associates, who designed a cluster randomized control trial study—a rarity in research on arts education. In the first year of implementation, 77 New York City public schools were assigned to treatment or status-quo control conditions using a stratified (art discipline and school level) random assignment process. Prior to the start of the second year of implementation, four treatment and six control schools dropped out, and 16 new schools were randomly assigned to the treatment or the control condition, for a total of 83 schools (Mastrorilli, Harnett, & Zhu, 2014).

One particularly striking feature of the Arts Achieve project was the use of performance assessments as pre- and post-tests. Benchmark Arts Assessments were developed for each of the four art forms in order to authentically measure students' conceptual understanding, literacy, application of knowledge, and analytical and performance skills. The majority of the tasks on the Benchmark Arts Assessments were performance-based (e.g., choreographing and performing a dance, composing a short piece of music, creating a collage, writing and acting a script) but the assessments also included multiple choice, short response, essay, and fill in the blank items. Scores could range from 0 to 100.

Metis Associates analyzed the data from the study (Mastrorilli, Harnett, & Zhu, 2014), and also provided access to de-identified data on the schools, student demographics, and outcome measures for additional analyses (Chen et al., 2017). Both sets of analyses revealed a significant effect of the professional development about formative assessment on student achievement in the arts as measured by the Benchmark Arts Assessments. Mastrorilli, Harnett, and Zhu (2014) report that, at the end of the first year of implementation, controlling for differences in demographics and previous achievement, students in the treatment schools performed 3.11 points higher on the post-Benchmark Arts Assessments than students in the control schools. The Year 1 predicted mean post-Benchmark Arts Assessment score for the average treatment student was 62.7, compared to 59.6 for the average control student. Glass's delta indicated that there was an effect size of 0.18.

In order to mitigate problems with the psychometric properties of some of the performance tasks, the analyses of Year 1 data by Chen et al. (2017) excluded tasks with kappas of less than 0.40. Using data from a propensity score matched sample of 611 pairs of students, the overall average treatment effect was $d = 0.26$. To put that effect in perspective, consider that a d of 0.25 would mean moving a group of students from the 50th to the 60th percentile—a significant outcome in an educational context.

Taken together, these analyses of the Arts Achieve experiment show that formative assessment had meaningful, positive effect on achievement. The study by Chen et al. (2017) also provides support for the claim that student learning in the arts is measurably deepened when students know the expectations for their learning (box 1), receive feedback from their teachers, themselves, and each other (boxes 4, 5, and 6), and have opportunities to revise (box 10)—all of which had to be occurring in the treatment classes in order for them to be included in the analysis. Written reflections by and conversations with the teachers indicate that formative assessment helped students not only to improve in their learning and performance but also to become more self-directed and self-sufficient (Valle et al., 2016).

Future Directions

The research on formative assessment in the arts is promising but limited. The Arts Achieve project was a study of formative assessment in the arts that foregrounded teachers' learning goals and success criteria (box 1 in Figure 6.4). Research is needed on the effects of formative assessment on arts learning when students' goals for their work are prioritized, as exemplified by the Liz Lerman protocols (Lerman & Borstel, 2003).

The Arts Achieve project included all four art forms: dance, theater, music, and visual arts, but the arts is not a discipline—it is a collection of disciplines—so even this chapter on formative assessment in the arts might be "too keen to find theories that embrace *all* the arts" (Schonmann, 2007, p. 414). Discipline-specific analyses of the effects of formative assessment on learning produced a stronger effect for music (Valle, 2015) than for theater (Chen & Andrade, 2016), but it cannot be assumed that disciplinary differences exist, because these studies did not directly compare music and theater using identical formative assessment practices or outcome measures. Closer examinations of the implementation and results of formative assessment in each art form are needed.

We also wonder if the generative tension between tradition and innovation experienced by arts teachers is or should be experienced by teachers in other disciplines as well. The primary goal of art education is to teach students to think creatively; this goal is not the stuff of the arts alone. In the field of science, for instance, there is a focus on innovation and radical change in theorizing about the nature of scientific discovery: Take Kuhn's (1962) notions of scientific revolutions as a primary example (Bailin, 2015). If innovation and novelty are thought of in terms of problem solving, every field demands them; yet it is not clear how teachers teach them in mathematics, history, literature, and other disciplines—or even if they should. The theory of action represented by Figure 6.4 could be a useful lens through which to examine the creative possibilities in core academic disciplines.

Conclusion

Teachers and their student-artists must know when and how to suspend judgment, and when and how to engage it (Borstel, Franz, & Johnson, 2011). The formative assessment literature currently favors feedback focused on standards, learning targets, or performance criteria, but formative assessment in an arts classroom must be a dynamic relationship between the freedom of imagination and the constraints of tradition (Bailin, 2015). For the theater, dance, visual arts, and music teachers with whom we have worked, formative assessment that honors student voice and choice provides a way to manage that dynamic. In fact, many of them have developed such sophisticated formative assessment cultures in their classrooms that they no longer feel a tension between hewing to standards and promoting creativity. We close this chapter with their insightful reflections, collected via email in 2017.

Formative Assessment in the Arts

Ron Sopyla, an elementary theater teacher, wrote to us to say, "I don't feel a tension here . . . Thoughtful formative assessment is another term for good direction." Like many of his colleagues, Ron involves his budding actors and playwrights in determining task-specific success criteria, setting goals for particular pieces of work, giving and receiving feedback, and making decisions about revision. (See Chen et al., 2015, for more about Ron's work.)

Christine Gross, a visual arts teacher, highlighted the role of co-creating expectations for learning in managing the tension between standards and artistic voice when she wrote about the risks of *not* developing learning goals and criteria with students: "Pre-determined [expectations] can feel contrived and not discovered. When expectations are placed, rather than developed, students look to checklists as formulas to meet rather than owning the process of creativity that is flexible, full of surprises and freeing." Similarly, Domenick Danza, a theater teacher, has found that "rubrics and checklists created in collaboration with students are highly valuable. They give students a voice in the assessment process, which creates an immediate buy-in to the revision process." Co-creating criteria also works in Helen Sorenson's music classes:

> Checklists and rubrics are an effective way to reveal to the students (and teacher) specifically what they are doing right and what they need to do in order to improve. Allowing them to be part of the process of creating the checklist or rubric gives them ownership of the process, deepens their understanding of the criteria, and helps them to internalize it.

The teachers are equally committed to student choice by allowing them to keep to their own goals for their work (box 3 in Figure 6.4) by deciding how to respond/react to feedback (the dotted lines to box 10). Christina Soriano, a visual arts teacher, echoes a common principle when she notes that, "ultimately, any revision made is a student choice." Suzanne Woodman, an assistant principal at a high school, reported that:

> This very situation came up in a beginning visual arts class I was observing. Students were giving feedback to each other in groups of four based on the criteria for the assigned project. The project was approximately 75% complete. The teacher instructed all students to listen to and consider all feedback, but ultimately it was their artistic choice as to whether or not they should adjust their project based on the feedback. I sat and listened to students give feedback to each artist after the artist briefly introduced their work. The feedback was thoughtful, respectful and insightful. Students were able to assist one another and give and take suggestions that were in their best interest. The carefully planned feedback activity took about 15 minutes, and all students were able to continue working afterward and adjust their projects if they chose to do so.

Again and again, teachers have told us that:

> Formative assessment acts as a mode that bridges the pre-determined standards and the creative process, provides the mechanism for revealing the creative process and its reflection of particular standards, and provides an evaluative process that is intrinsically constructivist and student-centered.
>
> *(Roberta Raymond, theater teacher)*

The results, as observed in their own classrooms, are true to the spirit of arts education and also preserve the core features of formative assessment:

> Since I started implementing formative assessment in my classroom, I have actually found that my students are more open to taking a risk and experimenting in my theater class.

They're excited to try out the feedback they've received from their peers, and they're more likely to try something that one of their peers suggested . . . My students' creativity and original thinking has taken off. Rather than stifle their creativity, I have found that peer feedback has encouraged them to take risks and push boundaries in ways that I was not witnessing before we began formative assessment. When given the opportunity to revise after receiving feedback from their peers, I have found that my students are eager and excited to push themselves. More often than not the work that comes out of revision post peer feedback is far superior to the work created in isolation. Since implementing co-created checklists in my classroom, I have found that performers' language surrounding the work has been elevated and feedback has gotten more specific and more actionable. We went from a chorus of "it was good" or "I liked it" to students being able to articulate what they enjoyed and how they would approach the next steps as artists.

(Naomi Avadanei, theater teacher)

Heightened student engagement in art-making is a very common theme in our collaborating teachers' reflections. When asked for evidence of increases in student engagement and love of learning, as well as in improvements in artwork due to her use of formative assessment, Barbara Canner, a dance teacher, pointed to the frequency with which her students now ask, *"Can we do it again?"*

References

Andrade, H. (2010). Students as the definitive source of formative assessment: Academic self-assessment and the self-regulation of learning. In H. Andrade & G. Cizek (Eds.), *Handbook of formative assessment* (pp. 90–105). New York, NY: Routledge.

Andrade, H., Du, Y., & Mycek, K. (2010). Rubric-referenced self-assessment and middle school students' writing. *Assessment in Education, 17*(2), 199–214.

Andrade, H., Du, Y., & Wang, X. (2008). Putting rubrics to the test: The effect of a model, criteria generation, and rubric-referenced self-assessment on elementary school students' writing. *Educational Measurement: Issues and Practices, 27*(2), 3–13.

Andrade, H., Hefferen, J., & Palma, M. (2014). Formative assessment in the visual arts. *Art Education Journal, 67*(1), 34–40.

Andrade, H. & Heritage, M. (2017). *Using assessment to enhance learning, achievement, and academic self-regulation.* New York, NY: Routledge.

Bailin, S. (2015). Developing creativity through critical inquiry. *Teachers College Record, 117*(10), 1–20. Retrieved from http://www.tcrecord.org, ID Number: 18083.

Bennett, R. (2011). Formative assessment: A critical review. *Assessment in Education: Principles, Policy and Practice, 18*(1), 5–25.

Borstel, J., Franz, J., & Johnson, E. (2011). The wonderful freedom of not being finished: Four values for constructive critique. *Youth Drama Ireland, 14*, 13–17.

Bresler, L. (2002). School art as a hybrid genre: Institutional contexts for art curriculum. In L. Bresler & C. M. Thompson (Eds.) (2002). *The arts in children's lives: Context, culture, curriculum* (pp. 169–183). Boston, MA: Kluwer.

Brookhart, S. M. (2013). *How to create and use rubrics for formative assessment and grading.* Alexandria, VA: Association for Supervision & Curriculum Development.

Chen, F. & Andrade, H. (2016). The impact of criteria-referenced formative assessment on fifth grade students' theater arts achievement. *Journal of Educational Research, 109*, 1–10.

Chen, F., Andrade, H., Hefferen, J., & Palma, M. (2015). Formative assessment in theater education: An application to practice. *Drama Research, 6*(1), 1–21.

Chen, F., Lui, A., Andrade, H., Valle, C., & Mir, H. (2017). Criteria-referenced formative assessment in the arts. *Educational Assessment, Evaluation, & Accountability.* DOI: 10.1007/s11092-017-9259-z.

Cizek, G. (2010). An introduction to formative assessment: History, characteristics, and challenges. In H. Andrade & G. Cizek (Eds.), *Handbook of formative assessment.* New York: Routledge.

Colwell, R. (2004). Evaluation in the arts is sheer madness. *ARTSPRAXIS, 1*, 1–12. Retrieved from http://steinhardt.nyu.edu/music/artspraxis

Council of Chief State School Officers (CCSSO) (2008). Attributes of effective formative assessment. Washington, DC: CCSSO. Retrieved from https://www.ccsso.org/sites/default/files/2017-12/Attributes_of_Effective_2008.pdf.

Eisner, E. (2007). Assessment and evaluation in education and the arts. In L. Bresler (Ed.), *International handbook of research in art education* (pp. 423–426). Dordrecht, The Netherlands: Springer.

Englebright, K. & M. R. Mahoney (2012). Assessment in elementary dance education. *Journal of Dance Education* 12(3): 87–92.

Hale, C. L. & Green, S. K. (2009). Six key principles for music assessment. *Music Educators Journal 95*, 27–31.

Harding, M. (2012). Assessment in the high school technique class: Creating thinking dancers. *Journal of Dance Education 12*(3), 93–98.

Hattie, J. & Timperley, H. (2007). The power of feedback. *Review of Educational Research*, 77, 81–112.

Hetland, L., Winner, E., Veenema, S., & Sheridan, K. (2013). *Studio Thinking 2: the real benefits of visual art education*. New York, NY: Teachers' College.

Hernandez, B. (2012). The case for multiple, authentic, evidence-based dance assessments. *JOPERD, 83*(1): 5–6, 55–56.

Kempe, A. & Ashwell, M. (2002). *Progression in secondary drama*. Oxford, UK: Heinemann.

Kohn, A. (2006). The trouble with rubrics. *English Journal*, *95*(4), 12–15.

Kuhn, T. (1962). *The structure of scientific revolutions*. Chicago, IL: University of Chicago Press.

Lerman, L. & Borstel, J. (2003). *Liz Lerman's critical response process: A method for getting useful feedback on anything you make, from dance to dessert*. Takoma Park, MD: Dance Exchange.

Mastrorilli, T. M., Harnett, S., & Zhu, J. (2014). *Arts Achieve* impacting student success in the arts: Preliminary findings after one year of implementation. *Journal for Learning through the Arts, 10*(1).

Moss, C. & Brookhart, S. (2012). *Learning targets: Helping students aim for understanding in today's lesson*. Alexandria, VA: Association for Supervision & Curriculum Development.

New York City Department of Education (2015). *Blueprints for teaching and learning in the arts: Prek-12*. Retrieved from: http://schools.nyc.gov/offices/teachlearn/arts/blueprints.html

Parkes, K. (2010). Performance assessment: Lessons from performers. *International Journal of Teacher and Learning in Higher Education, 22*, 98–106.

Penuel, W. R. & Shepard, L. A. (2016). Assessment and teaching. In D. H. Gitomer & C. A. Bell (Eds.), *Handbook of research on teaching* (5th ed.) (pp. 787–850). Washington, DC: American Educational Research Association.

Perkins, D. (2003). *King Arthur's round table: How collaborative conversations create smart organizations* (pp. 39v61). Hoboken, NJ: John Wiley & Sons.

Sadler, D. R. (1989). Formative assessment and the design of instructional systems. *Instructional Science*, 18, 119–144.

Schonmann, S. (2007). Wrestling with assessment in drama education. In L. Bresler (Ed.), *International handbook of research in art education* (pp. 409–422). Dordrecht, The Netherlands: Springer.

Shute, V. (2008). Focus on formative feedback. *Review of Educational Research*, *78*(1), 153–189.

Topping, K. (2013). Peers as a source of formative and summative assessment. In J. McMillan (Ed.), *SAGE handbook of research on classroom assessment* (pp. 395–412). New York, NY: SAGE.

Valle, C. (2015). Effects of criteria-referenced formative assessment on achievement in music. Proquest published doctoral dissertation: (3740126).

Valle, C., Andrade, H., Palma, M., & Hefferen, J. (2016). Applications of peer and self-assessment in music education. *Music Educators' Journal*, *102*(4), 41–49. DOI: 10.1177/0027432116644652.

Wilson, M. (2006). *Rethinking rubrics in writing assessment*. Portsmouth, NH: Heinemann.

Wiliam, D. & Thompson, M. (2007). Integrating assessment with instruction: What will it take to make it work? In C. A. Dwyer (Ed.), *The future of assessment: Shaping teaching and learning* (pp. 53–82). Mahwah, NJ: Erlbaum.

Zessoules, R. & Gardner, H. (1991). Authentic assessment: Beyond the buzzword and into the classroom. In V. Perrone (Ed.), *Expanding student assessment* (pp. 47–166). Alexandria, VA: ASCD.

7

FORMATIVE ASSESSMENT IN HIGHER EDUCATION
An Example from Astronomy

Anders Jönsson and Urban Eriksson

This chapter addresses the challenges and potential of implementing formative assessment in higher education with a specific focus on astronomy. We emphasize the use of formative assessment strategies as a coherent whole and a learning environment that encourages student autonomy and divergent thinking.

Background

In his analysis of the progress and prospects for formative assessment in higher education, Carless (2016) suggests that formative assessment is now a reasonably well-established part of higher education pedagogy. He points to the fact that there has been a range of research projects influenced explicitly or implicitly by formative assessment principles over the last two decades and also that the literature on formative assessment is rapidly expanding. He further acknowledges that it is difficult to estimate the extent to which the interest in formative assessment has led to any extensive implementations at the course level. Similar to the primary and secondary school contexts, there are long-standing traditions and legal requirements at the post-secondary level surrounding summative assessments and grading, which tend to counteract learning-oriented approaches to assessment (cf. Black & McCormick, 2010). Consequently, there is still much work to be done in scaling up the use of formative assessment in higher education.

However, the relationship between the interest in, and the implementation of, formative assessment in higher education is not the only tension in the literature. Rather, there has been some quite radical critique against research on formative assessment in higher education. Two of the most pertinent themes in this critique are what Bennett (2011) refers to as "the domain dependency issue" and the sometimes limited and mechanistic implementation of formative assessment strategies (see, e.g., Torrance, 2012).

The Domain Dependency Issue

One of the strongest claims made by some advocates of formative assessment is that the principles and strategies of formative assessment are universal. For instance, according to Wiliam and Leahy (2015), the strategies of formative assessment can be applied to learners of all ages and regardless of the content to be learned. This would suggest that the strategies are similar (or even identical) in widely diverse settings, such as primary schools and universities, as well as in different subjects, such as mathematics and physics education. Such universality might very well be the case because some formative assessment strategies are very general, but it is still a bold statement provided that the current empirical research base could be considered a bit too shaky for any substantiated extrapolations. Wiliam (2016) defends his position by arguing that practice does not have time to wait for empirical support in relation to all levels of the education system or all subject content. Instead, we need to act upon what we know today.

However, it is not only the lack of empirical support that is problematic here, but the lack of a coherent theoretical foundation to build upon. This is particularly true for the five key strategies by Wiliam and Thompson (2007), which are often used quite authoritatively. Even if presented as a common framework, there is not yet any robust theory binding these particular strategies together. On the contrary, they are typically presented, implemented, and investigated in isolation from each other. It is therefore not always possible to make any theoretically grounded predictions about how the strategies may strengthen or interfere with each other, or if there are any strategies that are superior or inferior in relation to the others.

As a consequence of the apparent lack of theoretical foundation, there have been a number of calls for theoretical developments with respect to formative assessment, as well as attempts to remedy the situation (e.g., Black & Wiliam, 2006). One of the most pervasive calls for theoretical development includes the demand for an account of the role of disciplinary epistemology in relation to the general principles, strategies, and techniques (e.g., Yorke, 2003). As shown by Cowie and Bell (1999) in a school-science context, to recognize the significance of what is noticed in the classroom as part of formative assessment, teachers must be able to interpret the information they have and to understand its implications, which requires both disciplinary knowledge in science and pedagogical content knowledge (PCK). In contrast, a teacher lacking disciplinary knowledge

> is less likely to know what questions to ask of students, what to look for in their performance, what inferences to make from that performance about student knowledge, and what actions to take to adjust instruction.
>
> *(Bennett, 2011, p. 15)*

As a minimum requirement, therefore, some of the general principles and techniques of formative assessment need to be adjusted in relation to the epistemological structure of a subject discipline, for instance in the formulation of criteria, the tasks and assessment situations designed to elicit student knowledge, or the focus of the feedback. An even stronger adaptation to the epistemological structure of a subject discipline may involve a negotiation of the strategies used.

It has also been suggested that instantiating formative assessment within the context of a specific domain could include a "cognitive-domain model" to guide the formative assessment process, by outlining a learning progression (Bennett, 2011; Yorke, 2003). By indicating important steps on the road from novice to expert (for examples from science and astronomy education, see, e.g., Krajcik, 2011, and Plummer and Maynard, 2014), this model could be used to support teachers' assessment and feedback, as well as facilitating students' self-regulation. The appropriateness of such a (more or less) linear model of progression would, however, also be a function of the epistemological structure of the discipline in question. When there is no predetermined path to advance along, a pre-set model of learning progression may instead limit students' freedom and narrow the space of performance outcomes. Note, however, that the absence of a pre-set model of learning progression does not imply that teachers' assessments and feedback are arbitrary. It is still possible to assess the quality of student performance, even if students may progress in different directions. This will be discussed further below.

Limited and Mechanistic Implementations of Formative Assessment

There are two different ways in which formative assessment practices in higher education have been branded as limited and/or mechanistic. First, the use of individual strategies in isolation from each other may be termed limited, since they do not make use of the potential added value of integrating the strategies into a coherent whole. For example, the students in some studies are given the opportunity to do formative assessments, which may be followed by either generic feedback on the structure of the questions and expectations for answers (Grosas et al., 2016) or feedback on their results (Carrillo-de-la-Peña et al., 2009). These studies do not involve, for instance, peer interaction and there is no explicit support for students' self-regulation. Instead, they focus more narrowly on student performance.

A second way to be termed limited and/or mechanistic is by structuring the learning environment too much, thereby – similar to providing pre-set models of learning progression – limiting students' freedom and narrowing the universe of potential outcomes. This perspective is voiced by Torrance (2012) in relation to transparency of expectations:

> With respect to the core aspirations of higher education, the issue can be stated very bluntly: Are we trying to get students to jump through pre-specified hoops, by making the nature of those hoops more apparent and encouraging students to better understand how the objectives of a course can be met; or are we trying to get students to think for themselves?
>
> *(p. 330)*

Although easy to express bluntly, this is a delicate problem. On the one hand, highly detailed rubrics may not leave enough space for creative and divergent thinking, but, on the other hand, relying on the transfer or tacit knowledge, guild knowledge, or connoisseurship means that we run the risk of making students more dependent on their teacher rather than the other way around. If the assessment criteria are concealed from the students, they are deprived of the possibility to take full responsibility for their work. We, therefore, need a middle way, where students are aware of the conditional nature and indeterminacy of criteria (Sadler, 2009). There is also a difference between "specifying criteria," dictating what students should do (and how), and criteria as indicators of quality. In the latter case, criteria help in communicating important aspects or dimensions of performance, without necessarily specifying how to perform. For example, a good hypothesis is testable and grounded in previous research, which means that "testability" and "grounding" are indicators of quality that can be used in order to evaluate a hypothesis. Knowing these criteria as a student, however, does not do the job for you if you are asked to formulate a hypothesis in relation to a new investigation.

Taken together, the main points of critique against formative assessment in higher education are that: (a) the principles, strategies, and techniques are too general, not taking the epistemological structure of the discipline into account; (b) implementations focus mainly on individual and isolated strategies, thereby being narrow and limited; and (c) implementations tend to encourage conformity and convergent thinking, rather than autonomy and divergent thinking.

The question is, therefore: What would an implementation of formative assessment in higher education look like, which takes the epistemological structure of the discipline into account, integrates the strategies of formative assessment into a coherent whole, and encourages student autonomy and divergent thinking? This is what this chapter aims to address, using a selected discipline (astronomy) as context.

The text is organized as follows: 1) we provide a brief description of what it means to be knowledgeable in science; 2) we present some of the distinctive features of astronomy, in relation to other natural sciences, such as physics and chemistry; and 3) we outline some important and common characteristics of the higher education context, which are thought to influence the use of formative assessment strategies. These first three aims are presented not only using astronomy as a context, but also using a specific formative assessment case drawn from classroom activities in astronomy, focusing on a particular aspect of science knowledge (i.e., using scientific concepts, theories, and models in astronomy). Fourth, two additional cases are presented (focusing on other aspects of science knowledge), where formative assessment strategies are used in the context of higher education astronomy; these cases provide the context for discussing formative assessment strategies for higher education. In a final section, implications for research on formative assessment in higher education are discussed.

The Epistemology of Science Learning

When educating students in science, what is it we want them to learn and be able to do? On the one hand, there is disciplinary-specific knowledge of the content (i.e., the concepts, theories, and models) and the methods of science (i.e., the experimental techniques and procedures used by scientists). Such knowledge is generally the foundation of undergraduate science and learning these aspects of science has been described as becoming fluent in using disciplinary-specific semiotic systems and resources, such as the representations, activities, and tools of the discipline (Airey & Linder, 2009, 2017). An essential aspect of this fluency is "disciplinary discernment" (Eriksson et al., 2014a, p. 168), i.e., to be able to discern and differentiate among the various qualities of some given phenomenon, in order to focus on what is most educationally relevant. As argued by Marton (2014), the development of disciplinary discernment is facilitated by experiencing pertinent patterns of variation of such relevant qualities. As will be discussed below, in relation to assessment criteria, relevant qualities in science may be the correctness and completeness of a scientific explanation, using appropriate disciplinary-specific semiotic resources (Airey & Linder, 2017), or the testability of a hypothesis. In order to discern these qualities, students need to experience explanations with a varying and increasing degree of correctness and completeness and, similarly, hypotheses with different degrees of testability. Basically, the students learn to discern a quality through the perception of difference and contrast. Learning science is thus a complex process, carrying similarities to learning a language, made up by a multitude of semiotic systems and resources, all created over time as social and cultural practices (Eriksson, 2014).

Another aspect of science learning is knowledge about science as a social and cultural practice, involving for instance how scientists decide which questions to investigate or how to communicate their findings. This facet of knowledge in science is often referred to as "nature of science" (Ryder, Leach, & Driver, 1999), and has increasingly been advocated as a means of educating for scientific literacy (Holbrook & Rannikmae, 2007). However, knowledge of the nature of science can also provide undergraduate students with insights about the social and cultural conditions of scientists in a specific discipline, leading to enhanced "disciplinary literacy" (Airey, 2011).

This broader conceptualization of science education, which includes "traditional science" (i.e., content knowledge and methods) as well as aspects of nature of science, is typically found in contemporary science curricula and assessment frameworks. Even though there may be some diversity in details, there is largely a consensus regarding overarching competencies to focus on in science education. For instance, in the PISA framework, scientific literacy is composed of three competencies, where students are supposed to be able to: (1) Explain phenomena scientifically, (2) Evaluate and design scientific inquiry, and (3) Interpret data and evidence (Organisation for Economic Co-operation and Development [OECD], 2016, p. 13). Similar competencies can be found in a number of national curricula, as well as the *Next Generation Science Standards* (National Research Council [NRC], 2012). According to the above view on the practice of science, there is an interplay between scientific concepts, theories, and models on the one hand, and planning, performing, and evaluating systematic investigations on the other. Scientific concepts, theories, and models can be used to formulate hypotheses or predictions, which are tested against empirical data, as well as to interpret evidence and draw conclusions. The bridge between the "product" and the "process" of science is evidence-based argumentation. As pointed out in the seminal paper by Newton, Driver, and Osborne (1999), claims for truth cannot be grounded in observations alone, but through the processes of argumentation; a view acknowledging that it is always humans who make disciplinary discernments and interpretations of data, and therefore that no science can be absolutely objective. Rather, the argument is used to create a link between the "imaginative conjectures of scientists and the available evidence" (p. 555).

Taken together, science learning as envisioned in this chapter involves knowledge of (1) the scientific concepts, theories, and models; (2) the methods of science, (3) evidence-based argumentation, and (4) science as a social practice. These aspects of science knowledge will be used in the cases below, where each case focus on a specific aspect.

Astronomy as a Discipline

Scientific method is commonly equated with experimental design and the testing of hypotheses in controlled laboratory settings. However, not all scientific hypotheses can be tested in this manner. Astronomy is one example of a scientific discipline that has to rely on investigations of existing natural phenomena that cannot be easily manipulated or even seen by the naked eye. Cleland (2002), among others, therefore, makes a distinction between experimental and historical sciences, where astronomy is seen to belong to the latter. Although astronomers, together with researchers in, for instance, geology, cosmology, paleontology, and evolutionary biology, cannot test their hypotheses directly by means of controlled experiments, they can formulate alternative explanations for their observations and then search for evidence to discriminate among them:

> Thus, the quality of this research is often based on the adequacy of the explanation [. . .] rather than successful prediction since it is based on the study of complex and unique entities (e.g., the big bang) that have a low probability of repeating exactly (if at all). [. . .]. In addition, reasoning in historical sciences consists largely of explanatory or reconstructive reasoning compared to predictive reasoning from causes to effects as is found in the experimental sciences.
>
> *(Gray, 2014, p. 331)*

The uniqueness of astronomy as a historical science lies partly in the sheer size of the three space dimensions, in combination with the time dimension. Learning about astronomy thus involves understanding and appreciating the vastness of the Universe as a function of its four-dimensional structure (Eriksson et al., 2014b). Since this structure is neither visible nor otherwise perceptible, experiences to facilitate the understanding of the Universe needs to be created for astronomy education purposes (Eriksson, 2014).

Another challenge for astronomy education is that most astronomical objects are either too far away, too faint to discern, or emit radiation in the non-visible part of the electromagnetic spectrum. A large part of astronomy, therefore, relies on the interpretation of indirect measurements. For example, the periodicity of variable Cepheid stars (which is observable) can be used to determine the actual luminosity (or brightness) of these stars (see arrows in Figure 7.1), which is *not* directly observable, since the apparent brightness changes with the distance to the star. If the actual luminosity is known, however, the distance to remote stars and galaxies can be calculated from the relationship between actual and apparent luminosity. As a consequence of the reliance on indirect measurements, astronomers need to create representations containing the information they gather from observations

Formative Assessment in Higher Education

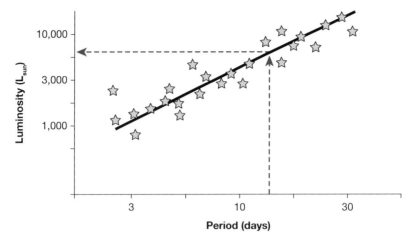

Figure 7.1 Astronomers have found that there is a relationship between the period and luminosity of variable stars that can be used for distance determinations. The type of representation in this figure holds several disciplinary affordances easily recognized by experienced astronomers, which students need to learn how to discern in order to use the graph for distance determination.

and measurements. These representations hold what is known as "disciplinary affordances," referring to the potential to provide access to disciplinary knowledge (Fredlund, Airey, & Linder, 2012), and play a central role in disciplinary communication and argumentation.

The above features of astronomy have several implications for teaching and learning in this subject. First, the inaccessibility of the Universe itself; second, the heavy reliance on instruments and computers for data collection and processing; and, third, the construction of representations to display disciplinary information for communication and argumentation, both within and outside the discipline. Furthermore, since astronomical instruments are extremely expensive and difficult to gain access to (such as space telescopes), and the fact that numerous phenomena occur only at very rare occasions (such as comets passing close to the sun), teaching and learning in astronomy has increasingly come to involve and rely on the use of computer simulations.

The Higher Education Context

This chapter has a particular focus on higher education. It is, therefore, necessary to make some distinctions between primary and secondary school settings and the higher education context.

First, from the information provided on the internet for future university students, it could be concluded that one of the major differences between primary and secondary school and higher education is student independence and personal responsibility (maybe with the exception of not having to wear school uniform in Australia and the UK). The main message is that at high school, the teacher is responsible for facilitating students' learning, whereas at university the students are responsible for their learning and for completing their assignments. The notion of increased student autonomy at university does not reside only in the minds of students, however, but it is also frequently suggested by university lecturers that university studies require students to become more autonomous. Still, as noted by for instance Macaskill and Taylor (2010), there does not appear to exist a common definition of what it means to be autonomous in this regard, and several authors discuss autonomous learning without defining what they mean. In this article, autonomous learning will be used more or less synonymously with *self-regulated learning* (SRL). There are several models of SRL (Panadero, 2017), but in its broadest meaning it refers to a process by which students plan their assignments by formulating goals, identifying resources, choose and implement appropriate strategies; monitor their performance; and evaluate the outcomes.

Another characteristic of higher education, also prevalent in information for future university students, is the large classes, resulting in less contact time with the lecturers. The large classes represent a challenge for the teachers as well, for instance when providing feedback to the students.

The final feature of higher education to be mentioned here, which is only occasionally mentioned on university web pages for future students, is the close connection to research. One aspect of this connection is the widespread conception that research enhances teaching, for instance since research-active academics are believed to teach from their first-hand research experience, rather than from textbooks (Coate, Barnett, & Williams, 2001). Regardless of whether it is true or not that research enhances teaching in a more general sense, researchers are able to introduce students to the specific scientific methods and instruments used in the particular subject. They are also able to introduce the students to the social and cultural practice of research.

In summary, this chapter will take into account some of the characteristics of higher education that are likely to influence teaching and learning, namely: (1) the goal of fostering independent learners, (2) the sometimes large classes of students, and (3) the close connection to research.

Formative Assessment in Higher Education

Carless (2016) discusses how formative assessment is conceptualized in higher education, as compared to school settings, where he notes that formative assessment strategies are generally more clearly defined and agreed upon in relation to schooling. Similar strategies can be traced in the literature on formative assessment in higher education, although some seem to be under-explored. For instance, Black and McCormick (2010) specifically highlight the need for further investigations regarding the lecture theater as a context for formative assessment, which is part of the strategy to engineer effective questioning and discussions.

Carless (2016) synthesizes work from different authors and proposes four main strategies for formative assessment in higher education:

1   Productive assessment task design.
2   Effective feedback processes.
3   Developing student understanding of the nature of quality.
4   Students practicing making judgments.

These strategies will be exemplified and further clarified in relation to three cases of teaching in astronomy below.

Formative Assessment in Astronomy

In this section, a teaching sequence focusing on one of the categories of science knowledge described above (i.e., scientific concepts, theories, and models in astronomy) is presented. This presentation is then followed by a discussion of the formative assessment strategies in higher education, highlighting the connections between these strategies and the case presented.

A Case of Teaching the Use of Concepts, Theories, and Models in Astronomy

There are a limited number of astronomical phenomena that are visible to the naked eye, such as the lunar phases, planetary movements, and the flickering light of close-to-horizon stars. Historically, different models have been used to explain these observations. One of the most elaborate concerns

Claudius Ptolemy's geocentric planetary model using epicycles, which was once introduced in order to explain puzzling planetary behavior, such as retrograde motion. Retrograde motion means that the planets are seen to move in the "wrong" direction across the sky for some time, before returning to move in the "correct" direction. As strange as that model might seem today, it could be used to predict planetary positions to, at the time, acceptable precision. Later, at the beginning of the seventeenth century, several of the apparent paradoxes in the sky were resolved by changing from a geocentric to a heliocentric worldview. Today, therefore, the retrograde motion, as well as changes in the apparent distances of the planets from the earth, can be easily explained by how the planets are organized around the sun. It is important to keep in mind, however, that the phenomena in themselves have not changed (i.e., they still look the same to the observer), even though we might perceive them differently when we observe them from another theoretical perspective (i.e., the disciplinary discernment by both astronomers and laypersons of today is more nuanced, due to access to more extensive disciplinary knowledge).

Using this as a point of departure, students are given a list of astronomical phenomena, all of which are observable in the sky by the naked eye. Their task is to explain the phenomena for younger students (i.e., lower secondary school students) by using visualizations (i.e., a semiotic system of different resources – static, dynamic, or in combination – that are presented visually). This means that the students have to transform abstract, scientific explanations into concrete visualizations, or as explained above, change the mode of representation (Figure 7.2).

Before being able to visualize the phenomena, the students have to find appropriate scientific explanations for these phenomena since, in this case, the explanations were not provided. Instead, the students are expected to find the explanations by themselves, for instance by using textbooks, the internet, or any other available sources. The reason for this is that the students need to learn how to choose an explanation that is appropriate for the specific purpose, which may not necessarily be an explanation from the textbook using mathematical symbols.

In order to support the students, they are asked to (anonymously) hand in their explanations to be reviewed by their peers. A number of peer groups are organized and a discussion is initiated on the quality criteria to be used in the review process. This discussion can be scaffolded by providing a number of different explanations for the same phenomenon, which differ in several dimensions, such as format, complexity, completeness, and correctness (Text Box 7.1). By comparing these examples, the following criteria can be formulated: The explanation should be "scientifically correct," "complete," and "adapted to the purpose." These criteria are then used by the peer groups to assess the explanations and provide written feedback. Text Box 7.2 shows some examples of

Astronomical phenomenon: Solar eclipse.

Scientific explanation: A solar eclipse occurs when the Moon passes between the Sun and Earth, and when the Moon fully or partially blocks the Sun for an observer on Earth.

Visualization:

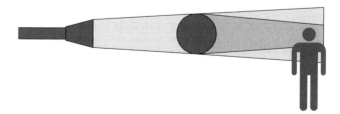

Figure 7.2 The scientific explanation for a solar eclipse visualized by blocking the light from a flashlight (representing the Sun) with a ball (representing the Moon). The figure shows a total eclipse, but a partial eclipse can also be visualized by moving either the ball or the observer.

explanations of why the Sun may have dark spots. (Note that it is not advisable to look directly at the Sun without any protection, such as special optical filters. For educational purposes, an image of the Sun can easily be projected onto a piece of paper using a small telescope or binoculars in order to see sunspots.)

Text Box 7.1

Different Versions of Explanations of Why an Apple Falls to the Ground

The apple falls because:

a) *There is a force (gravity) that pulls the apple toward the center of the Earth.*

b) $F = G \dfrac{m_1 m_2}{r^2}$

c) *There is a curvature of the space-time due to the presence of a massive object (the Earth) and the apple is accelerated relative to the observer on the ground.*

d) *Force equals mass times acceleration due to gravity.*

e) *All bodies move toward their natural place and since apples are made of mostly earth and water, their natural place is the center of the Earth.*

Text Box 7.2

Four Different Explanations of the Same Phenomenon (Sunspots).

There are dark spots on the surface of the Sun because:

1 Temporary concentrations of magnetic field flux may inhibit convection in the Sun's interior, thus preventing energy from the inside of the Sun to reach the surface at certain points. At these points, the temperature is reduced and consequently the luminosity of the photosphere decreases since the peak of the black-body radiation curve moves to lower intensities and longer wavelengths.

2 Parts of the photosphere temporarily have a lower temperature than the surroundings, making them appear darker (3400 K as compared to 5800 K).

3 The Sun is so hot that the gas enters a state of plasma, which means that electrons are dislocated from the atoms. The strong magnetic field in the sunspots interact with this electrically charged plasma, making the temperature drop, and creating a sunspot. Sunspots come in pairs with different magnetic poles. It is known that these magnetic fields interfere with each other. The sunspots are cooler than their surroundings (approximately 4000–3400K), the darkest part is called Umbra, and the magnetic field is also strongest there. The slightly lighter part is called penumbra. The sunspot period is approximately 22 years.

4 Sunspots appear as a result of the magnetic field in the Sun. A strong magnetic flux may displace significant portions of the gaseous surface, temporarily removing the burning fuel and creating (non-burning) holes that appear as dark spots. The gas will eventually, but slowly, re-enter these holes and ignite, which takes about 11 years.

As can be seen by comparing the explanations in Text Box 7.2, there are some important differences. Such differences can be referred to as disciplinary versus pedagogical affordances of the chosen semiotic resource, in this case written text. In contrast to disciplinary affordance (Fredlund et al., 2012), pedagogical affordance is the aptness of a semiotic resource for the teaching and learning of some particular educational content (Airey, 2015).

First, while three of the explanations are more or less scientifically correct (i.e., the sunspots appear as dark as a result of having a lower temperature as compared to the surroundings and that the drop in temperature is due to an interference between the plasma and the magnetic field), explanation number 4 is partly incorrect. While this explanation could still be assessed in relation to the other criteria (i.e., completeness, and adapted to the purpose), it may be considered doubtful whether time should be invested in providing such elaborated feedback for an incorrect response. Rather, efforts need to be made in order to address the misconception(s) expressed by the student. Incorrect responses also provide valuable input for the teacher, who can choose to address these misconceptions during lectures or other instructional activities.

Second, in terms of completeness, explanation number 2 does not include any information about the reasons for parts of the photosphere temporarily having a lower temperature than the surrounding solar surface, while explanations 1 and 3 both include information about the magnetic field causing the temperature to drop. Explanations 1 and 3 are therefore more complete than explanation 2. Another difference is that explanation 3 includes excessive information. Even if correct, this information is not necessary in order to explain the phenomenon in question.

Third, yet another difference between the explanations is that explanation number 1 is written in a language that might be less accessible for non-scientists (i.e., low in pedagogic affordance). Depending

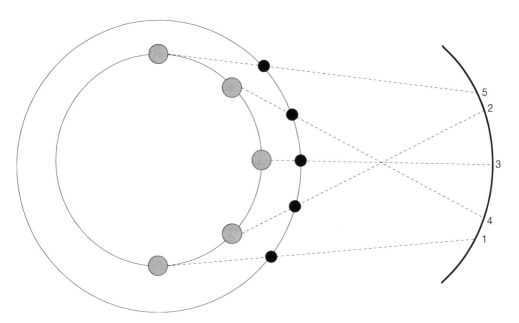

Figure 7.3 Diagram explaining the apparent retrograde motion of an outer planet as seen from Earth (gray circles), in this case Mars (black circles). Both planets move in a counterclockwise direction in the picture. The dotted lines are used to project the apparent position of Mars in the sky. As can be seen by the numbers to the right, the position of Mars will not appear in a uniform motion when the Earth "overtakes" superior planets (i.e., planets farther away from the Sun as compared to the Earth). Note that sizes and scales are incorrect in this representation.

on the target audience, this explanation may, therefore, fail to communicate the mechanisms behind the appearance of sunspots. Furthermore, explanation number 2 is not very detailed (i.e., lacks in completeness), which may also reduce the usefulness and accessibility of the explanation. Explanation number 3, on the other hand, provides an explanation that is both detailed and comprehensible, making it more accessible for non-scientists (i.e., high in pedagogic affordance).

By identifying differences such as the ones exemplified above, the students in the peer groups assessed the explanations and provided written feedback. The students could then collect their explanations, along with written feedback, and revise their explanations (if needed) before working with the visualizations.

Since the visualizations were supposed to explain the phenomena to younger students, they had to be quite simple and most were made from physical materials (i.e., not digital simulations or presentations), such as balloons, flashlights, and terrestrial globes. For example, the retrograde motion of planets mentioned above could be visualized by using papier-mâché spheres in strings and the apparent position in the sky projected on a piece of paper (Figure 7.3). These visualizations may also be subjected to peer- and/or teacher assessment, but since the quality of visualizations for younger students are not normally part of the disciplinary literacy, they will not be further discussed here.

Formative Assessment of Using Concepts, Theories, and Models in Astronomy

As mentioned, Carless (2016) has suggested four main strategies for formative assessment in higher education: productive assessment task design, effective feedback processes, developing student understanding of the nature of quality, and students practicing making judgments. The case presented above connects to all four of these strategies.

First, *productive assessment task design* involves securing alignment with intended learning outcomes, often encompassing complex knowledge, and designing tasks which encourage students' use of deep-learning approaches. The perceived importance of introducing such tasks is related to the value of designing and implementing "authentic assessments," which deal with "activities that can be direct models of the reality" (Black, 1998, p. 87). Such assessments are characterized by:

1   An ambition to reflect the complexity of real-world settings and thereby provide more valid data about student performance, by letting the students solve realistic problems (Darling-Hammond & Snyder, 2000).
2   Assessment criteria, as well as standards for excellent performance, which reflect what is considered quality within a specified "community of practice," which the students are to become participants of, so that the students can strive for what is considered excellent performance within these communities (Lave & Wenger, 1991; Wiggins, 1998).

By designing the assessment situation with as many authentic dimensions as possible (e.g., the task, the social or physical context, etc.) it has been argued that authentic assessment can provide more valid data about student competency, as well as having a positive impact on student motivation and learning (Gulikers, Bastiaens, & Kirschner, 2004). Furthermore, it could be assumed that authenticity facilitates transfer to the target domain (Havnes, 2008).

In the case presented here, the students were asked to visualize astronomical phenomena for younger students, which is a realistic and complex problem generating rich data on student performance. The task also involves the transduction of representations (Ariey & Linder, 2017), which is considered a fundamental part of disciplinary knowledge and learning in science. Furthermore, the criteria used to assess the explanations reflect what is considered quality within a scientific community.

Second, *effective feedback processes* involve giving formative feedback to students, but also to "close the feedback loop" by providing students with opportunities to use the feedback they receive. As has been suggested by research, a number of students do not use the feedback they receive and one of the main reasons seems to that they do not find the feedback to be useful (e.g., Carless, 2006; Sinclair & Cleland, 2007). Providing students with opportunities to use the feedback they receive therefore seems to be an important prerequisite for an active and productive use of feedback.

Regarding the provision of feedback, one of the most crucial factors for the effect of feedback seems to be whether it is about the student (self-level feedback) or about her/his performance (task-, and process-level feedback). Feedback at the self-level may not necessarily have any positive effect on student motivation or learning, or even negative effects. Feedback at the task-, or process-level, on the other hand, typically gives positive effects, although it may be more productive to focus on recurring processes (i.e., process-level feedback), so that the feedback can be utilized in future tasks, rather than focusing on details specific to the particular task (Hattie & Timperley, 2007). That task-related feedback is generally more productive than self-related feedback is not so difficult to understand. It does not help much to be told that you are talented or lazy when you need information on how to improve your performance. To repeatedly hear how good you are, or vice versa, tends to affect students' academic self-concept. And the feedback thus risks being self-fulfilling: "I can't do this, so there is no reason for me to invest any effort." Giving feedback on student performance, putting personal qualities aside, may, therefore, provide better opportunities for students to use their feedback constructively.

Another important factor for the effectiveness of feedback is the balance between a focus on past versus future performance. It is sometimes assumed that the students will be able to use information about past performance as a springboard for their continued learning. However, it has been found that some students find it difficult to transform information about past performance into strategies for their continued learning (Burke, 2009, Weaver 2006). There are several ways to support students in this process. For example, students can receive – and make use of – group feedback. It has also been shown that relatively short interventions can give good results, for example, in the form of workshops where students bring and process their own feedback (Burke & Pieterick, 2010). Feedback can be sorted into categories such as "strengths" and "improvement needed," and based on this categorization a plan for continued learning may be made.

In the case presented here, the feedback that students received was directed toward their task performance. There were no assessments of students' latent traits or personalities, thereby avoiding any self-level feedback. This was further emphasized by the criteria used, which all referred to task performance. All feedback provided also included both strengths and areas for improvement in relation to student performance, making the feedback easier to use for formative purposes. As an example, explanation number 3 in Text Box 7.2 has strengths in relation to some criteria (i.e., includes information about the reasons for parts of the photosphere temporarily having a lower temperature than the surrounding solar surface), but improvements can be made in relation to others' (i.e., includes excessive information).

It could also be noted that the feedback, in this case, included both task-level and process-level feedback. Task-level feedback is in part specific to the individual task, in the sense that feedback on the correctness of an explanation for sunspots may not easily transfer to other tasks involving different content knowledge. But as pointed out by Hattie and Timperley (2007), task-level feedback can be powerful for instance when it is about faulty interpretations or conceptual understanding. Process-level feedback, on the other hand, is more easily transferred between similar tasks (but with different content knowledge). In this case, process-level feedback refers to generic qualities in explanations.

Furthermore, it should be noted that the students in the case were given the opportunity to actively engage with and use the feedback they received as an integral part of instruction. Students receive feedback on their explanations, which they could use when working with the visualizations, thereby creating an incentive for the students to engage with their feedback.

The third strategy of formative assessment in higher education is *developing student understanding of the nature of quality*. At first thought, you may wonder what understanding the nature of quality has to do with assessment. But you soon realize that assessment and the nature of quality are intimately linked. When assessing student work, teachers look for indicators of quality (i.e., criteria) and only if student performance corresponds to the teacher's notion of quality, will she/he reward the performance with high grades or any other expression of judgment. Consequently, if the students do not share the teacher's notion of quality, they are not likely to succeed – at least not in terms of being high-performing.

A distinctive feature of qualities is that they are not static, but depend on values that may change over time and/or differ between cultures and contexts. What is considered high-quality work in one setting, may therefore not be acknowledged as such in another. Not even how we value academic work is constant, but have changed over time and differs between disciplines and cultures – sometimes even between universities in the same country. So how do we communicate to the students what it is that we value and what we expect of them?

Traditionally, and still very common, we rely on socialization. By inviting the students to participate in lectures, seminars, and other activities, by giving exams and feedback, we expose them to the implicit values of academia and hope that they will recognize and adopt these values. If they do, they are awarded with high grades and certifications. If they do not, we may think that they are not fit for higher education. But what if low performance does not depend on low ability, but on students not being able to extract the notion of quality by merely participating? And if they would understand the specific nature of quality in this particular context, would they improve their performance? These questions have spawned a lot of debate, not least since students with diverse backgrounds now enter academia in much larger numbers.

One way of addressing this problem has been to make efforts to increase transparency. For instance, it is now common to present the intended learning outcomes of a course to students, so that they know what they are supposed to learn. It has also become common practice to share explicit assessment criteria with the students, so that they know what is expected of them in terms of high-quality performance. As most academics are aware, however, quality is generally very difficult to communicate verbally and students may not necessarily profit from explicit criteria or scoring rubrics.

What is often disregarded is that quality criteria are often specific to defined communities of practice (Lave & Wenger, 1991) and cannot easily be removed from these contexts. This means that the words, and other semiotic systems, that signify the qualities (i.e., the criteria) are given meaning in a certain context by certain people. The semiotic resources are therefore more or less arbitrary and there is no direct relationship between the criteria and reality. Basically, in order to understand the criteria, you also have to have an understanding of the practice to which they belong (Airey & Linder, 2009). This is often obvious for communities of practice that are unfamiliar or obscure to us, as the art of wine tasting or martial arts may be to some. However, the concepts of connoisseurship and critique can also be used to describe the assessor's task in higher education, which is to make descriptions of the qualities and shortcomings of the work as an expert on the subject (Eisner, 1991). Assessments require a person that possesses a sense of relevant details and has the ability to judge and describe the performance in a versatile way.

What this means for communicating the notion of quality to students, is that they need to experience quality, but also acquire the multimodal language of the discipline to be able to identify and express the qualities sought for. If the students have never seen "a clear and justified conclusion" (Orsmond & Merry, 1996, p. 244), it is not easy to recognize one, even if they have such a conclusion just in front of them. The same applies to expressions such as "comprehensive and nuanced discussion" or "well-developed reasoning," where the language simply does not suffice and you need experience in order to understand what these terms really mean. But experience is not enough in itself, since without the proper multimodal language we do not know what to distinguish among our experiences. If you read a number of essays or laboratory reports, but do not know why some are considered good and some are considered less good, then experience will not help you very much. Criteria can, therefore, help us by drawing attention to the important qualities of the essays, the lab reports, or whatever they may apply to. This dynamic interplay between criteria and concrete examples is something that Sadler (1987) has argued for a long time, and there are a number of empirical studies supporting the use of criteria in combination with concrete examples of performance (e.g., Jonsson, 2010; Orsmond, Merry, & Reiling, 2002).

Another important prerequisite for communicating the notion of quality to students is variation. As Marton (2014) explains in his *variation theory*, we are able to discern the difference in quality through experiencing variation. Thus, if we are to understand what it means for a text to be "coherent and organized," we need to see a text that is coherent and organized, but also texts that are coherent and organized to a varying degree. Only then can we appreciate what "coherent and organized" really means.

According to Sadler (2010), the most natural way to access this variation is through peer assessment. If giving a number of students the same (open-ended) task, they will most likely solve it differently and presumably with varying quality. By letting the students compare and assess each other's performances based on criteria, they will experience a spectrum of quality for the criteria included in the assessment. In addition, by being involved in an assessment process, students work actively with the criteria, as compared to having the criteria passively presented to them. This engagement in the assessment process will be explored in relation to the next strategy.

In the case presented here, the students were provided with explicit criteria for scientific explanations, but they are not left alone with the criteria. Instead, the use of criteria is embedded in practice (i.e., peer review of explanations), where the meaning of the criteria can be discussed and negotiated with teachers and peers in relation to concrete examples of performance. Furthermore, the students are confronted with multiple performances, presumably of varying quality, which may facilitate the interpretation of the criteria.

Finally, the fourth strategy of formative assessment in higher education is *students practicing making judgments*. If student autonomy is the ultimate goal of higher education, students need to know both when and how to use the knowledge they acquired, to solve problems within the specific discipline or profession. Understanding the nature of quality is thus an essential component of autonomy, but students also need to engage actively with quality criteria in situations where the notion of quality come in to play. Examples of such situations are when reviewing someone else's work or when planning, monitoring, and evaluating own work.

Peer assessment is a typical example of reviewing someone else's work. As mentioned above, peer assessment is a useful pedagogical tool, not only to convey the notion of quality, but also to involve students in the assessment process. In addition, peer assessment is an established arrangement in higher education, where peers are asked to review each other's (mostly written) work and provide feedback. Students may then use this feedback to revise their work before handing it in for summative evaluation by the teacher. Empirical studies on peer assessment have shown that students initially may find this process difficult and uncomfortable, but also that they typically grow more positive and feel that they benefit from it (e.g., Barnard, de Luca, & Li, 2015; van den Berg, Admiraal, & Pilot, 2006). There are also a number of studies suggesting that the quality of students' performance may improve as a result of engagement in peer feedback (Panadero, Jonsson, & Alqassab, 2018), but also – interestingly – that students may actually benefit more from giving feedback than from receiving it (Cho & Cho, 2011). Consequently, there are several good reasons to make peer assessment a regular and integrated part of teaching in higher education.

When it comes to planning, monitoring, and evaluating own work, this process is often referred to as "self-regulated learning" (SRL). According to Nicol and Macfarlane-Dick (2006), SRL

> is manifested in the active monitoring and regulation of a number of different learning processes, e.g., the setting of, and orientation toward, learning goals; the strategies used to achieve goals; the management of resources; the effort exerted; reactions to external feedback; the products produced.
>
> *(p. 199)*

A number of studies have shown that SRL skills are important for the success of students and that the use of SRL strategies is a significant predictor of academic performance (Richardson, Abraham, & Bond, 2012).

Interestingly, there is increasing evidence that SRL skills can be learned as a set of generic skills, as shown by classroom interventions targeting the development of (school) students' SRL skills, either working with the students (Dignath & Büttner, 2008) and/or with the teachers (Kramarski & Michalsky, 2009). In particular, interventions to promote self-assessment has been shown to have a positive effect on students' SRL and, to a greater extent, on students' self-efficacy (Panadero, Jonsson, & Botella, 2017).

Self-assessment may involve a wide range of activities; from asking students to grade their own work without further reflection at one end of the spectrum, to having them make comprehensive analyses of their own performance on complex tasks at the other. Important to notice, however, is that self-assessment is about assessing own work, not about (for instance) estimating overall academic capacity or evaluating students' satisfaction with the instruction. Self-assessment involves making judgments of quality, identifying strengths and weaknesses, just as teachers' assessments – but in relation to own work (Boud & Falchikov, 1989).

Although it may seem obvious that self-assessment is a part of the (self-) evaluation phase of SRL, self-assessment is also used during task performance. According to research on students' use of scoring rubrics (e.g. Jonsson, 2014), it may be beneficial for students to have access to assessment criteria before starting the activity, so that they can use these criteria to set more realistic goals for the activity, as well as monitor their work as they progress (Panadero, Jonsson, & Strijbos, 2016).

In the case presented here, peer assessment has been used in order to: (a) provide formative feedback to a large number of students, (b) develop students' understanding of the nature of quality, and (c) practice making judgments. Self-regulation is also facilitated using an authentic task with room for divergent thinking, since there is a need to plan, monitor, and evaluate task performance, in a way that more closed assignments may not offer. Furthermore, the formative approach with peer assessment and peer feedback supports the monitoring and evaluation of performance.

Teaching Focusing on Other Categories of Science Knowledge

Above, a case of formative assessment in astronomy was presented and discussed. This case had a main focus on one of the categories of science knowledge (scientific concepts, theories, and models). In this section, two more cases are presented, focusing on the other categories of science knowledge: (2) methods of science, or (3) evidence-based argumentation. Knowledge in the fourth category, nature of science, is integrated into all three of the cases. The reader is encouraged to reflect on the connections between these cases and the strategies for formative assessment in higher education while reading the cases.

A Case of Teaching the Planning of Systematic Investigations

This case focuses on knowledge about the methods of science, by asking the students to plan systematic investigations using space telescopes. For astronomers, there are several good reasons for using space telescopes. In visible-light astronomy, space telescopes (such as the Hubble Space Telescope) are not affected by atmospheric effects or light pollution, thereby providing higher resolution images. Other telescopes, such as the Fermi Gamma-ray Space Telescope, are located in space because they measure electromagnetic radiation that is absorbed by the atmosphere. Unlike visible light and some radio wavelength bands, high-energy radiation, such as gamma rays and x-rays, cannot be measured from the ground and therefore demands space telescopes.

Some of the organizations behind space telescopes (such as European Space Agency [ESA] and National Aeronautics and Space Administration [NASA]) offer guest investigator programs, where scientists can submit proposals for data collection and be awarded observing time with the telescope and sometimes also funding for the analysis. Since the number of proposals often are large, the process may be highly competitive.

In this case, the students in a class are asked to design an investigation where they would need to collect data with the aid of a space, or remote, telescope (cf. Gomez & Fitzgerald, 2017). However, given the competition to access any of the telescopes, only one proposal will be selected and submitted from the class. The students, therefore, have to work together to decide which of the proposals that has the highest quality. The proposal will eventually be submitted, but the students are made aware of the very small probability of acceptance, since they are actually competing with experienced researchers.

The first step in such a teaching sequence involves coming up with questions to investigate. This is done as a whole class exercise, where students suggest topics and questions that they think would be interesting to investigate. In this discussion, the teacher helps by narrowing down the number of questions. When there is a manageable number, students form groups around these questions and search for previous research in order to formulate hypotheses and plan for investigations.

The students work with planning their investigations and prepare to present their research proposals for their peers. The next step of the teaching sequence, therefore, involves oral presentations in whole class, where the students present and argue for their research designs. When all groups have made their presentations, the students meet in groups and evaluate the research designs of the other groups according to criteria commonly used for scientific investigations, such as "providing a clear purpose and research questions," "adequate methods for collecting and analyzing data," "feasibility of the design," and the "awareness of potential problems, errors, and limitations." Each group also ranks the designs according to what they perceive as high to low quality, a decision they have to be able to justify by referring to both strengths and weaknesses in all research designs. When the groups come together again, they compare the ratings and try to prioritize which of the research projects to submit as an official proposal from the class. When a research design has been selected, all groups provide feedback, in order to improve the design and increase the likelihood of being awarded observation time with the telescope.

In the review process, students will most likely notice that it is very difficult to rank the research designs according to quality. The last step of the teaching sequence is, therefore, a discussion about the review process, in order to highlight the social processes of science, which becomes visible due to the formative assessment practices described above. For instance: How do we judge the overall quality of a research design? Why were certain research designs prioritized and not others? Are there other criteria at play besides the quality criteria, such as the social status of some students?

A Case of Teaching the Communication of Findings and Conclusions

This case focuses on evidence-based argumentation, by asking students to argue for their classification of stars. As described above, there are numerous practical problems with making observations in astronomy. Instead, there are computer simulations available to use in the teaching and learning of astronomy, where students can simulate the collection of data and then analyze this pre-arranged data, for example, the Slone Digital Sky Survey/SkyServer (http://cas.sdss.org/dr7/en/proj/) or the Hipparcos homepage (http://rssd.esa.int/index.php?project=HIPPARCOS&page=index).

In this case, the students collect data on stellar radiation through spectroscopy. This means that the light from a star passes through a prism or a diffraction grating, splitting the light into a spectrum. As compared to a continuous spectrum from a light source in a laboratory, the spectra from stars are interspersed with dark absorptions lines. These lines arise when the light from the star passes through the outer atmospheric layers of the emitting star, where elements in the gas or plasma may absorb electromagnetic radiation of certain wavelengths (Figure 7.4). Because elements only absorb radiation at specific wavelengths, the absorption lines provide information about which elements exist in the star, abundances, surface temperature of the star, and many other properties.

Stars can be classified into different spectral classes by their spectra. There are seven basic spectral classes (O, B, A, F, G, K, and M), which correspond to the surface temperature of the stars, such that O and B stars are very hot while K and M stars are cooler. Between the classes, there are ten subdivisions numbered 0 to 9. For example, our Sun is classified as a G2 star, Sirius A (the brightest star in the night sky) is a B3, and the red supergiant star Betelgeuse in the constellation Orion is an M2. A third classification is also added to the spectral class using Roman numerals, ranging from I (for super giants) to V (for main sequence stars; i.e., stars in their "middle ages," fusing hydrogen atoms to form helium atoms in their cores. Since about 90 percent of the stars in the universe are main sequence stars, they are in some sense ordinary stars), such as G2V for the Sun (a main sequence star) and M2I for Betelgeuse (a supergiant), to distinguish between stars with the same temperature but with different luminosity. This classification depends on the width of certain spectral lines; for giant stars, these lines are narrower than for main sequence stars. Generally, a small main sequence star (class V) does not shine as bright as a giant star (class III), even if they could have the same surface temperature.

In this teaching sequence, the students are asked to collect spectroscopic data on a number of stars, using a simulation software that provides them with both photographs and graphs (for example:

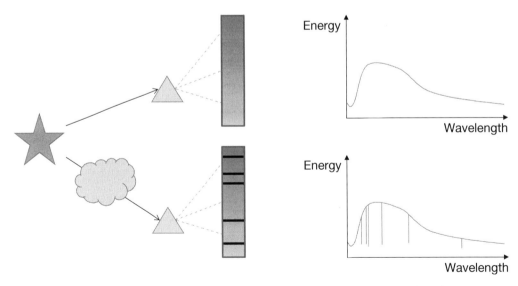

Figure 7.4 A hot source emits electromagnetic radiation, such as visible light. If passing through a prism or a diffraction grating, the light is split into a spectrum. However, if the continuous light from the surface of the star passes through cooler gas in the stellar atmosphere, elements in the gas may absorb certain specific wavelengths of radiation, seen as dark lines in the spectrum.

http://cas.sdss.org/dr7/en/proj/advanced/spectraltypes). They are first supposed to identify the absorption lines in the spectra by comparing to reference samples and use this information to make classifications of the stars in different spectral classes. In the next step, the students are to investigate the absorption lines in greater detail (i.e., calculate the relationship between width and depth) in order to determine the luminosity class of the stars. Both of these steps involve disciplinary discernment by the students and it is expected that students will discern different things, and in different detail, in those absorptions lines. However, in order to make this second classification, the students have to ascertain that they have identified the correct absorption lines. Before determining the luminosity class of the stars, the students, therefore, present their classification of the spectral classes to their peers. This is done by presenting the observed data, their conclusions, and arguments supporting the conclusions. At the end of the teaching sequence, the students have to hand in a written report to the teacher with their classifications and accompanying justifications for a summative evaluation.

Obviously, it is important that the classifications made by the students are correct and that they receive corrective feedback if they are not. However, in this case the students are also being assessed on the quality of their arguments. Similar to the previous case, the students are provided with criteria that they are supposed to use in order to assess each other's arguments.

The model for argumentation by Toulmin (1958) has been extensively used in the field of science education research. In the most basic form, the Toulmin model shows that claims/conclusions have to be supported by data, but also that data cannot speak for itself. Instead, the claims/conclusions have to be warranted by an argument connecting the data and the claims/conclusions (Figure 7.5). In a more elaborated form, the model may include qualifiers, which propose the conditions under which the argument holds, counter-arguments, and auxiliary statements that serve to support the warrants (called "backings").

For the present case, the following criteria (based on the Toulmin model) were used. As a baseline, arguments should be based on data and there should be more than one observation in favor of the claim/conclusion. For higher quality, counter-arguments should be presented and answered and arguments should be backed with scientific knowledge. Furthermore, for high quality, qualifiers could be addressed. Based on these criteria, the students peer assess each other's arguments and provide feedback.

Text Boxes 7.3 to 7.5 show a sequence of arguments with different qualities according to the abovementioned criteria. First, Text Box 7.3 shows an argument that is based on data (i.e., absorption lines) and includes two observations in favor of the conclusion (i.e., lines from ionized calcium as well as from hydrogen atoms). This argument, therefore, fulfills the baseline requirements according to the criteria. Second, in Text Box 7.4, a counter-argument is provided (i.e., lines from ionized calcium and hydrogen atoms can be found in A-class stars as well) and answered (i.e., the appearance of Fraunhofer G lines, which are not found in A-class stars). Finally, in Text Box 7.5, the arguments are backed by scientific knowledge (i.e., knowledge about the relationship between the appearance of lines and the surface temperature of the star). Qualifiers are not shown in the examples, but could, for instance, refer to the possibility of distinguishing between lines with approximately the same wavelength (such as the Hydrogen epsilon line with the Calcium H line).

Figure 7.5 Simplified version of the Toulmin model.

Text Box 7.3

Example of Argument Supporting the Conclusion That the Investigated Star is an F-Class Star.

"We have classified this star [showing photograph and graph of stellar spectrum] as an F-class star. As you can see here, there are strong absorption lines from ionized calcium, but also lines from hydrogen atoms."

Text Box 7.4

Example of Argument, and Answer to Counter-Argument, Supporting the Conclusion That the Investigated Star is an F-Class Star.

"We have classified this star [showing photograph and graph of stellar spectrum] as an F-class star. As you can see here, there are strong absorption lines from ionized calcium, but also lines from hydrogen atoms. These lines are not exclusively seen in F-class stars and can also be seen in A-class stars. However, the appearance of Fraunhofer G lines here provides further support for the conclusion that this is indeed an F-class star."

Text Box 7.5

Example of Argument That is Backed by Scientific Knowledge.

"We have classified this star [showing photograph and graph of stellar spectrum] as an F-class star. As you can see here, there are strong absorption lines from ionized calcium, but also lines from hydrogen atoms. Balmer lines from hydrogen are more prominent in stars with a surface temperature of about 10,000 K, while the H and K lines from ionized calcium tend to be stronger for somewhat lower temperatures. Together with the appearance of lines from neutral metals, which would typically be ionized at higher temperatures, this suggests that this is indeed an F-class star."

Discussion

Three cases have been presented above, which address different facets of knowledge in science. The first case addresses the use of scientific concepts, theories, and models in order to explain and visualize astronomical phenomena. The second case involves the methods of science by asking students to design an investigation, while the third case addresses evidence-based argumentation where students argue for their classification of stars. All three cases also involve "meta-knowledge" about science (i.e., nature of science) by introducing quality criteria for scientific explanations, research designs, and evidence-based arguments. Furthermore, the second case explicitly addresses the social processes of science by inviting students to discuss the review of research proposals and the potential influence of other factors than merely quality.

With regard to the higher education context, all cases involve peer assessment and peer feedback as a way to support autonomous learning, but also as a response to a teaching situation with large classes and less contact time, where the provision of individual formative feedback would be very time-consuming. As mentioned above, the cases also have a strong connection to research and disciplinary literacy.

Most importantly, however, all cases address the four main strategies for formative assessment in higher education as suggested by Carless (2016) (i.e., productive assessment task design, effective feedback processes, developing student understanding of the nature of quality, and students practicing making judgments). What these cases envision to illustrate, is the possibility to design teaching sequences where the formative assessment strategies work together as a whole to support students' learning of disciplinary knowledge. While there are some aspects of this teaching that are specific to the disciplinary knowledge being taught (such as the tasks, the criteria, and the content of the feedback), the principles and strategies are still the same. Furthermore, although the strategies can be implemented in a number of different ways, there are some specific operationalizations that have been used in all the above cases. This is not coincidental; rather it reflects either an adaptation to the higher education context or a pedagogical consideration. The recurring features are authentic tasks, formative feedback (including the opportunity to use their feedback), peer assessment and peer feedback, and the use of explicit assessment criteria.

Authentic Tasks

Productive assessment task design does not necessarily imply the use of authentic tasks. However, authentic tasks provide a rich material for formative feedback and also have a potential to support self-regulated learning, by inviting the students to plan, monitor, and evaluate their performance. All of the above cases are built around such authentic disciplinary-specific tasks. In the first case, the students are asked to visualize astronomical phenomena for younger students, simulating a teaching situation. In the second case, students plan an investigation and review research proposals, simulating the work of professional astronomers. Finally, in the third case, students work with stellar spectra to classify stars and learn how to base their arguments on observed data – again simulating the work of professional astronomers. This means that the students cannot rely solely on rote learning or memory knowledge in any of these situations. Instead, all of the tasks involve both divergent and convergent thinking (e.g., Torrance & Pryor, 2001). They are divergent in the sense that students can choose different ways to visualize astronomical phenomena, plan their investigations, or formulate their arguments. But they are also convergent in the sense that they have to rely on established concepts, theories, and models of science when explaining the astronomical phenomena or when backing their arguments. Even the criteria are to some extent fixed, although they are more open to interpretation and negotiation, as compared to scientific concepts, theories, and models.

Formative Feedback

All feedback provided to the students in these cases is in line with research on effective feedback, such as the feedback: (a) referring to task performance (i.e. not self-level feedback), (b) including information about both strengths and areas for improvement, and (c) including both task-level and process-level feedback. The students are also given the opportunity to use their feedback as an integral part of instruction. In the first case, the students received feedback on their explanations, so that they could use this information when working with the visualizations. In the second case, the students used feedback as a group to improve the research proposal that will be sent to ESA, NASA, or elsewhere. Finally, in the third case, the students received feedback on their arguments, so that they could use this information when working with the classifications and for the final report.

Peer Assessment and Peer Feedback

Peer assessment/feedback has great pedagogical potential by (a) providing both a larger amount and more timely formative feedback than the teacher is able to, (b) involving the students in the assessment process, (c) allowing for the discussion and negotiation of assessment criteria, and (d) providing a spectrum of performances with different quality.

In the cases above, peer assessment/feedback is used in order to support all of these functions by letting the students use criteria to evaluate each other's work. In the first case, students peer assess each other's scientific explanations and provide written feedback. In the second case, students peer assess each other's research designs and provide oral feedback. Finally, in the third case, students peer assess each other's arguments and provide oral feedback.

Explicit Assessment Criteria

Assessment criteria can guide the students in discerning indicators of quality performance, but also to provide formative feedback and as a support for planning, monitoring, and evaluating their performance.

All the cases above include the use of explicit assessment criteria (for scientific explanations, research designs, and evidence-based arguments) as a support for both peer assessment/feedback and for students' SRL, where the use of criteria are thought to facilitate all phases of the self-regulation cycle (Panadero, Jonsson, & Strijbos, 2016).

Furthermore, the use of criteria is embedded in practice (i.e., peer review of explanations, research designs, and evidence-based argumentation), where the meaning of the criteria can be discussed and negotiated with teachers and peers in relation to concrete examples of performance. In all cases, the students are also confronted with multiple performances, presumably of varying quality, which may facilitate the interpretation of the criteria.

Conclusions and Implications

This chapter took the critique against formative assessment in higher education as a starting point. Three cases of formative assessment in astronomy have been used to exemplify how implementations of formative assessment in higher education can take the epistemological structure of the discipline into account, integrate the strategies of formative assessment into a coherent whole, and encourage student autonomy and divergent thinking. This was done by combining the use of authentic tasks, formative feedback, peer assessment/feedback, and explicit quality criteria as strategies of formative assessment. One of the contributions made here is, therefore, to give inspiration to future research on how to integrate the strategies of formative assessment, where students' motivation, performance, and strategies for self-regulated learning can be studied.

Another implication for research on formative assessment in higher education is that, as a minimum requirement, researchers would need to spell out what it is they want the students to learn in relation to the epistemological structure of the discipline and justify how the selected strategies and techniques of formative assessment may support that learning. There would also be a need to make a distinction between short-term and long-term goals. Although improved performance in relation to expected learning outcomes is a good thing in a short-term perspective, it is not necessarily so if it compromises student autonomy, motivation, or creative thinking in a long-term perspective.

References

Airey, J. (2011). The disciplinary literacy discussion matrix: A heuristic tool for initiating collaboration in higher education. *Across the Disciplines, 8*, 1–9.

Airey, J. (2015, November). *Social semiotics in higher education: Examples from teaching and learning in undergraduate physics.* Presentation at the SACF Singapore-Sweden Excellence Seminars, Swedish Foundation for International Cooperation in Research in Higher Education (STINT). National Institute of Education, Singapore.

Airey, J. & Linder, C. (2009). A disciplinary discourse perspective on university science learning: Achieving fluency in a critical constellation of modes. *Journal of Research in Science Teaching, 46*, 27–49.

Airey, J. & Linder, C. (2017). Social semiotics in university physics education. In D. F. Treagust, R. Duit, & H. E. Fischer (Eds.), *Multiple representations in physics education* (pp. 95–122). Cham: Springer International Publishing.

Barnard, R., de Luca, R., & Li, J. (2015). First-year undergraduate students' perceptions of lecturer and peer feedback: A New Zealand action research project. *Studies in Higher Education, 40*, 933–944.

Bennett, R. E. (2011). Formative assessment: a critical review. *Assessment in Education: Principles, Policy & Practice, 18*, 5–25.

Black, P. (1998). *Testing: Friend or foe?* London: Falmer.

Black, P. & McCormick, R. (2010). Reflections and new directions. *Assessment & Evaluation in Higher Education, 35*, 493–499.

Black, P. & Wiliam, D. (2006). Developing a theory of formative assessment. In J. Gardner (Ed.), *Assessment and learning* (pp. 81–100). London: SAGE.

Boud, D. & Falchikov, N. (1989). Quantitative studies of self-assessment in higher education: a critical analysis of findings. *Higher Education, 18*, 529–549.

Burke, D. (2009). Strategies for using feedback students bring to higher education. *Assessment & Evaluation in Higher Education 34*, 41–50.

Burke, D. & Pieterick, J. (2010). *Giving students effective written feedback.* Maidenhead: Open University Press.

Carless, D. (2006). Differing perceptions in the feedback process. *Studies in Higher Education, 31*, 219–233.

Carless, D. (2016). Scaling up assessment for learning: Progress and prospects. In Carless, D., Bridges, S. M., Chan, C. K. Y., & Glofcheski, R. (Eds.), *Scaling up assessment for learning in higher education* (pp. 3–17). Singapore: Springer.

Carrillo-de-la-Peña, M. T., Baillès, E., Caseras, X., Martínez, À., Ortet, G., & Pérez, J. (2009). Formative assessment and academic achievement in pre-graduate students of health sciences. *Advances in Health Sciences Education, 14*, 61–67.

Cho, Y. H. & Cho, K. (2011). Peer reviewers learn from giving comments. *Instructional Science, 39*, 629–643.

Cleland, C. E. (2002). Methodological and epistemic differences between historical science and experimental science. *Philosophy of Science, 69*, 474–496.

Coate, K., Barnett, R., & Williams, G. (2001). Relationship between teaching and research in higher education in England. *Higher Education Quarterly, 55*, 158–174.

Cowie, B. & Bell, B. (1999). A model of formative assessment in science education. *Assessment in Education: Principles, Policy & Practice, 6*, 101–116.

Darling-Hammond, L. & Snyder, J. (2000). Authentic assessment of teaching in context. *Teaching and Teacher Education, 16*, 523–545.

Dignath, C. & Büttner, G. (2008). Components of fostering self-regulated learning among students. A meta-analysis on intervention studies at primary and secondary school level. *Metacognition and Learning, 3*, 231–264.

Eisner, E. (1991). Taking a second look: Educational connoisseurship revisited. In M. W. McLaughlin & D. C. Phillips (Eds.), *Yearbook of the national society for the study of education. Evaluation and education at quarter century* (pp. 169–187). Chicago, IL: The National Society for the Study of Education.

Eriksson, U. (2014). *Reading the sky: From starspots to spotting stars.* Doctoral dissertation. Uppsala University, Sweden.

Eriksson, U., Linder, C., Airey, J., & Redfors, A. (2014a). Introducing the anatomy of disciplinary discernment – An example for astronomy. *European Journal of Science and Mathematics Education, 2*, 167–182.

Eriksson, U., Linder, C., Airey, J., & Redfors, A. (2014b). Who needs 3D when the Universe is flat? *Science Education, 98*, 412–442.

Fredlund, T., Airey, J., & Linder, C. (2012). Exploring the role of physics representations: an illustrative example from students sharing knowledge about refraction. *European Journal of Physics, 33*, 657–666.

Gomez, E. L. & Fitzgerald, M. T. (2017). Robotic telescopes in education. *Astronomical Review, 13*, 28–68.

Gray, R. (2014). The distinction between experimental and historical sciences as a framework for improving classroom inquiry. *Science Education, 98*, 327–341.

Grosas, A. B., Raju, S. R., Schuett, B. S., Chuck, J-A., & Millar, T. J. (2016). Determining if active learning through a formative assessment process translates to better performance in summative assessment. *Studies in Higher Education, 41*, 1595–1611.

Gulikers, J. T. M., Bastiaens, T. J., & Kirschner, P. A. (2004). A five-dimensional framework for authentic assessment. *Educational Technology Research & Development, 52*, 67–86.

Hattie, J. & Timperley, H. (2007). The power of feedback. *Review of Educational Research, 77*, 81–112.

Havnes, A. (2008). Assessment. A boundary object linking professional education and work? In A. Havnes & L. McDowell (Eds.), *Balancing dilemmas in assessment and learning in contemporary education* (pp. 101–114). New York, NY: Routledge.

Holbrook, J. & Rannikmae, M. (2007). The nature of science education for enhancing scientific literacy. *International Journal of Science Education, 29*, 1347–1362.

Jonsson, A. (2010). The use of transparency in the "Interactive examination" for student teachers. *Assessment in Education: Principles, Policy & Practice, 17*, 185–199.

Jonsson, A. (2014). Rubrics as a way of providing transparency in assessment. *Assessment & Evaluation in Higher Education, 39*, 840–852.

Krajcik, J. (2011). Learning progressions provide road maps for the development and validity of assessments and curriculum materials. *Measurement: Interdisciplinary Research and Perspectives, 9*, 155–158.

Kramarski, B., & Michalsky, T. (2009). Three metacognitive approaches to training pre-service teachers in different learning phases of technological pedagogical content knowledge. *Educational Research and Evaluation: An International Journal on Theory and Practice, 15*, 465–485.

Lave, J. & Wenger, E. (1991). *Situated learning: legitimate peripheral participation.* Cambridge: Cambridge University Press.

Macaskill, A. & Taylor, E. (2010). The development of a brief measure of learner autonomy in university students. *Studies in Higher Education, 35*, 351–359.

Marton, F. (2014). *Necessary conditions of learning.* New York & London: Routledge.

National Research Council (2012). *A framework for K-12 science education: Practices, crosscutting concepts, and core ideas.* Washington, DC: The National Academies Press.

Newton, P., Driver, R., & Osborne, J. (1999). The place of argumentation in the pedagogy of school science. *International Journal of Science Education, 21*, 553–576.

Nicol, D. J. & Macfarlane-Dick, D. (2006). Formative assessment and self-regulated learning: a model and seven principles of good feedback practice. *Studies in Higher Education, 31*, 199–218.

OECD (2016). *PISA 2015 assessment and analytical framework: Science, reading, mathematic and financial Literacy.* Paris: OECD Publishing.

Orsmond, P. & Merry, S. (1996). The importance of marking criteria in the use of peer assessment. *Assessment & Evaluation in Higher Education, 21*, 239–250.

Orsmond, P., Merry, S., & Reiling, K. (2002). The use of exemplars and formative feedback when using student derived marking criteria in peer and self-assessment. *Assessment & Evaluation in Higher Education, 27*, 309–323.

Panadero, E. (2017). A review of self-regulated learning: Six models and four directions for research. *Frontiers in Psychology, 8*(422).

Panadero, E., Jonsson, A., & Alqassab, M. (2018). Peer feedback used for formative purposes: Review of findings. In A. Lipnevich & J. K. Smith (Eds.), *The Cambridge handbook of instructional feedback.* Cambridge: Cambridge University Press.

Panadero, E., Jonsson, A., & Botella, J. (2017). Effects of self-assessment on self-regulated learning and self-efficacy: Four meta-analyses. *Educational Research Review, 22*, 74–98.

Panadero, E., Jonsson, A., & Strijbos, J-W. (2016). Scaffolding self-regulated learning through self-assessment and peer assessment: Guidelines for classroom implementation. In D. Laveault & L. Allal (Eds.), *Assessment for learning: Meeting the challenge of implementation* (pp. 311–326). Dordrecht: Springer.

Plummer, J. D. & Maynard, L. (2014). Building a learning progression for celestial motion: An exploration of students' reasoning about the seasons. *Journal of Research in Science Teaching, 51*, 902–929.

Richardson, M., Abraham, C., & Bond, R. (2012). Psychological correlates of university students' academic performance: A systematic review and meta-analysis. *Psychological Bulletin, 138*, 353–387.

Ryder, J., Leach, J., & Driver, R. (1999). Undergraduate science students' images of science. *Journal of Research in Science Teaching, 36*, 201–219.

Sadler, R. D. (1987). Specifying and promulgating achievement standards. *Oxford Review of Education, 13*, 191–209.

Sadler, R. D. (2009). Indeterminacy in the use of preset criteria for assessment and grading. *Assessment & Evaluation in Higher Education, 34*, 159–179.

Sadler, R. D. (2010). Beyond feedback: Developing student capability in complex appraisal. *Assessment & Evaluation in Higher Education, 35*, 535–550.

Sinclair, H. K. & Cleland, J. A. (2007). Undergraduate medical students: Who seeks formative feedback? *Medical Education, 41*, 580–582.

Torrance, H. (2012). Formative assessment at the crossroads: conformative, deformative and transformative assessment. *Oxford Review of Education, 38*, 323–342.

Torrance, H. & Pryor, J. (2001). Developing formative assessment in the classroom: using action research to explore and modify theory. *British Educational Research Journal, 27,* 615–631.

Toulmin, S. E. (1958). *The uses of argument.* Cambridge: Cambridge University Press.

van den Berg, I., Admiraal, W., & Pilot, A. (2006). Designing student peer assessment in higher education: analysis of written and oral peer feedback. *Teaching in Higher Education, 11,* 135–147.

Weaver, M. R. (2006). Do students value feedback? Student perceptions of tutors written responses. *Assessment & Evaluation in Higher Education, 31,* 379–394.

Wiggins, G. (1998). *Educative assessment.* San Francisco, CA: Jossey-Bass.

Wiliam, D. (2016). *Leadership for teacher learning: Creating a culture where all teachers improve so that all students succeed.* West Palm Beach, FL: Learning Sciences International.

Wiliam, D. & Leahy, S. (2015). *Embedding formative assessment: practical techniques for K-12 classrooms.* West Palm Beach, FL: Learning Sciences International.

Wiliam, D. & Thompson, M. (2007). Integrating assessment with learning: What will it take to make it work? In C.A. Dwyer (Ed.), *The future of assessment* (pp. 53–82). New York, NY: Routledge.

Yorke, M. (2003). Formative assessment in higher education: Moves towards theory and the enhancement of pedagogic practice. *Higher Education, 45,* 477–501.

PART III

Professional Preparation in Formative Assessment

8

CREATING FORMATIVE ASSESSMENT SYSTEMS IN THE TEACHING OF WRITING, AND HARNESSING THEM AS PROFESSIONAL DEVELOPMENT

Lucy Calkins, Mary Ehrenworth, and Diana Akhmedjanova

The world of education has gone so data-crazy that many teachers flinch at just the mention of assessment. Sometimes it can seem, especially to teachers, as if there is more focus on data than on the children. However, there are good reasons for an emphasis on classroom writing assessment. Hattie (2011) reviewed studies of more than 20 million learners to understand the factors that maximize achievement, and found that it is important for a learner to have crystal-clear, ambitious goals, to receive feedback that highlights progress toward these goals, and to know next steps that are within reach. Formative assessment, or assessment for learning, including processes that rely on checklists, rubrics, and benchmark texts, allows teachers to provide students with potent assistance so that students work with deliberateness toward specific goals, and, as a result, improve their learning (Andrade, Du, & Mycek, 2010; Andrade, Du, & Wang, 2008).

Formative assessment has made its way to different disciplines and domains of knowledge, including English Language Arts (ELA) (Hattie, 2011; Kingston & Nash, 2011). In the teaching of writing, assessment practices have gone through qualitative changes, from focusing solely on the summative nature of assessment to using a wide array of formative, evidence-based practices (Graham, Harris, & Chambers, 2016; Graham, Hebert, & Harris, 2015; Graham et al., 2012; Parr, 2013). Writing teachers who use formative assessment set clear goals for their students, know their students' current levels of knowledge, tailor their instruction in accordance with their students' needs, and reflect on and refine their teaching based on formative feedback received from their students (Parr, 2013). Formative assessment is an ongoing process and can take various forms, for instance, self-assessment, peer assessment, teacher-student conferences, and teachers' written feedback on students' drafts (Graham, Harris, & Chambers, 2016; Hattie & Timperley, 2007; Parr, 2013). While some writing teachers develop formative assessment practices to use in their classrooms on their own, there are also published evidence-based materials such as *Writing Pathways* (Calkins, 2013a; Calkins, Boland Hohne, & Robb, 2015) aimed at supporting schools, districts, and states in formative assessment in writing.

In *Writing Pathways: Performance Assessments and Learning Progressions, Grades K-8*, the Teachers College Reading and Writing Project (TCRWP) documented a toolkit of on-demand prompts, normed student exemplars, student-facing checklists, scoring rubrics, and teacher demonstration texts for argument, information, and narrative writing in grades K-8. TCRWP is a not-for-profit literacy think tank housed at Teachers College, Columbia University. Its staff of approximately one 100 staff developers work in thousands of classrooms, providing professional development in literacy-based school reform, reading and writing workshops, and content-area literacy. The *Writing Pathways* toolkit combines formative assessment practices with performance assessments that prompt students to write on-demand pieces at the start and end of discrete curricular units of study. Both teachers and students assess this writing for the purposes of goal-setting at the start of a unit, and as a way to monitor progress across units of study.

Andrade (2008) describes how, when students have tools at hand to help them be more expert in the formative assessment process, they can "reflect on the quality of their work, judge the degree to which it reflects explicitly stated goals or criteria, and revise" (p. 60). Because *Writing Pathways* provides clear trajectories of writing development, the tools have allowed students to work toward improvement in their writing. *Writing Pathways* helps teachers realize that there is extraordinary power in rubrics, checklists, and benchmark exemplars that fit into a curriculum aligned to them. The student-facing checklists, combined with student exemplars, help students to become both more independent and expert at formative self-assessment and goal-setting – and these tools help them meet their learning goals.

Mosher and Heritage (2017) describe the intersection of this toolkit with writing instruction as "one of the best current examples of a literacy curriculum with an explicit grounding in ideas about [learning] progressions" (p. 41). While the progressions of skill descriptors, student exemplars, teacher demonstration texts, and checklists described in *Writing Pathways* can serve schools as a toolkit for teachers and students, schools can also use this toolkit as a model to seek and norm their own student exemplars and write their own teacher demonstration texts.

The questions we address in this chapter, then, are: What makes an assessment system such as *Writing Pathways* so valuable to teachers and students? And, how can *Writing Pathways* and assessment systems like it function as significant professional development, both for expert and new teachers? In that context, we will discuss the intersection of formative assessment and teaching writing, the significance of assessment systems as professional development in the teaching of writing, and the classroom application of a system such as *Writing Pathways*.

Formative Assessment in Writing

Formative assessment, or assessment for learning, is used to inform instructional decisions and to help students learn (Bennett, 2011; Stiggins, 2009). While there are inconsistencies in terms of the magnitude of the effect of formative assessment practices on student's achievement and learning (Bennett, 2011; Black & Wiliam, 1998; Hattie & Timperley, 2007; Kingston & Nash, 2011), there is a consensus among scholars that formative assessment practices improve student learning. A recent meta-analysis of 42 experimental studies investigating the effectiveness of formative assessment practices reports effect sizes with a mean of 0.32 in the area of ELA (Kingston & Nash, 2011). A second meta-analysis of true and quasi-experimental studies (n=39) reports positive average weighted effect sizes of feedback on student's quality of writing of 0.86 for feedback from teachers, 0.58 from peers, 0.62 from oneself, and 0.38 from a computer (Graham, Hebert, & Harris, 2015). That is, formative assessment is clearly associated with improvements in students' learning.

To serve the purposes of improving teaching and learning, formative assessment practices applied in classrooms should include: (1) clear purposes for assessing student work, (2) clear targets for what is being assessed, (3) high quality assessment designs for all assessment materials, (4) effective communication about what the results of assessment indicate about students' learning, and (5) students' active participation in formative assessment (Stiggins, 2009). Keeping these tenets in mind, we informally surveyed experts in the field of formative assessment to learn more about the ways in which these ideas can be implemented in practice. These individuals included Tom Corcoran and Fritz Mosher from the Consortium for Policy and Research in Education (CPRE); Ray Pecheone from the Stanford Center for Assessment, Learning, and Equity (SCALE); and Randy Bennett, Paul Deane, and Mary Fowles from the Cognitively Based Assessment of, for, and as Learning (CBAL) research initiative at ETS.

The Development and Structure of *Writing Pathways*

Tom Corcoran and Fritz Mosher of CPRE suggested that it was almost impossible for any single teacher to have access in her classroom to the resources that a university think tank such as TCRWP could put together: that is, student work gathered from hundreds of classrooms; time and people to study rubrics and assessments across states; a team of staff developers and pilot classrooms to pilot tools across grade levels, disciplines, and schools; and access to collaboration with other think tanks such as SCALE, CPRE, and CBAL. CPRE's response encouraged TCRWP to develop an assessment system for writing that teachers might be able to replicate from a model but would not be able to initially assemble on their own. Most important was the collection of normed student exemplars that marked grade level work. Inevitably, on their own teachers tend to compare student work within their own classroom, grade level, or school. Looking at student exemplars across not only classrooms but across schools helps teachers understand how their students are positioned as writers.

Ray Pecheone's response was a little different. He suggested developing these assessment and norming tools so that students are encouraged to work toward standards that are significant outside of the classroom, which would entail norming vertically up the grade levels, such as standards associated not only with state ELA assessments but also with successful high school performance on the ACT, the SAT, International Baccalaureate (IB), National Assessment of Educational Progress (NAEP), and the Advanced Placement (AP) program. That meant developing checklists, rubrics, and progressions of student exemplars aligned to K-12 benchmarks. Ray also suggested that while rubrics might be helpful for teachers, checklists were helpful for students. As a result, we combined student-facing checklists with student exemplars – tools that help students achieve rather than tools that only measure.

As we developed these tools, we were in close conversation with our colleagues at CBAL. Admittedly, when Randy Bennett, Paul Deane, and Mary Fowles suggested that assessment could act as instruction, we were skeptical, having been on the receiving end of years of rhetoric at the state level about how state tests were formative and productive when they were anything but. It turned out, however, that the pressure from CBAL to innovate a writing assessment system that would raise the level of achievement, led us to research student-facing tools, the role of artwork and graphics in making tools accessible, and the kinds of language and structures that help students use tools independently. CBAL shared their learning progressions, which for them were definitions of argumentation writing skills that became increasingly sophisticated, and gave us feedback on early drafts of our progressions, which were student-facing checklists and a ladder of student exemplars going up the grade levels, particularly in argument writing (Deane & Song, 2015). That collaboration offered us the chance to develop tools for teachers that they were unlikely to invent inside their classrooms but were easily adapted once teachers grasped the notion of a ladder of checklists and exemplars.

Our conversations with these colleagues and experts led to the development of an interlocking assessment system for writing that relies on formative assessment practices, offers teachers clear connections to state and global benchmarks, insists on internal vertical alignment across grade levels and lateral alignment across types of writing, and forges links between writing instruction, teacher assessment, and student self-assessment. So that educators can harness this system, adapt it, or duplicate it, we will describe the parts of this assessment system, as well as insights gained in its development. It is not crucial that teachers use *Writing Pathways* itself. What is essential is that teachers use a writing assessment system that increases teacher knowledge and student independence.

Lucy Calkins et al.

Writing Pathways includes: (1) student exemplar pieces grades Pre-K-8; (2) student-facing checklists for grades K-8; (3) teacher demonstration pieces for grades K-8; (4) rubrics that are aligned with the checklists; and (5) K-8 skill progressions of the qualities of writing described in the checklists and rubrics in argument, information, and narrative writing. TCRWP also created an extension toolkit for grades 9–12, which they offer to high schools who join the TCRWP thought collective, either through institutes or on-site professional development. The exemplars, demonstration writing, checklists, rubrics, and progressions are aligned from grades K-12 and across the types of writing (argument, information, and narrative) so that teachers and students encounter the same skill categories (Structure, Development, and Language Conventions) in every checklist, rubric, and skill progression, in each type of writing and grade level. As samples, the appendices of this chapter include: two strands of the learning progression for argument/opinion writing that stretch from Pre-K to fourth grade (Appendix A); two samples of fourth-grade student exemplars for argument/opinion writing (Appendix B); a student-facing checklist for argument/opinion writing (Appendices C1 and C2); a fourth-grade rubric for argument/opinion writing (Appendix D); and a teacher demonstration piece for fourth-grade argument/opinion writing (Appendix E).

TCRWP encourages teachers to collect on-demand writing from students at the start of the year, and/or before each unit of study in argument, information, or narrative writing. Teachers then study this writing, and students also study it to self-assess and set goals, often using the student-facing checklists. Teachers are encouraged to collect a second on-demand piece of writing at the end of each unit of study, so both teachers and students can celebrate and monitor growth and progress. If they want a more formal performance assessment, teachers can give an on-demand writing task at the end of a unit of study as a summative assessment, and use the rubrics to monitor students' growth in qualities of writing. By using the same assessment tools over time, the initial formative assessment becomes part of a performance assessment system, one which helps teachers, administrators, families, and students know how young writers are developing along a ladder of skill progressions in argument, information, and narrative writing.

Common Core State Standards

One of the first steps in the development of the *Writing Pathways* curriculum was looking at the details of the grade level writing standards for the Common Core State Standards (CCSS; National Governors Association, 2010), both because the CCSS has been highly influential in state standards, and because successful implementation of formative assessment practices depends on the definition of clear purposes and targets of assessment (Andrade & Heritage, 2017; Stiggins, 2009). We were drawn to the CCSS skill categories that spanned different types of writing. Orienting the reader, for example, exists in narrative, opinion, and information writing, as is providing a sense of closure. That certain qualities of writing are relevant to every type of writing helps teachers and students carry over large skill sets, and prevents a writing curriculum from devolving into separate, unconnected micro-skills.

For example, here is what the CCSS writing standards (para. 1) for third-grade *opinion* writing suggest:

1   Write opinion pieces on topics or texts, supporting a point of view with reasons.

    1   Introduce the topic or text they are writing about, state an opinion, and create an organizational structure that lists reasons.

    2   Provide reasons that support the opinion.

    3   Use linking words and phrases (e.g., *because, therefore, since, for example*) to connect opinion and reasons.

    4   Provide a concluding statement or section.

For third-grade *narrative* writing (para. 3), the CCSS suggest:

Writing and Professional Development

1　Write narratives to develop real or imagined experiences or events using effective technique, descriptive details, and clear event sequences.

    1　Establish a situation and introduce a narrator and/or characters; organize an event sequence that unfolds naturally.

    2　Use dialogue and descriptions of actions, thoughts, and feelings to develop experiences and events or the response of characters to situations.

    3　Use temporal words and phrases to signal event order.

    4　Provide a sense of closure.

You can see the thoughtful alignment of skills as you compare 1.a. in argument/opinion writing with 1.a. in narrative writing, and so on. In both types of writing, the CCSS ask writers to orient the reader, introducing the reader to the idea or to the scene. Whatever type of writing a student is tackling, she should orient her reader at the start of the piece, and provide a sense of closure at the end.

We found the logical matrix offered by the CCSS tremendously useful and worked to mirror it, using language that would be more comprehensible to young writers. At the same time, there were places where the CCSS benchmarks did not seem grounded in experience of developmental stages of young writers. For example, in growth from third to fourth grade in opinion writing, the third-grade opinion writing standard (para.1) suggests:

1　Write opinion pieces on topics or texts, supporting a point of view with reasons.

    1　Introduce the topic or text they are writing about, state an opinion, and create an organizational structure that lists reasons.

    2　Provide reasons that support the opinion.

    3　Use linking words and phrases (e.g., *because, therefore, since, for example*) to connect opinion and reasons.

    4　Provide a concluding statement or section.

While the fourth-grade opinion writing standard (para.1) suggests:

1　Write opinion pieces on topics or texts, supporting a point of view with reasons and information.

    2　Introduce a topic or text clearly, state an opinion, and create an organizational structure in which related ideas are grouped to support the writer's purpose.

    3　Provide reasons that are supported by facts and details.

    4　Link opinion and reasons using words and phrases (e.g., *for instance, in order to, in addition*).

    5　Provide a concluding statement or section related to the opinion presented.

That is, the CCSS suggests that in opinion writing, third graders should provide reasons, while fourth graders provide examples. Our work in thousands of third and fourth-grade classrooms suggested the opposite – concrete examples are much easier to provide than abstract reasons. Despite the CCSS articulation of this skill, when teachers try this work with children, they usually find that third graders create much stronger opinion pieces when they can elaborate their examples, whereas fourth graders are ready to consider reasons (Calkins, 2013b).

Work on learning progressions for *Writing Pathways* confirmed the importance of studying student work and comparing it with the more abstract benchmarks of standards such as the CCSS. As a result, we developed and refined learning progressions for *Writing Pathways*, and we advise teachers to continually study the work students do across grade levels to intuit developmental writing stages, rather than rely only on published benchmarks such as the CCSS (Calkins, Ehrenworth, & Lehman, 2012).

Learning Progressions: Articulating Skill Ladders to Inform Teaching

Intrinsic to all the tools in *Writing Pathways* are learning progressions in argument, information, and narrative writing, K-12 (see Appendix A for a sample). Learning progressions refer to the advancement of student's knowledge and skills as they gradually develop expertise in a given domain (Andrade & Heritage, 2017). The progressions in *Writing Pathways* inform the rubrics, the checklists, and the teacher demonstration pieces – these tools are all linked to the qualities of writing articulated in the learning progressions for writing.

Learning progressions give teachers ladders of skills, among other resources. In *Writing Pathways*, these skills are articulated vertically up the grade levels, and laterally across types of writing. The goal of these progressions is to help teachers envision what to teach next as they assess and confer with their writers. Gladwell (2007) explains that it is a mark of expertise to be able to make judgments in the blink of an eye. The reverse is also true: making judgments quickly is not easy for people whose expertise lies elsewhere. If teachers are new to the teaching of writing, it can be challenging to look at a student's text and to know the traits worth noting. The ability to grasp what a writer is trying to do and to see how to help the writer do that work better (or to tackle something else that is even more important) represents the epitome of effective writing instruction. But this work is not easy, and developing the expertise to do this well takes time. Having tools on hand can accelerate the development of expertise in analyzing the qualities of writing for teachers as well as students. Studying student exemplars, normed student-facing checklists, learning progressions, and talking about student work with teachers within and across grade levels helps teachers become more adept at understanding how student writers grow in different types of writing.

Learning progressions in writing give teachers and students one clear path forward. The path set out can be tremendously helpful for students and teachers, as it provides a vision of the next steps. It is, however, a hypothetical path, one of many possible ways that writing could improve. At TCRWP, we worry that checklists might become prescriptive and that learning progressions might unintentionally narrow teachers' vision. In the end, based on our work with thousands of teachers, many of whom are eager to expand their knowledge of writing, we found that having one clear path can be very helpful. With learning progressions, a teacher can place the writer's current work and skill set (what the writer is doing) somewhere on the learning progression. When she gives the writer feedback or suggests next steps, she is helping the writer to go from where the writer is on a learning progression toward whatever she believes might be next steps for that writer (Andrade & Heritage, 2017).

For example, if a strong fourth-grade writer has already written a lead to her argument in which she asked a question to hook her reader, and has given a surprising fact or bit of background information as well, a teacher who is wondering how to coach this strong writer can look to the strand for *Leads* in the learning progression for argument/opinion writing. From studying the fifth-grade descriptors, a teacher can see that one tip she could give her student would be that the writer might explain more about why this topic or issue is significant, or the writer could forecast the big points she will develop in her argument. This teacher, even if she is not yet an experienced teacher of argument writing, will be equipped with possibilities to coach her students.

We also wanted to work across rubrics, learning progressions, and student-facing checklists to bridge social and academic language, so that tools could be useful for novice and expert teachers of writing instructors. The skill descriptors in the student-facing checklists and rubrics are written to communicate expectations to students and novice teachers, so they are written in straight, clear language. On Ray Pecheone's advice, we wrote our checklists in the first person. We also found it helpful to use past tense. For example, "I wrote a beginning . . ." A young writer, holding his piece of writing and this checklist, can work between his piece and the checklist, not only self-assessing, but also finding tips for what he might do next.

The learning progressions and checklists not only help teachers track students' progress across the three kinds of writing, locating a student's current level of work and the next steps the student should take; they also help teachers see the cross-currents between the three types of writing, and enable teachers to help a student realize that lessons learned in narrative writing can transfer to information writing, and so forth. The CCSS benchmarks, the NAEP rubrics, or the IB rubrics are summative in nature: They help teachers assess. We wanted tools that would help teachers and students understand more about how to achieve as well. Our biggest advice to new teachers is to focus mostly on instruction and to hone their assessment tools so that they are formative and immediately inform instruction.

Communities of Practice

Having seen how rubrics and assessment tools can often become overwhelming, full of abstract and overly complex language, we strived to write all the tools – checklists, rubrics, and learning progressions – in simple yet academic language, providing detailed explanations and examples. Hence, we limited the master categories for qualities of writing to three: Structure, Development, and Language Conventions. Inside these categories, we created a limited number of subcategories, organizing them in a common-sense order that had less to do with a perfect match with the overarching category and more to do with the kind of work a writer does early and later in a piece. So, under *Structure*, we included Overall, Lead, Transitions, Ending, and Organization. *Structure* meant not only overt organizational structure, but deep structure – how the writer holds the parts of a piece together and leads the reader toward meaning. Under *Development*, we included Elaboration and Craft. Under *Language Conventions*, we included Spelling and Punctuation.

We ran these subcategories across all grade levels and all types of writing. This way, if a third-grade teacher wanted to look back to first grade to see what her students were grounded in, or what supports some of her below-grade level writers might need, she could look across familiar categories. If she wanted to look up to fourth grade, to see where her students would go next, or ways to support her higher-level writers, she would again find familiar categories.

One goal of creating familiar categories across types of writing and across grade levels was to foster a sense of a community of practice. All too often, teachers and students in a grade level might not share any similar tools. When fourth-grade teachers adopt a rubric that is radically different than the one fifth-grade teachers use, or when social studies teachers use a rubric for argument writing in eighth grade that differs dramatically from the one preferred in eighth-grade science, both teachers and students miss the opportunity to increase cohesion and collaborate in communities of practice. We found it to be empowering for students and liberating for teachers to come together around shared tools across types of writing and across grade levels.

When teachers do come together with shared tools and learning progressions, then clear lines of growth emerge. This alignment not only helps students as they move from one grade level to the next, but it also helps teachers to understand lines of growth inside their own grade level. With the enormous diversity of learners inside any one classroom, it is not enough for a teacher to simply know her grade level expectations. When she is familiar with qualities of writing in the grades below and above her own, then she is better prepared to coach students along a continuum of growth.

Finally, achieving cohesion in terms of normed student exemplars, checklists, rubrics, and learning progressions helps a community study and learn together in professional development around the teaching and learning of writing. Teachers can study across and within grade level teams, with common language and goals. Parents and families who study tools in one grade level find they can apply that knowledge as students move to the next grade level. What was most important to us was creating a matrix that would support a community of writing across grade levels and disciplines, teachers and families, as well as administration and teachers.

The learning progressions, then, are the framework that supports teachers being able to evaluate student work and student response to instruction (Andrade & Heritage, 2017). They create agreed-upon qualities for a community of writers and clear lines of growth for young writers to work within. They are the integral structure that supports cohesion of practice, so that teachers, students, and families work within a shared vision of qualities of writing and writing growth.

Normed Exemplars

In terms of putting learning progressions – whether they are a checklist, rubric, or written progression – into play inside of classrooms, we found that they are most valuable when combined with normed student exemplars (Appendix B). Teachers may vary widely in how they interpret a progression or rubric that they did not write (Hunter & Docherty, 2011; Sadler, 2005). Student exemplars help anchor teacher expectations (Orsmond, Merry, & Reiling, 2002). In addition, student exemplars can serve as models for students to emulate in their own writing as they improve their writing skills (Andrade, Du, & Wang, 2008; Orsmond, Merry, & Reiling, 2002).

For *Writing Pathways*, we collected and sorted thousands of pieces of student writing. All of the pieces were written under the same on-demand conditions, using a set of three open-ended prompts: one for narrative, one for information, and one for argument writing. We include these prompts in the toolkit for teachers as a way to initiate similar pre and post assessments in writing. These student pieces were collected in TCRWP schools that teach writing workshop, and for the first published version of *Writing Pathways* we collected pieces that were written in English, from public and independent schools. Looking across these many student pieces, we worked to assemble a ladder of pieces, initially from K–8th grade, later adding in a high school set, so that a piece that we normed at fourth grade was part of a clear pathway leading toward success at AP/IB/SAT/ACT writing in the eleventh and twelfth grades.

Since *Writing Pathways* was published, we have encouraged schools and districts to collect and sort their own student samples and to make their own toolkits, to highlight local writing. In collaboration with TCRWP schools in Columbia and Spain, we have translated the tools into Spanish and collected student writing in Spanish from Spanish-speaking schools. We encourage schools to use the *Writing Pathways* pieces to create their own normed collection, of local writing.

This local selection matters because it helps a community create a more culturally relevant collection of student pieces that reflects the histories, concerns, and joys of that community. Ladson-Billings (1995) argues that culturally relevant pedagogy must provide a way for students to maintain their cultural integrity while succeeding academically. It cannot be, then, that students everywhere need to use the same set of student exemplars. Instead, they should see themselves, their communities, and their stories inside of the exemplars at hand. It is also important to collect local exemplars because it shows the community that with cohesive instruction, students inside of the community can reach these same skill levels. Students find the student exemplars useful mentors to strive toward. Rather than pairing these with the entire writing progression, either in its cross-grade form or in the form of a rubric with four levels, student-facing checklists turned out to be the most useful when paired with student exemplars.

Student-Facing Checklists

When Ray Pecheone of SCALE was advising us in the creation of these assessments, he gave us an insight that has become a mantra. "Rubrics," he said, "might be helpful for teachers, but checklists are helpful for kids." For us, a checklist is a slice of the rubric in student-friendly language (Appendices C1 and C2). Gawande (2009) describes the power of checklists to transform practice. In his description of hospitals transforming something as seemingly simple but hard to put in practice as hand-washing, Gawande notes that simple checklists serve as important reminders to people, from nurses to pilots, of tasks or qualities of work that we want to remember. A checklist offers a palpable list of qualities. It is direct, concrete, and limited. It is not everything you could do to achieve success; it is the most essential things.

Student-facing checklists give students a way to self-assess and set immediate writing goals without the intervention of adults, and with remarkable efficacy. As Andrade (2008) puts it, "If students produce it, they can assess it; and if they can assess it, they can improve it" (p. 63). The process students in TCRWP schools follow is to write an on-demand piece before a unit of study and use a checklist to self-assess, marking a few things they are doing well and a few things that can be goals for their work during the unit. At the end of the unit of study, in which they have moved across the writing process and produced at least one published piece, students write another on-demand piece, this time using the checklist to self-assess their growth across the unit. Although the learning progressions are written in the third person, allowing a teacher using the tool to locate her students' writing, the checklists are written in the first person, helping a young writer use the tool to raise the level of her own writing. Each checklist lists the qualities of strong writing in each genre at each grade level and allows students to assess their own writing, set goals for themselves, and work to make palpable progress toward those goals.

It turns out that students love checklists. They love how useful they are. They love how contained they are. They love to color code the checklist and their essays as they self-assess. They love to move from one checklist to the next, or part of one checklist to another. For instance, a third grader might ask for the fourth-grade checklist to get an idea for a stronger lead. Students also love the freedom of sometimes moving "back" a checklist, so a fifth grader might ask for a fourth-grade checklist to see if there was an idea there for leads that might have been helpful. Teachers love them too, for two reasons. One is that checklists are tools that let students self-assess (Andrade & Du, 2007; Valle et al., 2016). They help lift the burden of assessment from the teacher's shoulders. Another reason is that by creating checklists that bridge social and academic language, we help to demystify writing for a lot of teachers.

For example, the CCSS suggested for third-grade narrative writing that writers "establish a situation and introduce a narrator and/or characters; organize an event sequence that unfolds naturally." Students and teachers would have to already know a lot about writing to envision what these terms describe. Our third-grade checklist offers these cues:

	Did I do it like a third grader?	NOT YET	STARTING TO	YES!
Lead	 I wrote a beginning in which I helped readers know who the characters were and what the setting was in my story.	☐	☐	☐

Figure 8.1 Excerpt from third-grade checklist for narrative writing.

181

We have found that a checklist is most helpful, in terms of its difficulty, if there are one or two things on it that a writer is already doing, and one or two things that could be goals. That means that in inclusive classrooms, students will need two or three levels of checklists in play at one time. The TCRWP checklists have a level listed at the top, which corresponds with grade level. Teachers, though, sometimes change the level to blue, red, or gold, if they want to de-emphasize grade level. Alongside the checklists, students also need access to related tools such as student exemplars. With these checklists and exemplars in hand, students can study ways to achieve their goals. All along the way, we found that teachers learn as much as students about qualities of writing, which brings us to the question of using an assessment toolkit as professional development.

Professional Development Using *Writing Pathways*

To improve student's learning with formative assessment practices in classrooms, teachers should be able to (1) collect accurate evidence about student's learning using high quality assessments; (2) interpret this evidence to adjust and refine their instructional practices; and (3) provide students with constructive feedback on how to improve their learning (Schneider & Randel, 2009). All of these processes work only if teachers can recognize qualities of writing across types of writing as well as within a variety of genres, and if they have in mind a progression within which these qualities fit.

In order to develop expertise in the above-mentioned formative assessment practices, teachers need significant opportunities for professional development (Bennett, 2011). With powerful tools such as learning progressions, student exemplars, and teacher demonstration texts, they can design some of this professional development themselves.

It is helpful to think about evidence-based practices for professional development to ensure successful implementation of formative assessment later on (Schneider & Randel, 2009). First, professional development needs administrative support. That is, district and school-level administration should show their interest and willingness to promote formative assessment practices in classrooms, which leads to higher fidelity of implementation by teachers (Moss, Brookhart, & Long, 2013). It is also important to personalize professional development workshops by letting teachers set their own learning goals, which will result in teachers' personal investment and interest. Another important aspect is increasing teachers' content knowledge of writing instruction, including methods of instruction as well as qualities of writing. In addition, teachers should spend time in professional development learning about formative assessment and have enough time to actually enact them in their classrooms. Teachers who have the opportunity to collaborate when applying formative assessment will be more likely to form a community of practice. They are more likely to support each other while implementing formative assessment in their classrooms. It is also important that formative assessment learned during professional development aligns with the existing state and district standards, infrastructure, and teaching methods to create a coherent system easy to implement in classrooms. Finally, it is essential to encourage teachers to be active participants of the professional development workshops, often by implementing some of the same formative assessment that teachers will implement in their classrooms (Schneider & Randel, 2009).

These aspects of successful professional development geared at promoting formative assessment informed the development of this expertise using *Writing Pathways*. The professional development for *Writing Pathways* takes place at administrative and teacher levels, is enacted in workshops and in classroom study, and centered on student and teacher participation, all of which are highlighted in evidence-based practices for professional development (Schneider & Randel, 2009).

Implementation of Professional Development

There are a variety of ways that we suggest integrating the tools from *Writing Pathways* (or ones like these) into professional development. These tools can help teachers to (1) norm their grade level expectations, (2) increase their familiarity with qualities of writing at each grade level, (3) develop language for describing student writing, and (4) become more ready to coach students within logical and attainable skill progressions. Administrators – district and school leaders – and teachers are invited to participate in professional development, where they engage in sorting, scoring, and double-scoring students' essays to illustrate the qualities of effective writing. In this way, professional development becomes more beneficial and transparent at all levels to ensure the successful implementation of formative assessment in writing classrooms (McCarthey & Geoghegan, 2016; Schneider & Randel, 2009).

District and School-Level Professional Development

Initially, we found that school districts were most interested in *Writing Pathways*, especially in the rubrics that allow teachers to score student writing, because of the districts' urge to gather, study, and record data. School and district leaders need to know how writing instruction is going in a building, and often they have to be able to quantify progress for state or district initiatives. In *Writing Pathways* there are rubrics for scoring each of the three types of writing (see Appendix D for a fourth-grade sample). These rubrics, grounded in the learning progressions, use numbers corresponding to grade levels and give appropriate weight to each category. In this way, school leaders can derive a point score for each student's work in a particular type of writing as well as examine students' progress statistically, both overall for types of writing and for individual qualities of writing.

Due to their urge (either personal or driven by outside forces) to gather quantifiable data, district and school leaders turned to the rubrics as the most essential tools. While rubric scores are reductive – reducing the complexity of the work to numbers – they can be helpful in measuring growth across time, noticing patterns that will help teachers inform whole-class and small-group instruction, and looking at the data from select groups (boys versus girls, for example, or strong writers versus struggling writers). For administrators, looking at data in this way also makes it easier to report according to the district or state mandates.

There is an implicit benefit to schools and districts scoring student pieces collaboratively, using shared rubrics. That benefit is that teachers come to a better shared understanding of grade level expectations. Double-scoring pieces and talking about scores leads to rich conversations about qualities of writing. Scoring pieces both formatively and summatively leads teachers to see small increments of growth that they might otherwise have missed. The scoring experience is time-consuming, but it can be valuable.

Over time, however, we have found that putting student exemplars and checklists into play in the curriculum are what most transform achievement, even more than scoring with rubrics. After all, writing down a number, recording a score, does not change achievement: Cohesive, expert instruction, student efficacy, and determined practice on the part of the learner change achievement. The tools in *Writing Pathways* provide students with clear pathways forward as writers, helping them answer not only the question, "How am I doing?" but also the more important question, "How can I improve?" By providing students with checklists and exemplars that illustrate a pathway forward, teachers help their students develop a sense of efficacy (Andrade & Brooke, 2010). That is why professional development for teachers is crucial, so that they move beyond scoring and into the intimate work of instilling a sense of agency in their young writers.

Teacher Level Professional Development

Fullan and Hargreaves (2012) point out that whole system change "absolutely requires individual and collective acts of investment in . . . a coherent set of actions that build everyone's capability and keep everyone learning" (p. xvii). One of the most surprising insights in our work with teachers and schools has been how implementing a systemic approach to writing assessment and writing progressions functions as transformative professional development. We knew that children benefit from learning to draft quickly and often, using all they know as writers. We also knew that young writers would benefit from a toolkit of exemplars and checklists that let them set goals and strive to reach those goals independently. What has been extraordinary is how studying student writing and committing to shared tools for assessment can result in whole buildings being transformed. The study of student work and the collaborative use of tools helps democratize teacher knowledge. We focused on increasing teacher knowledge and fostering transparency around student writing in our professional development, and we suggest this focus for transforming teaching.

Increasing Teacher Knowledge

The research on the teaching of writing has been crystal clear for 30 years, since Don Murray first researched and wrote *A Writer Teaches Writing* (2003). Murray's (at the time) radical suggestion was that all schools teach writing the way all professional writers write – through the writing process. Graves (2001) demonstrated that very young writers could learn the writing process and flourish in a writing workshop where teachers explicitly taught writing as a discipline. Calkins and Harwayne (1991) discussed launching writing workshops in elementary classrooms and described how students quickly internalized the writing process, becoming both more powerful and more independent writers.

Since that time, thousands of teachers have taught writing workshop. But thousands of teachers have not. Sometimes teachers work in a schedule that does not allocate time to the teaching of writing as a discipline. Sometimes they do not have access to professional development to help them study the teaching of writing. Sometimes they lack confidence in their own writing and knowledge of writing. At TCRWP, we work with thousands of classrooms and teachers around the country and around the globe. We know that a knowledgeable teacher can raise the level of writing quickly and keep students on a positive learning curve. We also know that when writing is not going well in a classroom or a building, it is almost always a problem of teacher knowledge.

Expectations for Teacher Knowledge

The expectations for teacher knowledge of writing have increased dramatically in the wake of the CCSS, yet teacher professional development has not always kept pace. Teachers need to be expert in argument, information, and narrative writing. They need to be able to coach a wide range of students in each of these types of writing. They need to know about the writing process and writing workshop. They also need to bring their students to higher levels of writing than ever. Students who take the ACT have approximately half an hour to write a well-constructed argument essay. On the SAT, they have about the same amount of time to write an analytical essay in response to a complex text. On the PARCC and Smarter Balanced and other state ELA exams, fourth graders are asked to write text-based arguments, to write well-crafted narratives, and to analyze the writing of published writers. When looking across the newest national and state assessments, it is clear that the level of writing that we are now teaching students has risen dramatically. The Common Core standards, with their grade level benchmarks for argument, information, and narrative writing; the Next Generation Science Standards, with their focus on evidence-based argumentation and explanation; and research suggest that writing is one of the most critical skills of the twenty-first-century workplace (Wagner, 2014).

We have come to realize that higher expectations mean that many teachers are insecure about writing. Supporting teachers of writing through strong professional development is especially important because teachers are often hesitant about their abilities to teach writing. Similarly, Fleischer (2004) has argued that "many writing teachers find writing a bit frightening" (pp. 24–28), which may be because they do not often write as adults other than in the service of routine tasks. They also may feel unsure of their knowledge of writing (Grisham & Wolsey, 2011). When teachers do not see themselves as writers, they can feel uncomfortable teaching writing. Part of professional development for the teaching of writing needs to include support for teachers as writers, and now that means writers of many kinds of texts.

Knowledge About Student Learning

To increase teacher knowledge, we suggest that teachers begin by capitalizing on formative assessment – that is, that they collect their students' on-demand pieces and study these pieces in comparison to a ladder of normed student exemplars. To do this work, teachers need a clear vision of what grade level exemplars look like, which is where *Writing Pathways* or a previously normed homegrown collection comes in. By comparing their own student pieces to a normed collection, teachers get a sense of where their students are on a ladder of skill development. We also suggest that teachers need professional development time to study exemplars even if they are not collecting their own on-demand pieces, as the study of exemplars serves as a primer in student writing in that genre. For instance, if second-grade teachers are setting out to teach information writing, they can study a set of student exemplars on information writing from kindergarten through third or fourth grade. They could turn to the pieces in *Writing Pathways*, or to a similar collection that has been collected and normed by their school, district, or state. What matters is that teachers are given professional development time to collectively study a progression of student exemplars in the genre they are teaching.

When we give teachers opportunities to study student pieces, we also have to coach teachers to talk aloud about student writing. To begin, it is often helpful to ask teachers to simply share what students are doing well – the qualities of writing that teachers see in each piece. One way to pose this question is to ask, "What does this child know about information writing?" Another is, "What is this writer doing well – what qualities of information writing can we see here?" We often find that some teachers slip into a deficit model, where they see and name all the things that students are not doing, thus getting caught in a vortex of limitation. Helping shift teachers to a readiness/growth model during professional development positions teachers to see their students' potential, moving them away from the limiting pathologies of deficit mindset (Harry & Klingner, 2007).

One of our main goals during professional development is to democratize knowledge of writing, so that teachers who are new to the teaching of writing share in the insights of more experienced teachers. To achieve this goal, we have to coach teachers to give specific examples of writing qualities from students' pieces. That means coaching teachers to say things like, "In first grade, it seems like the students are using technical vocabulary in their information writing. For example, this student writes, 'whales eat crill, the smallest animals on earth.'" Initially, some teachers will be quiet, unsure of what qualities they are looking for, or how to describe what they see, or how to find examples. This hesitancy matters, as the ability to talk about writing is intimately linked to the ability to teach writing. It helps to coach knowledgeable teachers to ask, "What is an example of that . . .," or to say, "For example, I see that quality right here, where the child writes . . ." When more knowledgeable teachers participate in sharing knowledge, it makes it more likely that all the teachers will be better prepared to teach and confer with children.

For example, groups of teachers, participating in professional development, turn student exemplars into conferring toolkits by marking up and annotating the student pieces, noting which ones they might use to teach leads and which ones they might use to teach endings, and so on. When teachers have had a chance to preview exemplars and to create instructional toolkits, they are more likely to teach small groups and conferences using these tools. Often, teachers find that students begin to mirror this process by personalizing tools, annotating them, and making choices as to what part of an exemplar or checklist will best help them as writers (Figure 8.2).

By studying progressions of student exemplars inside of a genre, teachers increase their understanding of qualities of writing across a progression. They are more expert in the genre, and better prepared to teach a wide range of students (Calkins & Ehrenworth, 2016).

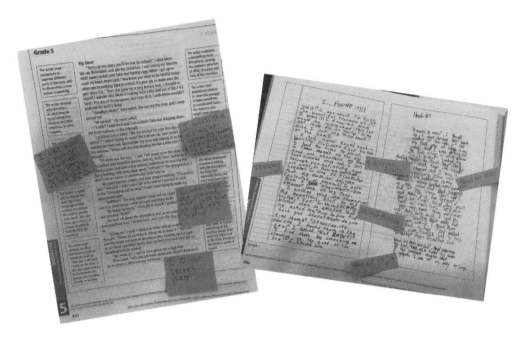

Figure 8.2 Teachers and students learn to annotate exemplars as tools to raise the level of writing.

Knowledge About Teaching Writing

We have also found it helpful to plan professional development time to study student writing over time for teachers to become more reflective about their own instruction. When teachers study writing over time – their students' on-demand writing before and after each curricular unit of study – they see the effect of their instruction over the year. This study requires a mindset wherein teachers examine student work not only as a reflection of *students'* progress but also as a reflection of the *teacher's* teaching. We suggest that professional development leads teachers to ask, "What groups of students have grown in leaps and bounds in this unit of study? Are there any students, or groups of students, who have not flourished?" The important thing is for teachers to observe student work, asking, "Why has some of my instruction led to visible results, while other teaching is not as visible in student writing?" As Hattie (2011) emphasizes, to become an expert, a teacher must be skilled at monitoring the current status of student understanding and progress toward the success criteria.

This one simple move, of studying a progression of student exemplars collected as assessments, dramatically increases and equalizes teacher knowledge of qualities of writing and of their own efficacy. It also fosters a sense of transparency around expectations – it helps teachers imagine what kind of writing they are aiming for.

Fostering Transparency

Students are encouraged to write on-demand pieces before and after each unit of study (and often at the start and end of the year) in order to monitor student progress and as a tool for professional development. These on-demand pieces give teachers and administrators immediate knowledge of students' current skills and their growth over time.

Studying on-demand writing creates transparency. When we work with teachers and school leaders, a question we often pose is: "How is writing going? How do you know?" It is important that teachers and administrators are able to answer that question meaningfully. It is possible to know how writing is going for a child, for a class, for a grade, and across a school. It is possible to know in which classrooms writers are thriving, what types of writing students are growing in the most, where there is rapid progress, and where there is not. To help teachers and school leaders understand what students know as writers, it is useful to pause on scoring with rubrics, and instead begin with professional development on rapidly studying student work to see how groups of students are doing – we call it thin-slicing (Gladwell, 2007).

Thin-slicing does not give teachers a quantitative score on every child's writing performance. However, it gives school leaders and teachers a quick view of how writing is going, overall, for groups of kids, for different grade levels, and for different types of writing. It gives a quick way to informally monitor growth, celebrate progress, see trouble, and find the powerful writing teachers in a building. For teachers, that information is helpful. For a principal, it is invaluable.

Thin-Slicing

We have used the term thin-slicing with teachers and administrators to describe a process of quickly examining student writing by studying a few pieces deeply and using these pieces to represent larger groups of students. Gladwell (2007) talks about how, with practice and familiarity, a brain learns to gather important information from quick bits of data to interpolate and suggest meaning. We took that notion to the study of student assessments by developing protocols for teachers to thin-slice assessments during professional development (Calkins & Ehrenworth, 2016).

To lead a professional development activity in thin-slicing student writing, teachers use a fast-paced protocol that takes them quickly through the work, one that lets them accomplish the task in one period, as in a grade level or planning meeting. It is a very simple protocol: (1) pre-sorting, (2) re-sorting, and (3) choosing exemplars. During the pre-sort, teachers rapidly sort student work into three piles according to what the writing looks like – mainly by length, which is a quick indicator of fluency. In the re-sort, they agree on some qualities of writing (e.g., for narrative writing, meaning, and visible craft), and then skim the pieces, this time moving some pieces up or down the piles. In the third round, teachers choose prototypical pieces for each pile and make photocopies of those pieces to represent groups of writers.

If we were to end the professional development right there, the process is already valuable for teachers. They have an overall view of where their writers are. They have a sense of the ways some writers are writing well and some others are struggling. They can move to reviewing their unit and imagining small-group work, especially for the lower and higher piles. They can plan quick conferences for students with what they have learned about them as writers. Without the enormous time it would take to score individual pieces, teachers have handled their students' on-demand pieces, become more familiar with groups of writers, and seen overall where their students are.

Norming Teachers' Expectations

There is more to be gained from this professional development experience, however. It is important that teachers in a grade level have a similar understanding of seventh-grade writing or fourth-grade writing, and so on. Two quick ways to check on and norm teachers' grade level expectations are by comparing their piles with each other or with the exemplars from *Writing Pathways*.

By comparing their piles or their exemplars with each other, teachers will often find that their piles are very closely aligned, and they (and the school leader) will be reassured. But sometimes there will be something askew. Perhaps a teacher has changed grade levels and has no pieces in her "high" pile.

Or a teacher only has looked for length and does not yet know how to look for craft. Sometimes teachers will argue for a piece being stronger or less so, pointing out the depth of meaning, or attention to craft, or effective structure. These conversations are all internal professional development. They create shared knowledge and shared vocabulary, they move teachers from a private to a collaborative mindset, and they help create a more collective vision of writing. By comparing their exemplars and the pieces in their sorted piles, teachers bring their expectations closer into alignment – all part of the process of democratizing teacher knowledge and the teaching of writing.

Another way to quickly sharpen teachers' grade level expectations is to give them a few minutes to compare their prototypical exemplars with the exemplars in *Writing Pathways*. The questions we push teachers to ask include, "If I had to assign a level to this piece, which level of text in *Pathways* does it come closest to matching? That is, if this piece is prototypical of the strongest writers in our fifth grade, are our fifth graders at the start of the year writing at the fourth-grade level (as we would hope)? Or is it more accurate to say they tend to be writing at the third-grade level? What are some of the big things the writer – these writers – is doing well? What might be next for them?"

An important lens highlighted in professional development is the cross-grade level lens. If teachers from different grade levels have the opportunity to do this work in the same room at the same time, a gallery walk across grades, focused on the prototypical pieces, is illuminating. Sometimes teachers realize that their highest-level writers are not really growing and changing across the grade. Sometimes they see growth they have not fully realized.

At the end of the unit, teachers have students write another on-demand piece. As a result, teachers can engage in thin-slicing again, this time as a summative assessment. Again, as professional development, teachers gather to study the on-demand writing of three students who represented groups of writers, asking, "How did our main group – most of our writers, grow across the unit? How did our higher writers respond to our instruction? How did our lower level writers respond?" Because these pieces have been chosen by a thin-slicing protocol, studying only these three writers' pre- and post- on-demands, teachers and school leaders will get a rapid impression of how groups of writers have grown or not grown across the unit. During the professional development, we encourage those teachers who are open to questioning how students have performed during norming to reflect on what they are noticing. They will be the first to say, "I feel like our higher-level writers have not changed that much." Leading teachers to that kind of transparency is transformative for growth (Calkins & Ehrenworth, 2016).

We have seen teachers bring the knowledge gained from thin-slicing immediately into their practice. By talking about qualities of writing, they are more ready to confer with kids. By studying normed exemplars, they are more likely to put these exemplars into specific writers' hands. By studying their own students' on-demand pieces, they learn to quickly sort writers into small groups for immediate, targeted instruction. Often, it makes sense to follow up professional development on studying student writing with professional development in the classroom and on-site in schools, on planning and rehearsing small groups and teacher-student conferences (Wiliam, 2007).

When school leaders ritualize the study of student work, they turn formative assessment into significant professional development. When they use tools that help teachers norm expectations, they create a sense of system-ness and cohesion.

Teacher-Written Demonstration Texts

One more set of tools in *Writing Pathways* that acts as professional development is the demonstration texts. The educator-written demonstration texts are created by TCRWP staff by writing opinion, information, and narrative pieces up the ladder from K through eighth grade, annotating these so teachers see how the qualities of writing grow (see Appendix E for a fourth-grade sample). It is easier for teachers, families, and students to see qualities of writing when the topic remains the same.

These texts, which progress with essentially the same content across K–8th grades, show how small revisions add up incrementally to texts that meet expectations for increasing sophistication in writing. In each instance, we wrote a text at a kindergarten level and then improved it up a notch to write it like a first-grader, then a second-grader, and so on through eighth grade. For each K–8 grade level, there is a text that matches the expectations for that grade. Here's how these educator-written demonstration texts are *not* like real writing from children, however: When a third-grade child writes an information text, her piece will include some of the qualities of writing on the information checklist, but not all. When we wrote these demonstration texts, we included all the qualities on the checklist, so that students could use these as mentors for the range of qualities of writing.

Teachers find it is helpful to show students how parts of a sixth-grade level text, for example, can be improved upon to a seventh-grade level conclusion, or a seventh-grade level structure. These teacher-written pieces illustrate the items on the checklist more precisely and completely than most single pieces of student writing can, and can be used to show students how they can revise their own writing to take it from one level to the next. Perhaps more significantly, they show teachers who are less experienced with some types of writing what changes as writing grows and strengthens.

A powerful professional development session gives teachers time to study these pieces and to duplicate them, writing about topics of their own choice. By shifting the topic, teachers need to articulate and mimic the qualities of writing. That practice helps teachers assimilate the qualities of the genre along a skill progression, and hones their ability to demonstrate writing. They then bring that confidence and those demonstration skills into their classroom instruction.

Professional Development for School Leaders

School leaders also need professional development in studying student writing as an assessment of how instruction is going. In professional development, we coach leaders to look for patterns, asking questions such as:

> Does the on-demand writing suggest that students who are becoming particularly strong writers are emerging from certain classrooms? Does the on-demand writing suggest that some teachers are producing students who are stronger in certain types of writing? If groups of children seem to lag in their proficiency, do patterns in their instruction suggest the need for targeted professional development support?

Studying patterns in on-demand writing helps principals find their teacher leaders and ask questions about possible trouble. The initial assessment, given in September, is a window into how writing developed in the prior grade. While teachers may thin-slice, studying a few pieces deeply to plan instruction and study growth, a school leader might want to study things like the ratio of groups of writers (proficient, below proficiency, above proficiency) as she looks up the grade levels or across the year, or study the relationship between groups of writers and patterns of prior teaching.

If, for instance, there are many pieces in the "high" pile in third grade, but hardly any in fourth grade, then the principal may want to investigate what is happening in third-grade writing. It might be helpful to norm some of these pieces. If, at the start of third grade, there are many pieces that norm as above second grade, then a principal knows that second-grade writing instruction is flourishing, and strong writers are growing. But if at the start of fourth grade, there are no longer many writers who norm above grade level, then third-grade writing instruction might need support. It is also interesting to look at which teachers taught the students whose pieces end up mostly in the "high" pile – those could possibly be teacher leaders in writing.

It can be helpful to have follow-up questions like those in Table 8.1 that let school leaders harness the wealth of information that emerges from systemic assessment.

Lucy Calkins et al.

Table 8.1 Follow-Up Questions for School Leaders Used During Professional Development.

Lenses for Studying On-Demand Writing	Follow-Up Questions
What does a quick sort of student writing indicate about the proficiency of groups of writers?	What qualities indicate inclusion in a higher group? How do typical pieces in each group compare among teachers – how are we norming expectations?
How does a typical piece from each group compare to a normed exemplar?	What is the overall grade level proficiency of most of the class? Of certain groups?
	What particular qualities of writing are writers getting stronger at (craft, structure, meaning, conventions)?
Does the ratio of proficient writers change across grade levels?	Are certain groups of writers growing than others? Are strong writers getting enough attention?
	Do certain grade levels produce more growth among certain groups?
Are there patterns in terms of who taught students who show powerful growth in writing?	Should certain teachers be teacher leaders in writing instruction?
	Do some teachers need support in writing instruction?
What kind of growth are writers showing across a unit of study?	Is there more growth among some groups than others?
	Is there more growth in some types of writing than others? Is there more growth in certain classrooms than others?

Conclusion

In this chapter, we have described the importance of professional development to encourage teachers to increase the use of formative assessment practices in their writing classrooms. The *Writing Pathways* toolkit provides an example system with resources in the form of learning progressions, normed exemplars, rubrics, and student-facing checklists to promote formative assessment. This toolkit is easily adapted by teachers in their own school or district. With professional development, teachers should be able to apply these resources in their classroom to improve students' quality of writing (McCarthey & Geoghegan, 2016). Therefore, opportunities for professional development at each level – administrative and teacher levels – can promote a better application of new skills (Schneider & Randel, 2009). The *Writing Pathways* professional development uses efficient tools to promote the successful implementation of this curriculum.

Of course, all of these tools, and the ways in which they can function as professional development, are going to be most useful when they are connected to a curriculum that explicitly teaches these qualities across the types of writing and grade levels. Fullan (2014) points out that the problem in education is not resistance to change but the presence of too many changes, uncoordinated with existing systems and with one another, implemented in superficial or ad hoc ways. The field of education is often characterized by a constant frenzy of efforts to grasp at yet one more magic solve-all – and this is premised on the hope that somewhere, there is a program to buy, to install, which will provide the magic solution. If there is a magic solution, it is an engagement in a persistent cycle of teaching, observing the results of teaching, and then responding thoughtfully to what one sees.

What's called for is that teachers study student work and develop and adapt curriculum in light of what the evidence shows. In the end, the greatest contribution made by the tools of a strong assessment system such as *Writing Pathways* is helping teachers and students self-assess, collaborate with other learners, learn from feedback, and work collectively toward challenging, clear goals. If there is a magic formula in education, a secret to success, it is this process of continuous improvement.

Fullan and Hargreaves (2012) point out that:

Writing and Professional Development

Teaching like a pro . . . cannot be sustained unless all your colleagues teach like pros too. Whether you are alone in your classroom or working in a team, teaching like a pro means that the confidence, competence, and critical feedback you get from your colleagues is always with you.

(p. xiv)

What we learned from working with *Writing Pathways* is that a normed, nested system of assessment works as professional development because it helps with vision-building, increases teacher knowledge, and creates collaborative communities of practice. Going forward, we hope that schools and teachers will be able to mirror the student progressions in *Writing Pathways* with their own, local student writing. We hope that district and school leaders dedicate professional development time for teachers to study student exemplars and their own students' writing, develop protocols for seeing growth over time, and, above all, increase teacher knowledge of writing. We also hope that, with increased knowledge and confidence, teachers shift assessment into students' hands, so that students learn to self-assess wisely, set ambitious goals, and strive to meet them as writers.

References

Andrade, H. (2008). Self-assessment through rubrics. *Educational Leadership, 65*(4), 60–63.

Andrade, H. & Brooke, G. (2010). Student self-assessment and learning to write. In N. L. Mertens (Ed.), *Writing: Processes, tools and techniques*. New York, NY: Nova Science.

Andrade, H. & Du, Y. (2007). Student responses to criteria-referenced self-assessment. *Assessment & Evaluation in Higher Education, 32*(2), 159–181.

Andrade, H. L., Du, Y., & Mycek, K. (2010). Rubric-referenced self-assessment and middle school students' writing. *Assessment in Education: Principles, Policy & Practice, 17*(2), 199–214.

Andrade, H. L., Du, Y., & Wang, X. (2008). Putting rubrics to the test: The effect of a model, criteria generation, and rubric-referenced self-assessment on elementary school students' writing. *Educational Measurement: Issues and Practice, 27*(2), 3–13.

Andrade, H. L. & Heritage, M. (2017). *Using formative assessment to enhance learning, achievement, and academic self-regulation*. New York, NY: Routledge.

Bennett, R. E. (2011). Formative assessment: A critical review. *Assessment in Education: Principles, Policy & Practice, 18*(1), 5–25.

Black, P. & Wiliam, D. (1998). Assessment and classroom learning. *Assessment in Education: Principles, Policy & Practice, 5*(1), 7–74.

Calkins, L. (2013a). *Writing pathways*. Portsmouth, NH: Heinemann.

Calkins, L. (2013b). *Units of study in opinion, information, and narrative writing*. Portsmouth, NH: Heinemann.

Calkins, L., Boland Hohne, K., & Robb, A. (2015). *Writing pathways: Performance assessments and learning progressions, Grades K-8*. Portsmouth, NH: Heinemann.

Calkins, L. & Ehrenworth, M. (2016). Growing extraordinary writers: Leadership decisions to raise the level of writing across a school and a district. *The Reading Teacher*, 60–63.

Calkins, L., Ehrenworth, M., & Lehman, C. (2012). *Pathways to the common core*. Portsmouth, NH: Heinemann.

Calkins, L. M. & Harwayne, S. (1991). *Living between the lines*. Portsmouth, NH: Heinemann.

Deane, P. & Song, Y. (2015). The key practice, discuss and debate ideas: Conceptual framework, literature review, and provisional learning progressions for argumentation. *ETS Research Report Series, 2015*(2), 1–21.

Fleischer, C. (2004). Professional development for teacher-writers. *Educational Leadership, 62* (2), 24–28.

Fullan, M. (2014, June 24). *Right versus wrong drivers in education*. Speech presented at June Writing Institute in Teachers College, Columbia University, New York.

Fullan, M. & Hargreaves, A. (2012). *Professional capital: Transforming teaching in every school*. New York: Teachers College Press.

Gawande, A. (2009). *The checklist manifesto*. New York: Metropolitan Books.

Gladwell, M. (2007). *Blink: The power of thinking without thinking*. New York, NY: Back Bay Books.

Graham, S., Harris, K.R., & Chambers, A.B. (2016). Evidence-based practice and writing instruction: A review of reviews. In C. A. MacArthur, S. Graham, J. Fitzgerald (Eds.) *Handbook of writing research* (5th ed., pp. 211–226). New York, NY: The Guilford Press.

Graham, S., Hebert, M., & Harris, K. R. (2015). Formative assessment and writing: A meta-analysis. *The Elementary School Journal, 115*(4), 523–547.

Graham, S., McKeown, D., Kiuhara, S., & Harris, K.R. (2012). A meta-analysis of writing instruction for students in the elementary grades. *Journal of Educational Psychology, 104*(4), 879–896.

Graves, D. (2001). *The energy to teach.* Portsmouth, NH: Heinemann.

Grisham, D.L., & Wolsey, T.D. (2011). Writing instruction for teacher candidates: Strengthening a weak curricular area. *Literacy Research and Instruction, 50*(4), 348–364.

Harry, B. & Klingner, J. (2007). Discarding the deficit model. *Educational Leadership, 64*(5), 16.

Hattie, J. (2011). *Visible learning for teachers.* New York, NY: Routledge.

Hattie, J. & Timperley, H. (2007). The power of feedback. *Review of Educational Research, 77*(1), 81–112.

Hunter, K. & Docherty, P. (2011). Reducing variation in the assessment of student writing. *Assessment & Evaluation in Higher Education, 36*(1), 109–124.

Kingston, N. & Nash, B. (2011). Formative assessment: A meta-analysis and a call for research. *Educational measurement: Issues and Practice, 30*(4), 28–37.

Ladson-Billings, G. (1995). Toward a theory of culturally relevant pedagogy. *American Educational Research Journal, 32*(3), 465–497.

McCarthey, S. J. & Geoghegan, C.M. (2016). The role of professional development for enhancing writing instruction. In C. A. MacArthur, S. Graham, & J. Fitzgerald (Eds.) *Handbook of writing research* (5th edition, pp. 330–345). New York, NY: The Guilford Press.

Mosher, F. & Heritage, M. (2017). A hitchhiker's guide to thinking about literacy, learning progressions, and instruction. *CPRE research reports.* Retrieved from https://repository.upenn.edu/cpre_researchreports/97

Moss, C., Brookhart, S., & Long, A. (2013). Administrators' roles in helping teachers use formative assessment information. *Applied Measurement in Education, 26*(3), 205–218.

Murray, D. (2003). *A writer teaches writing, revised.* Portsmouth, NH: Heinemann.

National Governors Association. (2010). Common core state standards. *Light, J, 19,* 19.

Orsmond, P., Merry, S., & Reiling, K. (2002). The use of exemplars and formative feedback when using student derived marking criteria in peer and self-assessment. *Assessment & Evaluation in Higher Education, 27*(4), 309–323.

Parr, J. M. (2013). Classroom assessment in writing. In J. H. McMillan (Ed.) *SAGE Handbook of Classroom Assessment* (pp. 489–501). Thousand Oaks, CA: SAGE.

Sadler, D. R. (2005). Interpretations of criteria-based assessment and grading in higher education. *Assessment & Evaluation in Higher Education, 30*(2), 175–194.

Schneider, M.C., & Randel, B. (2009). Research on characteristics of effective professional development programs for enhancing educators' skills in formative assessment. In H. L. Andrade & G. J. Cizek (Eds.) *Handbook of formative assessment* (pp. 251–276). New York, NY: Routledge.

Stiggins, R. J. (2009). Essential formative assessment competencies for teachers and school leaders. In H. L. Andrade & G. J. Cizek (Eds.) *Handbook of formative assessment* (pp. 233–250). New York, NY: Routledge.

Valle, C., Andrade, H., Palma, M., & Hefferen, J. (2016). Applications of peer assessment and self-assessment in music. *Music Educators Journal, 102*(4), 41–49.

Wagner, T. (2014). *The global achievement gap: Why even the best schools don't teach the new survival skills our children need, and what we can do about it.* New York, NY: Basic Books.

Wiliam, D. (2007). *Five "Key strategies" for effective formative assessment.* Reston, VA: National Council of Teachers of Mathematics. Retrieved from nwrcc.educationnorthwest.org/filesnwrcc/webfm/STEM/Formative_Assessment_Five_Key_Strategies.pdf.

Appendices

	Pre-Kindergarten	Kindergarten	Grade 1	Grade 2	Grade 3	Grade 4
DEVELOPMENT						
Elaboration	The writer put more and then more on the page.	The writer put everything she thought about the topic (or book) on the page.	The writer wrote at least one reason for his opinion.	The writer wrote at least two reasons and wrote at least a few sentences about each one.	The writer not only named her reasons to support her opinion, but also wrote more about each one.	The writer gave reasons to support his opinion. He chose the reasons to convince his readers. The writer included examples and information to support his reasons, perhaps from a text, his knowledge, or his life.
Craft	The writer said, drew, and "wrote" some things about what she liked and did not like.	The writer had details in pictures and words.	The writer used labels and words to give details.	The writer chose words that would make readers agree with her opinion.	The writer not only told readers to believe him, but also wrote in ways that got them thinking or feeling in certain ways.	The writer made deliberate word choices to convince her readers, perhaps by emphasizing or repeating words that made readers feel emotions. If it felt right to do so, the writer chose precise details and facts to help make her points and used figurative language to draw readers into her line of thought. The writer made choices about which evidence was best to include or not include to support her points. The writer used a convincing tone.

Appendix B Student On-Demand Exemplar, Grade 4 Argument/Opinion Writing,
   Writing Pathways

Television Shouldn't Be Over Watched

My strong opinion is that kids shouldn't watch too much television. Other people shouldn't too. I believe this is true because then you will have more time to study for a good education. Also, some shows on television are bad for kids to watch. Another reason this is true is that if you watch too much television you will get bad eyesight.

The first reason I will explain is that you will have more time to read and study if you're not always watching television. Then, you are more likely to do well on tests and get a good education. Education is important because if you do well in school, you will be able to get a good job and then you'll be able to buy a house and food so you don't starve. Education is important and so is not watching too much television.

An additional reason my opinion is true is that some shows on television are bad for kids to watch. Younger children might be scared of some shows. This is bad because then stuff that reminds them of the scary shows might make them cry. Also, some shows weren't made for children to watch but they may not know that and watch it anyway.

The last reason I will tell you about why people shouldn't watch too much television is that then you might develope bad eyesight. I have learnt before that staring at things like computer screens or televisions for a while can damage your eyes. You need your eyes to see other cars on the street and traffic lights. If you couldn't see those you might get in an accident. Also you need good eyesight to read important information like what to do if there is a fire in the building. If you don't know that information you could get hurt.

Sample 1, page 1

Even though I agree that television can be very entertaining and fun, too much of it can be very bad. I'm sure you now agree that this is true. So, if you want a good education, a healthy mind, and good eyesight, I would advise you to make sure that you're not always sitting on the couch with your eyes glued to a television screen.

Vote Against Math

Math is the worst subject in school! It is the worst subject in school for many reasons. The first reason is that if you have a calculater you won't need to know it. The second reason is it takes to much time out of the day and last but not least you won't really need to use math any where.

Before I said you have a calculater you won't need to know math, and it's true. If your having a party and you need two choclate bars for every one and theres 32 people just type in 32 x 2 and you've got your answer.

My second reason why math is the worst subject in shcool is it takes to long in class. In my class math a period and a half and in my oppinion thats to long. We should be useing that time to read or write or something more important. Last but not least we don't really need to use it.

Sample 2, page 1

Which is true. If you go to the store and by something for $5.21 and give them a 10 dollar bill you'll see on the little moniter that they are subtracting $5.21 from $10.00. but if you have some doubts that's where you use your culculater. If you still don't believe that math is the worst subject in school then try it for your self and see what a waste it is.

Sample 2, page 2

Appendix C 1. Fourth Grade Student-Facing Checklist, Argument/Opinion Writing, *Writing Pathways*

Name: _____ **Date:** _____

Opinion Writing Checklist

	Grade 4	NOT YET	STARTING TO	YES!
	Structure			
Overall	I made a claim about a topic or a text and tried to support my reasons.	☐	☐	☐
Lead	I wrote a few sentences to hook my readers, perhaps by asking a question, explaining why the topic mattered, telling a surprising fact, or giving background information.	☐	☐	☐
	I stated my claim.	☐	☐	☐
Transitions	I used words and phrases to glue parts of my piece together. I used phrases such as *for example, another example, one time,* and *for instance* to show when I was shifting from saying reasons to giving evidence and *in addition to, also,* and *another* to show when I wanted to make a new point.	☐	☐	☐
Ending	I wrote an ending for my piece in which I restated and reflected on my claim, perhaps suggesting an action or response based on what I had written.	☐	☐	☐
Organization	I separated sections of information using paragraphs.	☐	☐	☐
	Development			
Elaboration	I gave reasons to support my opinion. I chose the reasons to convince my readers.	☐	☐	☐
	I included examples and information to support my reasons, perhaps from a text, my knowledge, or my life.	☐	☐	☐
Craft	I made deliberate word choices to convince my readers, perhaps by emphasizing or repeating words that would make my readers feel emotions.	☐	☐	☐
	If it felt right to do so, I chose precise details and facts to help make my points and used figurative language to draw the readers into my line of thought.	☐	☐	☐
	I made choices about which evidence was best to include or not include to support my points.	☐	☐	☐
	I used a convincing tone.	☐	☐	☐
	Language Conventions			
Spelling	I used what I know about word families and spelling rules to help me spell and edit. I used the word wall and dictionaries to help me when needed.	☐	☐	☐
Punctuation	When writing long complex sentences, I used commas to make them clear and correct.	☐	☐	☐
	I used periods to fix my run-on sentences.	☐	☐	☐

May be photocopied for classroom use. © 2013 by Lucy Calkins and Colleagues from the Teachers College Reading and Writing Project from Units of Study in Opinion, Information, and Narrative Writing, Grade 4 (*firsthand*: Portsmouth, NH).

2. Excerpt, Illustrated Student-Facing Checklist, Grade 4 Argument/Opinion Writing, Writing Pathways

Name: _____ **Date:** _____

Opinion Writing Checklist

Grade 4

	STRUCTURE				
Overall	I made a claim about a topic or a text and tried to support my reasons.				
		Did I do it like a fourth grader?	NOT YET	STARTING TO	YES!
Lead		I wrote a few sentences to hook my readers, perhaps by asking a question, explaining why the topic mattered, telling a surprising fact, or giving background information.	☐	☐	☐
		I stated my claim.	☐	☐	☐
Transitions	for example another example one time for instance also in addition to another	I used words and phrases to glue parts of my piece together. I used phrases such as *for example*, *another example*, *one time*, and *for instance* to show when I was shifting from saying reasons to giving evidence and *in addition to*, *also*, and *another* to show when I wanted to make a new point.	☐	☐	☐
Ending	You should..	I wrote an ending for my piece in which I restated and reflected on my claim, perhaps suggesting an action or response based on what I had written.	☐	☐	☐
Organization		I separated sections of information using paragraphs.	☐	☐	☐

May be photocopied for classroom use. © 2014 by Lucy Calkins and Colleagues from the Teachers College Reading and Writing Project. *Writing Pathways: Performance Assessments and Learning Progressions, Grades K–8* (Heinemann: Portsmouth, NH).

Opinion Writing Checklist *(continued)*

Grade 4

		DEVELOPMENT			
		Did I do it like a fourth grader?	NOT YET	STARTING TO	YES!
Elaboration		I gave reasons to support my opinion. I chose the reasons to convince my readers.	☐	☐	☐
	For example... I read... I learned... One time...	I included examples and information to support my reasons, perhaps from a text, my knowledge, or my life.	☐	☐	☐
Craft	My father is my greatest teacher.	I made deliberate word choices to convince my readers, perhaps by emphasizing or repeating words that would make my readers feel emotions.	☐	☐	☐
	Family is like a puzzle.	If it felt right to do so, I chose precise details and facts to help make my points and used figurative language to draw the readers into my line of thought.	☐	☐	☐
		I made choices about which evidence was best to include or not include to support my points.	☐	☐	☐
	You must! Experts say... Why not... Do you realize... People should...	I used a convincing tone.	☐	☐	☐

May be photocopied for classroom use. © 2014 by Lucy Calkins and Colleagues from the Teachers College Reading and Writing Project. *Writing Pathways: Performance Assessments and Learning Progressions, Grades K–8* (Heinemann: Portsmouth, NH).

Opinion Writing Checklist *(continued)*

Grade 4

LANGUAGE CONVENTIONS

		Did I do it like a fourth grader?	NOT YET	STARTING TO	YES!
Spelling	~ing clapping sitting making loving	I used what I knew about word families and spelling rules to help me spell and edit.	☐	☐	☐
	Aa Bb Cc Dd Ee Ff Gg Hh Ii Jj	I used the word wall and dictionaries to help me when needed.	☐	☐	☐
Punctuation	Use commas to pause! For instance,	When writing long, complex sentences, I used commas to make them clear and correct.	☐	☐	☐
	Read + listen! and then so	I used periods to fix my run-on sentences.	☐	☐	☐

May be photocopied for classroom use. © 2014 by Lucy Calkins and Colleagues from the Teachers College Reading and Writing Project. *Writing Pathways: Performance Assessments and Learning Progressions, Grades K–8* (Heinemann: Portsmouth, NH).

Appendix D Grade 4 Rubric Argument/Opinion writing, *Writing Pathways*

Name: _____   Date: _____

Rubric for Opinion Writing—Fourth Grade

	Grade 2 (1 POINT)	1.5 PTS	Grade 3 (2 POINTS)	2.5 PTS	Grade 4 (3 POINTS)	3.5 PTS	Grade 5 (4 POINTS)	SCORE
STRUCTURE								
Overall	The writer wrote her opinion or her likes and dislikes and gave reasons for her opinion.	Mid-level	The writer told readers his opinion and ideas on a text or a topic and helped them understand his reasons.	Mid-level	The writer made a claim about a topic or a text and tried to support her reasons.	Mid-level	The writer made a claim or thesis on a topic or text, supported it with reasons, and provided a variety of evidence for each reason.	
Lead	The writer wrote a beginning in which he not only gave his opinion, but also set readers up to expect that his writing would try to convince them of it.	Mid-level	The writer wrote a beginning in which she not only set readers up to expect that this would be a piece of opinion writing, but also tried to hook them into caring about her opinion.	Mid-level	The writer wrote a few sentences to hook his readers, perhaps by asking a question, explaining why the topic mattered, telling a surprising fact, or giving background information. The writer stated his claim.	Mid-level	The writer wrote an introduction that led to a claim or thesis and got her readers to care about her opinion. She got readers to care by not only including a cool fact or jazzy question, but also figuring out what was significant in or around the topic and giving readers information about what was significant about the topic. The writer worked to find the precise words to state her claim; she let readers know the reasons she would develop later.	

	Grade 2 (1 POINT)	1.5 PTS	**Grade 3** (2 POINTS)	2.5 PTS	**Grade 4** (3 POINTS)	3.5 PTS	**Grade 5** (4 POINTS)	SCORE
STRUCTURE (cont.)								
Transitions	The writer connected parts of her piece using words such as *also*, *another*, and *because*.	Mid-level	The writer connected his ideas and reasons with his examples using words such as *for example* and *because*. He connected one reason or example using words such as *also* and *another*.	Mid-level	The writer used words and phrases to glue parts of her piece together. She used phrases such as *for example*, *another example*, *one time*, and *for instance* to show when she wanted to shift from saying reasons to giving evidence and *in addition to*, *also*, and *another* to show when she wanted to make a new point.	Mid-level	The writer used transition words and phrases to connect evidence back to his reasons using phrases such as *this shows that.* . . . The writer helped readers follow his thinking with phrases such as *another reason* and *the most important reason*. To show what happened he used phrases such as *consequently* and *because of*. The writer used words such as *specifically* and *in particular* to be more precise.	
Ending	The writer wrote an ending in which he reminded readers of his opinion.	Mid-level	The writer worked on an ending, perhaps a thought or comment related to her opinion.	Mid-level	The writer wrote an ending for his piece in which he restated and reflected on his claim, perhaps suggesting an action or response based on what he had written.	Mid-level	The writer worked on a conclusion in which he connected back to and highlighted what the text was mainly about, not just the preceding paragraph.	
Organization	The writer's piece had different parts; she wrote a lot of lines for each part.	Mid-level	The writer wrote several reasons or examples why readers should agree with his opinion and wrote at least several sentences about each reason. The writer organized his information so that each part of his writing was mostly about one thing.	Mid-level	The writer separated sections of information using paragraphs.	Mid-level	The writer grouped information and related ideas into paragraphs. He put the parts of his writing in the order that most suited his purpose and helped him prove his reasons and claim.	
								TOTAL

	Grade 2 (1 POINT)	1.5 PTS	Grade 3 (2 POINTS)	2.5 PTS	Grade 4 (3 POINTS)	3.5 PTS	Grade 5 (4 POINTS)	SCORE
				DEVELOPMENT				
Elaboration*	The writer wrote at least two reasons and wrote at least a few sentences about each one.	Mid-level	The writer not only named her reasons to support her opinion, but also wrote more about each one.	Mid-level	The writer gave reasons to support his opinion. He chose the reasons to convince his readers. The writer included examples and information to support his reasons, perhaps from a text, his knowledge, or his life.	Mid-level	The writer gave reasons to support her opinion that were parallel and did not overlap. She put them in an order that she thought would be most convincing. The writer included evidence such as facts, examples, quotations, micro-stories, and information to support her claim. The writer discussed and unpacked the way that the evidence went with the claim.	(X2)
Craft*	The writer chose words that would make readers agree with her opinion.	Mid-level	The writer not only told readers to believe him, but also wrote in ways that got them thinking or feeling in certain ways.	Mid-level	The writer made deliberate word choices to convince her readers, perhaps by emphasizing or repeating words that made readers feel emotions. If it felt right to do so, the writer chose precise details and facts to help make her points and used figurative language to draw readers into her line of thought. The writer made choices about which evidence was best to include or not include to support her points. The writer used a convincing tone.	Mid-level	The writer made deliberate word choices to have an effect on his readers. The writer reached for the precise phrase, metaphor, or image that would convey his ideas. The writer made choices about how to angle his evidence to support his points. When it seemed right to do so, the writer tried to use a scholarly voice and varied his sentences to create the pace and tone of the different sections of his piece.	(X2)
								TOTAL

* Elaboration and Craft are double-weighted categories: Whatever score a student would get in these categories is worth double the amount of points. For example, if a student exceeds expectations in Elaboration, then that student would receive 8 points instead of 4 points. If a student meets standards in Elaboration, then that student would receive 6 points instead of 3 points.

	Grade 2 (1 POINT)	1.5 PTS	Grade 3 (2 POINTS)	2.5 PTS	Grade 4 (3 POINTS)	3.5 PTS	Grade 5 (4 POINTS)	SCORE
LANGUAGE CONVENTIONS								
Spelling	To spell a word, the writer used what he knew about spelling patterns (*tion, er, ly,* etc.). The writer spelled all of the word wall words correctly and used the word wall to help him figure out how to spell other words.	Mid-level	The writer used what she knew about word families and spelling rules to help her spell and edit. The writer got help from others to check her spelling and punctuation before she wrote her final draft.	Mid-level	The writer used what he knew about word families and spelling rules to help him spell and edit. He used the word wall and dictionaries to help him when needed.	Mid-level	The writer used what she knew about word patterns to spell correctly and she used references to help her spell words when needed. She made sure to correctly spell words that were important to her topic.	
Punctuation	The writer used quotation marks to show what characters said. When the writer used words such as *can't* and *don't*, she put in the apostrophe.	Mid-level	The writer punctuated dialogue correctly with commas and quotation marks. While writing, the writer put punctuation at the end of every sentence. The writer wrote in ways that helped readers read with expression, reading some parts quickly, some slowly, some parts in one sort of voice and others in another.	Mid-level	When writing long, complex sentences, the writer used commas to make them clear and correct. The writer used periods to fix her run-on sentences.	Mid-level	The writer used commas to set off introductory parts of sentences, for example, *At this time in history,* and *it was common to . . . .* The writer used a variety of punctuation to fix any run-on sentences. The writer used punctuation to cite his sources.	
								TOTAL

Teachers, we created these rubrics so you will have your own place to pull together scores of student work. You can use these assessments immediately after giving the on-demands and also for self-assessment and setting goals.

If you want to translate this score into a grade, you can use the provided table to score each student on a scale of 0–4.

Scoring Guide

In each row, circle the descriptor in the column that matches the student work. Scores in the categories of Elaboration and Craft are worth double the point value (*2, 3, 4, 5, 6, 7,* or *8* instead of *1, 1.5, 2, 2.5, 3, 3.5,* or *4*).

Total the number of points and then track students' progress by seeing when the total points increase.

Total score: _____

Number of Points	Scaled Score
1–11	1
11.5–16.5	1.5
17–22	2
22.5–27.5	2.5
28–33	3
33.5–38.5	3.5
39–44	4

Appendix E Teacher Demonstration Text, Fourth Grade, Argument/Opinion Writing, *Writing Pathways*

Grade 4

The writer began with a few sentences to "hook" the reader. He may have done this by asking a question, explaining why the topic matters, telling a surprising fact, or giving background information.	Many people think that recess is fun for kids no matter what but I think it is boring because there isn't anything fun to do. Right now at recess a lot of kids just sit on the grass because they don't want to swing or play jump rope. We should have football at recess!

The writer stated his claim.

The first reason why we should have football is because it is good exercise. When you play, you get to run, throw, and catch. For instance, when I was playing football last week Anthony had the ball and we all had to run after him and try to get the ball to make a touchdown. My football coach says, "Football is a great workout." We should have football because it's good exercise.

The writer separated sections of information using paragraphs.

The writer used words and phrases to glue parts of his piece together. He used phrases such as *for example, another example, one time,* and *for instance* (to show a shift from reasons to evidence) and *in addition, also,* and *another* (to make a new point).

Another reason we should have football is because everyone can play football. I play with my brothers. Sometimes my sister plays. Sometimes my dog catches the ball! This shows that everyone can play. Also, if you don't know how to play it is an easy sport to learn. You can just start playing. All you need is a ball and a yard. We already have a yard at recess, we just need a ball. Our class says that five of us have balls at home that we can bring in. This shows that everyone can play.

The writer shows evidence of deliberate word and detail choice. He repeated and emphasized key words and used precise details to draw the reader into his line of thought.

The writer chose reasons that are convincing to the reader. He included examples and information to support those reasons. This information might be from a text, from personal experience, or from background knowledge.

The writer used a convincing tone.

The last and most important reason that we should have football is because it is fun for everyone. Even people that are just watching have fun! For instance, last weekend at Central Park I saw a game going on and the players were running and catching and throwing and giving each other high fives. And the fans were jumping up and down and screaming their heads off. We should have football because it is fun for everyone.

The writer used periods to fix run-on sentences.

The writer wrote an ending that doesn't just restate, but reflects on the claim. It reminds the reader of his point and suggests a solution for the problem.

Recess is supposed to be fun. If we have football at recess we will get more exercise, play more, and have more fun. When we were little we played on the swings or went down slides. But now everyone just sits around. It would be better if we could play football.

When writing long, complex sentences, the writer used commas to make them clear and correct.

9
TEACHER PREPARATION IN MATHEMATICS

Margaret Heritage and Caroline Wylie

There are many competing demands to consider in designing a preservice program that meets the two goals proposed by Hiebert, Morris, and Glass (2003) for mathematics teachers:

- Become more "mathematically proficient" (National Research Council [NRC], 2001);
- Develop the knowledge, competencies, and dispositions to learn to teach, with increasing effectiveness over time, in ways that help one's own students become more mathematically proficient.

(p. 202)

We take the view that because of the documented positive impact that formative assessment can have on student learning (Black et al., 2003; Black & Wiliam, 1998; Clark, 2012; Hattie & Timperley, 2007), the development of preservice teachers' knowledge and skills in this area should be considered as a priority in achieving these two goals. In this chapter, we outline an approach and present recommendations to help ensure that preservice teachers are prepared to implement formative assessment effectively as mathematics classroom teachers and are predisposed to continue their learning as they enter the profession.

To guide the design of preservice coursework for formative assessment in mathematics, we propose the framework shown in Figure 9.1. Our thesis is that the cultivation of teacher expertise to implement formative assessment effectively is grounded in three core, interrelated domains: formative assessment knowledge and skills, mathematics disciplinary knowledge, and habits of practice. In Figure 9.1, the core, interrelated domains are represented as three overlapping circles. Formative assessment is modulated and shaped by the discipline in which it is conducted (Bennett, 2011; Boaler, 2002; Cizek, Andrade, & Bennett, Chapter 1, this volume; Cowie & Moreland, 2015; Shepard, Penuel, & Pellegrino, 2018). Therefore, teachers' formative assessment knowledge and skills are inextricably connected with their disciplinary knowledge, which consists of their understanding of mathematics concepts, how these concepts relate to each other in a broader progression of learning, and the development of students' thinking about them (Bransford, Brown, & Cocking, 2000). Formative assessment knowledge and skills and disciplinary knowledge also overlap with habits of practice, the specific dispositions and patterns of behavior through which expertise in formative assessment within the discipline of mathematics is acquired and continuously refined. Associated with each of the domains are either knowledge representations or experiences (gray boxes) that support the development of expertise.

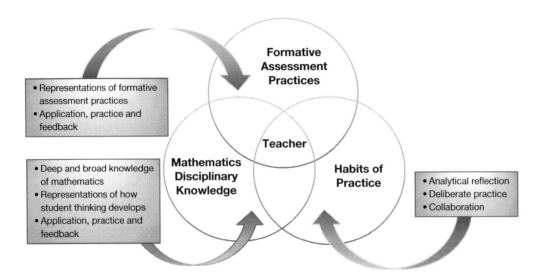

Figure 9.1 A framework for cultivating teachers' formative assessment expertise.

The chapter is divided into three main parts. In the first part, we provide a perspective on formative assessment as an ongoing classroom practice, along with a consideration of the role of disciplinary knowledge in its enactment, and describe the habits of practice that engender continued professional growth for its implementation. We also include an extended illustration of formative assessment in action with an analysis focused on the three interrelated domains of the framework (Figure 9.1). In the second part, we examine current, relevant professional standards for mathematics teachers that illustrate how the three core domains of the framework are woven throughout. In the third part of the chapter, we elaborate the proposed framework, and consider how it could guide the design of preservice mathematics teacher education programs.

Part One: Perspective on Formative Assessment

We define formative assessment following the Council of Chief State School Officers, Formative Assessment for Students and Teachers (FAST) State Collaborative on Assessment and Student Standards (SCASS) definition (CCSSO, 2018). The FAST SCASS is comprised of members of state departments of education, and its purpose is to provide guidance and resources to state-level personnel on formative assessment. While there is significant alignment across many research- and practice-based definitions of formative assessment in the literature (e.g., Bell & Cowie, 2001; Black & Wiliam, 2009; Brookhart & Moss, 2009; Cizek, Andrade, & Bennett, Chapter 1, this volume; Leahy et al., 2005), we adopt the FAST SCASS definition because it represents a professional view from state-level personnel of their expectations for teachers' implementation of formative assessment, and consequently for what preservice teachers ought to be learning about in their preservice programs.

The FAST SCASS definition (CCSSO, 2018, p. 2), in common with many others, represents formative assessment as a set of practices that engage both students and teachers in a process of eliciting evidence of learning related to specific goals, and acting on that evidence to advance learning toward those goals.

> *Formative assessment is a planned, ongoing process used by all students and teachers during learning and teaching to elicit and use evidence of student learning to improve student understanding of intended disciplinary learning outcomes, and support students to become self-directed learners.*

Teacher Preparation in Mathematics

Effective use of the formative assessment process requires students and teachers to integrate and embed the following practices in a collaborative and respectful classroom environment:

- *Clarifying learning goals and success criteria within a broader progression of learning;*
- *Eliciting and analyzing evidence of student thinking;*
- *Engaging in self-assessment and peer feedback;*
- *Providing actionable feedback; and*
- *Using evidence and feedback to move learning forward by adjusting learning strategies, goals or next instructional steps.*

Mathematics Disciplinary Knowledge and the FAST SCASS Definition of Formative Assessment

The FAST SCASS definition clearly references disciplinary learning as an outcome of formative assessment, underscoring that the five delineated practices are grounded in the discipline of focus.

Clarifying Learning Goals and Success Criteria Within a Broader Progression of Learning

The process of formative assessment begins with establishing clear learning goals and success criteria (Absolum, 2010; Black et al., 2003; Leahy et al., 2005; Heritage, 2010, 2013). With strong mathematics disciplinary knowledge, teachers are better able to establish meaningful learning goals and success criteria within a broader progression of learning as emphasized in the FAST SCASS definition. Such a progression describes the typical pathways that students move along to achieve mathematical understanding and the typical difficulties or misconceptions they might encounter along the way (Hill, Schilling, & Ball, 2004).

The level of teachers' disciplinary knowledge will also impact their capacity to integrate into learning goals the analytical practices (e.g., reasoning and proof, problem solving, strategic competence) that characterize mathematical expertise. Figure 9.2 briefly illustrates how learning goals and success criteria are shaped by mathematics disciplinary knowledge or the lack thereof. Example 1 represents how a teacher with stronger disciplinary knowledge describes a learning goal and success criteria for a lesson, while Example 2 shows a learning goal and success criteria from a teacher with weaker disciplinary knowledge.

In Example 1, the learning goal requires students to access relevant mathematical understanding and apply it to problem solving. The success criteria reflect higher-level thinking and foster problem solving through the use of different representations and explanations without suggesting a predictable

Example 1	Example 2
Learning goal I can use division to solve word problems	*Learning goal* I can shade fractions of shapes
Success criteria – Represent the problem with a visual representation – Represent the problem using numbers – Write a clear explanation of how I solved the problem – Use appropriate math vocabulary in my explanation	*Success criteria* – Know what number is the denominator – Know how many pieces the shape needs to be divided into – Know what number is the numerator – Know how many pieces need to be shaded

Figure 9.2 Contrasting examples of learning goals and success criteria.

pathway (National Council of Teachers of Mathematics [NCTM], 2014). In Example 2, the learning goal and the success criteria have no connections to the meaning that underlies the procedures being used, and the success criteria are focused on producing correct answers rather than on developing mathematical understanding.

Eliciting and Analyzing Evidence of Student Thinking

The descriptors *planned* and *ongoing* included in the FAST SCASS definition emphasize formative assessment as intentional and continuous assessment that occurs while learning is in development. Teachers who are skilled in formative assessment plan opportunities within the lesson to obtain evidence about how student learning is progressing so that they can take action intended to keep learning moving forward to desired goals (e.g., Bell & Cowie, 2001; Heritage, 2016; Heritage & Wylie, 2018). Teacher planning for obtaining evidence can involve:

- determining what formative opportunities are already embedded in the flow of activity and transactions in the lesson (Swaffield, 2011);
- deciding how to promote dialogue through questions or activities that provoke a range of responses, and encourage students to clarify, compare, challenge or defend their ideas (Black, Wilson, & Yao, 2011);
- creating or using curriculum-embedded tasks designed to reveal misconceptions (Arieli-Attali, Wylie & Bauer, 2012; Shavelson et al., 2008; Wylie & Ciofalo, 2008).

In each case, the purpose of gathering evidence is for teachers to gain substantive, qualitative insights into their students' current learning status while they are still in the process of learning,

When teachers plan formative assessment opportunities during a lesson, they draw on a deep and broad knowledge of mathematics, an understanding of the multiple modes of mathematical thinking, and the challenges and misconceptions that students commonly have in learning particular topics. For instance, in Example 1 (Figure 9.2), the representations and explanation reflected in the success criteria guide formative opportunities in the lesson while students engage in their mathematics learning. These opportunities can be deepened when teachers engage students in dialogue about their representations and explanations. Productive dialogue is reliant on teachers' abilities to pose questions, informed by their disciplinary knowledge, which are broad in nature and permit them to explore the full range of student thinking (Black, Wilson, & Yao, 2011).

Disciplinary knowledge also supports teachers' engagement in interpretive listening (Davis, 1997) during dialogue in order to understand students' partially formed or not fully articulated explanations. In addition, knowledge of how students learn mathematics assists teachers in interpreting students' problem solving strategies and their reasoning and justifications so as to gain insights into their thinking.

Engaging in Self-Assessment and Peer Feedback

A key component of the FAST SCASS definition is that formative assessment supports students to become self-directed learners, developing the self-regulatory learning processes needed for success in school and in life beyond school (NRC, 2012; Organisation for Economic Cooperation and Development, 2013). These include goal setting, making plans to achieve goals, monitoring progress toward goals, and, when necessary, adapting learning approaches to move closer to desired goals (Allal, 2011; Andrade & Brookhart, 2016; Bailey & Heritage, 2018; Clark, 2012; Heritage, 2016).

Self-assessment is essential to students' self-regulatory learning processes. To engage in self-assessment of their current learning state in comparison to the learning goal and make judgments about their progress so they can take action (Nicol & MacFarlane-Dick, 2006), students need to understand what they are learning and how they will know if they have learned it. In other words, they need to be clear about learning goals and success criteria for the lesson. Teachers with strong disciplinary knowledge have an understanding of what meeting the goals and criteria entail and therefore can support students to internalize them for self-assessment purposes. Similarly, students' ability to provide peer feedback is dependent on their understanding of the goals and criteria.

Providing Actionable Feedback

Teachers' capacity to provide actionable feedback to students that helps them recognize a discrepancy between their current status and the goal (Sadler, 1989) and take steps to move learning forward is also grounded in understanding what is involved in meeting the goal and criteria. Actionable feedback is not intended to indicate to students that their mathematical solution is either correct or incorrect. Rather, the purpose of feedback is to help students understand what they are doing well in relation to the learning goal and success criteria and what they can do in order to improve. For instance, the Example 1 teacher (Figure 9.2) might say "I see you have represented the division problem as the number of groups of 4 in 28. Can you use what you know about multiplication to check if your solution is accurate?" Or she might ask "can you revise your explanation of your strategy to include what the numbers left over – the remainder – means in this context?" This kind of feedback does not take over student thinking – students have to do the thinking to take the next steps. It also has the advantage of increasing the student's metacognition and promoting self-monitoring, a necessary skill for self-regulation. In contrast to Example 1 teacher's feedback, because of the nature of the learning goals and success criteria created by the Example 2 teacher, his feedback is more likely to focus on correctness (e.g., "yes that is the denominator," "no that is not the denominator"), thus limiting the prospects of both deeper learning and strategic action on the part of the student.

Using Evidence and Feedback to Move Learning Forward by Adjusting Learning Strategies, Goals or Next Instructional Steps

Research has suggested that a stumbling block for teachers in formative assessment is their capacity to decide appropriate next steps in learning based on the evidence they have interpreted (Heritage et al., 2009). Teachers' abilities to take effective action is grounded in disciplinary knowledge (Coffey et al., 2011; Cowie & Moreland, 2015; Shepard, Penuel, & Davidson, 2017) and manifests in several ways:

1   Disciplinary knowledge helps teachers to recognize what is likely to be an effective pedagogical action, for example, a prompt, explanation, or a model to challenge misconceptions or resolve difficulties.
2   Knowledge of how students learn mathematics helps teachers anticipate the range of possible student responses to a particular task, or question, and consider beforehand what contingent pedagogical action they might take in the event of these responses (Threlfall, 2005; Wiliam, 2011). The net result of anticipating responses is that a teacher who appears to be taking contingent action in the moment, may, in fact, be enacting one of several plans that she has prepared prior to the lesson.
3   Understanding how mathematics learning progresses advantages teachers in their capacity to respond to their interpretations of evidence in ways that foreshadow how mathematical ideas develop beyond the current level of the students' learning, and assist students to make connections between and among mathematical ideas to deepen their understanding.
4   Disciplinary knowledge can also impact lesson planning informed by evidence, for example, which mathematical representations to select and how to use them both to support students' mathematical understanding and to reveal their thinking during the lesson (Burton & Audrict, 2018).

Of particular note in the FAST SCASS definition is the integrated and embedded nature of these practices, indicating that they are not a set of discrete steps, but rather are interdependent elements of ongoing classroom teaching and learning. While a novice in formative assessment may focus on a specific practice for the purpose of developing fluency with that practice, it is the integration of all the practices, underpinned by disciplinary knowledge, which leads to effective enactment of formative assessment (Wylie & Lyon, 2015a).

Habits of Practice

We use the term *habits of practice* to refer to the specific dispositions and patterns of behavior that predispose teachers for continued learning throughout their professional careers. We propose that three habits of practice, in particular, should be inculcated in preservice teachers during their preservice programs: (1) a commitment to engage in continued inquiry about, and reflection on, their formative assessment practice; (2) a willingness to de-privatize teaching and engage in collaboration with colleagues (Darling-Hammond, Hyler, & Gardner, 2017; Hayden, Moore-Russo, & Marino, 2013); and (3) a willingness to engage in deliberate practice (Ericsson, Krampe, & Tesch-Römer, 1993).

A Commitment to Engage in Continued Inquiry About, and Reflection on, Formative Assessment Practice

A broad interest has developed in the educational literature around the idea of a "reflective practitioner" (Schön, 1983), a theory of how teachers learn and develop expertise in their professional practices (Gillies, 2016). Schön (1983) argued that professional practice should be characterized by reflection-in-action, which involves teachers in thinking quickly about a situation that is occurring as they are teaching, and reflection-on-action, which occurs outside the classroom when teachers consider the situation again and more deeply. The process of reflection-in-action characterizes much of what teachers do in formative assessment; they interpret evidence of learning *in situ* and take immediate contingent action to advance learning. As a result of post-lesson reflection-on-action, teachers might decide that their interpretation of evidence was incorrect, or that their pedagogical action was not appropriate; they can reinterpret the evidence or take different actions without any detrimental consequences for students. This kind of reflection-on-action might also result in teachers' increased awareness of student thinking and the instructional action that was ultimately effective in advancing their thinking from its present state.

From Schön's (1983) perspective, "research is an activity of practitioners" (p. 308), undertaken by teachers as action researchers in the context of their own classrooms to provide a source of theory that is valuable for their teaching work. This perspective stands in contrast to other theories of professional practice that marginalize the role of teachers in favor of implementing the reflections of external experts, essentially reducing teachers to mere technicians (cf. Palincsar, 1999). The notion of research as an activity of practitioners underscores that formative assessment is honed by teachers through deliberate practice and reflection. In preservice education, an orientation to formative assessment as requiring ongoing reflection about its implementation lays the groundwork for continued professional learning.

A Willingness to De-Privatize Teaching and Engage in Collaboration with Colleagues

While the literature endorses the notion of individual inquiry and reflection, there is also support for the notion of collective reflection (Zeichner, 2003). When diverse groups of teachers come together in discourse communities, they can draw upon each other's expertise to engage in reflective examination of teaching practice (Putnam & Borko, 2000). Collaborating with colleagues in joint inquiry about authentic work in their classrooms enables teachers to co-construct knowledge about teaching and learning, develop new ways of teaching, and critically reflect on their practice (Ball, 1995; Borko & Putnam, 1998; Englert & Tarrant, 1995). Without opportunities to collaborate, teachers' views often go unchallenged. As a result, teachers may remain trapped in unexamined judgments, interpretations, and expectations (Larrivee, 2010).

Collaborating with colleagues and using each other as resources can strengthen teachers' formative assessment implementation in several ways. For instance, teachers can review together the mathematics learning goals and success criteria for each other's lessons to help refine them and engage in post-lesson reflections about the degree to which the goals and criteria were appropriate; they can create rich mathematics tasks and activities that are likely to provide formative assessment opportunities during the lesson; they can anticipate student responses to those tasks and later compare them to actual student responses; they can examine sources of evidence together to develop interpretive skills; and they can consider potential pedagogical actions, including feedback, and reflect on their success or otherwise. Such instances of collaborative reflection need to be built in as a routine part of preservice education, both to support preservice teachers' skills in formative assessment and apprentice them to the practices, procedures, and standards of their professional community (Lave & Wenger, 1991).

A Willingness to Engage in Deliberate Practice

Anders Ericsson and colleagues (1993) argued "that the differences between expert performers and normal adults reflect a life-long period of deliberate effort to improve performance" (p. 400). The characteristics of deliberate practice (in any area, not specifically teaching) have been identified as: (1) a motivated subject who is attending to the task at hand and willing to exert effort to improve; (2) a scaffolded task that takes into account the prior learning of the subject; (3) the opportunity for brief instruction to support the performance of the task; (4) the provision of informative feedback to the subject about his or her performance; and (5) the opportunity to repeatedly engage in similar tasks over time (Ericsson, Krampe, & Tesch-Römer, 1993).

These characteristics of deliberate practice can be applied to preservice teachers' learning. In terms of a motivated subject, we can assume that an individual who wishes to attend a preservice program is motivated to be apprenticed into a community of teachers and learn the craft of teaching. When learning about the work of teaching is undertaken with opportunities for repeated practice and informative feedback about the practice, preservice teachers are likely to exert effort to improve. Furthermore, deliberate practice can develop a mindset of continuous growth, a necessary outlook for preservice teachers to carry with them into the profession to advance their knowledge and skills.

In summary, we propose that teacher preparation for formative assessment in mathematics should be approached from the perspective of deepening preservice teachers' disciplinary knowledge, including their knowledge of how students learn in the discipline, their pedagogical knowledge and skills, and their knowledge of, and skills in, formative assessment. Preservice programs should also foster habits of practice that will equip preservice teachers to become reflective practitioners who subscribe to continual professional learning. We now turn to a practice-based example of mathematics teaching to illustrate the knowledge and skills we have presented thus far.

An Example of Practice

The example is taken from a larger data collection conducted for the purpose of analyzing formative assessment in classroom practice (Heritage, 2016). The lesson took place in a combined first- and second-grade class (students aged 6–8) in a university laboratory school where the student population mirrors the demographics of public schools in a very diverse state in the United States. From this data corpus, a one-hour long video-taped mathematics lesson and a post-lesson conversation with the teacher were transcribed and examined independently by both authors for instances of formative assessment. The FAST SCASS definition of formative assessment bounded the case and our analysis (Yin, 2003). The second author reduced the initial transcription to a case study (Hays & Singh, 2012), using deductive coding (Saldaña, 2009; Shank, 2006) to identify occasions of formative assessment practice. The first author reviewed the description for accuracy and consistency of how instances of formative assessment were described (Creswell, 2012), and any areas of disagreement were resolved through discussion and further refinement to the analysis.

The English word for assessment is derived from the Latin verb *assidere*, which means to sit beside. Formative assessment often occurs as a teacher sits with a student to help him or her articulate and extend ideas. Such opportunities can provide insights for teachers about what students can do on their own, and what they might be able to do with assistance. Indeed, interaction between teacher and student has been characterized as a primary source of evidence in formative assessment (e.g., Allal, 2010; Black & Wiliam, 2009; Heritage & Heritage, 2013; Ruiz-Primo, 2011; Torrance & Pryor, 1998). In the following example, there are multiple instances of the teacher *sitting alongside* her students to elicit evidence of their mathematical understanding and responding to that evidence to extend and deepen their thinking.

Prior to this lesson, the students had been working on *decomposing* (breaking down) and *composing* (regrouping) two- and three-digit numbers into units, tens, and hundreds. The teacher began the lesson with a warm-up discussion about grouping eight beads of two different colors to make patterns for a necklace. The conversation took an interesting turn when one student proposed the idea of eight as an "equal" number because it could be divided evenly into two groups of four. This led to an extended and sophisticated mathematical discussion, involving mathematical argumentation and justification, as another student proposed "I think every number is an even number, because if you take a five, for example, you can split it into two and two, but then you take the extra one and you split it in half." The discussion culminated by students concluding that an even number was "a number made up of two of the same whole numbers."

After this discussion, the teacher made connections among the ideas of even, equal and groupings to the day's learning goal which she stated as: "As a mathematician today, I will understand how a group of objects can be partitioned into equal shares." She discussed with the class the term *partition*, calling on multiple students to propose ideas about what it meant, and helping them connect their ideas to the lesson learning goal. The teacher then introduced the task that the students were going to work on independently.

> You're going to be able to show me and yourself that, as a mathematician, you understand how to group objects and how a group of objects can be partitioned into equal shares by identifying what the problem is asking you to do. Can you represent your strategy for solving the problem and can you explain and justify why your strategy worked?

The mathematics task they worked on was:

> Camillo went apple picking. He gathered __ apples and put them in __ baskets. Each basket had the same amount of apples. How many apples were in each basket? Fill in the blanks with one of the number pairs to create a problem the right size for you: [28, 4] or [292, 4], or [568, 4]

This was a familiar task format that the students used on many occasions during the school year, that is, word problems with blanks for them to insert their choice of number pairs provided by the teacher – [28, 4] or [292, 4], or [568, 4] – to create a problem that was the "right size" for them in terms of the level of challenge that it presented.

214

Teacher Preparation in Mathematics

As students started working, the teacher circulated to hear their explanations, sitting beside individuals to assist in identifying manipulatives to use, or pose questions to help them think about how to justify their problem solving strategies. For example, she interacted with one student by asking her to describe the approach she was taking to divide the 292 apples among the four baskets. The student had divided 100 into four groups of 25 and was starting to divide another 100 among four baskets. With some gentle probing from the teacher, the student realized that she needed to continue to group the second 100 into the four original baskets rather than starting another set of four groupings. The teacher ended this interaction by saying, "I'm going to check in very quickly with Kaya. I'm going to come back and see how you partitioned that 92 into the four groups. Because I'm pretty curious. I noticed the strategy you used with hundreds. Now I want to see what that strategy looks like with tens and two ones."

The teacher moved to sit beside Kaya, who was working on the same version of the task. This student had quickly decomposed 200 (of 292) into four groups of 50 but was then struggling with how to divide 92 (of 292). She had identified that she had nine tens and two ones, and had also divided one of the tens into two fives but was now stuck. With some prompting from the teacher, she reconsidered her approach and divided ten into units. She then realized she had 12 ones in total, which led her then to the insight about how to regroup them: "That into three. That into three. That into three. That into three. Four threes." With a little more encouragement and support, the student recognized that she had four groups of 50s, 20s, and three ones so that the total number of apples per group was 73. The teacher ended her interaction with this student by restating the process that the student had used, and by suggesting a next step for her, "So here's what I want you to think about. Now 73 was your answer. So 73 apples in each basket. What strategy might you be able to use, to see if that 73 is actually the right answer?"

Other students were able to engage more easily with the task, and the teacher provided feedback that was targeted at helping them to communicate their mathematical approach to others. As they sat together, one student, who tackled the most challenging of the versions of the task (working with the [568, 4] number pair), explained his approach to her, and also how he checked his answer to prove to himself that he was correct. Focusing on the communication part of the learning goal, the teacher provided the following feedback:

> Now, each of these numbers and the boxes represent something. Right? Now I know we ask you to explain and we ask you to justify. One thing that mathematicians also do is organize their work. So how would you use labels to help identify what each of these parts represent? How might you label your strategy to help someone who's coming in understand your strategy?

After individual work time, the students paired up to explain their strategies to each other, while the teacher continued to help them to figure out how to communicate their ideas and, in the process, gained additional insights into their learning. Toward the end of the lesson, the teacher brought the students together to listen to one student's strategy and offer feedback. She asked them to use their PQS (i.e., Put up, Question, Suggest) strategy, a structure for providing peer feedback, starting with a positive comment about what their peers were doing well (put up), asking about something they were confused about in their peers' work (question), and suggesting a next learning step (suggest). A student who shared her strategy explained how she initially struggled through several approaches to solve the problem. Another student, an English learner, complimented her, "*I liked how Nina didn't like when she didn't know what to do, she didn't say, I can't do this. She never gave up.*" The teacher reinforced this idea of productive struggle, "Sometimes as mathematicians we try one strategy and sometimes that just doesn't work. Sometimes we might think of that second strategy . . . until you find a strategy that's just right for you." The teacher ended the lesson by returning to the learning goal, asking students to reflect on whether they felt they had met it yet, and noting how this mathematics topic was going to be the focus of their learning all week.

Analysis of the Critical Aspects of Formative Assessment in the Vignette

Using the practices from the FAST SCASS definition of formative assessment, we next identify noteworthy features in this vignette (with the specific practices from the definition in italics for reference). The teacher had *clear learning goals* for the lesson and primed students for the ideas of grouping and regrouping with the example of beads on the necklace. She noted in the interview that, although the discussion extended beyond her original expectation for this opening activity, she gained insights into which students were able to engage in a mathematically rich discussion about odd and even numbers, divide a whole number in half, and support their argument.

The mathematics task that the teacher used to *elicit evidence* of her students' understanding of decomposing and composing two- and three-digit numbers was structured using what she called the "just-right" strategy. The number pairs she provided for the students were based on her previous observations that some students were ready to work with hundreds, while others still needed to make sense of problems using tens and units. Thus, the teacher was able to challenge all the students in her class while simultaneously eliciting evidence of their learning. As the teacher interacted with individual students and small groups (*eliciting evidence*), she observed how they approached the problem, whether they needed to use manipulatives, and how successful their problem solving strategies were. During her interactions with students, she served as a sounding board to help them clarify their own thinking, or she provided just enough scaffolding or *actionable feedback* to get them past a point if they were stuck, or she challenged them to think about how to explain and justify their reasoning if they had solved the problem (*eliciting evidence*). She always left the students with something worthwhile to do next or think about.

The teacher used both *self-assessment and peer feedback* throughout the lesson. During the lesson opening, she invited peers to respond to the initial proposal about an "equal" number and provide feedback to their peers on the ideas that were emerging. The task design gave students a self-assessment opportunity to identify the version of the mathematics task that would make it the "right size" for where they determined they were in their own learning. At the end of the lesson, she used the PQS structure for peers to provide feedback on one student's strategy, and invited students informally to reflect on whether they had each met the learning goal. Collectively, these strategies illustrate how the teacher demonstrated to students that they were valued participants in the learning process.

The wrap-up discussion at the end of the lesson provides a clear example of the development of academic self-regulatory processes (*self-direction*). During the discussion, one student recognized that her peer, Nina, persevered when her initial attempts to solve the problem were unsuccessful, a characteristic of academic self-regulation. The teacher then amplified this idea by reminding the class that, as mathematicians, they will often have to try different strategies. The supportive nature of the student's comment is an indication of the *collaborative classroom culture* that this teacher had engineered with her students, which the FAST SCASS definition notes as a condition for formative assessment.

Throughout this lesson the teacher drew on a knowledge base that went beyond simple mathematics, allowing her to efficiently assess and respond to students (Loewenberg Ball, Thames, & Phelps, 2008). She demonstrated this knowledge in how she devised the task, identifying number pairs that would provide an appropriate level of challenge for each student; during the opening discussion she shaped the conversation around the idea of an "equal" number by identifying productive student comments to be further explored; as she observed students while they worked individually, she reviewed student strategies, and by interacting with them to hear their explanations and justifications, she was able to gain insights about their thinking to provide appropriate, in-the-moment feedback and scaffolding. The teacher's content knowledge for teaching combined an understanding of the ways in which students think when learning mathematics and targeted knowledge of appropriate instructional and assessment strategies, evidenced by how she was able to listen to students' strategies and emerging ideas, make sense of their thinking, even when not fully articulated, and provide meaningful mathematical feedback to help them continue with their productive struggles.

The Teacher's Perspective on the Development of Expertise

One aspect of the observed teacher's practice that is not apparent from the description of the lesson is how she developed her practice to its current level. However, in a post-lesson interview, she provided some insights into some of the supports and structures that helped her refine her skills over time. The interview was not structured around the framework presented earlier (Figure 9.1), but in her explanations she touched on several of the themes identified in the prior section on habits of practice, in particular.

The teacher talked about how she did not develop her skills in isolation, explaining that their development occurred over many years with her co-teacher:

> I benefited from having a partner, someone that I can bounce ideas off of, someone I can go to for advice, someone that can give me feedback. I really feel that it mirrors what we expect of our students. I feel that the journey that I took with my colleague is one of learning, one of trial and error, one of determination and perseverance. One that was a lengthy journey. It started 15 years ago.

She further explained how after a one-day workshop on formative assessment from an expert professional development provider, she and her partner teacher initially identified just one content area, and a specific aspect of formative assessment on which to focus.

> We first started by just crafting learning goals and success criteria and practicing that and how that felt in our lessons, and we would share our learning goals and share our success criteria. To this day, we feel like we still need to share them with one another and get feedback because they're not always 100%.

She continued to provide other examples of aspects of classroom practices that she and her colleague developed together, such as creating the PQS strategy for students, and working collaboratively to help students understand and use the "just-right" strategy. She and her partner teacher eventually applied both of these strategies across content areas in their teaching.

In summary, several critical factors contributed to this teacher's development of expertise in formative assessment: (1) she had a trusted colleague with whom she worked; (2) she started in a limited way, only focusing on one aspect of practice in one content area; (3) her focus integrated content with formative assessment; (4) there was an infusion of some expertise through the professional learning provider; (5) she had the habits of practice to sustain commitment to the development of her knowledge and skills.

Next, in part two of the chapter, we explore the integration of teacher knowledge, skills, and habits of practice that are needed for effective formative assessment through an examination of current professional standards for mathematics teachers. Across these foundational documents there is broad agreement that knowledge of formative assessment practices, disciplinary knowledge (including both knowledge of mathematics and knowledge of how students learn mathematics), and particular dispositions or habits of practice are requirements for teaching, and therefore important components of professional learning trajectories that start in preservice education.

Part Two: Current Professional Standards

Profiles of expertise provide a framework for guiding initial teacher education programs, teacher certification, teachers' ongoing professional learning, and career advancement (OECD, 2005). To inform our proposals for preservice programs, we draw from three key sources that elaborate the profession-wide standards of practice for mathematics teachers: (1) National Board for Professional Teaching Standards (NBPTS): Mathematics Standards (NBPTS, 2010); (2) National Council of Teachers of Mathematics (NCTM), *Principles to Action* (NCTM, 2014); and (3) The Interstate Teacher Assessment and Support Consortium (InTASC) Model Core Teaching Standards (InTASC, 2011).

We selected these standards because, taken as a whole, they represent a shared understanding of what is considered to be accomplished teaching in mathematics. The Council for the Accreditation of Teacher Preparation (CAEP) specifies that preservice teachers demonstrate an understanding of the InTASC standards, and that professional learning providers ensure that preservice teachers can apply content and pedagogical knowledge as reflected in outcome assessments in response to NBPTS or other specialized professional associations (CAEP, 2013). We included the NCTM *Principles to Action* (2014) because they have been developed by a leading professional organization to specifically bridge the gap "between the development and adoption of CCSSM [Common Core State Standards for Mathematics] and other standards and the enactment of practices, policies, programs, and actions required for their widespread and successful implementation" (p. 4).

National Board for Professional Teaching Standards: Mathematics Standards

Table 9.1 summarizes the knowledge and skills for mathematics teachers of students aged 11 to 18+ as described in the National Board for Professional Teaching Standards Mathematics Standards (NBPTS, 2010). The excerpts from the standards are organized in our framework's categories of formative assessment, disciplinary knowledge, and habits of practice (see Figure 9.1).

Consistent with the earlier discussion, the conception of formative assessment threaded through the NBPTS mathematics standards (2010) emphasizes the centrality of intentionally eliciting evidence of learning and using that evidence to inform both teaching and learning. For example, assessment is described in the standards as an integral part of daily instruction; teachers are expected to use questioning strategies to explore students' understanding of mathematics, and to take instructional action, including providing feedback, in response to evidence.

Notably, the NBPTS (2010) standards specify a knowledge of mathematics "well beyond the level they teach" (p. 21), an understanding of "significant connections" (p. 21) among mathematical ideas and their application, and an awareness of "the challenges and difficulties that students commonly encounter in learning particular mathematical topics" (p. 33) as requisite for accomplished teaching. As we discussed in part one of this chapter, understanding a broader progression of mathematics learning and common challenges and difficulties are forms of disciplinary knowledge that will advantage teachers' formative assessment implementation.

Deepening disciplinary knowledge is a continuous process that benefits from the habits of practice associated with collaboration and reflection. Engaging with colleagues in discussions of how students' mathematical thinking develops, how best to elicit that thinking in the context of specific

Table 9.1 Knowledge and Skills for Mathematics Teachers, as Defined by NBPTS (2010) in Three Domains of Expertise.

Formative Assessment	Disciplinary Knowledge	Habits of Practice
− View ongoing assessment as an integral part of their instruction, benefiting both the teacher and the student. − Identify and make explicit the learning goals for each lesson. − Skillfully incorporate opportunities for assessing students' progress into daily instruction. − Use knowledge of misconceptions to plan their assessment of students' understanding. − Demonstrate the use of appropriate questioning strategies by knowing how, when, and why to question students about their understanding of mathematics. − Recognize and respond to the mathematical potential of student questions and comments and pursue ideas of interest that emerge during classroom discussion. − Help students develop the ability to self-monitor and evaluate personal progress. − Use assessment strategies to identify student strengths and areas for improvement, and provide timely and constructive feedback. − Analyze student work to identify current mathematical understandings and use that information to drive instruction. − Adjust instruction, either because unforeseen difficulties suggest that a path they planned to take will not succeed, or a classroom discussion points to a beneficial alternative.	− Deep and broad knowledge of the concepts, principles, techniques and reasoning methods of mathematics well beyond the level they teach. − Understand the major ideas in the core domains of mathematics. − Understand significant connections among mathematical ideas and the application of those ideas. − Have a broad and rich understanding of the knowledge base that informs the mathematics curriculum. − [Understand that] thinking mathematically includes representing, modeling, proving, experimenting, conjecturing, classifying, visualizing, and computing. − Know multiple ways to represent mathematical concepts, and organize tasks so that students will learn that a single problem may have many representations. − Know the challenges and difficulties that students commonly encounter in learning particular mathematical topics; anticipate underlying misconceptions. − Know the ways of thinking, talking, and writing about mathematics.	− Recognize that every class and every course provide the opportunity to reflect and improve on an ongoing basis. − Modify teaching practices based on one's experiences and on the continuous process of self-examination, using a variety of strategies to collect data about one's own teaching. − Identify areas for self-improvement and seek strategies for reaching one's own educational and instructional goals. − Recognize that collaborating in a professional learning community contributes to one's own professional growth, as well as to the growth of peers for the benefit of student learning. − Seek to make teaching an open community activity. − Observe and study other teachers' practices, engage colleagues in dialogue about professional issues, and may serve as mentors to new teachers as well as coaches to experienced colleagues.

lessons, and reflecting on the results of pedagogical actions in terms of advancing learning all provide critical support for the development of teacher expertise.

National Council of Teachers of Mathematics, Principles to Action

The dimensions of formative assessment and disciplinary knowledge from the NBPTS mathematics standards are echoed by the NCTM in its recommendations for high-quality mathematics teaching practices (NCTM, 2014), listed in Table 9.2.

Two of the NCTM practices, establishing mathematics goals to focus learning (1) and eliciting and using evidence of thinking (8), use very similar language to two of the practices named in the FAST SCASS definition of formative assessment. Notably, and unlike the NBPTS (2010) discussed above and the InTASC standards (2011) that follow, the NCTM practices call out that learning goals are situated within a learning progression. Earlier, we identified the knowledge and skills needed to establish learning goals within a progression of learning as a significant component of teachers' disciplinary knowledge. Similarly, the knowledge and skills needed to interpret and act on evidence are supported when learning progressions are used as an interpretative framework (Heritage, 2008).

In addition to identifying the eight teaching practices, the NCTM principles draw attention to essential elements that are needed to support those practices. Of most relevance to this chapter, and echoing the habit of practice related to a commitment to shared inquiry, is *Professionalism*:

> Effective schools communicate a tangible sense of the professional imperative to grow personally and collectively and to hold one another accountable for this growth . . . they cultivate and support a culture of professional collaboration and continual improvement that is driven by an abiding sense of interdependence and collective responsibility.
>
> *(NCTM, 2014, p. 99)*

The NCTM principles also affirm the value placed on ongoing professional learning reflected in the NBPTS mathematics standards, and support the habits of practice of commitment to growth, inquiry, reflection, and collaboration.

Table 9.2 Eight Mathematics Teaching Practices (NCTM, 2014)

NCTM Practices
1   Establish mathematics goals to focus learning; goals are situated within a learning progression.
2   Implement tasks that promote reasoning and problem solving; tasks should allow multiple entry points and varied solution strategies.
3   Use and connect mathematical representations; deepen students' understanding of mathematics concepts and procedures and as tools for problem solving.
4   Facilitate meaningful mathematical discourse; build a shared understanding of mathematical ideas.
5   Pose purposeful questions; to assess and advance students' reasoning and sense-making.
6   Build procedural fluency from conceptual understanding; students become skillful, over time, in using procedures flexibly as they solve problems.
7   Support productive struggle in learning mathematics; opportunities to grapple with mathematical ideas and relationships.
8   Elicit and use evidence of student thinking; assess progress toward mathematical understanding and adjust instruction continually in ways that support and extend learning.

The Interstate Teacher Assessment and Support Consortium (InTASC) Model Core Teaching Standards

In the professional documents described above, mathematics is a specific focus, whereas the InTASC (2011) standards are content agnostic. While some of the core ideas represented in the NBPTS mathematics standards and the NCTM practices are reflected in the wide-ranging InTASC standards, they lack the specificity from which the requirements of disciplinary expertise can be derived. However, the essential knowledge and performances that are necessary to meet each InTASC standard are broadly consistent with both the NBPTS mathematics standards and the NCTM practices. For example, teachers are expected to:

- know how learning occurs and how to use instructional strategies that promote student learning;
- understand major concepts, assumptions, debates, processes of inquiry, and ways of knowing that are central to the discipline(s) s/he teaches;
- understand common misconceptions in learning the discipline;
- regularly assess individual and group performance in order to design and modify instruction to meet learners' needs;
- understand the difference between formative and summative applications of assessment and know how and when to use each (pp. 9–15).

The InTASC standards (2011) also include critical dispositions needed to meet each of the standards. Two, in particular, are pertinent to the notion of habits of practice because they relate to ongoing learning and to learning within a community of colleagues:

- "The teacher sees him/herself as a learner, continuously seeking opportunities to draw upon current education policy and research as sources of analysis and reflection to improve practice" (p. 18);
- "The teacher takes initiative to grow and develop with colleagues through interactions that enhance practice and support student learning" (p. 19).

The general agreement across these three documents is echoed by the Association of Mathematics Teacher Educators (AMTE), which advocates that well-prepared beginning teachers should robustly understand mathematical content, know how students think about and learn mathematics, including possible misconceptions and creative pathways they might take in learning, and know how to assess student understanding and use assessment information to plan and modify instruction (AMTE, 2017).

Professional Learning Standards

We suggested earlier preservice teachers' experiences are at the beginning of a continuum of professional learning that extends into ongoing in-service. In this regard, the Standards for Professional Learning (Learning Forward, 2011) outline the characteristics of professional learning that lead to effective teaching practices, and make explicit that the purpose of professional learning is to assist teachers in developing the knowledge, skills, practices, and dispositions they need to be effective in their classrooms. Noting that for too long approaches to professional development have treated educators as individual, passive recipients of information, the Standards are referred to as Standards for Professional Learning rather than Standards for Professional Development, pointing to the importance of educators taking an active role in their continuous development and placing emphasis on their learning (Learning Forward, 2011).

There are seven Standards for Professional Learning, three of which are germane to this chapter: (1) Learning Communities; (2) Learning Designs; and (3) Implementation. The *Learning Communities* standard describes such communities as contexts for continuous improvement in which teachers engage in inquiry, action research, reflection, and evaluation, and collective participation and peer-to-peer support is fostered. The *Learning Designs* standard describes common features of professional learning designs that incorporate theory, research, and models. These include active engagement, modeling, reflection, metacognition, application, feedback, and ongoing support. The *Implementation* standard also underscores the importance of constructive feedback and reflection to support teachers' movement along a continuum from novice to expert.

These three standards suggest that preservice learning should be grounded in sociocultural theory, with its emphasis on mediated learning (Vygotsky, 1962). In our recommendations for the development of expertise which follow in part three, ideas of mediated learning through collaboration, scaffolding, and application accompanied by feedback are threaded throughout.

Part Three: Developing Teacher Expertise by Setting the Groundwork in Preservice Education

In the introduction to this chapter, we proposed a framework (Figure 9.1) for developing formative assessment expertise for mathematics teachers that comprises three interrelated domains: formative assessment knowledge and skills, disciplinary knowledge (both knowledge of mathematics and knowledge of how students learn mathematics), and habits of practice. Table 9.3 expands on the three domains of expertise and presents ways in which knowledge can be represented to preservice teachers, and experiences provided to support the development of their skills in each domain.

We now consider each of the knowledge representations and experiences for the three domains, in turn.

Table 9.3 Summary of Knowledge Representations and Experiences in Three Domains of Expertise

	Formative assessment		*Disciplinary knowledge*		*Habits of practice*	
Knowledge Representations	1	A shared definition of formative assessment.	1	Mathematics standards.	1	Professional standards (e.g., dispositions).
	2	Rubrics that describe a continuum of expertise.	2	Representations of how student learn (e.g., learning progressions).		
Experiences	3	Examine beliefs that influence formative assessment.	3	Analyze mathematics content standards.	2	Supported by the experiences for acquiring formative assessment knowledge and skills and disciplinary knowledge.
	4	Observe and analyze expert formative assessment practice.	4	Use standards and learning progressions to create learning goals and success criteria.		
	5	Observe and analyze peers' formative assessment implementation.	5	Analyze diagnostic items to understand student thinking.		
	6	Learn and practice specific formative assessment skills.	6	Use learning progressions to analyze student work.		
	7	Reflect on one's own formative assessment implementation.	7	Use learning progressions to plan next instructional steps, including feedback.		
			8	Examine model curriculum materials.		

Knowledge Representations: Developing Expertise in Formative Assessment

To support mathematics preservice teachers as they begin the process of developing expertise in formative assessment, we suggest two representations of knowledge: (1) definitions of formative assessment that provide clarity about what it is, as distinct from other types of assessment; and (2) a rubric of expertise describing what more or less sophisticated formative assessment practice looks like, both holistically and by discrete dimensions. These two representations of knowledge should be consistent with each other, with use of one reciprocally supporting a deeper understanding of the other.

Definitions of Formative Assessment

The FAST SCASS definition (CCSSO, 2018) introduced in part one is one example of a definition that aims to provide clarity about formative assessment. Other congruent definitions are provided in various chapters of this volume (e.g., Burkhardt & Schoenfeld, 2019) and elsewhere (e.g., Klenowski, 2009; Smarter Balanced Assessment Consortium, n.d.). Deconstructing the definition, discussing its elements, reading associated literature, and seeing examples of the definition in action, for example, through video exemplars of mathematics lessons, are ways in which a developing understanding of formative assessment can be supported.

Preservice teachers' understanding gained from analyses of definitions can be augmented by considering existing instructional frameworks that embed formative assessment. For instance, in a recent volume edited by Mills and Silver (2018), chapter authors connect formative assessment in mathematics with specific instructional perspectives, including Cognitively Guided Instruction (Levi & Ambrose, 2018), culturally responsive teaching (Lott Adams & Bonner, 2018), response to intervention (Kobett & Karp, 2018), the mathematical tasks framework (Steele & Smith, 2018), and the NCTM mathematical practices (Burton & Audrict, 2018). Across the volume, it is clear how formative assessment is central to the work of mathematics teaching, whether focusing on classroom discourse, the tasks that students complete, or analyzing student work.

A way to further expand preservice teachers' understanding of formative assessment definitions is to distinguish formative assessment from other assessment types in the context of a broader system of assessment (Klinger et al., 2015). Examination of comprehensive, coherent and continuous assessment systems (NRC, 2001) to understand the purpose of various assessments will be an important component of developing assessment literacy and understanding the specific role that formative assessment plays in student learning.

Rubrics That Describe a Continuum of Expertise

An example of rubrics that describe a continuum of expertise is the *Formative Assessment Rubrics, Resources, and Observation Protocol* (FARROP) (Wylie & Lyon, 2015b), a resource commissioned by the FAST SCASS members to support teachers' engagement in structured self-reflection and peer observation of their formative assessment practices. The FARROP breaks the domain of formative assessment into discrete dimensions that provide a level of specificity, enable teachers to focus on particular aspects (Wylie, 2016), and provide targeted feedback (Brinko, 1993). Preliminary evidence suggests that the FARROP is an effective tool for supporting formative assessment implementation among classroom teachers (Ziker, 2017), and for this reason we recommend its use in preservice programs.

The FARROP comprises ten dimensions of formative assessment, all of which are reflected in the FAST SCASS definition. These dimensions range from learning goals and success criteria, to questions, tasks, and activities to elicit evidence, to a collaborative culture for learning. The rubric for each FARROP dimension has four levels (beginning, developing, progressing, and extending) and a "not observed" category, which allow for reasonable discrimination among practices while not requiring teachers (the ultimate users) to make such fine distinctions that training and use would be burdensome. By way of illustration, the rubric and observation notes for the *Tasks and Activities to Elicit Evidence of Student Learning* dimension is provided in the Appendix.

The benefit gained by individuals using rubrics to evaluate their own work and that of peers when they have clear descriptions of what constitutes quality work has been largely researched in the context of K-12 students (e.g., Andrade, Du, & Mycek, 2010; Fontana & Fernandes, 1994; Mercer et al., 2004; White & Frederiksen, 1998). In a parallel approach for teachers, the theory of action for the use of the FARROP posits that high-quality descriptions of the domain of formative assessment (codified by a set of rubrics) will help teachers better understand the characteristics of effective formative assessment in practice. Reading only the highest levels of practice articulated by each dimension in the rubric can help a preservice teacher begin to conceptualize what characterizes effective formative assessment implementation. Reading all the rubric levels for a particular dimension gives teachers a picture of what increasingly skillful practice might look like on that dimension as well as common pitfalls of practice to avoid (seen in the lower rubric level descriptors).

We believe that tools such as a clear and elaborated definition of formative assessment and a representation of practice in action such as the FARROP can help preservice teachers develop a schema for formative assessment that will progressively increase in sophistication as they implement formative assessment in their classrooms.

Experiences to Support the Development of Skills

We recognize that schema development is unlikely to occur without experiences in applying the kinds of knowledge representations we have described. We now consider five experiences for this purpose that can be included in preservice programs.

Examine Beliefs That Influence Formative Assessment

Preservice teachers will inevitably enter their preservice programs with beliefs about teaching that are likely to predict their practice instructional and assessment practices. These beliefs are informed in part by their "apprenticeship-of-observation" (Lortie, 1975) that began when they were students of mathematics themselves. Previous research suggests that teachers' beliefs tend not to change much from the time they enter their preservice programs until the time they leave (Stipek et al., 2001). Their beliefs serve as filters through which new information is processed (Cohen & Ball, 1990; Kagan, 1992), which probably accounts for their persistence.

To ensure that preservice teachers' beliefs do not become obstacles to effective teaching and assessment, program faculty need to help preservice teachers resolve any conflicts between their previously established beliefs and the knowledge representations and experiences they are exposed to in their program. For instance, preservice can examine the beliefs held by individuals that might negatively impact student learning and formative assessment, with a view to internally examining their own beliefs. Such examinations can encompass (1) beliefs that impede the mathematical empowerment of particular groups of students (e.g., students living in poverty, English language learners); (2) beliefs about learning mathematics that may be instilled as a result of their own school experience, for example, drill and repetition make you better at mathematics, there is only one way to solve a problem, learning mathematics is about memorization and speed (Strutchens & Silver, 2018); (3) beliefs that students possess innate levels of mathematics ability that cannot be changed by instruction (NCTM, 2014); and (4) beliefs about assessment, such as that weekly quizzes are the best type of assessment, that assessment always requires a score, that assessment occurs to figure out if students "got it" or "didn't get it," (Otero, 2006), and that grades are the best forms of feedback.

Clearly, any examination of beliefs needs to be undertaken with sensitivity and care. A community of practice, in which preservice teachers have created mutual trust and collaborative relationships, is a context in which the participants can engage in this examination without feeling undermined or threatened.

Observe and Analyze Expert Formative Assessment Practice

Lave and Wenger (1991) note the importance of expert models to support learning during the apprentice stage in a community of practice. In this regard, preservice teachers, as apprentices to the profession, need opportunities to engage in structured observation and analysis of expert implementation of formative assessment. This need is further underscored by indications from research about the supports that preservice teachers require to identify critical features of classroom interactions (Star & Strickland, 2008; Star, Lynch, & Perova, 2011). Recognizing interactions between teacher and student and among students as sources of evidence for formative assessment will necessitate carefully selected exemplars and models from mathematics teaching. The example of practice and analysis provided in part one of this chapter can serve this purpose.

The FARROP or other similar observational protocols may help preservice teachers more readily identify features of formative assessment to which they should attend. After developing their observational skills in general, preservice teachers can observe video recordings of expert practice which provides opportunities for rich discussion that help them make the connections between the aspects of practices named in an observational protocol and how they are represented in actual classroom teaching and learning (Bliss & Reynolds, 2004). These discussions of expert formative assessment practice need to be grounded in the mathematics content of the lesson, starting from the relevance and importance of the mathematical learning goals and how they relate to the standards, the activities, tasks, and questions that both support and elicit evidence of those goals, how the teacher analyzes students' mathematical understanding, and the type of feedback that the teacher provides to support productive mathematical struggle and deeper learning (Burton & Audrict, 2018).

Observe and Analyze Peers' Formative Assessment Implementation

The process of peer assessment can positively impact teaching practices for both the observed teacher and the observer (Kohut, Burnap, & Yon, 2007; Ross & Bruce, 2007). Using rubrics such as the FARROP for observing and discussing a peer's practice can also make the dimensions of formative assessment more explicit and concrete for the peer carrying out the observation. Providing feedback to peers is also valuable practice for when preservice teachers give feedback to their students in the context of formative assessment.

After an observation, preservice teachers may also examine their own practice, informed by the rubrics as well as in contrast to the practice of others (Educational Testing Service, 2009). Additionally, peer observation has been studied as one component of the Peer Assistance and Review (PAR) program that has been used as both part of teacher evaluation and teacher improvement systems (Johnson et al., 2010). The PAR implementation has resulted in positive outcomes primarily with novice and struggling teachers (Stroot et al., 1999). The experience of peer observation in preservice programs not only helps beginning teachers develop their knowledge of formative assessment, but also encourages them in developing an important habit of practice, a willingness to de-privatize teaching, and engage in collaboration with colleagues. Similar to discussions of expert implementation of formative assessment, preservice teachers should be supported in their examination of peers' teaching to consider how the mathematics embedded within the lesson interacts with each aspect of formative assessment. As part of the examination, attention will need to be given to anticipating the range of student mathematical responses, and how this anticipation can support formative assessment practice.

Learn and Practice Specific Formative Assessment Skills

In terms of apprenticing preservice teachers to implement formative assessment in their teaching practice, Duckor and Holmberg (2017) suggest they learn certain specific skills that focus primarily on eliciting evidence of student understanding through class discussion. They propose preservice teachers acquire a series of moves which they term, *priming, posing, pausing, probing, bouncing, tagging,* and *binning*. These moves contribute to a preservice teacher's ability to appropriately set up a discussion (*priming*), engage all students in a meaningful discussion (*posing, pausing, probing, bouncing*), and make sense of the evidence of student thinking that arises in the discussion (*tagging, binning*) to inform next instructional steps. In this approach to formative assessment, Duckor and Holmberg (2017) focus less on some aspects of formative assessment practice, such as student self-assessment or peer feedback, leaving those for in-service development. These moves appear to have a payoff for preservice teachers and provide them with early success in their implementation of formative assessment.

Some aspects of these moves can be either approximations or decompositions of practice (Grossman, Hammerness, & McDonald, 2009) and practiced in isolation without actual students. For example, preservice teachers could be given key mathematical ideas from the standards and asked to develop an engaging, relevant and mathematically accurate introduction to a new discussion (*priming*), with the preservice teachers acting as students. Rehearsing individual components can build confidence for when preservice teachers apply this knowledge in classroom practice.

Reflect on One's Own Formative Assessment Implementation

During their teaching practice, preservice teachers should all be provided with structured time to support reflection on their own developing formative assessment practice. Structured time means that reflection time is not an afterthought but rather allocated as an explicit and rigorous part of their teaching experience, indicating that it is valued by the preservice teacher, mentor teacher, and program faculty.

When lessons are thought of as "experiments" (Hiebert, Morris, & Glass, 2003, p. 207) preservice teachers' reflection can be supported through use of tools such as the FARROP or, in the case of the moves discussed in the previous section, by reflecting on the lesson in terms of which moves worked well and why, and which were less effective and why, followed by revisions to strengthen their practice (Duckor & Holmberg, 2017). Program faculty or mentor teachers can also provide protocols to guide preservice teachers' reflection incorporating guiding questions such as:

> Did you think that your learning goals and success criteria guided your lesson and helped you obtain evidence of students' understanding of the mathematical concept? Did students have opportunities to engage in productive mathematical struggle? What evidence do you have that your students' learned or did not learn the mathematics that you intended? How did you interpret the evidence? Did any student responses surprise you? Why? What contingent action did you take to a student or a group of students based on the analysis? Was your response effective? How do you know? How might you modify your response in the event of similar evidence in the future? How does your analysis of this lesson impact your planning for the next mathematics lesson?

Protocols for reflection often require members of a community of practice to share teaching artifacts, including samples of student work, with their colleagues. Sharing student work makes both the mathematics tasks used and the student responses readily accessible for analysis. Examples of protocols for this purpose include the *Guided Reflection Protocol* which provides a series of steps for teachers to reflect alone on classroom episodes; a *Critical Incidents Protocol*, which provides similar steps for reflection but this time with colleagues (Tripp, 1993); a tuning protocol (Allen & McDonald, 1997), which outlines a series of steps for teachers to present student work to colleagues in a structured, reflective discourse aimed at tuning the work to a higher standard; and a questioning protocol, designed to engage teachers in examining their teaching experiences from different perspectives to generate new thinking (Moss, Springer, & Dehr, 2008). Each of these protocols could be used to focus on one or more dimensions of formative assessment, using mathematics tasks or activities that help preservice teachers reflect on their effectiveness of implementation and what they could do to make improvements.

Experiences in the use of tools and protocols focused on formative assessment implementation sow the seeds for the preservice teachers' uptake of reflection-in-action and reflection-on-action that becomes an important and indigenous habit of practice in their teaching. Next, we turn to knowledge representations that preservice teachers can use to deepen their disciplinary knowledge along with experiences to support that development.

Developing Expertise in Disciplinary Knowledge

As we have noted, disciplinary knowledge for mathematics teachers comprises both subject matter knowledge and knowledge of how students think about and learn mathematics. We suggest two specific representations of knowledge and six experiences that can be integrated into a preservice program to assist preservice teachers in beginning to develop mathematics disciplinary knowledge for formative assessment.

Mathematics Standards

Beginning mathematics teachers will be responsible for their students' achievement of state mathematics standards, just as their more experienced colleagues are, so a starting point for developing disciplinary knowledge is becoming familiar with the student-level mathematics detailed in mathematics content standards adopted by the U.S. state in which they will receive teacher certification. Acquiring a knowledge of the standards includes tracing the development of mathematical concepts across grade-level standards to understand how they progressively increase in sophistication, as well as examining how the mathematical practice standards interact with the content standards.

As important as deep knowledge of the mathematics content and practice standards is, the standards have limitations for the purpose of formative assessment. This is because, by their nature, standards describe the learning expectations for the end of a grade level rather than identifying the intra-grade development of concepts, skills, and analytical practices. Consequently, standards lack the specificity needed to understand the incremental development of mathematics learning, which is necessary for both teaching and formative assessment. In contrast, learning progressions describe in more detail how mathematics learning develops over time and can add to preservice teachers' mathematical knowledge in important ways to support formative assessment.

Mathematics Learning Progressions

In their landmark review of studies of formative assessment, Black and Wiliam (1998) called for "sound models of students' progression in the learning of the subject matter" (p. 37) so that teachers could interpret and respond to assessment evidence in a formative way. Along these lines, the idea of learning progressions – descriptions of how student thinking about a concept typically evolves over time – has recently gained ground as a way to provide more detailed and nuanced descriptions of learning in support of instruction and assessment in mathematics (e.g., Arieli-Attali, Wylie, & Bauer, 2012; Sztajn, et al., 2012). Including an analysis of mathematics learning progressions in conjunction with examining related standards offers preservice teachers a deeper perspective on how students' mathematical learning develops. To make preservice teachers' experience with learning progressions productive, particularly as they are being prepared to teach a range of grade levels, we propose that they examine a few progressions in depth, rather than superficially addressing many. Once they understand the nature of mathematics progressions and how they can be used for teaching, learning, and formative assessment, they can take advantage of them for continued professional learning as mathematics teachers.

One example of how progressions that preservice teachers could profitably examine to understand how progressions can both undergird and augment standards is the Progressions for the Common Core State Standards in Mathematics (Common Core Standards Writing Team [CCSWT], 2013). The Common Core State Standards for Mathematics (CCSSM) were created from research on how students' mathematical understanding develops, and the logical structure in mathematics. The progressions provide a level of detail that can support the development of deeper disciplinary knowledge about the standards. They are a valuable resource for both teachers and preservice teachers because they "explain why standards are sequenced the way they are, point out cognitive difficulties and pedagogical solutions, and give more detail on particularly knotty areas of the mathematics" (CCSWT, 2013, p. 3). Understanding cognitive difficulties and knotty areas is likely to benefit formative assessment – teachers can pay attention to the possibility of their presence during learning and make appropriate pedagogical responses when necessary.

A second example is an empirically validated mathematics progression that describes student understanding of proportional reasoning, shown in abbreviated form in Table 9.4 below (Arieli-Attali, Wylie, & Bauer, 2012). While mathematical standards will help a preservice teacher identify that proportional reasoning is part of the expectations for students at grades 6 and 7, the standards will not provide insight into how students misunderstand critical concepts or hold naïve or partial understandings (Hill, Schilling, & Ball, 2004). Askew and Wiliam (1995) found that "learning is more effective when common misconceptions are addressed, exposed, and discussed" (p. 8). In this progression, for example, the additive misconception is a common one, which entails students considering the ratios 2:3 and 4:5 as equivalent because they both add one to the first number of the ratio to get the second number. Beginning teachers need to understand commonly held misconceptions so they so they can anticipate, recognize, and respond to them when they arise during teaching and learning.

A third example of a knowledge representation resource describes a growth and development trajectory (progression) of student ideas from informal understandings to increasingly complex ones (Confrey, Maloney, & Corley, 2014). The learning maps, available at TurnOnCCMath.net, include students' misconceptions and instructional strategies to productively address or build on naïve understandings (Confrey, Maloney, & Corley, 2014). An in-depth examination of this progression could assist preservice teachers in understanding the development of student thinking and support their interpretation of evidence and potential contingent pedagogical responses designed to move learning forward.

In addition to examining the details of progressions to enhance their disciplinary knowledge, preservice teachers need to leave their programs with several core understandings about progressions. First, progressions are pathways that students typically follow, although they may not hold true for each student. Second, while progressions trace the development of concepts and skills, progressions are not developmentally inevitable, but rather are dependent on effective instruction. Third, the nature of progressions takes account of the axiom that learning does not proceed in lockstep. Students will likely not all reach the same point in learning at the same time, but all students can

Teacher Preparation in Mathematics

Table 9.4 Abbreviated Proportional Reasoning Learning Progression

Level		Proportional Reasoning
1	Intuitive understanding	Students have an intuitive understanding that allows them to make a qualitative comparison of more or less.
2	Begin to quantify, work with single ratios	Students attempt at quantifying, beginning to recognizing the inner relation within the "mixture," i.e., the single ratio. They understand that changing the ratio results in a changed outcome, but mostly focus on one part of the ratio (the numerator), which may be perceived as the "cause" of the outcome. Students may incorrectly assume additive relationships to compare ratios (e.g., incorrectly assume 2:3 is equivalent to 3:4).
3	Recognition of multiplicative relationship	Students have recognition of a multiplicative relationship, i.e., they understand the inner symmetric relation within the ratio so much as to map it to another ratio but also may use build-up (scale-up) additive strategies to solve problems.
4	Accommodating covariance and invariance	Students are able to accommodate covariance and invariance, i.e., they understand the model behind the proportional ratios. They understand the "constant" or invariant aspect of the ratio (i.e., the inner structure of the ratio) – mapped (as is) to other ratios, building the covariance quantities.
5	Generalized model of proportionality	Students acquire a generalized model of proportionality, i.e., they understand that a proportional relationship can be represented with more than two quantities. They would be able to detect proportionality in different situations, using different strategies.

progress from where they are. This idea goes to the heart of formative assessment: Teachers find the status of student learning and match their instructional response to where the learning currently stands. Finally, and again critical for formative assessment, learning is not best characterized in a binary got it/didn't get it manner, but rather evolves from partial and naïve understandings that can be productively built on through pedagogical actions, including feedback that students can use to move their own learning forward. Next, we discuss the six specific experiences to support preservice teachers' analyses of standards and progressions for the purpose of formative assessment.

Analyze Mathematics Standards

For the purpose of deeply understanding the standards, we draw from professional learning experiences provided by *Talking Teaching Network* (TTN), designed to help teachers become familiar with college- and career-ready mathematics content standards (TTN Math Study Guide, n.d.). These experiences are equally applicable to preservice teachers. Following TTN, we recommend a series of reviews of the standards, increasing in depth on each successive occasion, to build familiarity and help preservice teachers identify areas where they need additional learning opportunities:

- Browse the standards and mathematical practices and form general impressions about the nature of the standards and practices, noting points of interest; discussions among the group;
- Identify the standards that are least familiar for further examination;
- Think about which of the mathematical practice standards might support specific content standards;
- Analyze standards (depending on elementary, middle, high school preferences) domain by domain, categorizing them into facts, procedure, concept, and/or a combination;

- Identify standards at the grade below and above that connect into the set being analyzed;
- Discuss the categories in terms of the different teaching and learning they require;
- Consider what evidence would be required to indicate students had met the content standards and mathematical practices.

Use Standards and Learning Progressions to Develop Learning Goals and Success Criteria

After preservice teachers have closely examined the standards, they should have opportunities to deconstruct standards into lesson-sized component goals or subgoals. While learning progressions are not usually at a grain-size to inform learning goals directly, they can be used in conjunction with the standards to provide support in two ways. First, they often articulate naïve ways of thinking for which teachers ought to be alert (Davis, 1997) as students make progress toward the goals. Second, they support the development of "horizon knowledge" (Loewenberg Ball, Thames, & Phelps, 2008, p. 403) which can help preservice teachers envision how an individual lesson goal fits into a larger view of learning within and across grades.

In the process of creating goals, preservice teachers need to learn that goals are specific and use the language of mathematics. For example, a goal of "80% correct by each student on the quiz at the end of the lesson" is not a useful one because it does not specify the mathematics that students will learn, whereas the goal *students should construct relationships between the value of a decimal fraction, the sum of the values of each of its digits, and increasing (and decreasing) powers of ten* makes clear the intended mathematical learning (Hiebert et al., 2007). When learning goals are specific, preservice teachers can be helped, with reference to standards and progressions, to think about what counts as evidence for achieving the goal – what are the learning performances that will indicate that students are meeting the goal?

Spending time on learning goals should help preservice students develop the habit of creating learning goals that are both mathematically meaningful and at an appropriate grain-size for formative assessment and to guide decisions both within and between lessons (Hiebert, Morris, & Glass, 2003).

Analyze Diagnostic Items to Understand Student Thinking

Analyzing student responses from items designed to pinpoint student misconceptions is another way to focus preservice teachers' attention on student thinking in the discipline as foundational support for formative assessment. Underscoring the importance of this kind of experience in preservice programs are findings from a project aimed at developing classroom teachers' awareness of student misconceptions (Wylie & Ciofalo, 2008). Participating teachers expressed a lack of familiarity with mathematical misconceptions. For example, one fourth-grade mathematics teacher stated, "I never really thought much about misconceptions before [this project]. Listening to student thinking and ideas has been great."

In this project, teachers were provided with multiple-choice items that were developed using common student misconceptions for several of the distractors. The items were intended to help teachers uncover students' mathematical misconceptions and provided a way for them to consider students' thinking about concepts and not just the correctness of an answer. Using the items helped teachers develop disciplinary insights that went beyond knowledge of the subject, and supported their interpretative listening during class discussions. As an eighth-grade teacher said, "I enjoyed the free ride these questions granted me into the minds of my students."

Figure 9.3 illustrates a relatively simple item that can help a teacher identify more or less sophisticated understanding of a concept.

Teacher Preparation in Mathematics

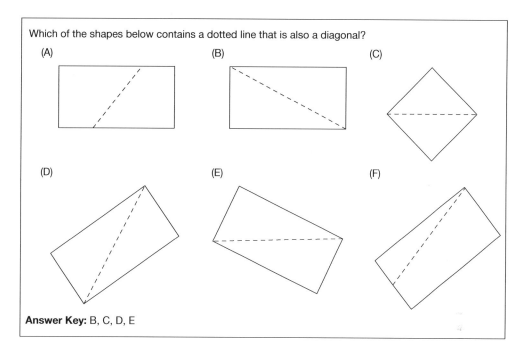

Figure 9.3 A misconception item targeting understanding of a diagonal.

A student with a rudimentary understanding of a diagonal might only identify shape B, whereas a student with a more sophisticated understanding could identify all of the correct shapes and would not be distracted by their orientation. A student who selects F may think that a diagonal is any line that starts from a corner. A student who selects A may believe that a diagonal is a line that is oriented at 45° to the horizontal regardless of where it starts. Understanding the misconceptions revealed by this item would enhance preservice teachers' knowledge about student understanding of a diagonal.

Similarly, if teachers were asked to consider the answer choices in the item in Figure 9.4, their knowledge of student thinking about fractions could be deepened. Students will likely choose answer (a) if they understand that the relationship between the numerator and the denominator that determines size. Students who use the denominator to determine size will likely choose answer (b). Students who use the numerator to determine size will likely answer (c) (Chappuis, 2015, p. 212). Following their analysis, preservice teachers could discuss together what pedagogical responses would be appropriate for each answer choice.

Use Learning Progressions to Examine Student Work

Student work illustrating critical aspects of the mathematics progression can be examined to help preservice teachers understand the qualitative distinctions in the levels of a specific progression. It is

---

Which fraction is the largest?

a) $\dfrac{2}{1}$ b) $\dfrac{3}{8}$ c) $\dfrac{4}{3}$

Figure 9.4 An item targeting understanding of fractions.

also helpful for preservice teachers to use the progression to examine student work and gain insights into the students' mathematics reasoning and understanding, and think about how they could build on the students' current learning status. This approach is similar to how others have used learning progressions with teachers. For example, Ebby and Petit (2018) used research-based mathematics learning trajectories in the *Ongoing Assessment Project* (OGAP) to support the development of teacher knowledge and their capacity to elicit, interpret, and respond to student thinking. This use of progressions led to more differentiated teaching that better met the learning needs of individual students. Levi and Ambrose (2018) describe a similar approach in the context of Cognitively Guided Instruction.

By way of illustration, the learning progression for proportional reasoning shown previously in Table 9.4 can be used to examine student responses to a proportional reasoning item (Figure 9.5) and help a teacher gain insights into students' reasoning.

The first student did not provide a lengthy explanation, but "it is plus 8" suggests that the student looked at the 12 quarters and 20 pieces of candy and identified that the difference is eight. The student then applied the rule of plus 8 to the new context of 15 quarters to arrive at the answer 23 pieces of candy. This approach suggests evidence of the learning progression level 2 where the student assumes an additive relationship between the numbers rather than a multiplicative relationship. The second and third responses are both correct but differ in their sophistication. One student used a build-up strategy to recognize that every three quarters can increase by five pieces of candy, so 15 quarters is one more group of three quarters more than the original 12 quarters, and so the resulting amount of candy must be one more group of five candies more than the original 20. The third student used a unit rate approach to the problem, after converting quarters to cents. The first student, if the response is typical of his or her reasoning, will require different learning opportunities than the other two students who, for example, may benefit from hearing each other explain their reasoning so that they can both develop a robust and flexible repertoire of approaches.

Use Learning Progressions to Plan Next Instructional Steps, Including Feedback

Learning progressions can help preservice teachers identify and group student thinking (e.g., what Duckor and Holmberg [2017] called *binning*), but this is only a first stage in planning next instructional steps. An essential, and often challenging, second stage is to identify how to productively build on the current status of student understanding. While learning progressions can help preservice teachers understand what learning a particular concept entails, and what the next level of understanding might be, they do not generally define the specific learning opportunities to advance learning. One exception is *The Enhanced Learning Maps* materials for mathematics that include progressions, illustrating the connections among concepts and skills that students need to construct; instructional activities that suggest ideas for teaching; and solution guides to provide insights for diagnosing misconceptions and informing next steps in learning (Kingston & Broaddus, 2017). In the absence of such materials, once preservice teachers understand the current status of student thinking, working

---

Question: Brenda bought 20 pieces of candy with 12 quarters. Marisa has 15 quarters. How many pieces of candy can Marisa buy with her money? Explain how you found your answer.

23 pieces. there is a rule and it is plus 8

25 pieces of candy. for every three quarters its five pieces of candy so i just added five more pieces of candies

12 quarters is equal to 3 dollars. 300 pennies divided by 20 pieces of candy is equal to 15 cents per piece of candy. Marisa's 15 quarters are equal to $3.75 at 15 cents a piece she can get 25 pieces of candy

---

Figure 9.5 Proportional reasoning problem and three student responses.

collaboratively with peers, mentor teachers, and program faculty can help them identify possible instructional responses, including the feedback that could be provided to students to assist their next steps. This same group can also provide opportunities for post-lesson reflection on the success or otherwise of their actions.

Examine Model Mathematics Curriculum Materials

In most districts, mathematics teachers are expected to follow a specific curriculum. It is unlikely that preservice programs can familiarize participants with all the curricula they may encounter as teachers. However, preservice teachers can engage as learners with model curricular activities that teachers employ with their students (e.g., Buczynski & Hansen, 2010; Heller et al., 2012). Such first-hand experiences may provide insights into the design of curricular materials and how they describe the development of mathematical learning. When combined with analysis of their own experience, preservice teachers can think about student mathematics learning, how it develops as a result of the activities, and what student misconceptions or partial understandings students might have as they engage in the activities. They can also become familiar with how to find and use resources to obtain insights into student thinking.

In the next section, we focus on our third area of expertise for formative assessment, habits of practice.

Expertise in Habits of Practice

Earlier in this chapter, we identified three critical habits of practice that we believe are essential for teachers, both beginning and more experienced, as they develop and deepen their disciplinary knowledge in conjunction with formative assessment expertise: (1) a commitment to participate in continued inquiry about, and reflection on, their practice; (2) a willingness to de-privatize teaching and engage in collaboration with colleagues; and (3) a willingness to engage in deliberate practice (see Figure 9.1). Orienting preservice teachers to the acquisition of these habits of practice lays a foundation on which they can continue to build over the course of their careers, as exemplified in the interview with the teacher we described earlier. One main source of knowledge for developing habits of practice in support of formative assessment implementation is professional standards.

Recognizing that professional standards are more expectations to aspire to than knowledge representations, we nonetheless regard them as valuable sources for considering the habits of practice that preservice teachers need to acquire. As we have seen, examination of professional standards reveals the importance of educators being actively involved in their continuous development and placing emphasis on their own learning. According to the professional standards, this active involvement is accomplished through inquiry, action research, reflection, self-evaluation, and receiving constructive feedback.

Preservice teachers need to be exposed to the standards that describe habits of practice and be made aware of their significance to their continuing professional lives and, in particular, to the development of formative assessment expertise. In this regard, throughout the third part of the chapter, we have highlighted the experiences that preservice teacher programs can provide that not only support the development of formative assessment knowledge and skills and disciplinary knowledge, but also simultaneously promote desired habits of practice. Among these experiences are enabling beginning teachers to collaborate in assisting each other's learning, for example, by sharing problems of practice related to formative assessment implementation from their field experiences and collaboratively finding solutions guided by program faculty, and by creating opportunities for reflection and revision through a cyclical process of learn, practice, revise (Lyon & Wylie, 2009; Wylie, Lyon, & Mavronikolas, 2008).

Preservice teachers are not only learning about teaching and formative assessment, but are also beginning to develop their identities as teachers. The habits of practice promoted in their preservice programs will go a long way to influencing and shaping their identities as professionals who are committed to progress on the continuum of expertise that they have just begun.

Conclusion

In this chapter, we have advanced proposals for how preservice teachers can develop a baseline competency for formative assessment. Currently, there is an absence of research evidence to support the idea of sufficient teacher preparation, and more broadly, there is not agreement about what constitutes readiness to practice. Nonetheless, we regard our proposals as sound and doable. We believe that implementing the proposed framework and suggestions for developing baseline competence in formative assessment (Figure 9.1) is achievable within the confines of a traditional teacher preparation program, and necessary for preservice teachers to be ready to enter the classroom. While preservice teachers will need to wait for their own classrooms to establish a culture for learning and formative assessment, including expectations and routines for student interaction and collaboration, and to develop skills in fostering student self-regulation, the baseline competency we have proposed will equip them to engage in formative assessment immediately. This is surely in the interests of all their students.

We have proposed that preservice teachers learn to implement the practices of formative assessment through inquiry, active engagement, collaboration, feedback, reflection, and the development of their own agency in learning, an approach which we believe can lead them to develop critical habits for ongoing professional growth.

Our proposals for learning experiences in preservice programs are consistent with the requirements of professional standards for teaching, assessment, and professional learning, which we described in the chapter. In terms of the content of the program, we proposed the development of a foundational understanding of formative assessment practice, through the use of definitions and rubrics that help preservice teachers understand what formative assessment is, how it relates to other aspects of teaching practice, and what characterizes expert versus novice practice. We recommended that beginning mathematics teachers have opportunities to apply these definitions and rubrics to the practice of others, experts and novice peers, and also to use them to reflect on their own teaching practice. In this way, preservice students develop strategies for using these tools to support deliberate, reflective practice.

We also emphasized that formative assessment is grounded in disciplinary knowledge and proposed several ways in which this knowledge can be acquired. We recommended close analysis of both mathematics standards and of targeted learning progressions as resources for developing disciplinary knowledge and suggested a range of experiences for preservice teachers to use them to use them for the purposes of formative assessment. Additionally, we proposed reviewing model curricula as a means of developing disciplinary knowledge. We also suggested exposure to ways of eliciting student misconceptions, using learning progressions to examine student work and planning next steps in response to evidence of students' mathematical thinking.

One further proposal remains: program faculty and mentor teachers must model formative assessment for their students – they must practice what they preach. While this proposal may seem self-evident, it is instructive to recall the results a survey of preservice teachers and faculty members at one institute of higher education in the United Kingdom, which reported a disconnect between the perceptions of faculty members and preservice students in the use of formative assessment (MacLellan, 2001). Faculty member responses indicated that they were using formative assessment in their courses, whereas preservice teacher responses suggested that formative assessment was not used as often as the faculty thought, and, in instances where it was used, it was not

Teacher Preparation in Mathematics

beneficial to their learning. If preservice teachers are going to adopt formative assessment as part of their pedagogy, then, at the very least, their preservice programs should provide some experiential learning on its value.

Expert teachers are able to engage in an almost seamless dance among teaching, learning, and assessment (Hayward, 2007; Willis & Cowie, 2014). In the classroom vignette we described, the teacher had reached a level of seamless dancing, which had taken time and commitment to ongoing professional learning. We close this chapter by posing a challenge for the wider educational community: to ensure that teachers, through induction and in-service programs, have opportunities to continue along a professional learning continuum to develop and deepen formative assessment knowledge and skills in the context of disciplinary knowledge, to enable them to reach that seamless dance in their mathematics teaching.

References

Absolum, M. (2010). *Clarity in the classroom: Using formative assessment for building learner-focused relationships.* Winnipeg, MB Canada: Portage & Main Press.

Allal, L. (2010). Assessment and the regulation of learning. In E.B.P. Peterson (Ed.), *International encyclopedia of education* (Vol. 3, pp. 348–352). Oxford: Elsevier.

Allal, L. (2011). Pedagogy, didactics and the co-regulation of learning: A perspective from the French-language world of educational research. *Research Papers in Education, 26*(3), 329–336.

Allen, D. & McDonald, J. (1997). Tuning protocol: A process for reflection on teacher and student work. *Horace 13*(2).

Andrade, H. L., Du, Y., & Mycek, K. (2010). Rubric-referenced self-assessment and middle school students' writing. *Assessment in Education: Principles, Policy & Practice, 17*(2), 199–214.

Andrade, H. & Brookhart, S. M. (2016). The role of classroom assessment in supporting self-regulated learning. In D. Laveault & L. Allal (Eds.), *Assessment for learning: Meeting the challenge of implementation* (pp. 293–309). Heidelberg, Germany: Springer.

Arieli-Attali, M., Wylie, E. C., Bauer, M. I. (2012, April). *The use of three learning progressions in supporting formative assessment in middle school mathematics.* Paper presented at the annual meeting of the American Educational Research Association, Vancouver, Canada.

Askew, M. & D. Wiliam (1995). *Recent research in mathematics education 5–16.* London, UK: Her Majesty's Stationery Office.

AMTE. (2017). Standards for preparing teachers of mathematics. Raleigh, NC: Association of Mathematics Teacher Educators. Retrieved from https://amte.net/standards.

Bailey, A. L. & Heritage, M. (2018). *Self-regulation in learning: The role of language and formative assessment.* Cambridge, MA: Harvard Education Press.

Ball, D. L. (1995). *Developing mathematics reform: What don't we know about teacher learning – but would make good working hypotheses?* Paper presented at the conference on Teacher Enhancement in Mathematics K–6. Arlington, VA.

Bell, B. & Cowie, B. (2001). *Formative assessment and science education.* Dordrecht, The Netherlands: Kluwer.

Bennett, R. E. (2011). Formative assessment: A critical review. *Assessment in Education: Principles, Policy & Practice, 18*(1), 5–25.

Black, P., Harrison, C., Lee, C., Marshall, B., & Wiliam, D. (2003). *Assessment for learning.* Maidenhead: Open University Press.

Black, P. J. & Wiliam, D. (1998). Assessment and classroom learning. *Assessment in Education: Principles Policy and Practice* (5) *1*, 7–74.

Black, P. & Wiliam, D. (2009). Developing the theory of formative assessment. *Educational Assessment, Evaluation and Accountability, 21*(1), 5.

Black, P., Wilson, M., & Yao, S.-Y. (2011). Road maps for learning: A guide to the navigation of learning progressions. *Measurement: Interdisciplinary Research & Perspective, 9*(2–3), 71–123.

Bliss, T. & Reynolds, A. (2004). Quality visions and focused imagination. In J. Brophy (Ed.), *Using video in teacher education* (1st edition, pp. 29–52). Boston, M|A: Elsevier.

Boaler, J. (2002). The development of disciplinary relationships: Knowledge, practice and identify in mathematics classrooms. *For the Learning of Mathematics, 22*(1), 42–47.

Borko, H. & Putnam, R. (1998). Professional development and reform-based teaching: Introduction to theme issue. *Teaching and Teacher Education, 14*(1), 1–3.

Bransford, J., Brown, A. L., & Cocking, R. R. (2000). *How People Learn: Brain, Mind, Experience, and School.* Commission on Behavioral and Social Sciences and Education National Research Council: Washington, DC: National Academy Press.

Brinko, K. T. (1993). The practice of giving feedback to improve teaching: What is effective? *The Journal of Higher Education, 64*(5), 574–593.

Brookhart, S. & Moss, C. (2009). *Advancing formative assessment in every classroom.* Alexandria VA: ASCD.

Buczynski, S. & Hansen, C. B. (2010). Impact of professional development on teacher practice: Uncovering connections. *Teaching and Teacher Education, 26*(3), 599–607.

Burkhardt, H. & Schoenfeld, A. (2019). Formative Assessment in Mathematics. In H. Andrade, G. Cizek, R. Bennett (Eds.), *The Handbook of Formative Assessment in the Disciplines.* New York, NY: Routledge.

Burton, M. & Audrict, W. (2018). Focusing on formative assessment to improve mathematics teaching and learning. In V. Mills & E. Silver (Eds.), *A fresh look at formative assessment in mathematics teaching* (pp. 147–157). Reston, VA: National Council of Mathematics Teachers.

Chappuis, J. (2015). *Seven strategies of assessment for learning* (2nd edition). Upper Saddle River, NJ: Pearson Education.

Clark, I. (2012). Formative assessment: Assessment is for self-regulated learning. *Educational Psychology Review, 24*(2), 205–249.

Coffey, J. E., Hammer, D., Levin, D. M., & Grant, T. (2011). The missing disciplinary substance of formative assessment. *Journal of Research in Science Teaching, 48*(10), 1109–1136.

Cohen, D. K. & Ball, D. L. (1990). Relations between policy and practice: A commentary. *Educational Evaluation and Policy Analysis, 12*(3), 331–338.

Common Core Standards Writing Team. (2013). *Progressions documents for the Common Core Mathematics Standards.* Retrieved from http://ime.math.arizona.edu/progressions/#products.

Confrey, J., Maloney, A.P. & Corley, A. K. (2014). Learning trajectories: a framework for connecting standards with curriculum. *ZDM Mathematics Education, 46*(5), 719–733. DOI 10.1007/s11858-014-0598-7.

CCSSO (2018). *Revising the definition of formative assessment.* Washington, DC: Council of Chief State School Officers.

Council for the Accreditation of Educator Preparation. (2013). *CAEP accreditation standards and evidence: Aspirations for educator preparation.* Retrieved from http://caepnet.org/~/media/Files/caep/standards/commrpt.pdf?la=en.

Cowie, B., & Moreland, J. (2015). Leveraging disciplinary practices to support students' active participation in formative assessment. *Assessment in Education: Principles, Policy & Practice, 22*(2), 247–264.

Creswell, J. W. (2012). *Qualitative inquiry and research design: Choosing among five approaches.* Thousand Oaks, CA: Sage.

Darling-Hammond, L., Hyler, M. E., & Gardner, M. (2017). *Effective teacher professional development.* Palo Alto, CA: Learning Policy Institute.

Davis, B. (1997). Listening for differences: An evolving conception of mathematics teaching. *Journal for Research in Mathematics Education, 28*(3), 355–376.

Duckor, B. & Holmberg, C. (2017). *Mastering formative assessment moves: 7 high-leverage practices to advance student learning.* Alexandria, VA: ASCD.

Ebby, C. & Petit, M. (2018). Using learning trajectories to elicit, interpret and respond to student thinking. In V. Mills & E. Silver (Eds.), *A fresh look at formative assessment in mathematics teaching* (pp. 81–103). Reston, VA: National Council of Mathematics Teachers.

Educational Testing Service. (2009). *TLC Leader Handbook.* Portland, OR: Author.

Englert, S. C. & Tarrant, K. L. (1995). Creating collaborative cultures for educational change. *Remedial and Special Education, 16*(6), 325–336.

Ericsson, K. A., Krampe, R. T., & Tesch-Römer, C. (1993). The role of deliberate practice in the acquisition of expert performance. *Psychological Review, 100*(3), 363–406.

Fontana, D., & Fernandes, M. (1994). Improvements in the mathematics performance as a consequence of self-assessment in Portuguese primary school pupils. *British Journal of Educational Psychology, 64*, 407–417.

Gillies, D. (2016). Developing the thoughtful practitioner. In M. Peters, B. Cowie, I. Mentor. (Eds.), *A Companion to research in teacher education* (pp. 23–35). Singapore: Springer.

Grossman, P., Hammerness, K., & McDonald, M. (2009). Redefining teaching, re-imagining teacher education. *Teachers and Teaching: theory and practice, 15*(2), 273–289.

Hattie, J. & Timperley, H. (2007). The power of feedback. *Review of Educational Research, 77*(1), 81–112.

Hayden, E. H., Moore-Russo, D., & Marino, M. R. (2013). One teacher's reflective journey and the evolution of a lesson: Systematic reflection as a catalyst for adaptive expertise. *Reflective Practice, 14*(1), 144–156.

Hays, D. G. & Singh, A. A. (2012). *Qualitative inquiry in clinical and educational settings.* New York, NY: Guilford.

Hayward, E. L. (2007).Curriculum, pedagogies and assessment in Scotland: the quest for social justice. "Ah kent yir faither." *Assessment in Education: Principles, Policy & Practice, 14*(2), 251–268.

Heller, J. I., Daehler, K. R., Wong, N., Shinohara, M., & Miratrix, L. W. (2012). Differential effects of three professional development models on teacher knowledge and student achievement in elementary science. *Journal of Research in Science Teaching, 49*(3), 333–362.

Heritage, M. (2008). Learning Progressions: Supporting Instruction and Formative Assessment. Washington, DC: CCSSO.

Heritage, M. (2010). *Formative assessment and next-generation assessment systems: Are we losing an opportunity?* Washington, DC: The Council of Chief State School Officers.

Heritage, M. (2013). *Formative assessment: A process of inquiry and action.* Cambridge, MA: Harvard Education Press.

Heritage, M. (2016). Assessment for learning: Co-regulation in and as student-teacher interactions. In D. Laveault & V. L. Allal. (Eds). *Assessment for learning: Meeting the challenge of implementation.* (pp. 311–327). New York, NY: Springer.

Heritage, M. & Heritage, J. (2013). Teacher questioning: The epicenter of instruction and assessment. *Applied Measurement in Education, 26,* 176–190.

Heritage, M., Kim, J., Vendlinski, T., & Herman, J. (2009). From evidence to action: a seamless process in formative assessment? *Education Measurement: Issues and Practice, 28*(3), 24–31.

Heritage, M. & Wylie, E. C. (2018). Reaping the benefits of assessment for learning: Achievement, equity and identity. *ZDM Mathematics Education, 50*(4), 729–741. DOI: 10.1007/s11858-018-0943-3.

Hiebert, J., Morris, A. K., & Glass, B. (2003). Learning to learn to teach: An "experiment" model for teaching and teacher preparation in mathematics. *Journal of mathematics teacher education, 6*(3), 201–222.

Hiebert, J., Morris, A. K., Berk, D., & Jansen, A. (2007). Preparing teachers to learn from teaching. *Journal of Teacher Education, 58*(1), 47–61.

Hill, H. C., Schilling, S. G., & Ball, D. L. (2004). Developing measures of teachers' mathematics knowledge for teaching. *The Elementary School Journal, 105*(1), 11–30.

Interstate Teacher Assessment and Support Consortium (InTASC). (2011). *InTASC model core teaching standards: A resource for state dialogue.* Washington, DC: Council of Chief State School Officers.

Johnson, S. M., Papay, J. P., Fiarman, S. E., Munger, M. S., & Qazilbash, E. K. (2010). *Teacher to teacher: Realizing the potential of peer assistance and review.* Washington, DC: *Center for American Progress.*

Kagan, D. M. (1992). Implication of research on teacher belief. *Educational Psychologist, 27*(1), 65–90.

Kingston, N. M. & Broaddus, A. (2017). The use of learning map systems to support formative assessment in mathematics. *Education Sciences, 7*(1), 41.

Klenowski, V. (2009). Assessment for learning revisited: An Asia-Pacific perspective. *Assessment in Education: Principles, Policy, & Practice, 16*(3), 263–268.

Klinger, D.A., McDivitt, P.J., Howard, B.B., Munoz, M.A., Roger, W.T., Wylie, E.C. (2015). *Classroom assessment standards for preK-12 teachers: Joint Committee on Standards for Educational Evaluation.* Published as a Kindle e-Book.

Kobett, B.M. & Karp, K. (2018). Using formative assessment to guide the effective implementation of response to intervention (RtI). In V. Mills & E. Silver (Eds.), *A fresh look at formative assessment in mathematics teaching* (pp. 127–145). Reston, VA: National Council of Mathematics Teachers.

Kohut, G. F., Burnap, C., & Yon, M. G. (2007). Peer observation of teaching: Perceptions of the observer and the observed. *College Teaching, 55*(1), 19–25.

Larrivee, B. (2010). What we know and don't know about teacher reflection. In E. Pultorak (Ed.), *The purposes, practices, and professionalism of teacher reflectivity: Insights for twenty-first-century teachers and students* (pp. 137–162). Lanham, MD: Rowman & Littlefield.

Lave, J. & Wenger, E. (1991). *Situated learning: Legitimate peripheral participation.* New York, NY: Cambridge University Press.

Leahy, S., Lyon, C., Thompson, M., & Wiliam, D. (2005). Classroom assessment minute by minute, day by day. *Educational Leadership, 63*(3), 18–24.

Learning Forward. (2011). *Standards for professional learning.* Oxford, OH: Learning Forward.

Levi, L. & Ambrose, R. (2018). Cognitively guided instruction and formative assessment. In V. Mills & E. Silver (Eds.), *A fresh look at formative assessment in mathematics teaching* (pp. 41–61). Reston, VA: National Council of Mathematics Teachers.

Loewenberg Ball, D., Thames, M. H., & Phelps, G. (2008). Content knowledge for teaching: What makes it special? *Journal of Teacher Education, 59*(5), 389–407.

Lortie, D. (1975) *Schoolteacher: A sociological study.* London: University of Chicago Press.

Lott Adams, T. & Bonner, E. (2018). Distinguishing features of culturally responsive pedagogy related to formative assessment in mathematics instruction. In V. Mills & E. Silver (Eds.), *A fresh look at formative assessment in mathematics teaching* (pp. 61–81). Reston, VA: National Council of Mathematics Teachers.

Lyon, C.J &Wylie, E.C. (2009). How structure and focus support teacher learning. *ETS Research Memorandum No. RM-09-02*. Princeton, NJ: ETS.

Maclellan, E. (2001). Assessment for learning: The differing perceptions of tutors and students. *Assessment & Evaluation in Higher Education, 26*(4), 307–318.

Mercer, N., Dawes, L., Wegerif, R., & Sams, C. (2004). Reasoning as a scientist: Ways of helping children to use language to learn science. *British Educational Research Journal, 30*(3), 359–377.

Mills, V. & Silver, E. (Eds.). (2018). *A fresh look at formative assessment in mathematics teaching*. Reston, VA: National Council of Mathematics Teachers.

Moss, G., Springer, T., & Dehr, K. (2008). Guided reflection protocol as narrative inquiry and teacher professional development, *Reflective Practice, 9*(4), 497–508.

National Board for Professional Teaching Standards (NBPTS) (2010). Mathematics standards (3rd edition): for teachers of students ages 11–18+. National Board for Professional Teaching Standards, Retrieved from http://www.nbpts.org/wp-content/uploads/EAYA-MATH.pdf.

National Council of Teachers of Mathematics (NCTM) (2014). *Principles to actions: Ensuring mathematical success for all*. Reston, VA: Author.

National Research Council (NRC) (2001). *Adding it up: Helping children learn mathematics*. J. Kilpatrick, J. Swafford, & B. Findell (Eds.). Mathematics Learning Study Committee, Center for Education, Division of Behavioral and Social Sciences and Education. Washington, DC: National Academy Press.

National Research Council (2012). *Education for life and work: Developing transferable knowledge and skills in the 21st century*. Committee on Defining Deeper Learning and 21st Century Skills, J.W. Pellegrino and M.L. Hilton, Editors. Board on Testing and Assessment and Board on Science Education, Division of Behavioral and Social Sciences and Education. Washington, DC: The National Academies Press.

Nicol, D. J. & Macfarlane-Dick, D. (2006). Formative assessment and self-regulated learning: A model and seven principles of good feedback practice. *Studies in Higher Education, 31*(2), 199–218.

Organisation for Economic Cooperation and Development (2005). *Teachers matter: Attracting, retaining and developing effective teachers*. Paris, France: OECD Publishing.

Organisation for Economic Cooperation and Development (2013). *Synergies for better learning; An international perspective on evaluation and assessment. OECD reviews and assessment in education*. Paris, France: OECD Publishing.

Otero, V. K. (2006). Moving beyond the "get it or don't" conception of formative assessment. *Journal of Teacher Education, 57*(3), 247–255.

Palincsar, A. (1999). Response: A community of practice. *Teacher Education and Special Education, 22*(4), 272–274.

Putnam, R. T. & Borko, H. (2000). What do new views of knowledge and thinking have to say about research on teacher learning? *Educational Researcher, 29*(1), 4–15.

Ross, J. & Bruce, C. (2007). Professional development effects on teacher efficacy: Results of randomized field trial. *The Journal of Educational Research, 101*(1), 50–60.

Ruiz-Primo, M. A. (2011). Informal formative assessment: The role of instructional dialogues in assessing students' learning. *Studies in Educational Evaluation, 37*(1), 15–24.

Sadler, D. R. (1989). Formative assessment and the design of instructional systems. *Instructional Science, 18*(2), 119–144.

Saldaña, J. (2009). *The coding manual for qualitative researchers*. Thousand Oaks, CA: SAGE.

Shank, G. D. (2006). *Qualitative research: A personal skills approach* (2nd edition). Upper Saddle River, NJ: Pearson.

Schön, D. (1983). *The reflective practitioner*. New York: Basic Books.

Shavelson, R. J., Young, D. B., Ayala, C. C., Brandon, P. R., Furtak, E. M., Ruiz-Primo, M. A., Tomita, M. K., Yin, Y. (2008). On the impact of curriculum-embedded formative assessment on learning: A collaboration between curriculum and assessment developers. *Applied Measurement in Education, 21*(4), 295–314.

Shepard, L. A., Penuel, W. R., & Davidson, K. L. (2017). Design principles for new systems of assessment. *Phi Delta Kappan, 98*(6), 47–52.

Shepard, L. A., Penuel, W. R. & Pellegrino, J. W. (2018). Using learning and motivation theories to coherently link formative assessment, grading practices, and large-scale assessment. *Education Measurement: Issues and Practice, 37*(1), 21–34.

Smarter Balanced Assessment Consortium. (n.d.). *The formative assessment process*. Retrieved from https://portal.smarterbalanced.org/library/en/formative-assessment-process.pdf.

Star, J. R. & Strickland, S. K. (2008). Learning to observe: Using video to improve preservice mathematics teachers' ability to notice. *Journal of Mathematics Teacher Education, 11*(2), 107–125.

Star, J. R., Lynch, K. H., & Perova, N. (2011). Using video to improve mathematics' teachers' abilities to attend to classroom features: A replication study. In *Mathematics teacher noticing: Seeing through teachers' eyes.* In M. G. Sherin, V. R. Jacobs & R. A. Philipp (Eds.), *Mathematics teacher noticing: seeing through teachers' eyes* (pp. 117–133). New York, NY: Routledge.

Steele, M. & Smith, M. (2018). The mathematical tasks framework and formative assessment. In V. Mills & E. Silver (Eds.), *A fresh look at formative assessment in mathematics teaching* (pp. 103–127). Reston, VA: National Council of Mathematics Teachers.

Stipek, D. J., Givvin, K. B., Salmon, J. M., & MacGyvers, V. L. (2001). Teachers' beliefs and practices related to mathematics instruction. *Teaching and Teacher Education, 17*(2), 213–226.

Stroot, S. A., Fowlkes, J., Langholz, J., Paxton, S., Stedman, P., Steffes, L., & Valtman, A. (1999). Impact of a collaborative peer assistance and review model on entry-year teachers in a large urban school setting. *Journal of Teacher Education, 50*(1), 27–41.

Strutchens, M. E. & Silver, E. A. (2018). Formative assessment and equitable mathematics classrooms: Probing the intersection. In V. Mills & E. Silver (Eds.), *A fresh look at formative assessment in mathematics teaching* (pp. 157–170). Reston, VA: National Council of Mathematics Teachers.

Swaffield, S. (2011). Getting to the heart of authentic assessment for learning. *Assessment in Education: Principles, Policy & Practice, 18*(4), 433–449.

Sztajn, P., Confrey, J., Holt Wilson, P. H., & Edgington, C. (2012). Learning trajectory based instruction: Toward a theory of teaching. *Educational Research, 41*,147–156. DOI: 10.3102/0013189X12442801.

Threlfall, J. (2005). The formative use of assessment information in planning – the notion of contingent planning. *British Journal of Educational Studies, 53*(1), 54–65.

Torrance, H. & Pryor, J. (1998). *Investigating formative assessment: Teaching, learning and assessment in the classroom.* New York, NY: McGraw-Hill Education.

Tripp, D. (1993). *Critical incidents in teaching: Developing professional judgment.* New York, NY: Routledge.

Talking Teaching Network (n.d.). *TTN CA CC Math Study Guide.* Retrieved from http://talkingteaching.org/publications/.

Vygotsky, L. S. (1962). *Language and thought.* Ontario, Canada: Massachusetts Institute of Technology Press.

White, B. Y. & Frederiksen, J. R. (1998). Inquiry, modeling, and metacognition. Making science accessible to all students. *Cognition and Instruction, 16*(1), 3–118.

Wiliam, D. (2011). *Embedded formative assessment.* Bloomington, IN: Solution Tree.

Willis J., & Cowie B. (2014) Assessment as a generative dance. In: Wyatt-Smith C., Klenowski V., Colbert P. (Eds.), *Designing assessment for quality learning. The enabling power of assessment, Vol 1* (pp. 23–37). Dordrecht: Springer.

Wylie, E.C. (2016). *Supporting teacher learning through self and peer observation.* Presentation at the Chief Council of State School Officers (CCSSO) National Conference on Student Assessment, Philadelphia, PA.

Wylie, E. C. & Ciofalo, J. F. (2008). Supporting teachers' use of individual diagnostic items. *Teachers College Record.* Retrieved from http://www.tcrecord.org/content.asp?contentid=15363.

Wylie, E. C. & Lyon, C. J. (2015a). The fidelity of formative assessment implementation: issues of breadth and quality. *Assessment in Education: Principles, Policy & Practice, 22*(1), 140–160.

Wylie, E.C. & Lyon, C. (2015b). Using the formative assessment rubrics, reflection and observation tools to support professional reflection on practice. Created for the Formative Assessment for Teachers and Students (FAST) State Collaborative on Assessment and Student Standards (SCASS) of the Council of Chief State School Officers (CCSSO), Washington, DC.

Wylie, E.C., Lyon, C.J, Mavronikolas, E. (2008). Effective and scalable teacher professional development: A report of the formative research and development. *ETS Research Rep. No. RR-08-65.* Princeton, NJ: ETS.

Yin, R. K. (2003). *Case study research: Design and methods.* Thousands Oaks: Sage.

Zeichner, K. M. (2003) Teacher research as professional development for P–12 educators in the USA. *Educational Action Research, 11*(2), 301–326. DOI: 10.1080/09650790300200211.

Ziker, C. (2017). *FASTER grant summary report.* Menlo Park, CA: SRI International.

Appendix: FARROP Rubric Example

III. Tasks and Activities that Elicit Evidence of Student Learning

The focus of this dimension is on those things with which students engage that potentially produce evidence of student learning (except classroom discussions, as this is discussed in the *Questioning Strategies that Elicit Evidence of Student Learning* and the *Extending Thinking During Discourse* dimensions). Research indicates that student learning improves when teachers have rich evidence of student learning and make instructional adjustments based on that evidence.

Teachers need to use a range of tasks and activities to collect relevant and sufficient evidence of student understanding and/or progress toward the learning goals. When students are engaged in tasks and activities that are aligned with the learning goals (on their own, with another student, or in a small group), the work products provide evidence of student understanding. In order for a task to be effective, students need to have access to appropriate support from either the teacher or from their peers to complete the task. In addition, the teacher needs to have a mechanism for synthesizing evidence from across the class, whether through a formal review process or through an informal on-the-fly review.

Observation Notes

Tasks and Activities that Elicit Evidence of Student Learning:

- Tasks and activities include any learning opportunities that students engage in that potentially produce evidence of student learning that can be used to adjust instruction (except classroom discussions, as this is discussed in the *Questioning Strategies that Elicit Evidence of Student Learning* and *Extending Thinking During Discourse* dimensions). Tasks and activities that are formative do not include summative assessments or graded assignments that do not allow for revision or additional learning opportunities (e.g., graded quizzes). Furthermore, if the focus is on the overall outcome (e.g., the grade) rather than on understanding what students should know and what students need to know, then the task is higher stakes than a formative assessment should be. Examples of potential tasks and activities that can be used to elicit evidence of learning for formative purposes include worksheets, lab experiments, performance tasks (e.g., playing a C-major scale, learning to serve a volleyball, reading a poem with expression), commercially produced formative assessment tasks, essays, quizzes, group projects, and/or journaling. The decision regarding the purpose of the task and the use of the evidence will be a professional judgment made by the observer.
- It is possible (although not common) for an observed lesson to not include any tasks or activities that elicited evidence of student learning. For example, this could be the case if the entire lesson was a class discussion or teacher lecture, or if the entire class was devoted to independent silent reading.
- There are references across the levels to whether students are clear or unclear about the directions for the task. The focus here is not on the clarity of the learning goals but rather on whether the students have a clear understanding of how to begin the task itself.
- The rubric also asks observers to consider the directions that a teacher provides for a task and how quickly students are able to engage with the task or whether they need extensive re-explanations. The focus of this dimension is on how well the tasks and activities that a teacher selects provide evidence of student learning. Directions are important to the extent that if students don't understand the task they cannot engage with it to provide evidence of learning. Tasks that are more complex may require students to consider and plan how to

Not Observed	Beginning	Developing	Progressing	Extending
The teacher does not engage the class with any tasks or activities to elicit evidence of student learning.	The teacher uses tasks or activities that are not aligned to the learning goals or will not provide evidence of student progress toward those goals.	The teacher uses tasks or activities that are loosely aligned to the learning goals and will provide limited evidence of student progress toward those goals.	The teacher uses well-crafted tasks and activities that are mostly aligned to the learning goals and will provide evidence of student progress toward those goals.	The teacher uses a series of integrated, well-crafted tasks and activities that are tightly aligned to the learning goals and will provide evidence of student progress toward those goals.
	....	....	....	....
	Most students are unclear about how they need to approach the task, and students require extensive repeated or revised explanations.	Many students are unclear about how they need to approach the task, and the teacher takes some time to repeat or revise explanations.	A few students are unclear about how they need to approach the task, and the teacher takes minimal time to repeat or revise explanations.	Most or all students are clear about how they need to approach the task and are able to begin work efficiently.
	....	....	....	....
	The teacher does not review student work products during the lesson or does not indicate when they will be reviewed.	The teacher occasionally or haphazardly reviews student work products during the lesson or makes a vague reference to when they will be reviewed.	The teacher reviews student work products during the lesson in a way that provides insight into most students' progress or indicates how work products will be reviewed later.	The teacher systematically reviews student work products during the lesson in a way that provides insight into most or all students' progress or clearly indicates how they will be reviewed and how the information will be used to inform instruction.

approach them, and professional judgment should be used to distinguish between genuine confusion about the task that could have been avoided and productive confusion as students grapple with complex ideas. Students may be off-task due to reasons unrelated to the clarity of the task or directions, but that is not part of the scoring considerations for this dimension.

- You may observe cases of the teacher working with a small group of students (while other students are working independently). Apply the Tasks rubric to the small-group work as if the small group is the whole class. While the teacher could score high on this dimension, if the teacher does not collect any evidence of the other students' learning, that will be reflected in the *Use of Evidence to Inform Instruction* dimension.

The final row of this rubric discusses the teacher's review of (or intent to review) the student work products. The highest level of the rubric requires a teacher to indicate how the student work products will be reviewed; however, it does not require the teacher to make inferences about student progress or to adjust instruction. Evidence of the latter practice will be captured in the *Use of Evidence to Inform Instruction* dimension.

10

CONCLUSION

Why Formative Assessment is Always Both Domain-General and Domain-Specific and What Matters is the Balance Between the Two

Dylan Wiliam

Over the last 50 years, evidence has mounted that assessment can be used to improve the quality of instruction as well as measure its effects. While there is some debate about the magnitude of that improvement, there appears to be an increasing consensus that the use of classroom formative assessment needs to be part of any attempt to improve the quality of schools and teachers, and to increase student achievement. As a result of this consensus, attention has shifted to consideration of how teachers can best be supported in developing their use of classroom formative assessment. While providing this support requires addressing a number of complex issues regarding the nature and feasibility of formative assessment, one issue that has been a particular focus of recent debate has been the domain-specificity of formative assessment. Can formative assessment be regarded as a more-or-less generic process, with professional development support for teachers being provided in a similar way to all teachers? Or, on the other hand, must support for teachers in their development of formative assessment practice be designed and delivered in a domain-specific way, with teachers of different subjects given different kinds of support?

The tendency in the research literature has been toward the former approach, while the chapters in this book offer helpful illustrations of how formative assessment can be implemented in different domains. The authors of the contributions to this collection take different positions on the extent to which formative assessment needs to be treated as a generic process. Some, such as Heritage and Wylie, adopt a generic definition of formative assessment and explore how the generic processes can be implemented in a particular domain, while others, such as Jönsson and Eriksson, argue that formative assessment needs to be defined in a way that is specific to the domain under consideration. In their chapter, Deane and Sparks suggest that, according generic aspects of formative assessment anything more than a minor role fundamentally undermines its potential, and that formative assessment must be discipline-specific. In their different ways, each of the chapters provide a useful counterbalance to arguments that formative assessment is an essentially generic process.

In this chapter, I want to argue for an intermediate position. I want to suggest that the best answer to the question of the domain-specificity of formative assessment is that formative assessment is irreducibly both domain-specific *and* domain-general, as implemented in the King's-Medway-Oxfordshire Formative Assessment Project (Black, et al., 2003). In that project, a group of 24 (later 36) science and math teachers met every six weeks to explore formative assessment practice, with each one-day workshop including generic sessions, where teachers were introduced to central ideas about formative assessment, and domain-specific sessions, where teachers explored the implications of those generic principles for their subject. In other words, following Bennett (2011), I want to suggest that the answer to the question about the domain-specificity of formative assessment is "both/and" rather than "either/or."

I begin by briefly reviewing the development of formative assessment, and then discussing two central issues about how formative assessment should be defined. First, should formative assessment be defined descriptively or prescriptively: should definitions of formative assessment describe how the term is actually used, or should they provide guidance about how formative assessment should be implemented? Second, I discuss whether definitions of formative assessment should take into account what students should learn, how we decide what it means to know something, what happens when learning takes place or the instructional activities that students should engage in. The chapter concludes with a report of a large-scale randomized controlled trial of a generic approach to formative assessment that produced significant increases in student achievement at minimal cost (Speckesser et al., 2018), suggesting that the optimal approach to using formative assessment to improve student achievement at scale has to recognize that formative assessment is both domain-general and domain-specific.

Formative Assessment: Origins and Antecedents

Half a century ago, David Ausubel (1968) suggested that formative assessment was at the heart of effective instruction: "If I had to reduce all of educational psychology to just one principle, I would say this: The most important single factor influencing learning is what the learner already knows. Ascertain this and teach him [or her] accordingly" (Ausubel, 1968, p. vi). The same year, Benjamin Bloom outlined an approach to instruction that he called *mastery learning* (B. S. Bloom, 1968). The key idea in Bloom's approach was that perhaps as many as 90% of students could master what they were being taught in schools if their educational experiences were explicitly designed to achieve this goal. At the time, it was widely believed that high levels of educational achievement were possible only for the most able students, a belief that was no doubt in part reinforced by the high correlations observed between aptitude test scores and measures of educational achievement.

Rejecting such a belief, Bloom adopted John Carroll's definition of aptitude as the amount of time needed to attain mastery of a learning task under optimal conditions so that, given enough time, any student could attain mastery of a learning task, although Carroll himself (1963) acknowledged that the amount of extra time needed might be very great. He estimated that a student at the 5th percentile of aptitude would take five years to learn what would take a student at the 95th percentile of aptitude just one year to learn.[1]

This represented a profound shift in perspective. With the old model, teachers taught, and some students learned the material and others did not, with the result that educational achievement was normally distributed. Under Bloom's mastery model, a normal distribution was a sign of instructional failure: "In fact, we may even insist that our educational efforts have been unsuccessful to the extent to which our distribution of achievement approximates the normal distribution" (B. S. Bloom, 1968, p. 3).

The reason that this shift was so profound, at least from the point of view of teaching, was that, with such a perspective, teaching became a *contingent* activity. However carefully teachers planned their instruction, they would not be able to predict in advance how much time would be needed by each of their students. Some form of assessment of the achievement of students would be needed to determine whether the required level of mastery had been reached. Assessment was now an integral part of instruction.

Of course, the idea that students do not always learn what they are taught has probably been around for as long as people have been trying to teach others to do anything. And where instruction was individualized—as it was, for example in Frederic Burk's Individual System (Reiser, 1986), the Winnetka Plan (Washburne, 1941), the Dalton Plan (Parkhurst, 1922), or the Kent Mathematics Project (Banks, 1991)—the idea that the next steps in learning would be determined by the student's current level of achievement was an inherent feature. In such schemes, teaching was always a contingent activity. But such an approach was not common within the educational mainstream, and that is why Bloom's proposals were so radical.

In Bloom's approach, the time needed for a student to gain mastery would be revealed by periodic assessments of student progress:

> Much of what we have been discussing in the section on the effects of examinations has been concerned with what may be termed "summative evaluation." This is the evaluation which is used at the end of a course, term, or educational program. Although the procedures for such evaluation may have a profound effect on the learning and instruction, much of this effect may be in anticipation of the examination or as a short- or long-term consequence of the examination after it has been given.
>
> Quite in contrast is the use of "formative evaluation" to provide feedback and correctives at each stage in the teaching-learning process. By formative evaluation, we mean evaluation by brief tests used by teachers and students as aids in the learning process. While such tests may be graded and used as part of the judging and classificatory function of evaluation, we see much more effective use of formative evaluation if it is separated from the grading process and used primarily as an aid to teaching.
>
> (B. S. Bloom, 1969, pp. 47–48)

The terms *formative* and *summative* had been proposed by Michael Scriven in response to a paper in which Lee Cronbach (1963) had suggested that asking an evaluator to determine the effectiveness of an educational program at the end of the development process was to offer the evaluator "a menial role and to make meager use of his services" (Cronbach, 1963, p. 3). Scriven (1963) pointed out that "there are many contexts in which calling in an evaluator to perform a final evaluation of the project or person is an act of proper recognition of responsibility to the person, product, or taxpayers" (Scriven, 1963, p. 7). Rejecting the idea that this was a menial role, he said, "It is obviously a great service if this kind of terminal evaluation (we might call it *summative* as opposed to *formative* evaluation) can demonstrate that an expensive textbook is not significantly better than the competition, or that it is enormously better than any competitor" (p. 5). In this context it is worth noting that this paper (or a revised version published some years later by the American Educational Research Association) are often cited as the source of the term *formative evaluation* when, in fact, it seems that it was the term *summative* that Scriven was proposing as novel.

It is also worth noting that while it is appropriate to attribute the formative-summative distinction to Scriven (in terms of curriculum, texts, or individual teachers) and Bloom (in terms of students), it is important to realize that the qualifiers formative and summative did not represent new distinctions in the role that evaluation might play—in fact, these ideas had been around for decades. What was new was the labels, as a way of clarifying the debate.

Defining Formative Assessment

Since the pioneering work of Bloom, the idea that assessment can improve instruction as well as measure its results has become an important element in efforts to improve the educational achievement of students all around the world. Some authors (for example, Broadfoot et al., 1999) have suggested using the term *assessment for learning* in place of formative assessment, while others such as Calkins, Ehrenworth, and Akhmedjanova (Chapter 8, this volume) use the terms interchangeably. However, as Bennett (2011) has pointed out, this change merely shifts the definitional burden. More importantly, at least in the way the term is typically used, assessment for learning is a much broader term than formative assessment, as Black et al., (2004) explained:

Assessment for learning is any assessment for which the first priority in its design and practice is to serve the purpose of promoting students' learning. It thus differs from assessment designed primarily to serve the purposes of accountability, or of ranking, or of certifying competence. An assessment activity can help learning if it provides information that teachers, and their students, can use as feedback in assessing themselves and one another, and in modifying the teaching and learning activities in which they are engaged. Such assessment becomes "formative assessment" when the evidence is actually used to adapt the teaching work to meet learning needs.

(p. 10)

This is an important distinction because assessments that are given to motivate students (see, for example, Assessment Reform Group, 2002) or to provide retrieval practice (see, for example, Roediger III & Butler, 2011) would, under many if not most definitions, be regarded as assessment for learning. However, it seems unlikely that many people would regard an assessment that was scheduled but not administered, or administered but not looked at further by either teachers or students, as formative.

Still others (Earl & Katz, 2006) have used the term assessment for learning more restrictively, to focus on the role of teachers, suggesting that the learner's role should be described as *assessment as learning* (Dann, 2002; Earl, 2003). While it is obviously attractive that students might be learning something while they are being assessed, as Bennett (Chapter 2, this volume) points out, equating assessment with learning undermines the idea that both assessment for learning and assessment as learning should be regarded first and foremost as *assessment*. To equate assessment—probably best defined as a process of evidentiary reasoning (Mislevy, Almond, & Lukas, 2003)—with learning—defined by Kirschner, Sweller, and Clark (2006) as "a change in long-term memory" (p. 75) is unlikely to be helpful in clarifying the debate.

More importantly, as Cizek, Andrade, and Bennett (Chapter 1, this volume) note, not only is there no agreement about the terms that we should use, there is also no agreement about how to define formative assessment. This is not because people have not tried to define formative assessment. Indeed, there is no shortage of proposed definitions, and several of these are discussed by Cizek, Andrade, and Bennett. In my view, one of the most important reasons for the lack of agreement about the definition of formative assessment is because most of the definitions of formative assessment that have been proposed over the years, including those in the chapters of this volume, are, in essence, prescriptive. The desire for such prescriptive formulations is, of course, understandable, not least because it is natural to want to ensure that formative assessment is as effective as possible. Indeed, a major strength of the chapters in this volume, and a reason that they make important contributions to how we might improve formative assessment practice, is that they lay out in great detail how formative assessment might be implemented in particular disciplines, and these proposals seem to me to be eminently sensible. However, where such prescriptions are treated as definitions, the effect is to treat all approaches that do not conform to the definition as not being formative assessment, which is unfortunate for at least two reasons.

The first reason is that such an approach leaves little room for the creativity of teachers. For example, Cizek, Andrade, and Bennett acknowledge that

Whereas an assessment that was explicitly designed as a summative assessment *could* be used in a formative manner (and vice versa), that would clearly not be an optimal situation. Rather, a characteristic of any sound assessment is that it is used in the way it was designed.

(Chapter 1, this book, p. 4; emphasis in the original)

This may be good general advice, but as an empirical statement, it is unlikely to be correct.[2] For example, if a teacher were preparing a group of students for the College Board's Advanced

Conclusion

Placement (AP) examination in history, the teacher might ask the students to take a practice test under formal test conditions. As well as providing an opportunity to familiarize the students with the test, such an occasion would also provide retrieval practice for the students, thus increasing their learning (Brown, Roediger III, & McDaniel, 2014). At the end of the allocated time, the teacher could collect and grade the students' responses, but an alternative would be to collect the responses and, several days later, give the completed response sheets back to the students and ask them, in groups of four, to compare their responses for each of the questions in the test and produce the best possible composite response. For students with incorrect answers, especially where they were confident their answers were correct, this exercise would lead to further learning via the hypercorrection effect (Butterfield & Metcalfe, 2001). Mindful of the work of Graham Nuthall (2007) that showed that the advice given by a student's peers was often misleading at best, and often just incorrect, the teacher might then lead a whole class discussion in which each group shares its answer with the class and the teacher ensures that the students' understanding of the material is appropriate.

This use of the AP exam would appear to be one that is unlikely to have been envisaged by its designers, since the program was originally created to allow advanced high school students to earn college placement and course credit at higher education institutions. And yet, given that for many students the goal is to gain the highest score they can on the test, it seems perverse to regard this use of the AP test as inappropriate. Indeed, given the goals of the students, it might very well be optimal in terms of the additional learning generated and the time taken.

For another example of how a prescriptive definition leaves little room for the creativity of teachers, consider the definition of formative assessment proposed by the Council of Chief State School Officers (2008): "Formative assessment is a process used by teachers and students during instruction that provides feedback to adjust ongoing teaching and learning to improve students' achievements of intended instructional outcomes" (p. 3). While this definition is attractive as guidance for how to implement effective formative assessment, any assessment that was used by a teacher to improve her instruction without the involvement of her students would not, under this definition, qualify as formative assessment. Clearly, for a number of reasons, the involvement of students in their own learning is desirable, but the CCSSO definition decrees that any use of assessment that is not shared by both teachers and students is not formative.

This problem is even more marked in the revised CCSSO definition adopted by Heritage and Wylie (Chapter 9, this volume):

> formative assessment is a planned, ongoing process used by all students and teachers during learning and teaching to elicit and use evidence of student learning to improve student understanding of intended disciplinary learning outcomes, and support students to become self-directed learners.
>
> Effective use of the formative assessment process requires students and teachers to integrate and embed the following practices in a collaborative and respectful classroom environment:
>
> - Clarifying learning goals and success criteria within a broader progression of learning;
> - Eliciting and analyzing evidence of student thinking;
> - Engaging in self-assessment and peer feedback;
> - Providing actionable feedback; and
> - Using evidence and feedback to move learning forward by adjusting learning strategies, goals or next instructional steps.
>
> *(Council of Chief State School Officers, 2018)*

While these are clearly helpful suggestions for improving the use of formative assessment in practice, the normative element here is particularly strong—and in my view, unhelpful. For example:

- if an assessment process is not planned, then according to this definition, it cannot be formative;
- if all students are not involved, it cannot be formative;
- if the assessment process helps teachers adjust instruction in a way that improves learning but does not support students in becoming self-directed learners, then it is not formative;
- if the five listed practices are not integrated, then the process is not formative assessment.
- if the classroom environment is not collaborative and respectful, then there can be no formative assessment;
- if the learning goals are not located within a broader progression of learning, then there can be no formative assessment. In this context, it is worth noting that, as Calkins, Ehrenworth, and Akhmedjanova (Chapter 8, this volume) point out, the learning progressions provided in the Common Core State Standards for opinion writing do not appear to reflect the developmental sequence followed by the majority of learners;
- if the assessment is used to improve non-disciplinary goals, such as well-being or mindfulness, then the assessment cannot be formative.

It is also worth noting that the second paragraph, in its use of the word "effective," makes a strong empirical claim for which no evidence is presented, and is unlikely, in fact, to be true, since the claim being made here is that where the five listed processes are not integrated and embedded, the formative assessment process will not be effective. In the KMOFAP project, participating teachers were explicitly required to focus their development efforts on just one or two strategies, and yet the project appears to have had a substantial impact on student achievement, improving student achievement on the English national school leaving examinations by around 0.32 standard deviations (Wiliam et al., 2004).

Similar arguments can be made about the definition of formative assessment adopted by Calkins, Ehrenworth, and Akhmedjanova (Chapter 8, this volume), which is adapted from Stiggins (2010), although it is worth noting that Stiggins proposed the definition as applying to all classroom assessment, including assessment for summative purposes, and not only formative assessment. Calkins, Ehrenworth, and Akhmedjanova suggest that:

> formative assessment practices applied in classrooms should include: (1) clear purposes for assessing student work, (2) clear targets for what is being assessed, (3) high-quality assessment designs for all assessment materials, (4) effective communication about what the results of assessment indicate about student learning, and (5) students' active participation in formative assessment.
>
> *(Chapter 8, this volume, p. 174)*

The implication here again is that assessment that does not, for example, require students' active participation cannot be formative.

To be clear, I am not objecting to any of the features of these different definitions as being ways to maximize the power of formative assessment. But to claim that these features *define* formative assessment is to render any practices that do not conform to a particular vision as not being formative assessment. Such a restrictive definition of formative assessment is at best unhelpful, and possibly completely counterproductive.

A second, and perhaps even more important, objection to the use of normative or prescriptive definitions is that they merely serve to perpetuate the definitional debate. As Cizek, Andrade, and Bennett (Chapter 2, this volume) point out, several writers, such as Shepard (2008) and Popham (2006), have quite rightly criticized the use of the term formative assessment when used to claim legitimacy for something that is not supported by the research cited, as when research on classroom formative assessment is asserted to support the use of benchmark or interim tests as mechanisms for improving student achievement—a version of Kelley's jingle fallacy in which two things with the

Conclusion

same name are assumed to be the same (Kelley, 1927). However, while the evidence often cited in support of benchmark or interim testing does not support the claims being made, it does not follow that the claims are not true—absence of evidence is not necessarily evidence of absence. In this particular case, there are both logical and empirical arguments that show that benchmark or interim assessment can improve student achievement.

Start with the logical basis. It is obviously useful for school leaders to know whether students are actually learning anything in their schools, and the assurances of teachers that everything is on track are unlikely to be enough, so some kind of reasonably objective measure of student progress is essential to effective management of a school—after all any well-run organization should have ways of determining whether it is making progress toward its goals. And if different teachers of students in the same grade set their own assessments, it is difficult to compare results across classes, which is why the idea that teachers should create, curate, or adopt common assessments across their classes is so powerful. When some students are found to be making less progress than needed to be ready for the next grade, then appropriate action can be taken.

Moreover, there is empirical evidence that such approaches have been successful in improving student achievement. Saunders, Goldenberg, and Gallimore (2009) worked with instructional data teams in nine elementary schools in Southern California and found that, over a five-year period, students in these schools made significantly greater progress on standardized tests and other achievement measures than students in six comparable schools. They reported an effect size of 0.79 at the teacher level. Assuming a correlation of 0.15 between teacher quality and student achievement (Hanushek & Rivkin, 2010), this would represent an increase in student achievement of 0.12 standard deviations. Using norms developed by H. S. Bloom, et al., (2008) for children in third through fifth grade, such an effect size would represent an increase in the rate of learning somewhere between 20% and 40%. Given the time invested by the teachers, such an intervention could be a highly cost-effective way of improving student achievement. Similar benefits of the use of interim or benchmark assessments were found by Barry and Leslie Pulliam in the Focus on Standards program, which involved teachers comparing student performance on tests with their state standards, and their curriculum resources (Goe & Bridgeman, 2006). So while Shepard and Popham are quite correct to point out that the use of benchmark and interim assessments is not justified by the research that is generally cited, it is not correct to say that such uses have no evidence in their support.

In response, it could be argued that the term formative assessment should be reserved for uses of assessment that are relatively close to instruction, and a term such as formative evaluation could be used to describe more distal uses of assessment to improve learning. However, given that those advocating for interim and benchmark assessment have substantial investments in the term "formative assessment" (DuFour, 2007), it seems unlikely that calls for such definitional clarity will be heeded.

To summarize, while it is clearly a matter of judgment whether formative assessment is defined descriptively or prescriptively, defining formative assessment prescriptively is likely to result in the exclusion of many uses of assessment that do, in fact, improve learning, and which many people would regard as formative. Whatever one thinks about the use of benchmark or interim tests to monitor student progress and to align curriculum, such assessments are, in the literal sense of the term, functioning formatively, especially when such tests are keyed to the instruction that students have received as they were in the work of the Pulliams. Evidence of achievement is being elicited, interpreted, and used to make decisions about instruction that are likely to benefit students. To say that such assessment processes are not formative is to redefine the term *formative* in a way that is completely at variance with its use in natural language, and indeed, at variance with the sense that the term was proposed by Scriven and Bloom.

A prescriptive definition of formative assessment will, therefore, in my view, make it harder for academics and practitioners ever to reach an agreed definition. It would, of course, be wonderful if—upon being told that what they regard as formative assessment is not, in fact, formative assessment—those individuals and entities with different views accepted this, stopped using the term, and looked for another term to describe their practices. It seems to me, however, that this is extremely unlikely. Rather, restricting the definition of formative assessment to a subset of the ways in which it is currently used practically guarantees that no agreed definition will ever be established. Instead, what is needed is to develop an inclusive definition of formative assessment that excludes none of the processes that are, within reason, described as formative assessment. Put bluntly, we should not make the word *formative* work too hard. Formative should just mean formative, so that we can then focus on the features that make formative assessment more-or-less effective.

As a matter of practical necessity, therefore, formative assessment needs to be defined in a descriptive and inclusive way, rather than in a prescriptive, normative manner. The next issue that arises is the scope of the definition. As each of the chapters in this volume have pointed out, formative assessment practices must take account of the domain being assessed. What is less clear, however, is whether the nature of the domain entails any commitments about how formative assessment should be defined.

Four Issues About How We Define Formative Assessment

The next section addresses four questions about how formative assessment can or should be defined, and in particular examines whether commitments to formative assessment necessarily entail a particular view of what students should be learning, what it means to know something, what happens when learning takes place, and what kinds of pedagogical activities teachers should arrange for their students.

Does a Commitment to Formative Assessment Entail a Commitment About What is to be Learned?

Most of the chapters in this collection discuss aspects of formative assessment from a particular set of assumptions about what is to be learned. Bennett (Chapter 2., this volume) suggests that "reasoning about assessment design starts with articulating the claims to be made from assessment results about individuals or institutions" and that "Those claims should derive directly from state content standards, cognitive-domain theory, curriculum frameworks, learning objectives, or some combination of these sources" (p. 20).

While such clarity about educational outcomes may well be desirable, as Calkins, Ehrenworth, and Akhmedjanova (Chapter 8, this volume) and Andrade, Hefferend, and Palma (Chapter 6, this volume) point out, sometimes it is not possible to codify the quality of work in formal standards, theories, curriculum frameworks, or learning objectives. Sometimes, the best that we can do is to help students develop what Claxton (1995) describes as a "nose" for quality. Students become enculturated into a particular community of practice in which their teachers are already participants. Effective formative assessment then requires teachers to possess, in addition to a shared construct of quality, an understanding of the "anatomy" of quality, so that they can identify instructional next steps that may not be related in any obvious way to the goal, but do help students to progress (see discussion of cognitive load theory below).

Moreover, in many parts of the world, teachers determine their instructional goals not by reference to formal standards or curriculum frameworks of learning objectives, but by reference to the examinations their students need to pass. In many countries, these examinations are accompanied by examination syllabuses that specify what may, and may not, be assessed, but typically these are written at a level of generality that provides little guidance for teachers. For this reason, teachers determine priorities for instruction by looking at the examination papers that have been set in previous years (which are usually readily available and accessible). Even in countries like the US,

Conclusion

where state content standards are provided, the relationship between what is specified and what is assessed is far from straightforward. Sometimes this ambiguity is due to the technical inadequacy of the assessments used in that state, but often it arises from a mismatch between the specified content and the means of assessment. For example, Common Core state standard number 8(c) for mathematics requires students to "design and use a simulation to generate frequencies for compound events" (Common Core State Standards Initiative, 2010, p. 51). However, whether this could be meaningfully assessed in a standardized test, especially one that relied on multiple-choice items, is doubtful. Where teachers are under pressure to raise test scores, especially given the fact that most state content standards contain more content than most students can learn in a year, teachers may well choose not to spend time on material like this that is unlikely to be assessed. This is not to condone such behavior, but merely to point out that what a particular teacher is trying to achieve cannot be determined by the officially mandated curricula that are in place.

The two chapters in this collection that address science education (Jönsson and Eriksson, Chapter 7, this volume; Furtak, Heredia and Morrison, Chapter 5, this volume) define the goals of science education so as to include knowledge about science as a social and cultural practice, as well as the concepts, theories, and models that scientists have generated. In particular, Furtak, Heredia and Morrison show that, around the world, there is increasing consensus that science education should include both the things that scientists have found out and how such knowledge is generated. However, it is important to note that these are arbitrary choices (in the original sense of requiring judgment). In many countries, science education does not include science as a cultural and social practice. Any approach to formative assessment that entails an acceptance of a particular definition of what students should learn is likely to be unhelpful to those who define science, or for whom science is defined, in a different way.

In a similar vein, Jönsson and Eriksson (Chapter 7, this volume) draw three distinctions between higher education and earlier phases of education, in terms of the autonomy of the learner, the size of classes, and connections to research. First, while it is certainly true that many of those involved in teaching in higher education see the development of learner autonomy as a key outcome, others do not, and many elementary school teachers would also claim that learner autonomy is a key aim for them and their students too. The *extent* to which autonomy is a goal for education may vary from one phase of education to another, but it is a difference in degree, rather than kind. Second, while classes in undergraduate education can be very large, they are often not, with seminar groups often composed of 20 or fewer students. And in sub-Saharan Africa, classes of 70 or more are common in elementary schools. Again, the variation within each phase is much greater than the difference between the phases. Third, while it is true that many higher education institutions do claim that having students being taught by active researchers is a benefit, there is little evidence to show this belief is true, and, in most higher education institutions in the US, let alone the rest of the world, research is a marginal activity for those involved in teaching undergraduates (and teaching is often a marginal activity for those involved in research).

As a third example, Andrade, Hefferen, and Palma (Chapter 6, this volume) define arts education as focusing on creativity, and while such a view may well be agreed to by many, and perhaps almost all, arts teachers, it is far from clear whether this stipulation is essential. For example, many instrumental music teachers do not regard creativity as particularly important, at least while a student is learning an instrument.

If we are to have broadly agreed definitions of formative assessment, it, therefore, seems essential that a commitment to formative assessment entails nothing about what students are to be learning, since different teachers may well have different goals. State standards include far more material for each grade than most students can learn—presumably because the standards are designed to keep the fastest-learning students occupied for the whole year. But, following Carroll (1963), this position means that there is far too much for most students to learn, and so teachers have to make choices about what to teach. Such choices will depend on the kinds of state tests in place, and even such prosaic factors as whether the teacher has tenure. Teachers are placed in an impossible position, and have to make compromises, taking a number of factors into account, and so teachers do need to be clear about what their students are to learn—in fact, formative assessment can only begin once the teacher is clear about the purpose of instruction. But, as noted above, any approach to defining formative assessment that entails a particular set of assumptions about what students are to learn renders formative assessment irrelevant in many settings. Given the reasonably clear evidence about the effectiveness of formative assessment to raise student achievement even where such achievement is measured through standardized tests, anything that dissuades teachers from embracing formative assessment because of the restrictions applied is, in effect, a way of lowering student achievement.

Does a Commitment to Formative Assessment Entail a Commitment About What it Means to Know Something?

As well as making assumptions about what students should be learning, most of the chapters in this volume also make a number of epistemological assumptions—assumptions about what it means to know or understand something. Most science curricula require that, at some point in their school careers, students learn Archimedes' principle. However, what is often less clear is what it means to know Archimedes' principle. At one level, we might be content that a student can recite the principle in the standard form: "Any object, wholly or partially immersed in a fluid, is buoyed up by a force equal to the weight of the fluid displaced by the object."

A student who can recite this definition could be said to "know" Archimedes' principle, but others, such as Gobert et al. (2011) have argued that while knowing science does require knowing how to state scientific principles, students also have to be able to use the principles to reason scientifically. Even here, quite what we mean by being able to use a principle varies. We might say that a student knows Archimedes' principle if she can use it to explain why ice floats, or we could be more demanding and say that they only really know it if they can use it to answer questions such as the following:

> Someone sits in a boat in a swimming pool holding a 10kg mass. What happens to the level of the water in the pool if the mass is dropped into the swimming pool?

Being able to answer such questions would entail a far deeper knowledge of the subject matter than just being able to answer simple questions about why ice floats, although the basic concepts are identical.

The important point here is that people may reasonably disagree about what it means to understand Archimedes' principle, and so in that same way that a commitment to formative assessment cannot entail any particular commitment about what students are to learn, a commitment to formative assessment cannot entail any commitment about what it means to know. Those ideas must be clarified before formative assessment can begin.

Does a Commitment to Formative Assessment Entail Any View About What Happens When Learning Takes Place?

In recent years, a number of authors have suggested that a commitment to formative assessment necessitates a socio-cognitive, or a socio-cultural perspective on psychology (see, for example, Shepard, Penuel, & Pellegrino, 2018), but again, whether such commitments are necessarily entailed is open to question, and depends on one's views about what happens when learning takes place.

In the 1960s, the prevalent idea that learning was simply making links between stimuli and responses came into question because such a model would predict that students' errors should be random, whereas, particularly in mathematics and science education, students' errors were to a significant extent predictable (Driver & Easley, 1978; Hart, 1981). Students were not "misremembering" what they had been taught but were rather constructing their own knowledge on the basis of their experience of the world. Learning was an active "constructive" process. Constructivism, as a view of what happens what learning takes place, accounted for many observed phenomena, such as misconceptions, that were not explained well by associationist views of learning. However, constructivism was not particularly effective in explaining aspects of learning, such as learning number facts, that associationist approaches explained well. In psychology, each new theory about what happens when learning takes place is very good at explaining things that the pre-existing theories did not, but are often not very good at explaining what the pre-existing theories explained well. Unlike in science—where newer theories tend to subsume previous theories, in the way that Einstein's approach to physics includes Newton's ideas as special cases—in psychology, new theories tend to provide different perspectives rather than more complete solutions. This is why Anna Sfard (1998) stresses that we need multiple—often incommensurable—perspectives on learning, rather than trying to figure out which is the best, or more complete theory.

For example, when students learn that there is a single electron in the outer shell of a sodium atom, which is why it bonds with a single atom of chlorine to make salt, there is not much to "understand" here. There is no point in asking why an atom of sodium has a single electron in its outer shell. Students just need to know that the atoms of the element that we call sodium happen to have a single electron in the outer shell. If, on the other hand, we are trying to figure out why many young children believe that wind is caused by the movement of trees, then associationist approaches are unhelpful. This "misconception" is not the result of poor-quality science instruction, nor is it the result of insufficient reinforcement of the correct links between stimuli and responses. Rather it is the result of students creating schemas to make sense of their experience. While some people adopt entrenched positions on such issues, it probably makes more sense to acknowledge that some aspects of learning science are best described by the former approach, which we might call an associationist approach, while some are more like the latter which we might call a constructivist approach.

A commitment to formative assessment, therefore, should not entail any particular commitment to what happens when learning takes place. Formative assessment is necessary, because, as Ausubel (1968) noted, good instruction starts from where the learner is, and because what students learn as a result of any particular sequence of instruction is impossible to predict with any certainty. For those who believe that learning is a matter of making associations between stimuli and responses, then it is impossible to predict in advance how much reinforcement will be required before the associations are established, so establishing what has been learned and then taking appropriate remedial action is essential. For those who believe that students construct their own knowledge about the world, then we need to find out what sense the students have made of their instructional experiences. For those who adopt situated perspectives on learning, it is necessary to determine the extent to which a student's performance in a particular task is the result of attunements to affordances or constraints in a particular environment. Those with different views about what happens when learning takes place may have different reasons for using formative assessment, but a commitment to formative assessment cannot entail a commitment about what happens when learning takes place.

Does a Commitment to Formative Assessment Entail Any Commitment About How Students Should Be Taught?

Several of the chapters make implicit claims about the kinds of pedagogical activities that are likely to promote strong disciplinary learning. For example, Burkhardt and Schoenfeld (Chapter 3, this volume) suggest that widely employed imitative methods such as "I do, we do, you do" "cannot address the now-generally-accepted importance of extended autonomous reasoning, including non-routine thinking and problem solving" (p. 35). No evidence is provided in support of this claim, and recent work in cognitive psychology suggests that it may be incorrect. For example, John Sweller and his colleagues have provided considerable evidence that, for novices, worked examples, with guidance being progressively faded, result in superior learning about mathematical problem solving than more "authentic" activities (Sweller, Kalyuga, & Ayres, 2011). While the full implications of cognitive load theory are still being explored, there is now considerable evidence that in many cases, inquiry-based approaches to learning may be less effective, at least for some learners.

Similar arguments apply in the context of attempts to make science more interesting to students through the use of more inquiry-based approaches to instruction, and especially those that attempt to engage students with "real" contexts, such as the Red Fox task discussed by Furtak, Heredia, and Morrison (Chapter 5, this volume). The task was developed by a group of high school biology teachers "to connect with students' lived experiences in observing red foxes in the communities around their homes" (p. 100). Where students are not particularly interested in science, then approaches of this sort may be necessary to increase student engagement, but it is important to note that while inquiry-based instruction appears to increase student engagement in science, its impact on student achievement is far from clear. Indeed, in the most recent round of the Programme for International Student Assessment (PISA), the prevalence of inquiry-based instruction was negatively correlated with student achievement in science (Organisation for Economic Co-operation and Development, 2016: Figure II.7.2). Now, of course, it could be that teachers who teach low-achieving students make greater use of inquiry-based instruction in order to increase student engagement—the direction of causality is unclear—but it does at least raise questions about what makes for effective instruction.

My aim here is not to present arguments for or against the respective merits of different approaches to instruction. Rather it is to point out that, given the great uncertainty about what kinds of instructional approaches work best, and in which circumstances, a definition of formative assessment that entails any commitment about what kinds of learning activities should be employed immediately condemns itself to irrelevance in many settings.

The rather extended discussion of these four questions leads, inevitably, I believe, to the conclusion that any definition of formative assessment should entail absolutely no commitments whatsoever about what students are to learn, what it means to know, what happens when learning takes place, and what activities are likely to be most effective in getting students to learn. A commitment to formative assessment does, to be sure, require that we take into account what students are to learn, what it means to know, what happens when learning takes place, and what kinds of instructional activities are likely to be successful. But we should not define formative assessment in a way that, for example, rejects as illegitimate a belief that history is about learning facts and dates, that knowing simply means being able to reproduce what one has been taught, that learning is just making links between stimuli and responses, and that students learn best through lectures. For the avoidance of doubt, these are not positions that I am defending—in fact, I disagree with each of these propositions. What I am saying is that debates about the adequacy of such ideas should be discussed separately, and should not be smuggled in through the way we define formative assessment.

If we are to maximize the power of formative assessment to improve student learning, we need to frame definitions that include, rather than exclude, and encompass all the ways that the term formative assessment is used. It was this concern to be inclusive that led Paul Black and myself (2009) to suggest that assessment functions formatively

> to the extent that evidence about student achievement is elicited, interpreted, and used by teachers, learners, or their peers, to make decisions about the next steps in instruction that are likely to be better, or better founded, than the decisions they would have taken in the absence of the evidence that was elicited
>
> *(Black & Wiliam, 2009, p. 9)*

Conclusion

A full description of the rationale for this definition can be found in Black and Wiliam (2009), but for the purpose of the present discussion the important feature of this definition is that it is inclusive of all the ways that the term formative assessment is currently used: from interim or benchmark assessments administered monthly or even quarterly and used to align curriculum and monitor student progress, to the minute-by-minute use of assessment to judge the level of understanding of a particular concept in a group of students. It focuses on assessment as measurement, as advocated by Bennett (Chapter 2, this volume) and its role in evidentiary reasoning, and does not require that the assessment actually improves learning—only that it is likely to. This definition is also consistent with the idea that the formative-summative distinction is a distinction about the kinds of inferences supported by assessments, rather than in terms of assessment instruments, or assessment outcomes (Black & Wiliam, 2018).

Adopting an inclusive definition matters, because discussion can then move on from the relatively unproductive boundary disputes about whether certain practices are, or are not, examples of formative assessment to the more important and substantive issues about whether, and if so, by how much, and under what circumstances, student achievement is increased through the use of such assessment. In particular, given the focus of this book, it is important to discuss the extent to which formative assessment can be successfully implemented as a domain-general process and the extent to which student learning is improved by emphasizing the idea of formative assessment as a domain-specific process.

Before further discussing the extent to which it is helpful to regard formative assessment as domain-specific versus domain-general, it is important to point out that the terms *domain*-specific and *discipline*-specific are not equivalent. Good formative assessment in science looks different from good formative assessment in English language arts at least partly because of the differences in the subject matter being taught. However, it is important to note that while some of those differences are inherent in the discipline, others are not. For example, in the teaching of science in most countries, more time is spent teaching students about the knowledge that science has generated than on how science generated that knowledge. It is therefore not surprising that formative assessment practices in science classrooms often bear strong similarities to formative assessment practices in math classrooms, with, for example, a focus on alternative conceptions or facets of knowledge (Minstrell, 1992). In contrast, particularly in the Anglophone countries, English language arts instruction focuses on students' experiences, and their personal responses to text, so that formative assessment practices often look very different from those in math and science classrooms. However, it is important to recognize that the ways that school curricula are developed represent a series of choices about what students should be learning in school—in Denis Lawton's memorable phrase, a curriculum is "essentially a selection from the culture of a society" (Lawton, 1975, p. 7)—and that different choices could have been made. For example, in the second half of the nineteenth century, it was common to find students in English language arts classrooms analyzing sentences by drawing diagrams (Edgar, 1915). The kinds of formative assessment practices that would be used in such a classroom would resemble much more closely those used today in science and math classrooms than those used in English language arts classrooms. In contrast, if a class were discussing the ethical implications of, say, genetically-modified foods, the discussion would resemble the kind of discussions common in English language arts and social studies classrooms, with consequent implications for the most appropriate formative assessment practices.

The important point here is that different ways of defining a school subject will result in different implications for formative assessment practice. Knowing which *discipline* is being taught tells us very little about what kinds of formative assessment practice would be appropriate. Knowing how the discipline has been defined within the school curriculum, on the other hand, would be much more informative. The *domain* matters much more than the *discipline*.

Dylan Wiliam

Domain-General and Domain-Specific Approaches to Professional Development for Formative Assessment: Empirical Evidence

In debating the respective merits of domain-general and domain-specific approaches to formative assessment, it is important to note that the extreme positions in this debate—that formative assessment is entirely domain-specific or entirely domain-general—are demonstrably absurd. Formative assessment is, obviously, both domain-general and domain-specific. The idea that a teacher's instructional decisions are likely to be better if evidence about current understandings are collected from all the students in a group, rather than just the individuals who are confident enough to volunteer answers, can be applied to any group teaching situation, and so as a technique is completely generic. I do not need to know what you are teaching to know that evidence from all the students in the group about their current level of understanding of the material being taught is likely to result in better instructional decisions. At the other extreme, the questions that teachers need to ask to determine whether their students have understood the material being taught can only be determined with substantial content knowledge. As has been said several times, what is important, therefore, are the trade-offs that occur when we treat formative assessment as more generic or more subject-specific.

The chapters in this volume clearly demonstrate the advantages, for teachers and for students, of operationalizing formative assessment in a domain-specific way. However, there are also a number of disadvantages. First, it makes it more difficult for teachers to learn from teachers of other subjects, since a common language of description is less likely to be developed (Black et al., 2003). Second, students' experiences in school will become less coherent, since teachers in different domains may define the same processes differently, and different processes may be defined similarly (Kelley's "jingle-jangle" fallacies again). Third, administrators are likely to find it more difficult to support teachers, and getting access to the domain-specific expertise is likely to be challenging, particularly in small school districts, and for domains outside the core subjects of math, English language arts, science, and social studies. Fourth, developing whole-school policies is likely to be more difficult, making system-wide implementation of formative assessment more difficult to secure (Thompson & Wiliam, 2008).

The challenge, then, is to define formative assessment as a generic process, but to do it in a way that accommodates domain-specific definitions and practices that are, as far as possible, both consistent with the generic approach, and do not conflict with definitions and practices that are used in other domains. Or, to put it another way, we need to determine the extent to which formative assessment can be usefully and productively defined and operationalized as a generic process, and to what extent it is necessary for the practice of formative assessment to take into account the discipline or the domain.

One way to achieve such a framework would be to survey practice in different disciplines and look for commonalities. As Jönsson and Eriksson (Chapter 7, this volume) point out, many approaches to formative assessment in effect do exactly that. The result is that any collection of practices thus identified will lack a strong theoretical foundation which makes it more difficult to identify whether different techniques conflict, and it is also impossible to determine whether the totality of practices is complete.

To provide a theoretically-grounded approach to the operationalization of formative assessment, my colleagues and I began by identifying what we thought would be more-or-less universally agreed assumptions.

We began by looking at formative assessment as a process of closing the gap between current and desired levels of achievement as suggested by Ramaprasad (1983) and D. R. Sadler (1989). However, while this idea seemed to be acceptable to many teachers, some teachers, particularly those from English language arts and the creative arts (art, music, dance, drama) found the idea of a "gap" between current and desired levels of achievement an unhelpful way of thinking about their practice (Marshall, 2000).

For this reason, when we sought to theorize formative assessment, we looked for starting points that would be likely to be agreed by all teachers. As an absolute minimum, it seemed to us that teaching should be an intentional process. In other words, the teacher should have some idea of what

Conclusion

kinds of changes they seek to effect in their students. These ideas might be expressed as learning targets, goals, aims, or objectives, but could also take the form of implicit understandings of what it means to participate in a particular domain (Sfard, 1998). Whether or not they can be expressed in words, any instruction should start with some intentions about what students should learn.

Once the intentions have been defined, then, returning to Ausubel's (1968) principle for instruction, the crucial processes are to establish:

1 Where the learners are in their learning
2 Where they are going
3 How to get there

Crossing these three processes with the three kinds of agents in the classroom—the student, their peers, and the teacher—produces a 3 × 3 grid, which can be simplified to yield five strategies of formative assessment, as shown in Table 10.1 (Leahy et al., 2005; Wiliam & Thompson, 2008).

This framework provides a useful way of integrating research literature from a number of fields (Education Endowment Foundation, 2018), and, most important, seems to be accessible to teachers, and useful in their daily work. As just one example, this framework has been adopted by the Singapore Ministry of Education as a central element of its Primary Education Review and Implementation—Holistic Assessment (PERI-HA) program, and has been implemented in over two-thirds of the nation's elementary schools (Tan et al., 2014).

In addition, while some of the original nine cells have been merged in order to make the framework easier to use and apply, as a study by Chen et al. (2017) discussed by Andrade, Hefferen, and Palma (Chapter 6, this volume) shows, the merged cells can be unmerged in order to make important distinctions in particular contexts. However, perhaps the main strength of this framework is as a general one for thinking about formative assessment that applies to all disciplines, allowing the specificities of each discipline or domain to be honored within a coherent structure.

Ultimately, however, the argument about the extent to which formative assessment needs to be conceptualized in a domain-specific way, or can be treated generically, is, at its heart, an empirical question. Most of the chapters in this collection argue that student learning is enhanced when formative assessment is conceptualized in a discipline-specific, or domain-specific way. Now at one level, as mentioned earlier, this is obviously true. Formative assessment has to be conceptualized in a domain-specific way. Formative assessment involves the collection of evidence about student achievement, and without a clear idea about what students should be learning, it is impossible to know what evidence would be relevant. And while Furtak, Heredia, and Morrison (Chapter 5, this volume) note that many science educators have objected to the term "misconception" for describing students' non-standard or incomplete ideas about scientific topics, students do seem to learn more when they are taught by teachers who know the misconceptions that students are likely to have (P. M. Sadler et al., 2013). Similarly, while it is possible to formulate general principles about good feedback such as "make feedback into detective work" (Wiliam & Leahy, 2015, p. 124), actually doing this requires detailed subject knowledge, as does activating students as learning resources for one another, and as owners of their

Table 10.1 Five Strategies of Formative Assessment (Wiliam & Thompson, 2008)

	Where learner is going	*Where learner is now*	*How to get the learner there*
Teacher	Clarifying, sharing, and understanding learning intentions and criteria for success	Eliciting evidence	Providing feedback that moves learning forward
Peer		Activating students as learning resources for one another	
Learner		Activating students as owners of their own learning	

own learning. This is what prompted Paul Black, myself, and our colleagues to co-author a series of short booklets for teachers with subject-specialists in English (Marshall & Wiliam, 2006), mathematics (Hodgen & Wiliam, 2006), science (Black & Harrison, 2002), modern foreign languages (Jones & Wiliam, 2007), geography (Lambert & Weeden, 2006), information and communications technology (Cox & Webb, 2007), design and technology (Moreland, Jones, & Barlex, 2008) as well as a similar booklet for elementary school teachers (Harrison & Howard, 2009).

But the arguments about the necessity for domain-specific approaches to formative assessment made in this collection are, implicitly, making a stronger claim. They are arguing that it is necessary to draw out the implications of generic strategies for particular domains in order to help teachers implement formative assessment more effectively. After all, if defining formative assessment in a subject-specific way, or drawing out the domain-specific implications of particular strategies, had no impact on student achievement, there would be little point in doing so.

The key question, therefore, is to what extent providing guidance to practitioners about the implementation of formative assessment practices in specific domains increases the impact on student achievement? This is the focus of the remainder of this chapter.

First, it is worth pointing out while the chapters in this collection present thoughtful ways of implementing formative assessment in the disciplines that are consistent with the research evidence, the majority of the chapters present little or no empirical evidence that domain-specific approaches to the development of formative assessment are in fact more effective.

As Burkhardt and Schoenfeld (Chapter 3, this volume) report, the 8 to 12 days devoted to "formative assessment lessons" developed by the Mathematics Assessment Project resulted in increased student achievement. However, it is not clear whether this can be attributed to formative assessment, since the intervention also included a series of high-quality lesson plans, which may have made a substantial contribution to the improvements in achievement (Jackson & Makarin, 2016). The project evaluators (Herman et al., 2015) found that the mathematics achievement of students working with the formative assessment lessons was 0.13 standard deviations higher than comparable students, which they equate to an extra 4.6 months of learning, using norms derived by Howard Bloom and his colleagues from standardized tests (H. S. Bloom et al., 2008; Hill et al., 2007). However, the tests used to evaluate the formative assessment lessons were developed by the Mathematics Development Collaborative and, because of the way the tests were developed, they are likely to be more sensitive to the effects of instruction than the traditional standardized tests analyzed by Bloom and his colleagues. As a result, the effect of the formative assessment lessons may be somewhat overestimated.

More positively, Andrade, Hefferen, and Palma (Chapter 6, this volume) report on studies undertaken through the Arts Achieve project that showed students taught by teachers receiving a two-year professional development program focused on formative assessment made more progress than students taught by other teachers. Although the study was designed as a cluster-randomized trial, the low fidelity of implementation by some teachers led the researchers to use propensity-score matching to compare teachers who implemented the program with fidelity to matched teachers who were not exposed to the program, and found a net effect of 0.26 standard deviations. Interpreting this result is not straightforward for several reasons. First, the teachers who did not implement the program with fidelity may be less competent, and so it is not possible to attribute the effects to the professional development. Second, since the project included elementary, middle, and high school teachers, it is not clear what kinds of norms would be most appropriate to convert the effect size into a rate measure such as the number of extra months of learning. Third, the assessments used in the study may have been, like the measures used by Burkhardt and Schoenfeld, more sensitive to the effects of instruction. Nevertheless, this result represents a substantial increase in the rate of learning, and close to the median found for formative assessment programs in other subjects (Kingston & Nash, 2011, 2015).

To examine the empirical claim that teacher professional development in formative assessment needs to be domain-specific, it is instructive to compare the effect sizes reported by Burkhardt and

Conclusion

Schoenfeld and by Andrade, Hefferen, and Palma with those obtained from a recently conducted evaluation of a generic, whole-school professional development program.

Embedding Formative Assessment (EFA; Leahy & Wiliam, 2013) is a two-year professional development program developed from the Keeping Learning on Track program discussed by Andrade, Hefferen, and Palma (Chapter 6, this volume). The EFA program was designed to be delivered within schools with minimal additional cost, and without any external facilitation, not because such facilitation would not be helpful, but rather because, in many local education authorities, particularly in the United States, such additional resources cannot easily be found from school budgets. Even where such funds are available at a particular point in time, budgets are often volatile, and where cuts have to be made quickly, professional development appears to be a particularly convenient place to make them. For this reason, it was determined that to be sustainable, a teacher professional development program could not require anything more than minimal additional cost.

The EFA program consists of all the materials and handouts needed to run 18 monthly Teacher Learning Community (TLC) meetings of 75 to 90 minutes duration, over a two-year period, together with videos of classroom practice exemplifying formative assessment practices, interviews with educators, administrators and students, and a variety of other relevant resources.

Through the EFA program, teachers are introduced to the five strategies of formative assessment suggested by Leahy et al. (2005) and shown in Table 10.1 above. At each meeting, each TLC member commits to trying out at least one strategy in their classroom, and at the next meeting, the following month, they report back to their peers on their experiences. Teachers are also encouraged to observe each other and give each other feedback on their development of formative assessment.

While the program has been implemented in a number of countries, including Sweden, Australia, England, and Scotland, and was found to be helpful by teachers and administrators, there was little more than anecdotal evidence that the program actually increased student achievement. Accordingly, the Education Endowment Foundation—a UK-based philanthropic organization—funded an evaluation of the program in secondary schools in England, which was awarded to the UK's National Institute for Economic and Social Research (NIESR).

The NIESR estimated that a cluster-randomized trial of the program with an 80% chance to detect an effect size of 0.2 standard deviations would require 140 schools, since randomization would need to take place at the school level (as teachers in the same school could be expected to talk to each other). The study took the form of a preregistered "intention to treat" study,[3] with half the schools allocated at random to receive the EFA materials, and the other half being given the cash equivalent of the cost of the materials (approximately $500 at the exchange rate prevailing at the start of the study). This last feature is particularly important because the analysis took no account of the fidelity of implementation in the experimental schools. The performance of all students in the study cohort in the schools allocated to the experimental group was compared to that of all students in the control group, unlike the study reported in Andrade, Hefferen, and Palma (Chapter 6, this volume).

After schools had been recruited, and allocated to either the treatment or control group, it was discovered that some of the schools had already participated in a professional development program titled the Teacher Effectiveness Enhancement Programme (TEEP), which included many elements of the EFA program. It was decided that these schools should not be included in the main analysis, leaving a total of 58 schools assigned to receive the EFA material, and 66 schools receiving the cash equivalent.

The measure of achievement used in the study was the average grade (on a nine-point scale) received by students in England's national school leaving examination, the General Certificate of Secondary Education (GCSE), in mathematics, English, and their best six other subjects.[4] This composite measure, which is called Attainment 8, is the key measure that is used to hold schools accountable for the academic achievement of their students and the grades that students achieve on their GCSE examinations are also important determinants of their options for future study and employment. The outcome measure that was used in this evaluation is, therefore, a measure that is of great concern both to schools and to their students. In total data were collected on 22,709 students in the participating schools who commenced their studies in September 2015 and took their school leaving examinations in June 2017.

A full description of the research protocols can be found in Speckesser et al. (2018). The primary analysis consisted of fitting two models to the data:

> A "simple" model, including prior attainment and allocation dummy variables as fixed covariates, with school as a random effect.
>
> A "precise" model, including prior attainment, the allocation dummy and indicator variables specifying membership of the randomization blocks (all fixed effects) and schools as a random effect.

The average Attainment 8 scores for students in the original 70 treatment schools were 0.10 standard deviations higher than for those in the original 70 control schools, and this result was not statistically significant. However, when comparing the 58 experimental schools and the 66 control schools that had not been exposed to the TEEP program—arguably a fairer comparison of the effect of the EFA program—students in the experimental schools scored 0.13 standard deviations higher, and the result was statistically significant ($p=0.04$).

To interpret this effect in terms of increases in the rate of learning, it is necessary to estimate the progress made over two years by students in the control group. These students were 15 years old at the beginning of the trial. The norms produced by H. S. Bloom et al. (2008) discussed above suggest that one year's progress for 15-year-old students is approximately 0.2 standard deviations, while NAEP scores increase by about one standard deviation over four years, suggesting an annual equivalent of 0.25 standard deviations (National Assessment of Educational Progress, 2013). On the other hand, Rodriguez (2004) estimates that for eighth-grade students on the mathematics tests used in the Trends in Mathematics and Science Study, one year's progress is 0.36 standard deviations. Finally, the Organisation for Economic Co-operation and Development assumes that one year's growth for 15-year-olds on the tests used in the Programme for International Student Assessment (PISA) is 0.3 standard deviations (Andreas Schleicher, personal communication, November 14th, 2018). Given these results, it seems reasonable to assume that one year's progress for students in the control group would be in the range of 0.2 to 0.4 standard deviations, with 0.3 as a reasonable central estimate.

Since the program spanned two school years, it is necessary to make some allowance for the attrition of student learning from the first to the second year of students' GCSE studies. In a meta-analysis of 39 studies, mostly from the 1970s and 1980s, Cooper et al. (1996) found an attrition of around 10% of learning from one year to the next. However, other studies have found much larger estimates. For example, using data from the North West Evaluation Association's Measures of Academic Progress test, Thum and Hauser (2015) found attrition rates of 25% for reading and as much as 40% for math. Given this, it would appear that assuming an attrition rate of 10% is conservative.

Students in England take their GCSE examinations half-way through the third and final term of the English academic year—in other words, the final year of the GCSE program is really only five-sixths of a year, so over the two years of their GCSE studies, students in the control group could be expected to increase their achievement by:

> First-year growth × 0.9 [to account for attrition] + second year growth × 5/6 [to account for the shorter second year]

Using the range of estimates of annual growth from 0.2 to 0.4 discussed above yields an expected increase in the range of 0.35 to 0.69, with a central value of 0.52. Since the effect of the EFA program

Conclusion

over the two years was to increase student achievement by 0.13 standard deviations, this suggests that the program increased the rate of student learning between 19% and 38%, with a central estimate of 25%. Given that this increase is the average across all students in the experimental group—not just those who implemented the program with fidelity—this is an important finding. Given also that the additional cost of the program is less than $2 per student per year, this suggests that the program is highly cost-effective. Moreover, the fact that the EFA is a generic program, which was delivered at scale with minimal support provided to schools, suggests that it has the potential to significantly increase student achievement, at scale, in a sustainable way, within existing resources constraints.

Conclusion

The main argument of this chapter is that the most productive way of implementing formative assessment at scale is to recognize that formative assessment has both generic and domain-specific elements. The chapters in this volume provide detailed, important, and useful guidance on the practical issues that need to be considered when implementing classroom formative assessment. Formative assessment in English is different from formative assessment in mathematics, which is in turn different from formative assessment in science. While some of these differences are more to do with the way that the subjects have been defined in school curricula rather than anything inherent in the discipline, supporting teachers in their development of classroom formative assessment has to recognize the realities of their classrooms. However, to make students' school experiences more coherent, to allow schools to create a shared language of description in order to improve communication between teachers, it is also important to recognize that many aspects of formative assessment—including its definition—can and should be addressed generically.

Moreover, as the evaluation of the EFA project above shows, there is now clear evidence that generic approaches to teacher professional development can be effective. However, the available empirical evidence does also suggest that approaches to formative assessment that take into account the particular issues involved in implementing formative assessment in different disciplines and domains do produce somewhat larger effect sizes. Obviously, more research will be needed to refine the somewhat limited evidence of effectiveness that has been discussed here, but it does seem to indicate that attempts to harness the power of formative assessment need to recognize that it is both subject-specific and generic.

Perhaps the fundamental question, in taking this work forward, is whether it is more fruitful, in the development of formative assessment practice, to work top-down or bottom-up. In other words, should we start with generic approaches to formative assessment, and explore how these approaches can best be implemented in particular domains? Or would it be better to begin with detailed conceptualizations of domains, and then select particular formative assessment strategies that would appear to be especially relevant for that domain? Further work in articulating the differences between these two approaches, and their implications for practice, would allow the strengths and weakness of the two approaches to be investigated empirically. What the available evidence does show is that formative assessment represents an extremely powerful focus for effective, scalable, teacher professional development. While finding the optimum balance between generic and domain-specific approaches is likely to be challenging, the potential benefits for learners suggest that it is likely to be a highly productive focus for future work.

Notes

1 This might seem like a strong claim, but it is consistent with some other estimates of the differences in rates of learning between high achievers and low achievers (see, for example, Wiliam, 1992)

2 The use of the word "sound" here in effect renders the statement unfalsifiable, since any exceptions can be defined as unsound—a debating technique that that Anthony Flew (1975) describes as a "no true Scotsman" move (p. 47).

3 The study was pre-registered as ISRCTN ISRCTN10973392 at https://www.isrctn.com/ISRCTN10973392.
4 This is, in fact, a slight simplification. The Attainment 8 score is based on the student's grade in math, English language, the three best grades in the subjects included in the English baccalaureate (science, foreign languages, history, geography), and their three best GCSE or equivalent grades in other subjects, with the grades for math and English being double-weighted.

References

Assessment Reform Group. (2002). *Assessment for learning: Ten research-based principles to guide classroom practice.* Cambridge, UK: University of Cambridge Faculty of Education.

Ausubel, D. P. (1968). *Educational psychology: A cognitive view.* New York, NY: Holt, Rinehart & Winston.

Banks, B. (1991). *The KMP way to learn maths: A history of the early development of the Kent Mathematics Project.* Maidstone, UK: Bertram Banks.

Bennett, R. E. (2011). Formative assessment: A critical review. *Assessment in Education: Principles Policy and Practice, 18*(1), 5–25.

Black, P. & Harrison, C. (2002). *Science inside the black box: Assessment for learning in the science classroom.* London, UK: King's College London Department of Education and Professional Studies.

Black, P., Harrison, C., Lee, C., Marshall, B., & Wiliam, D. (2003). *Assessment for learning: Putting it into practice.* Buckingham, UK: Open University Press.

Black, P., Harrison, C., Lee, C., Marshall, B., & Wiliam, D. (2004). Working inside the black box: Assessment for learning in the classroom. *Phi Delta Kappan, 86*(1), 8–21.

Black, P. & Wiliam, D. (2009). Developing the theory of formative assessment. *Educational Assessment, Evaluation and Accountability, 21*(1), 5–31.

Black, P. & Wiliam, D. (2018). Classroom assessment and pedagogy. *Assessment in Education: Principles, Policy & Practice, 25.* DOI 10.1080/0969594X.2018.1441807.

Bloom, B. S. (1968). Learning for mastery. *Evaluation Comment, 1*(2), 1–12.

Bloom, B. S. (1969). Some theoretical issues relating to educational evaluation. In R. W. Tyler (Ed.), *Educational evaluation: New roles, new means* (Vol. 68(2), pp. 26–50). Chicago, IL: University of Chicago Press.

Bloom, H. S., Hill, C. J., Black, A. R., & Lipsey, M. W. (2008). Performance trajectories and performance gaps as achievement effect-size benchmarks for educational interventions. *Journal of Research on Educational Effectiveness, 1*(4), 289–328.

Broadfoot, P. M., Daugherty, R., Gardner, J., Gipps, C. V., Harlen, W., James, M., & Stobart, G. (1999). *Assessment for learning: Beyond the black box.* Cambridge, UK: University of Cambridge School of Education.

Brown, P. C., Roediger III, H. L., & McDaniel, M. A. (2014). *Make it stick: The science of successful learning.* Cambridge, MA: Belknap Press.

Butterfield, B. & Metcalfe, J. (2001). Errors committed with high confidence are hypercorrected. *Journal of Experimental Psychology: Learning, Memory, and Cognition, 27*(6), 1491–1494.

Carroll, J. B. (1963). A model for school learning. *Teachers College Record, 64*(8), 723–733.

Chen, F., Lui, A. M., Andrade, H., Valle, C., & Mir, H. (2017). Criteria-referenced formative assessment in the arts. *Educational Assessment, Evaluation and Accountability, 29*(3), 297–314. DOI 10.1007/s11092-017-9259-z.

Claxton, G. L. (1995). What kind of learning does self-assessment drive? Developing a "nose" for quality: Comments on Klenowski. *Assessment in Education: principles, policy and practice, 2*(3), 339–343.

Common Core State Standards Initiative. (2010). *Common core state standards for mathematics.* Washington, DC: National Governors Association/Council of Chief State School Officers.

Cooper, H., Nye, B. A., Charlton, K., Lindsay, J., & Greathouse, S. (1996). The effects of summer vacation on achievement test scores: A narrative and meta-analytic review. *Review of Educational Research, 66*(3), 227–268.

Council of Chief State School Officers. (2008). *Attributes of effective formative assessment.* Washington, DC: Council of Chief State School Officers.

Council of Chief State School Officers. (2018). *Revising the definition of formative assessment.* Washington, DC: Council of Chief State School Officers.

Cox, M. & Webb, M. (2007). *Information and communication technology inside the black box: Assessment for learning in the ICT classroom.* London, UK: NFER-Nelson.

Cronbach, L. J. (1963). Course improvements through evaluation. *Teachers College Record, 64*(8), 672–683.

Dann, R. (2002). *Promoting assessment as learning: improving the learning process.* London, UK: RoutledgeFalmer.

Driver, R. & Easley, J. (1978). Pupils and paradigms: A review of literature related to concept development in adolescent science students. *Studies in Science Education, 5*(1), 61–84. DOI: 10.1080/03057267808559857.

DuFour, R. (2007, July 30). Common formative assessments. *All Things PLC.* Retrieved from http://www.allthingsplc.info/blog/view/14/common-formative-assessments.

Conclusion

Earl, L. M. (2003). *Assessment as learning: Using classroom assessment to maximize student learning.* Thousand Oaks, CA: Corwin.

Earl, L. M. & Katz, S. (2006). *Rethinking classroom assessment with purpose in mind: Assessment for learning, assessment as learning, assessment of learning.* Winnipeg, MB: Manitoba Education, Citizenship and Youth.

Edgar, H. C. (1915). *Sentence analysis by diagram: A handbook for the rapid review of English syntax.* New York, NY: Newson & Company.

Education Endowment Foundation. (2018). Teaching and learning toolkit. Retrieved January 8, 2018, from https://educationendowmentfoundation.org.uk/evidence-summaries/teaching-learning-toolkit.

Flew, A. (1975). *Thinking about thinking: Do I sincerely want to be right?* London, UK: Fontana.

Gobert, J. D., O'Dwyer, L., Horwitz, P., Buckley, B. C., Levy, S. T., & Wilensky, U. (2011). Examining the relationship between students' understanding of the nature of models and conceptual learning in biology, physics, and chemistry. *International Journal of Science Education, 33*(5), 653–684. DOI 10.1080/09500691003720671.

Goe, L. & Bridgeman, B. (2006). *Effects of Focus on Standards on academic performance.* Princeton, NJ: Educational Testing Service.

Hanushek, E. A. & Rivkin, S. G. (2010). Generalizations about using value-added measures of teacher quality. *American Economic Review, 100*(2), 267–271.

Harrison, C. & Howard, S. (2009). *Inside the primary black box: Assessment for learning in primary and early years classrooms.* London, UK: NFER-Nelson.

Hart, K. M. (Ed.). (1981). *Children's understanding of mathematics: 11–16.* London, UK: John Murray.

Herman, J., Matrundola, D. L. T., Epstein, S., Leon, S., Dai, Y., Reber, S., & Choi, K. (2015). *The implementation and effects of the mathematics design collaborative (MDC): Early findings from Kentucky ninth-grade Algebra 1 courses.* Los Angeles, CA: National Center for Research on Evaluation, Standards, and Student Testing.

Hill, C. J., Bloom, H. S., Black, A. R., & Lipsey, M. W. (2007). *Empirical benchmarks for interpreting effect sizes in research.* New York, NY: MDRC.

Hodgen, J. & Wiliam, D. (2006). *Mathematics inside the black box: Assessment for learning in the mathematics classroom.* London, UK: NFER-Nelson.

Jackson, C. K. & Makarin, A. (2016). *Simplifying teaching: A field experiment with online "off-the-shelf" lessons.* Cambridge, MA: National Bureau of Economic Research.

Jones, J. & Wiliam, D. (2007). *Modern foreign languages inside the black box: Assessment for learning in the modern foreign languages classroom.* London, UK: Granada.

Kelley, T. L. (1927). *Interpretation of educational measurements.* Yonkers-on-Hudson, NY: World Book Company.

Kingston, N. M. & Nash, B. (2011). Formative assessment: A meta-analysis and a call for research. *Educational Measurement: Issues and Practice, 30*(4), 28–37.

Kingston, N. M. & Nash, B. (2015). Erratum. *Educational Measurement: Issues and Practice, 34*(1), 55.

Kirschner, P. A., Sweller, J., & Clark, R. E. (2006). Why minimal guidance during instruction does not work: An analysis of the failure of constructivist, problem-based, experiential, and inquiry-based teaching. *Educational Psychologist, 41*(2), 75–86.

Lambert, D. & Weeden, P. (2006). *Geography inside the black box.* London, UK: NFER-Nelson.

Lawton, D. L. (1975). *Class, culture and the curriculum.* London, UK: Routledge and Kegan Paul.

Leahy, S., Lyon, C., Thompson, M., & Wiliam, D. (2005). Classroom assessment: Minute-by-minute and day-by-day. *Educational Leadership, 63*(3), 18–24.

Leahy, S. & Wiliam, D. (2013). *Embedding formative assessment.* London, UK: Specialist Schools and Academies Trust.

Marshall, B. (2000). A rough guide to English teachers. *English in Education, 34*(1), 24–41.

Marshall, B. & Wiliam, D. (2006). *English inside the black box: Assessment for learning in the English classroom.* London, UK: NFER-Nelson.

Minstrell, J. (1992). Facets of students' knowledge and relevant instruction. In R. Duit, F. M. Goldberg & H. Niedderer (Eds.), *Research in physics learning: Theoretical issues and empirical studies (Proceedings of an international workshop held at the University of Bremen, March 4–8, 1991)* (pp. 110–128). Kiel, Germany: Institut für die Pädagogik der Naturwissenschaften an der Universität Kiel.

Mislevy, R. J., Almond, R. G., & Lukas, J. F. (2003). *A brief introduction to evidence centered design* (Vol. RR-03-16). Princeton, NJ: Educational Testing Service.

Moreland, J., Jones, A., & Barlex, D. (2008). *Design and technology inside the black box: Assessment for learning in the design and technology classroom.* London, UK: NFER-Nelson.

National Assessment of Educational Progress. (2013). *Trends in academic progress: Reading 1971–2012, mathematics 1973–2012.* Washington, DC: United States Department of Education.

Nuthall, G. (2007). *The hidden lives of learners.* Wellington, NZ: New Zealand Council for Educational Research.

Organisation for Economic Co-operation and Development. (2016). *PISA 2015 results: Policies and practices for successful schools* (Vol. 2). Paris, France: Organisation for Economic Co-operation and Development.

Parkhurst, H. (1922). *Education on the Dalton Plan*. London, UK: G. Bell and Sons, Ltd.

Popham, W. J. (2006). Phony formative assessments: Buyer beware! *Educational Leadership, 64*(3), 86–87.

Ramaprasad, A. (1983). On the definition of feedback. *Behavioral Science, 28*(1), 4–13.

Reiser, R. A. (1986). Instructional technology: A history. In R. M. Gagné (Ed.), *Instructional technology: Foundations* (pp. 11–48). Hillsdale, NJ: Lawrence Erlbaum Associates.

Rodriguez, M. C. (2004). The role of classroom assessment in student performance on TIMSS. *Applied Measurement in Education, 17*(1), 1–24.

Roediger III, H. L. & Butler, A. C. (2011). The critical role of retrieval practice in long-term retention. *Trends in Cognitive Sciences, 15*(1), 20–27. DOI: 10.1016/j.tics.2010.09.003.

Sadler, D. R. (1989). Formative assessment and the design of instructional systems. *Instructional Science, 18*, 119–144.

Sadler, P. M., Sonnert, G., Coyle, H. P., Cook-Smith, N., & Miller, J. L. (2013). The influence of teachers' knowledge on student learning in middle school physical science classrooms. *American Educational Research Journal, 50*(5), 1020–1049. DOI: 10.3102/0002831213477680.

Saunders, W. M., Goldenberg, C. N., & Gallimore, R. (2009). Increasing achievement by focusing grade level teams on improving classroom learning: A prospective, quasi-experimental study of title 1 schools. *American Educational Research Journal, 46*(4), 1006–1033.

Scriven, M. (1963). *The methodology of evaluation*. Lafayette, IN: Purdue University.

Schleicher, A. personal communication, November *14*, 2018.

Sfard, A. (1998). On two metaphors for learning and on the dangers of choosing just one. *Educational Researcher, 27*(2), 4–13.

Shepard, L. A. (2008). Formative assessment: Caveat emptor. In C. A. Dwyer (Ed.), *The future of assessment: shaping teaching and learning* (pp. 279–303). Mahwah, NJ: Lawrence Erlbaum Associates.

Shepard, L. A., Penuel, W. R., & Pellegrino, J. W. (2018). Using learning and motivation theories to coherently link formative assessment, grading practices, and large-scale assessment. *Educational Measurement: Issues and Practice, 37*(1), 21–34. DOI: 10.1111/emip.12189.

Speckesser, S., Runge, J., Foliano, F., Bursnall, M., Hudson-Sharp, N., Rolfe, H., & Anders, J. (2018). *Embedding Formative Assessment: Evaluation report and executive summary*. London, UK: Education Endowment Foundation.

Stiggins, R. (2010). Essential formative assessment competencies for teachers and school leaders. In H. L. Andrade & G. J. Cizek (Eds.), *Handbook of formative assessment* (pp. 233–250). New York, NY: Taylor & Francis.

Sweller, J., Kalyuga, S., & Ayres, P. (2011). *Cognitive load theory*. New York, NY: Springer.

Tan, F., Teng, E., Tan, J., & Peng, Y. W. (2014, May). *Holistic assessment implementation in Singapore primary schools part II: Developing teacher assessment capacity to improve student learning*. Paper presented at the Annual meeting of the International Association for Education Assessment,, Singapore.

Thompson, M. & Wiliam, D. (2008). Tight but loose: A conceptual framework for scaling up school reforms. In E. C. Wylie (Ed.), *Tight but loose: Scaling up teacher professional development in diverse contexts* (Vol. RR-08-29, pp. 1–44). Princeton, NJ: Educational Testing Service.

Thum, Y. M. & Hauser, C. H. (2015). *NWEA 2015 MAP norms for student and school achievement status and growth*. Portland, OR: North West Evaluation Association.

Washburne, C. (1941). *A living philosophy of education*. Chicago, IL: University of Chicago Press.

Wiliam, D. (1992). Special needs and the distribution of attainment in the national curriculum. *British Journal of Educational Psychology, 62*, 397–403.

Wiliam, D. & Leahy, S. (2015). *Embedding formative assessment: Practical techniques for K-12 classrooms*. West Palm Beach, FL: Learning Sciences International.

Wiliam, D., Lee, C., Harrison, C., & Black, P. J. (2004). Teachers developing assessment for learning: impact on student achievement. *Assessment in Education: Principles Policy and Practice, 11*(1), 49–65.

Wiliam, D. & Thompson, M. (2008). Integrating assessment with instruction: what will it take to make it work? In C. A. Dwyer (Ed.), *The future of assessment: shaping teaching and learning* (pp. 53–82). Mahwah, NJ: Lawrence Erlbaum Associates.

CONTRIBUTORS

Diana Akhmedjanova is a Doctoral Candidate in Educational Psychology and Methodology at the University at Albany/SUNY. She is originally from Tashkent, Uzbekistan, where she taught English as a foreign language. Her work focuses on self-regulated learning and formative assessment. Diana's dissertation is an examination of the effects of self-regulated learning on the quality of persuasive essays written by freshman international students. She is also involved in two projects: one on new ways of analyzing single-case experimental data, and one on diagnostic assessment and feedback for college students: https://demo.daacs.net/.

Heidi L. Andrade is a Professor and the Division Director of Educational Psychology and Methodology at the University at Albany/SUNY. Her work focuses on the relationships between learning and assessment, with emphases on student self-assessment and self-regulated learning. She has written many articles, including an award-winning article on rubrics for *Educational Leadership* (1996). She has authored, edited, and co-edited several books on classroom assessment, including the *Using Assessment to Enhance Learning, Achievement, and Academic Self-Regulation* (2017), the *SAGE Handbook of Research on Classroom Assessment* (2013), and the *Handbook of Formative Assessment* (2010). She has edited or co-edited special issues of *Theory Into Practice* (2009) and *Applied Measurement in Education* (2013). A long-term working relationship with arts educators in New York City has produced a collection of formative assessments for the arts: http://artsassessmentforlearning.org/about-assessment/. A current project involves the development of diagnostic assessments and feedback for newly enrolled college students: https://demo.daacs.net/.

Randy E. Bennett is Norman O. Frederiksen Chair in Assessment Innovation in the Research & Development Division at Educational Testing Service in Princeton, New Jersey. Dr. Bennett's work has focused on integrating advances in cognitive science, technology, and educational measurement to create approaches to assessment that have a positive impact on teaching and learning. From 1999 through 2005, he directed the National Assessment of Educational Progress (NAEP) Technology Based Assessment project, which included the first administration of computer-based performance assessments with nationally representative samples of school students, and the first use of "clickstream," or logfile, data in such samples to measure the processes used in problem solving. From 2007 to 2016, he directed an integrated research initiative titled Cognitively-Based Assessment of, for, and as Learning (CBAL), which focused on creating theory-based summative and formative assessment intended to model good teaching and learning practice. Randy Bennett is president of the International Association for Educational Assessment (IAEA), an organization primarily constituted of governmental and non-governmental nonprofit measurement organizations throughout the world, and past president of the National Council on Measurement in Education (NCME) (2017–2018), whose members are individuals employed primarily in universities, testing organizations, state education departments, and school districts. He is a Fellow of the American Educational Research Association.

Hugh Burkhardt is an Educational Engineer. His long career leading the team at the University of Nottingham's Shell Centre for Mathematical Education has been focused on research and development aimed at direct impact on educational practice around the world. This was recognized by the International Commission on Mathematical Instruction with its first Emma Castelnuovo Award for "the practice of mathematical education." His long-running collaboration with Alan Schoenfeld on assessment-led curriculum improvement embraced both balanced assessment—tests worth teaching to—and teaching materials that support both formative assessment and teacher development. Hugh founded the International Society for Design and Development in Education. He is currently focused on developing ways to improve the systemic process of research-based improvement— "making education more like medicine."

Lucy Calkins is the Founding Director of the Reading and Writing Project at Teachers College, Columbia University. For more than 30 years, the Project has been both a think tank, developing state-of-the-art teaching methods, and a provider of professional development. As the leader of this renowned organization, Lucy works closely with policy makers, school principals, and teachers to initiate and support schoolwide and system-wide reform in the teaching of reading and writing. Lucy is also the Robinson Professor of Children's Literacy and the co-director of the Literacy Specialist program at Teachers College, Columbia University. Lucy's many books include the seminal texts *The Art of Teaching Writing* and *The Art of Teaching Reading*, as well as the *Units of Study for Teaching Reading* (Grades K–8), *Units of Study in Opinion/Argument, Information, and Narrative Writing* (Grades K–8), the *Up the Ladder* writing units (Grades 3–6), the *Units of Study in Phonics* (Grades K–2), and *Leading Well: Building Schoolwide Excellence in Reading and Writing*.

Gregory J. Cizek is Guy B. Phillips Distinguished Professor of Educational Measurement and Evaluation at the University of North Carolina-Chapel Hill. His scholarly interests include standard setting, validity, test security, and testing policy. He is editor of the *Handbook of Educational Policy* (1999) and *Setting Performance Standards* (2001, 2012); co-editor of the *Handbook of Formative Assessment* (2010), and author of *Filling in the Blanks* (1999), *Cheating on Tests: How to Do It, Detect It, and Prevent It* (1999), *Detecting and Preventing Classroom Cheating* (2003), *Addressing Test Anxiety in a High-Stakes Environment* (with S. Burg, 2005), and co-author of *Standard Setting: A Practitioner's Guide* (2007). He provides expert consultation on testing programs and policy, including service on an advisory panel for the Smarter Balanced Assessment Consortium and as a member of the National Assessment Governing Board which oversees the National Assessment of Educational Progress (NAEP). He has held leadership positions in the American Educational Research Association (AERA) and is past President of the National Council on Measurement in Education (NCME). Dr. Cizek has worked on test development for a statewide testing program, for national licensure and certification programs, and has served as an elected member of a local board of education. He began his career as an elementary school teacher.

Paul D. Deane, a principal research scientist in Research & Development, earned a Ph.D. in linguistics at the University of Chicago in 1987. He is author of *Grammar in Mind and Brain* (1994), a study of the interaction of cognitive structures in syntax and semantics, and is co-author of

Contributors

Vocabulary Assessment to Support Instruction (McKeown, Deane, Scott, Krovetz, & Lawless, 2017). He taught English composition and linguistics at the University of Central Florida from 1986 to 1994. From 1994 to 2001, he worked in industrial natural language processing, where he focused on lexicon development, parser design, and semantic information retrieval. He joined Educational Testing Service in 2001. Deane's research interests include formative assessment design in the English Language Arts, cognitive models of writing skill, automated essay scoring, and vocabulary assessment. During his career at ETS he has worked on a variety of natural language processing and assessment projects, including automated item generation, tools to support verbal test development, scoring of collocation errors, reading and vocabulary assessment, and automated essay scoring. His work currently focuses on the assessment of English Language Arts skills and analysis of student digital logs that capture student writing processes.

Mary Ehrenworth is the Senior Deputy Director of the Reading and Writing Project at Teachers College, Columbia University. She works nationally and globally to empower teachers and students through critical literacy skills. Mary has authored or co-authored *Looking to Write, The Power of Grammar, Pathways to the Common Core*, many units of study in *Units of Study for Teaching Reading* (Grades K–8), and *Units of Study in Opinion/Argument, Information, and Narrative Writing* (Grades K–8), and *Leading Well: Building Schoolwide Excellence in Reading and Writing*. Among articles she has authored, recent publications include: "Those Who Can Coach Can Teach," in the *Journal of Adolescent Literacy*, "Unlocking the Secrets of Complex Texts," in *Educational Leadership*, "Growing Extraordinary Writers," in *The Reading Teacher*, and "Why Argue," in *Educational Leadership*.

Urban Eriksson, Ph.D., completed his teaching diploma at Lund University in 1992 in physics, astronomy, and mathematics for the upper secondary school level. He taught physics, astronomy, and mathematics for five years at an adult school and then, in 1997, got a permanent position as a lecturer at Kristianstad University. At Kristianstad University he taught physics and astronomy at various teacher education programs, from pre-school to upper secondary school teachers. During this period, he entered a Ph.D. program and graduated in 2014 at Uppsala University on a combined thesis in astronomy and astronomy education research, focusing on disciplinary discernment from semiotic resources, and in particular the competency to extrapolate three-dimensionality from 1D and 2D semiotic resources. He was promoted to Associate Professor in physics with a specialization in astronomy education research. In 2017, he got a position as researcher at the National Resource Center for Physics Education in Sweden, responsible for developing the center into a physics and astronomy education research division.

Erin Marie Furtak is the Associate Dean of Faculty and Professor of Science Education in the School of Education at the University of Colorado Boulder. Her research investigates the ways that secondary science teachers design and enact formative assessments, how this process informs teachers' learning and, in turn, how improvements in teachers' formative assessment practice over time relates to student achievement. Her findings have appeared in *Review of Educational Research*, the *Journal of Research in Science Teaching, Educational Measurement: Issues and Practice, Science Education*, and other venues. She has also written several books focused on formative assessment and science education reform, including *Formative Assessment for Secondary Science Teachers* (2009), *The Feedback Loop* (2016), and *Supporting Teachers' Formative Assessment Practice with Learning Progressions* (2018). She received the 2011 Presidential Early Career Award for Scientists and Engineers in recognition of her research investigating learning progressions as supports for teachers' formative assessment design and practice. She currently directs a long-term research-practice partnership, funded by the National Science Foundation and the Spencer Foundation, with a large, economically, culturally, linguistically, and ethnically diverse school district focused on supporting high school teachers' classroom assessment practices.

Contributors

Joanna Hefferen is the Director of Professional Development at ArtsConnection in NYC, where she oversees all professional learning programs. Ms. Hefferen has worked on nine US ED-funded arts education research initiatives focused on arts assessment. In partnership with NYC DOE Deputy Director of the Arts Maria Palma, she has co-directed *Artful Learning Communities (ALC I & II), Connected Learning Communities*, and curated a website: www.artsassessmentforlearning.org. She also designs and facilitates professional development on ArtsConnection's *Digital DELLTA (Developing English Language Literacy through the Arts)* a US ED initiative that engages middle school English Learners in theater and dance residencies focused on language acquisition through the use of student collaborative digital portfolios. A contributing writer on formative assessment articles published in arts education professional journals, Ms. Hefferen also contributed to *The New York City Blueprint for Teaching and Learning in Theater*. In addition, she has consulted with Henry Street Settlement, The New Jersey State Council on the Arts, the Boston Public Schools and the University of Massachusetts. She earned a B.A. in Theater Arts and Masters in Education from SUNY-Geneseo.

Sara C. Heredia is an Assistant Professor of Science Education in the School of Education at the University of North Carolina at Greensboro. Her research focuses on the design of professional learning opportunities that engage secondary science teachers in experiences that support them to facilitate student sense-making in their classrooms. She focuses on the ways in which teachers' school and district contexts matter for how they make decisions about reform implementation. She works in partnership with teachers, schools, and informal science institutions to create a network of support for implementation of science education reform. Her work has been published in research journals including the *Journal of Research in Science Teaching* and the *Journal of Science Teacher Education*, as well as practitioner journals such as *Science Scope* and *Connected Science Learning*.

Margaret Heritage is an independent consultant in education. For her entire career, her work has spanned both research and practice. In addition to spending many years in her native England as a practitioner, a university teacher, and an inspector of schools, she had an extensive period at UCLA, first as principal of the laboratory school of the Graduate School of Education and Information Students and then as an Assistant Director at the National Center for Research on Evaluation, Standards and Student Testing (CRESST) UCLA. She has also taught in the Departments of Education at UCLA and Stanford. Her current work centers on formative assessment and how formative assessment supports regulatory processes. Her recent books include *Using assessment to enhance learning, achievement, and academic self-regulation* (Routledge) with Heidi Andrade, and *Self-regulation: The role of language and formative assessment* (Harvard Education Press) with Alison Bailey

Anders Jönsson is a Professor of Education at Kristianstad University, Sweden, and Director of the research platform, Learning in Cooperation, which funds and facilitates educational research performed in collaboration between academia and schools/pre-schools. Previously, he was responsible for the development of national tests in science for 12-year-olds in Sweden, as well as support material for assessing science in Swedish compulsory school. Anders' research focuses on the relationships between learning and assessment, with emphases on communicating expectations through explicit criteria and students' use of feedback, but also on the impact on student learning from summative assessment practices, such as grading and national testing. Anders has authored, edited, and co-edited several books on classroom assessment in Swedish, including *Lärande bedömning* [Educational Assessment], *4th edition* (2017), *Prov eller bedömning* [Measurement or Assessment] (2018), and *Att bedöma och sätta betyg* [Assessing and Grading] (2013). He has also published a number of articles and book chapters in English.

Contributors

Deb Morrison collaborates with those involved in K-12 education to design equitable learning experiences for students and teachers, primarily within science education. Her research focuses on the ways in which those involved in systems of education navigate new identities and narratives of the way they engage in equitable educational practices. Dr. Morrison centers her research in practice, working with teachers, administrators and teacher educators in the use of formative assessment to uncover inequity and design equitable learning experiences. She is currently working at the University of Washington's Institute of Math and Science Education. She has a growing number of publications based empirical work as well as conceptual writing emerging from her theoretical grounding in critical race theory, design-based research, and action research. More information can be found at www.debmorrison.me.

Maria Palma, a Deputy Director in the New York City Department of Education Office of Arts and Special Projects, is an experienced arts educator and seasoned administrator. Ms. Palma has designed numerous professional development initiatives in the arts. She was part of the team that supported the NYCDOE's *Blueprints* and rolled out related professional development initiatives for arts educators in NYC. In her current role, she supports schools, administrators, and teachers in implementing quality standards-based arts education citywide. She has managed several USDOE grants including AEMDD 2004, PDAE 2005, PDAE 2008, and PDAE 2017. A highlight of her career has been working with Heidi Andrade and Joanna Hefferen to deepen arts educators' practice around formative assessment and harnessing the power of feedback to nurture students to think and work like artists.

Alan Schoenfeld is the Elizabeth and Edward Conner Professor of Education and Affiliated Professor of Mathematics at the University of California at Berkeley. He is a Fellow of AAAS and AERA, and a Laureate of the education honor society Kappa Delta Pi. He has served as President of AERA and Vice President of the National Academy of Education. Among his awards are the International Commission on Mathematics Instruction's Klein Medal, the highest international distinction in mathematics education, and AERA's Distinguished Contributions to Research in Education award. Schoenfeld's work is aimed at understanding and improving learning environments. He has focused on mathematical problem solving and mathematics assessments, both summative and formative. Formative assessment is one of five dimensions of his Teaching for Robust Understanding framework, known as TRU.

Jesse R. Sparks is a Research Scientist in the Cognitive Science Group in the Research & Development Division at Educational Testing Service (ETS) in Princeton, New Jersey. Her research leverages theories and findings from cognitive and learning sciences research to develop innovative assessments of 21st century skills that seek both to measure and to enhance students' critical reading, writing, and thinking skills when learning from texts or multimedia sources. Jesse received her Ph.D. in Learning Sciences from Northwestern University, focusing on students' critical evaluation of source credibility. Since joining ETS in 2013 to work on the Cognitively-Based Assessment of, for, and as Learning (CBAL) research initiative as an AERA-ETS postdoctoral fellow, her work has emphasized the development of cognitively-based frameworks and engaging task designs to measure critical research and inquiry skills in English language arts, science, and social science domains. This includes developing conceptual assessment frameworks for K-12 and higher education competencies, consulting on NAEP Reading and Social Sciences assessments in the design of interactive, scenario based tasks, conducting empirical studies examining effects of task designs on performance, and leading a multi-year project funded by the NAEP Survey Assessment Innovations Lab (SAIL). The SAIL initiative involves developing a virtual world environment for assessing and examining relationships among middle school students' multiple-document inquiry processes and final products using logfile data.

Contributors

Dylan Wiliam is the Emeritus Professor of Educational Assessment at UCL (University College London). In a varied career, he has taught in private and public schools, coordinated a large scale testing program, and served a number of roles in university administration, including Provost and Dean of a School of Education. From 2003 to 2006 he served as Senior Research Director at Educational Testing Service in Princeton, New Jersey. For the past 20 years, his work has focused on helping teachers develop their use of assessment in support of learning, often called *formative assessment* or *assessment for learning*. In addition to numerous academic and professional publications, he is the author of a number of books for educators and key stakeholders, including *Embedded Formative Assessment, Leadership for Teacher Learning,* and *Creating the Schools Our Children Need,* and the co-author, with Siobhan Leahy, of *Embedding Formative Assessment: Practical Techniques for K-12 Classrooms.*

Caroline Wylie is a Research Director in the Student and Teacher Research Center and Senior Research Scientist at ETS. Her current research centers on issues around balanced assessment systems, with a focus on the use of formative assessment to improve classroom teaching and learning. She has led studies related to the creation of effective, scalable, and sustainable teacher professional development focused on formative assessment, on the formative use of diagnostic questions for classroom-based assessment, assessment literacy, and on the role of learning progressions to support formative assessment in mathematics and science. She is specifically interested in issues of rater quality as it relates to formative classroom observations, and the relationship between observations, feedback, and changes to assessment practice. She began her career in education training to be a mathematics teacher in Belfast, Northern Ireland.

INDEX

Note: page numbers in italic type refer to Figures; those in bold type refer to Tables.

ACESSE project 119
ACT 175, 180, 184
action: on characterizations 21, 27–28; *see also* theory of action
Advanced Placement (AP) program 175, 180, 246–247
AEMDD (Arts in Education Model Development and Dissemination) 141
AERA (American Educational Research Association), *Standards for Educational and Psychological Testing* 4–5
Akhmedjanova, Diana 173–206, 245, 248, 250
ALC (Artful Learning Communities: Assessing Learning in the Arts) 131–132, 141
Allal, L. 15–16
Ambitious Science Teaching tools 103–104
Ambrose, R. 232
American Educational Research Association (AERA), *Standards for Educational and Psychological Testing* 4–5
American Psychological Association (APA), *Standards for Educational and Psychological Testing* 4–5
AMTE (Association of Mathematics Teacher Educators) 221
Analysis, Evaluation, and Synthesis 77, **77, 81,** 85; Evaluating Sources learning progression 77, **77,** 78, **78,** 83–84, **84**
Anderson, C. W. 113–114
Andrade, Heidi L. 3–19, 126–145, 174, 181, 246, 248, 250, 251, 257, 258, 259
AP (Advanced Placement) program 175, 180, 246–247
APA (American Psychological Association), *Standards for Educational and Psychological Testing* 4–5
applied practices 72
apps 111–112

aptitude 244
argumentative essays *24,* 24–25
Artful Learning Communities: Assessing Learning in the Arts (ALC) 131–132, 141
Arts Achieve: Impacting Student Success in the Arts 141–142, 258
arts disciplines 126–129, 142–144, 251; effectiveness of 141–142; feedback 127, 130–131, 137, *137,* 140, *140;* future directions 142; learning goals and expectations 127, 130, 132–135, *133,* **134;** participation 132–133; peer assessment/feedback 130–131, 137–138, *138, 139,* 140, *140;* practices 131–138, *133,* **134,** *137, 138, 139,* 140, *140;* rubrics 128, *133,* 133–134, **134,** 143; self-assessment 130–131; summative assessment 127; theory of action *129,* 129–131, *130, 131*
Arts in Education Model Development and Dissemination (AEMDD) 141
ArtsConnection 131
Askew, M. 228
Asking Guiding Questions learning progression (ELA) **77,** 80
assessment: assessment as learning 246; assessment conversations 101, *102;* assessment for learning 245–246; benchmark assessment **9–10,** 11, 248–249, 255; *embedded assessments* 5; interim assessment **9–10,** 11, 248–249, 255; Smarter Balanced assessment 73, 184; *see also* formative assessment; peer assessment; self-assessment; summative assessment
assessment criteria, transparency in 158, 166
Association of Mathematics Teacher Educators (AMTE) 221
astronomy discipline 148–149, 164–166; authentic tasks 165; concepts, theories and models case 152–160, *153, 155,* 164; as a discipline 150–151,

151; evidence-based argumentation case 161–164, *162, 163,* 164; methods of science case 160–161, 164; peer assessment/feedback 153–154, 156, 164, 165–166

Atkin, J. M. 106

Ausubel, David 244, 257

autonomy, of students in higher education 151–152, 251

Avadanei, Naomi 143–144

Ayendiz, M. 113

Bailin, S. 128, 129

Baxter, G. P. 27

Beatty, I. D. 111

Bell, Alan 44, 147

Benchmark Arts Assessments 141

benchmark assessment **9–10,** 11, 248–249, 255

Bennett, Randy E. 3–19, 20–31, 68–69, 99, 130, 146, 147, 175, 245, 246, 248, 250, 255

biases 26, 29, 69

Biggers, M. 109

Bill and Melinda Gates Foundation 59, 60

Black, Paul 12, 15, 36, 37, 38, 56, 69, 71, 97, 98, 147, 152, 227, 245–246, 254–255, 258

Bloom, Benjamin 6–7, 244, 245, 249

Bloom, H. S. 249, 258, 260

Blueprint for Teaching and Learning in the Arts (New York City Department of Education) 132, 134

Boeckaerts, M. 16

Borstel, J. 134–135

Box, C. 108–109

Brigs, D. C. 69

Brown, B. A. 116

Buck, G. A. 106, 109, 113

Burk, Frederic 244

Burkhardt, Hugh 35–67, 253–254, 258–259

CAEP (Council for the Accreditation of Teacher Preparation) 218

Calkins, Lucy M. 173–206, 245, 248, 250

Canner, Barbara 133

CAPITAL project 106

Carless, D. 146, 152

Carroll, John B. 244, 251

CBAL™ (Cognitively Based Assessment of, for, and as Learning) 75–76, 175; *Clouds* task 85, *86,* 87–88, *88, 89,* 90, *90, 91,* 92; independent learning progression tasks 83–85, **84**; key practice definition 76–77, **77**; learning progressions **77,** 77–78, **78**; Roman Meal SBT 78–82, *79, 80,* **81**

CCSS (Common Core State Standards): CCSSM (Common Core State Standards for Mathematics) 50, 56, 218, 228, 251; ELA (English Language Arts) discipline 71, 72, 75, 82; writing discipline 176–178, 179, 181, 184, 248

CCSSO (Council of Chief State School Officers) 127, 247; *see also* FAST SCASS (Formative Assessment for Students and Teachers [FAST]

State Collaborative on Assessment and Student Standards [SCASS])

CGI (Cognitively Guided Instruction) 38, 43, 223, 232

characterizations 29; acting on 21, 27–28; inferentially connecting evidence to 21, 25–27

checklists 110, 143; writing discipline 174, 176, 178–179, 180–182, *181,* 183

Chen, F. 141, 142, 143, 257

Cizek, Gregory J. 3–19, 246, 248

CLA+ (Collegiate Learning Assessment) 73

Clark, I. 16

Clark, R. E. 246

Classroom Challenges *see* MAP FALS (Mathematics Assessment Project formative assessment lessons)

classroom resources: science disciplines 109–112; *see also* tools

Claxton, G. L. 250

Cleland, C. E. 150

clickers 111

Clouds task 85, *86,* 87–88, *88, 89,* 90, *90, 91,* 92

Coffey, J. E. 69, 114

cognitive-domain model 147

cognitive-domain theory 24, 29

cognitive load theory 254

Cognitively Based Assessment of, for, and as Learning *see* CBAL™ (Cognitively Based Assessment of, for, and as Learning)

Cognitively Guided Instruction (CGI) 38, 43, 223, 232

collaboration, with colleagues 212–213

College and Work Readiness Assessment (CWRA+) 73

Collegiate Learning Assessment (CLA+) 73

Common Core State Standards *see* CCSS (Common Core State Standards)

Communication and Presentation of Results key practice (ELA) 77, **77, 81**

communities of practice: astronomy discipline 156, 158; writing discipline 179–180

concept development lessons, MAP FALS 50, 51–52, *52, 53, 54,* 54–56, *55*

concept maps 111

conceptual domain for student science learning 99

Conducting Research and Inquiry key practice (ELA) 75, 76–78, **77, 78**; independent learning progression tasks 83–85, **84**; Roman Meal SBT 78–82, *79, 80,* **81**

Consortium for Policy and Research in Education (CPRE) 175

Cooper, H. 260

Corcoran, Tom 175

Council for the Accreditation of Teacher Preparation (CAEP) 218

Council of Chief State School Officers *see* CCSSO (Council of Chief State School Officers)

Council of State Science Supervisors (CSSS) 119

Cowie, B. 69, 116, 147

Index

CPRE (Consortium for Policy and Research in Education) 175
creative process 126–127
CRESST (National Center for Research on Evaluation, Standards, and Student Testing), UCLA 59
Critical Incident Protocol 227
critical inquiry 128
Critical Response Process 134, 135–136, 140
Cronbach, Lee 6, 245
CSSS (Council of State Science Supervisors) 119
culture: science disciplines 115–117; socio-cultural perspective 21, 22, 26, 98–99, 119, 222, 252
curriculum developers 17
curriculum-embedded formative assessment 106–107
CWRA+ (College and Work Readiness Assessment) 73

Dabbs, J. M. 108–109
Dalton Plan 244
Danza, Dominic 143
Daro, Phil 50
data-driven decision making 13, 21, 22
Deane, Paul 23–24, 25, 68–96, 175, 243
DeNisi, A. S. 12
design and technology discipline 258
design of formative assessment 4, 16, 21–22, 25, 104–105, *105*; ELA (English Language Arts) discipline 75–76; evidentiary reasoning as basis for 21–22; Formative Assessment Design Cycle 104–105, *105*; mathematics discipline 35, 39, 44, 46, **47**, *48*, 48–49, *49*, 51–52, *52, 53, 54,* 54–56, *57, 58,* 58–59, 60–64, *61,* **62**; productive assessment task design (formative assessment strategy in higher education) 152, 156, 165; of summative assessments 73
developing student understanding of the nature of quality (formative assessment strategy in higher education) 152, 156, 158–159, 165
DIAGNOSER software 112
disability status, and biases 26
disciplinary affordances 151, 155
disciplinary discernment 149
disciplinary literacy 149
discipline-specific nature of formative assessment 16, 17, 255, 256, 257, 258, 261
Dogan, A. 113
domain-general characteristic of formative assessment 243–244, 255, 256, 257, 261
domain proficiency theory 22
domain-specific characteristic of formative assessment 22, 243–244, 255, 258
domain theory 22
Donnelly, D. F. 117
Driver, R. 150
Duckor, B. 226
Dunn, K. E. 8
Durán, R. P. 119
Duschl, R. A. 99

Ebby, C. 232
ECD (Evidence Centered Design) 20, 21, 73, 92; *see also* evidentiary reasoning
Education Endowment Foundation 259
EFA (Embedding Formative Assessment) 259–261
effective feedback process (formative assessment strategy in higher education) 152, 156, 157, 165
Ehrenworth, Mary 173–206, 245, 248, 250
Eisner, E. 126
ELA (English Language Arts) discipline 255, 258; *Analysis, Evaluation, and Synthesis* 77, **77, 81,** 85; *Clouds* task 85, *86,* 87–88, *88, 89,* 90, *90, 91,* 92; *Communication and Presentation of Results* 77, **77, 81;** *Conducting Research and Inquiry* key practice 75, 76–78, **77, 78;** domain analysis 70–73, 76, 92; Evaluating Sources learning progression 77, **77, 78, 78,** 83–84, **84;** formative task models 75; independent learning progression tasks 83–85, **84;** *Inquiry and Information Gathering* 77, **77, 81;** integrating model tasks into formative assessment cycle 85, *86,* 87–88, *88, 89,* 90, *90, 91,* 92; key practices 23, 29, 70, 72–73, 76–77, **77;** learning progressions 70–71, 73, 75, **77,** 77–78, **78,** 80; model task design 75–76; PCK (pedagogical content knowledge) 69, 70, 75, 76, 92; performance tasks 73–74; *Roman Meal SBT* 78–82, *79, 80,* **81;** SBTs (scenario-based tasks) 74; task analysis 73–75, 76; *Testing Hypotheses* learning progression **77,** 80; *see also* writing
ELL (English Language Learners) 114
embedded assessments 5
embedded-in-the-curriculum formative assessment 13
Embedding Formative Assessment (EFA) 259–261
end-of-course testing 5
English Language Arts *see* ELA (English Language Arts) discipline
English Language Learners (ELL) 114
Enhanced Learning Maps, mathematics 232
epistemic domain for student science learning 99
equity 114, 118–119
Ericsson, Anders 213
Eriksson, Urban 146–169, 243, 251, 256
errors 27–28, 44–45, *47,* 47–48, 253–254
ethnicity, and biases 26
ETS 130, *130,* 175
Evaluating Sources learning progression (ELA) 77, **77,** 78, **78,** 83–84, **84**
Every Student Succeeds Act (2015) 3
evidence 22–23; inferential connection to characterizations 21, 25–27; mathematics discipline 210, 216; *see also* evidentiary reasoning
Evidence Centered Design (ECD) 20, 21, 73, 92; *see also* evidentiary reasoning
evidentiary reasoning 246, 255; acting on characterizations 21, 27–28; and assessment 20–21; as design basis for formative assessment 21–22; engineering opportunities to observe evidence

Index

21, 22–25, *24*; evaluating quality and impact 21, 28–29; inferentially connecting evidence to characterizations 21, 25–27

exemplars, in writing discipline 174, 176, 178, 180, 183, 188–189

FARROP *(Formative Assessment Rubrics, Resources, and Observation Protocol)* 223–224, 225, 226, 240, **241,** 242

FAST SCASS (Formative Assessment for Students and Teachers [FAST] State Collaborative on Assessment and Student Standards [SCASS]) 208–212, 214, 216, 220, 223

feedback 27, 29, 113, 257; arts disciplines 127, 130–131, 137, *137,* 140, *140*; effective feedback process (formative assessment strategy in higher education) 152, 156, 157, 165; impact on performance 12; mathematics discipline 211, 232–233; qualitative 62; self-level feedback 157; task-level feedback 157; *see also* peer assessment/ feedback

Fleischer, C. 184

Focus on Standards program 249

Forbes, C. T. 109, 113

Ford, M. J. 99

Forman, E. A. 99

format of task, and evidence 27

formative assessment 245; characteristics of 5–6, 8, **8,** 127; contemporary typologies of 12–13; critiques of 68–69; curriculum-embedded 106–107; definitions and definitional issues 4–6, 11, 21, 36, 69, 126, 223, 244, 245–255; design of 4, 16, 21–22, 25, 104–105, *105*; diagnostic teaching approach 44–46, *46*; domain dependency of 16, 17, 69, 146–147; domain-general characteristic of 243–244, 255, 256, 257, 261; domain-specific characteristic of 22, 243–244, 255, 258; effectiveness of in ELA 92; future of 16–17; historical review 6–8, **7, 8, 9–10,** 11; inclusive definitions 254–255; as inferential activity 14–15, 17; limited and mechanistic implementations 148–149; next-generation definition 14–16; origins and antecedents 244–245; pre-service teachers' beliefs about 224–225; principles of 68–70; purpose of 4–5, 16; research literature on 11–12; uses of 5, 16; *see also* design of formative assessment; measurement principles

Formative Assessment Design Cycle 104–105, *105*

Formative Assessment for Students and Teachers [FAST] State Collaborative on Assessment and Student Standards [SCASS] (FAST SCASS) 208–212, 214, 216, 220, 223

Formative Assessment Rubrics, Resources, and Observation Protocol (FARROP) 223–224, 225, 226, 240, **241,** 242

Formative Diagnostic Assessment **9–10**

formative evaluation 6–7

formative hypothesis 27

Formative Learning Assessment **9–10,** 16

FOSS (Full Option Science System) 112

Foundational Approaches to Science Teaching Curriculum 107

Fowles, Mary 175

Framework for K-12 Science Education, A. (Board on Science Education) 97, 119

Franz, J. 134–135

Fremont, Angela 140

Full Option Science System (FOSS) 112

Fullan, M. 183–184, 190–191

fundamental literacy practices (ELA key practice) 72

Furtak, Erin Marie 97–125, 251, 254, 257

Gallimore, R. 249

Gao, X. 27

Gawande, A. 181

gender and biases 26

geography discipline 258

Gerace, W. J. 111

Gladwell, M. 178

Glass, B. 207

goals *see* learning goals

Gobert, J. D. 252

Goldenberg, C. N. 249

Gopal, N. 117

Gotwals, A. W. 108

Graves, D. 184

Gray, R. 150

Gross, Christine 143

Guided Reflection Protocol 227

habits of practice, mathematics teachers 207, 208, *208,* 212–213, 222, **222,** 233–234

Handbook of Formative and Summative Evaluation of Student Learning (Bloom, Hastings, and Madaus) 6–7

Handbook of Formative Assessment (Andrade & Cizek, 2010) 14, 105

Hargreaves, A. 183–184, 190–191

Harnett, S. 141

Harrison, C. 109

Harwayne, S. 184

Hastings, J. T. 6–7

Hattie, J. A. C. 12, 157, 173, 186

Hauser, C. H. 260

Hefferen, Joanna 126–145, 250, 251, 257, 258, 259

Heredia, Sara C. 97–125, 251, 254, 257

Heritage, Margaret 71, 174, 207–242, 243, 247

Herman, J. 115

Hiebert, J. 207

higher education 146, 166, 234–235, 251; astronomy discipline 150–151, *151,* 152–166; context of 151–152; domain dependency 146–147; epistemology of science learning 149–150; limited and mechanistic implementations 148–149

Holmberg, C. 226

Holmeier, M. 111

Hondrich, A. L. 107, 118
hypothesis testing 148, 150; *Testing Hypotheses* learning progression (ELA) **77**, 80

IB (International Baccalaureate) 175, 179, 180
identity, and science disciplines 115–117
impact, evaluation of 21, 28–29
inclusive definitions of formative assessment 254–255
Individual System 244
inference, and formative assessment 14–15, 17; inferentially connecting evidence to characterizations 21, 25–27; validity of 69
information and communications technology discipline 258
Inquiry and Information Gathering key practice (ELA) 77, **77**, 81; learning progression **77**, 80; *Testing Hypotheses* learning progression **77**, 80
InTASC (Interstate Teacher Assessment and Support Consortium) Model Core Teaching Standards 218, 220, 221
interim assessment **9–10,** 11, 248–249, 255
International Baccalaureate (IB) 175, 179, 180
Inverness Research Associates 60
ITMA *(Investigations on Teaching with Microcomputers as an Aid) 61,* 61–62

Jin, H. 110
Johnson, E. 134–135
Jones, A. 116
Jönsson, Anders 146–169, 243, 251, 256
judgment, in arts disciplines 134–135

Kaftan, J. 113
Kang, H. 103–104, 110, 113–114, 118
Keeley, Paige 100, 106
Keeping Learning on Track 259
Kent Mathematics Project 244
key practices 23, 72
Kings College Professional Development Project 38
Kingston, N. 12, 69
Kirschner, P. A. 246
Kluger, A. N. 12
KMOFAP (Kings-Medway-Oxfordshire Formative Assessment Project) 243–244, 248
knowledge, types of 98
Kuhn, T. 142

lack of understanding 28
Ladder of Feedback 137, *137,* 140, *140*
Ladson-Billings, G. 180
language: and biases 26; *see also* ELA (English Language Arts) discipline
Lave, J. 225
Lawton, Denis 255
Leahy, S. 146, 259
learning, definition of 246
learning expectations, in arts disciplines 132–134, *133,* **134**

learning goals: arts disciplines 127, 130, 134–135; mathematics discipline *209,* 209–210, 211–212, 216, 230; science disciplines 98–99
learning progressions 23–24, 70–71; cognitive-domain model 147; ELA (English Language Arts) discipline 70–71, 73, 75, **77,** 77–78, **78,** 80; independent learning progression tasks 83–85, *84;* mathematics discipline *209,* 209–210, 227–229, *229,* 230, *231,* 231–233, *232;* science disciplines 110; writing discipline 176, 177–180
Lerman, Liz 134, 135–136
Levi, L. 232
Li, M. 98
literacy learning *see* ELA (English Language Arts) discipline; writing discipline
Living History Day events 79; *see also* Roman Meal SBT
Lyon, C. J. 108
Lyon, E. G. 114

Macaskill, A. 151
Macfarlane-Dick, D. 160
Madaus, G. F. 6–7
Maddy, Emily 133, 136–138
MAP FALS (Mathematics Assessment Project formative assessment lessons) 35, 46, 50–51, 59–60, 64, 258; concept development lessons 50, 51–52, *52, 53, 54,* 54–56, *55;* non-routine problem solving lessons 50, 56, *57, 58,* 58–59
Marton, F. 149, 159
mastery learning 244
Mastrorilli, T. M. 141
Mathematics Development Collaborative (MDC) 59, 258
mathematics discipline 35–36, 64–65, 255, 258; definitions and interpretations 36–37; design 35, 39, 44, 46, **47,** *48,* 48–49, *49,* 51–52, *52, 53, 54,* 54–56, *57, 58,* 58–59, 60–64, *61,* **62;** diagnostic teaching approach 44–46, *46;* feedback 211, 232–233; learning goals *209,* 209–210, 211–212, 216, 230; learning progressions *209,* 209–210, 227–229, *229,* 230, *231,* 231–233, *232;* MAP (Mathematics Assessment Project) 50–52, *52, 53, 54,* 54–56, *55, 57, 58,* 58–65, *61,* **62;** misconceptions in 44–45, *47,* 47–48, 230–231, *231;* PCK (pedagogical content knowledge) 43, 207, 208, *208, 209,* 209–212, 213, 222, **222,** 227–233, **229,** *231, 232,* 234; peer assessment/feedback 210–211, 216; practice example 213–218; pre-service teacher learning 207–242; professional development 35, 37–38, 49; professional standards 50, 56, 218, **219, 220,** 220–222, 227, 229–230; rubrics 223–224, 240, **241,** 242; self-assessment 210–211, 216; success criteria *209,* 209–210, 230; teacher's formative assessment knowledge and skills 207, 208, *208,* 222, **222,** 223–227, 234; teachers' habits of practice 207, 208, *208,* 212–213, 222, **222,**

Index

233–234; theoretical basis 38–39; TRU (Teaching for Robust Understanding) Framework 39, **40, 41,** 41–44, **42,** *43,* 45, 46, 49, 56, 59, 64–65

McCormick, R. 152

McGarr, O. 117

MDC (Mathematics Development Collaborative) 59, 258

measurement principles 20, 29, 255; acting on characterizations 21, 27–28; engineering opportunities to observe evidence 21, 22–25, *24;* evaluating quality and impact 21, 28–29; evidentiary reasoning and assessment 20–21; evidentiary reasoning as design basis 21–22; inferentially connecting evidence to characterizations 21, 25–27

mediated learning 222

Metis Associates 141

Mills, V. 223

Minstrell, J. 112

misconceptions 28, 114–115, 257; mathematics discipline 44–45, *47,* 47–48, 230–231, *231*

Mislevy, R. J. 20, 22, 25, 73, 119

model-building practices (ELA key practice) 72

modern foreign languages disciplines 258

Moreland, J. 69

Morris, A. K. 207

Morrison, Deb 97–125, 251, 254, 257

Mosher, Fritz 71, 174, 175

Mulvenon, S. W. 8

Murray, Don 184

Mutual Coaching Strategy 134–135, 137

My Science Tutor program 112

NAEP (National Assessment of Educational Progress) 175, 179, 260

Nash, B. 12, 69

Nathan, M. J. 112–113

National Assessment of Educational Progress (NAEP) 175, 179, 260

National Board for Professional Teaching Standards (NBPTS): Mathematics Standards 218, **219,** 220, 221

National Center for Research on Evaluation, Standards, and Student Testing (CRESST), UCLA 59

National Council of Teachers of Mathematics (NCTM) *Principles to Action* 218, 220, **220,** 221

National Council on Measurement in Education (NCME), *Standards for Educational and Psychological Testing* 4–5

National Institute for Economic and Social Research (NIESR) 259

National Research Council (NRC) 98, 99, 149

National Science Education Standards (National Research Council) 98

nature of science 149

NBPTS (National Board for Professional Teaching Standards): Mathematics Standards 218, **219,** 220, 221

NCME (National Council on Measurement in Education), *Standards for Educational and Psychological Testing* 4–5

NCTM (National Council of Teachers of Mathematics) *Principles to Action* 218, 220, **220,** 221

New York City Department of Education 131, 132; *Arts Achieve: Impacting Student Success in the Arts* 141–142

New Zealand Ministry of Education 71

Newton, P. 150

Next Generation Science Standards (NRC) 149, 184

Nicol, D. J. 160

NIESR (National Institute for Economic and Social Research) 259

No Child Left Behind Act (2001) 3, 8

noise 25–26

non-routine problem solving lessons, MAP FALS 50, 56, *57, 58,* 58–59

North West Evaluation Association, Measures of Academic Progress test 260

NRC (National Research Council) 98, 99, 149

Nuthall, Graham 247

OECD (Organisation for Economic Co-operation and Development), PISA (Programme for International Student Assessment) 149, 254, 260

OGAP *(Ongoing Assessment Project)* 232

on-the-fly formative assessment 13

O'Reilly, J. 117

O'Reilly, T. 23

Osborne, J. 150

Otero, V. K. 112–113

Otrel-Cass, K. 116

Palma, Maria 126–145, 250, 251, 257, 258, 259

Panizzon, D. 109

PAR (Peer Assistance and Review) 225

PARCC CCSS assessment 73, 184

participation: arts disciplines 132–133; science disciplines 102–103, 118

PCK (pedagogical content knowledge): ELA (English Language Arts) discipline 69, 70, 75, 76, 92; mathematics discipline 43, 207, 208, *208, 209,* 209–212, 213, 222, **222,** 227–233, **229,** *231, 232,* 234; science disciplines 109, 113, 115, 147

Pecheone, Ray 175, 179, 180–181

pedagogical affordances 155

peer assessment/feedback 159–160; arts disciplines 130–131, 137–138, *138, 139,* 140, *140;* astronomy discipline 153–154, 156, 164, 165–166; mathematics discipline 210–211, 216; students practicing making judgments (formative assessment strategy in higher education) 152, 156, 159–160, 165

Peer Assistance and Review (PAR) 225

Pegg, J. 109

Penuel, W. R. 13, 21, 107, 129

Index

PERI-HA (Primary Education Review and Implementation Holistic Assessment) program, Singapore 257

personal practice assessment theory (PPAT) 108–109

Petit, M. 232

Phillips, R. 61

PISA (Programme for International Student Assessment), OECD 149, 254, 260

planned-for interaction formative assessment 13

policy makers 17

Popham, W. J. 248, 249

posters 60

power, and science disciplines 115–117

PPAT (personal practice assessment theory) 108–109

practices: arts disciplines 131–138, *133,* **134,** *137, 138, 139,* 140, *140*; science disciplines 101–102, 103, 107–108, 118

pre-service teacher learning 17, 69; mathematics discipline 207–242; science disciplines 112–114

Primary Education Review and Implementation Holistic Assessment (PERI-HA) program, Singapore 257

procedural knowledge 98

process-level feedback 157

productive assessment task design (formative assessment strategy in higher education) 152, 156, 165

professional development 69; empirical evidence 256–261, **257**; Formative Assessment Design Cycle 104–105, *105*; mathematics discipline 35, 37–38, 49; school leaders 183, 189, **190**; science disciplines 104–105, *105,* 108–109; writing/*Writing Pathways: Performance Assessments and Learning Progression, Grades K-8* (TCRWP, Teachers College Reading and Writing Project) 182–189, *186,* **190**

professional standards: mathematics discipline 50, 56, 218, **219, 220,** 220–222, 227, 229–230; *Standards for Educational and Psychological Testing* (AERA, APA, NCME) 4–5; Standards for Professional Learning (Learning Forward) 221–222; *see also* CCSS (Common Core State Standards)

Programme for International Student Assessment (PISA), OECD 149, 254, 260

progress assessment 11

Progressions for the Common Core Standards in Mathematics (CCSWT) 228

Pulliam, Barry 249

Pulliam, Leslie 249

quality: developing student understanding of the nature of quality (formative assessment strategy in higher education) 152, 156, 158–159, 165; evaluation of 21, 28–29

Quellmalz, E. S. 27

race, and biases 26

Ramaprasad, A. 256

Raymond, Roberta 143

reflective practitioner 212

rehearsals 126–127

Research for Action 59

Rivas, C. 107

Rodriguez, A. J. 118, 260

role shifting *61,* 61–62, **62**

Roman Meal SBT 78–82, *79, 80,* **81**

Rondinelli Jason 133, 136–138

rubrics 110; arts disciplines 128, *133,* 133–134, **134,** 143; mathematics discipline 223–224, 240, **241,** 242; writing discipline 128, 174, 176, 178–179, 181, 183

Ruiz-Primo, M. A. 110–111

Sabatini, J. 23

Sabel, J. L. 109, 113

Sadler, D. R. 72, 132, 159, 256

Sadler, P. M. 115

SAT 175, 180, 184

Saunders, W. M. 249

SBTs (scenario-based tasks), ELA 74; Roman Meal 78–82, *79, 80,* **81**

SCALE (Stanford Center for Assessment, Learning, and Equity) 175, 180–181

schematic knowledge 98

Schleicher, Andreas 260

Schoenfeld, Alan 35–67, 253–254, 258–259

Schön, D. 212

Schonmann, ? 141

school leaders 17; professional development 183, 189, **190**

science disciplines 97–98, 251, 252, 254, 255, 258; Ambitious Science Teaching tools 103–104; classroom resources 109–112; curriculum-embedded formative assessment 106–107; epistemology of science learning 149–150; Formative Assessment Design Cycle 104–105, *105*; future research directions 118–119; learning goals 98–99; learning progressions 110; literature review 105–118; nature of science 149; participation 102–103, 118; PCK (pedagogical content knowledge) 109, 113, 115, 147; power, culture, and identity 115–117; practices 101–102, 103, 107–108, 118; pre-service teacher learning 112–114; professional development 104–105, *105,* 108–109; sensemaking of student ideas 114–115; task formats 110–111; tools, practices and participants 99–103; *see also* astronomy discipline

scientific revolutions 142

Scriven, Michael 6, 7, 245, 249

self-assessment: arts disciplines 130–131; mathematics discipline 210–211, 216; students practicing making judgments (formative assessment strategy in higher education) 152, 156, 159–160, 165; writing discipline 181

self-level feedback 157

self-reflection 28–29, 212, 226–227

Index

self-regulated learning (SRL) 15–16, 17, 68, 151–152, 160
sensemaking of student ideas 114–115
Shavelson, R. J. 13, 27, 107
Shell Centre 44, 45, 56, 61; *see also* TLL (Teaching for Long-Term Learning)
Shepard, L. A. 8, 11, 129, 248, 249
Shirley, M. L. 111–112
Shute, V. J. 12
Silver, E. 223
Singapore Ministry of Education 257
Skoog, G. 108–109
slips 27–28
Smarter Balanced assessment 73, 184
Smarter Balanced Formative Task Library 75
smartphone apps 111–112
social class, and biases 26
social domain for student science learning 99
socialization 158
socio-cognitive perspective 13, 21, 22, 252
socio-cultural perspective 21, 22, 26, 98–99, 119, 222, 252
software: and evidentiary reasoning 22; student response systems 111
Song, Y. 23–24, 25
Sopyla, Ron 143
Sorenson, Helen 143
Soriano, Christine 143
sorting and matching tasks 60
Sparks, Jesse R. 25, 68–96, 243
Speckesser, S. 260
SRL (self-regulated learning) 15–16, 17, 68, 151–152, 160
Stake, Robert 5
standards *see* professional standards
Standards for Educational and Psychological Testing (AERA, APA, NCME) 4–5
Standards for Professional Learning (Learning Forward) 221–222
Stanford Center for Assessment, Learning, and Equity (SCALE) 175, 180–181
Stears, M. 117
STEM education 39; STEM Teaching Tools 112; *see also* astronomy discipline; mathematics discipline; science disciplines
Stiggins, R. 248
strategic knowledge 98
strategy-focused formative assessment 13, 21, 22
student autonomy in higher education 151–152, 251
student performance, reasoning about 20–21
student response systems 111
students: lived experiences of 115; participants in formative assessment 17, 102–103; students practicing making judgments (formative assessment strategy in higher education) 152, 156, 159–160, 165; *see also* peer assessment/feedback; self-assessment; SRL (self-regulated learning)

success criteria, mathematics discipline *209,* 209–210, 230
summative assessment 5, 245, 246; arts disciplines 127; changing attitudes towards 3–4; comparative analysis **9–10**; definition 4; design of 73; and noise 25
summative evaluation 6
Swan, Malcolm 36, 44, 49, 50, 64
Sweller, John 246, 254

Taking Science to School (NRC) 105
Talking Teaching Network (TTN) 229–230
task formats, science disciplines 110–111
task-level feedback 157
task specificity 26–27
Taylor, E. 151
TCRWP (Teachers College Reading and Writing Project) *see* writing disciplines/*Writing Pathways: Performance Assessments and Learning Progression, Grades K-8* (TCRWP, Teachers College Reading and Writing Project)
Teacher Learning Community (TLC) 259
teachers: beliefs about formative assessment 224–225; biases 26; challenges of formative assessment for 35–36, 43–44; design tactics for 61–63; impact of MAP FALS on 59–60; strategies for formative assessment 68; *see also* PCK (pedagogical content knowledge); pre-service teacher learning; professional development
Teachers College Reading and Writing Project (TCRWP) *see* writing disciplines/*Writing Pathways: Performance Assessments and Learning Progression, Grades K-8* (TCRWP, Teachers College Reading and Writing Project)
Teaching Excellence Enhancement Programme (TEEP) 259–260
Teaching for Long-Term Learning (TLL) 44–46, *46*
Teaching for Robust Understanding Framework *see* TRU (Teaching for Robust Understanding) Framework
technology, science disciplines 111–112
technology-enhanced formative assessment 111
TEEP (Teaching Excellence Enhancement Programme) 259–260
Terrazas-Arellanes, F. E. 107
Testing Hypotheses learning progression (ELA) **77,** 80
theory of action 28, 69, 75, *129,* 129–131, *130, 131*
thin-slicing, in writing discipline 187
Thompson, M. 147
Thum, Y. M. 260
Timperley, H. 157
TLC (Teacher Learning Community) 259
TLL (Teaching for Long-Term Learning) 44–46, *46*
tools: science disciplines *100,* 100–101, 103–104, 117; *see also* classroom resources
Torrance, H. 148
Toulmin, S. E. 163, *163*
transparency 158; writing discipline 186–187

Index

Trauth-Nare, A. 109, 113, 117
Trends in Mathematics and Science Study 260
TRU (Teaching for Robust Understanding) Framework 39, **40,** 41, 45, 46, 49, 59, 64–65; comparison with MAP FALs 56; discipline specificity 43–44; and formative assessment 42, *43*; Toolkit **41,** 41–42
TTN *(Talking Teaching Network)* 229–230

uncertainty 25, 29, 69
U.S. Department of Education 131; Investing in Innovation 141

variation theory 159
Vygotsky, L. S. 98–99, 222

Ward, W. 112
websites 111–112
Wenger, E. 225
Wiggins, G. P. 22
Wiliam, Dylan 12, 15, 16, 36, 37, 38, 56, 69, 71, 97, 98, 146, 147, 227, 228, 243–264

Winnetka Plan 244
Woodman, Suzanne 143
Wright, B. D. 15
writing discipline/*Writing Pathways: Performance Assessments and Learning Progression, Grades K-8* (TCRWP, Teachers College Reading and Writing Project) 71, 173–174, 173–175, 190–191; CCSS (Common Core State Standards) 176–178, 179, 181, 184; development and structure 175–176; examples (appendices) 193–206; learning progressions 176, 177–180; professional development 182–189, *186,* **190**; rubrics 128, 174, 176, 178–179, 181, 183; self-assessment 181; *see also* ELA (English Language Arts) discipline
Wylie, Caroline 108, 207–242, 243, 247

Yin, X. 106
Yin, Y. 107

Zangori, L. 113
Zhu, J. 141